Bringing SYSTEMS THINKING *to Life*

D1595923

Routledge Titles of Related Interest

"Good leaders are always looking for novel ways to deepen their understanding of how things work and how they might be able to achieve ever better results in their lives and their work. This book provides exactly the right kind of stimulation for anyone seeking that kind of growth. It is a thoughtful compendium designed to stir the brain and heart to better understanding and better leadership."
—Bob Watt, Vice President of State and Local Government Relations and Global Corporate Citizenship (retired), The Boeing Company

"Bowen formulated a way of thinking about 'homo sapiens' that he believed was unique and potentially capable, over time, of revolutionizing the way people think about their lives and their relationships. Although he knew it would take a long, long time, he hoped his theory would continue to develop until society would be ready to 'hear' the theory's message. With the publication of this text, Bregman and White have emerged as new members of an elite group of 'keepers of the flame.' Their efforts at presenting various contexts in which Bowen theory can be fruitfully applied deserve your sustained attention. If Bowen's key concepts intrigue your brain, this book will stimulate your thinking and perhaps lead to the development of other creative applications of the theory."
—Philip J. Guerin, MD, Distinguished Lecturer and Practitioner of Family Systems Psychiatry; Founding Director of the Center for Family Learning in Rye Brook, New York; former faculty member at Albert Einstein College of Medicine, Bronx, New York; Senior Author: *The Evaluation and Treatment of Marital Conflict,* & *Working with Relationship Triangles*

"Bowen's systems theory is the dominant paradigm in the field of family enterprise. Many of the field's leading theorists and practitioners are so educated— including several authors in this powerfully comprehensive collection. Everyone working with families will find this book invaluably rich."
—John L. Ward, PhD, Clinical Professor of Family Enterprises, Kellogg School of Management, Northwestern University, Evanston, Illinois

"For those interested in learning about Bowen theory, Mr. White and Ms. Bregmans' book offers both a broad range of topics and in-depth study of its application. The chapters span the breadth from theoretical perspectives by internationally known leaders to its application in education, research, supervision, clinical work, pastoral work, the workplace, and society. *Bringing Systems Thinking to Life* offers a wealth of knowledge for students, professionals, and those interested in the many realms where Bowen theory can be applied to understand the underlying emotional process in relationship systems."
—Anne S. McKnight, LCSW, EdD, Faculty, Bowen Center for the Study of the Family, Washington, DC

"*Bringing Systems Thinking to Life* clearly demonstrates the saying that 'nothing is more practical than a good theory.' Family systems theory is meant to be lived, and this deeply thoughtful, outstanding collection of articles by recognized leaders demonstrates, as the editors say, 'the breadth and universality of Bowen theory.'"
—Dr. Ronald W. Richardson, former Clinical Director, North Shore Counseling Center, North Vancouver, British Columbia; Pastoral Counselor and Pastor (retired); Author: *Couples in Conflict, Becoming a Healthier Pastor, Creating a Healthier Church,* & *Becoming Your Best*

"This collection of edited papers by Bowen practitioners demonstrates the remarkable depth of Bowen family system theory and its many applications to family life, the work place, and local and national governments. Collectively, these contributions reveal Bowen's greatest intellectual contribution to science—his belief that humans are subject to the same natural forces that govern all life forms, and that emotional functioning governs all relationship existing within and among families, their societies, and the planet Earth. Included in these contributions are transcriptions of Bowen's lectures given in the late 1980s, years after papers in *Family Therapy in Clinical Practice* were written. Here, Bowen describes in his elegant and often direct language the growth of his theory. This book is a must read for anyone interested in the human condition."
—Joanne Bowen, PhD, Curator, Zooarcheology Collections, Conservation, and Museums, Colonial Williamsburg Foundation; Research Professor, Anthropology, College of William and Mary, Williamsburg, Virginia

"Systems thinking ... surpasses being an interesting way to analyze organizations—it is necessary for healthy survival in many workplaces *and* families.... *Bringing Systems Thinking to Life* ably introduces systems theory to newcomers, as well as charts its present standing among organizational theorists and therapists, and anticipates the increasing role it will enjoy as leaders continue to discover how their role is strengthened by self-definition, clarity, and a nonanxious presence."
—Howard Stringfellow III, Archdeacon, The Episcopal Diocese of Bethlehem, Pennsylvania

"A remarkable work! The authors of *Bringing Systems Thinking to Life* provide fresh observations on family emotional process and the importance of family systems theory to understanding human functioning."
—Charles W. Collier, Senior Philanthropic Adviser, Harvard University, Cambridge, Massachusetts; Author: *Wealth in Families*

Bringing
SYSTEMS
THINKING
to Life

EXPANDING THE HORIZONS FOR BOWEN FAMILY SYSTEMS THEORY

EDITED BY

ONA COHN BREGMAN   CHARLES M. WHITE

Routledge
Taylor & Francis Group
New York   London

Routledge
Taylor & Francis Group
270 Madison Avenue
New York, NY 10016

Routledge
Taylor & Francis Group
27 Church Road
Hove, East Sussex BN3 2FA

© 2011 by Taylor and Francis Group, LLC
Routledge is an imprint of Taylor & Francis Group, an Informa business

Printed in the United States of America on acid-free paper
10 9 8 7 6 5 4 3 2 1

International Standard Book Number: 978-0-415-80046-4 (Hardback) 978-0-415-80047-1 (Paperback)

Library of Congress Cataloging-in-Publication Data

Bringing systems thinking to life : expanding the horizons for bowen family
   systems theory / edited by Ona Cohn Bregman, Charles M. White.
      p. cm.
   Includes bibliographical references and index.
   ISBN 978-0-415-80046-4 (hardback : alk. paper) -- ISBN 978-0-415-80047-1
   (pbk. : alk. paper)
   1. Systemic therapy (Family therapy) I. Bregman, Ona Cohn. II. White,
Charles M. III. Title.

RC388.5.B747 2010
616.89'156--dc22   2010013399

Visit the Taylor & Francis Web site at
http://www.taylorandfrancis.com

and the Routledge Web site at
http://www.routledgementalhealth.com

To the memory and life legacies of

Roberta Baxter "Bobbie" Holt, DSW
March 14, 1941—March 15, 2009
Faculty, Bowen Center for the Study of
the Family, Washington, DC

and

Tamara Jeanne "Tammi" Hawk, MSW
August 5, 1952—July 18, 2010
Director, The Prairie Center for Family
Studies, Manhattan, Kansas

Two colleagues who understood that the best "bringing
systems thinking to life" efforts always began and ended with
themselves as they worked to actualize a way of thinking
into a way of being in relation to their own families.

Contents

Foreword

Dr. Murray Bowen (1913–1990) originated Bowen family systems theory and would have been especially pleased with the efforts of Ona Bregman and Charlie White to edit this particular book about his theory. Bowen often emphasized that this new theory of human behavior was relevant far beyond the field of family therapy. The diverse contributions in this book clearly demonstrate that. Rather than focus on the wide range of issues presented in the book, I make a few comments related to one of my principal research interests through the years. I do this because my area of interest highlights key obstacles to the acceptance of Bowen theory. One of the obstacles is the medical model, and the other is the notion of human emotional autonomy.

Understanding Bowen theory's challenge to the medical model begins with discoveries in the fields of mind–body medicine and stress research. The body's stress response systems are activated to deal with challenges such as fleeing a predator, healing a wound, or fighting an infection. One aspect of the stress response is immune system activation. An acute stress response is adaptive, but if it becomes chronic, it can sometimes activate and help sustain a wide range of diseases. For example, chronic inflammation is a frequent component of a prolonged stress response and plays a key role in both mental and physical illnesses. Factors such as genes, toxins, and pathogens may govern *where* in the body inflammation occurs, but such factors do not explain *when* it occurs.

It has long been recognized that no matter what disease a patient has, involvement of the nervous, endocrine, and immune systems is necessary to support the disease process. Myriad components of these three systems are part of the stress response system. It had generally been assumed that a disease process itself emitted signals that kept these systems activated. This is true, but it now appears that it is not a one-way process. The myriad chemical signals generated by a chronic stress response may do as much to activate and sustain a disease as signals from the disease itself do to activate the chronic stress response. It is a reciprocal interaction, with no one component being its cause. Additionally, given that psychological factors are prime activators of the stress response, it is necessary to understand mind–body interactions to understand a disease process at the organ or tissue level. From this perspective, the cause of a disease does not reside in biological processes at the organ or tissue level. Bowen's (1957) early research on the family indicated that the cause of a disease does not even reside within the person of the patient—a finding that subsequent research (Sternberg, 2000; McEwan & Lasley, 2002) seems to substantiate.

Freudian theory reinforced a cultural attitude that people are fairly autonomous psychological entities, each motivated by his or her particular psychological mechanisms and conflicts. In contrast, family research led to the development of Bowen family systems theory, which views *emotional interdependence* as a more accurate description of human nature. Human beings profoundly affect one another's thoughts, feelings, moods, decisions, and actions. This is especially true in the family, where how one member functions can powerfully affect how others function. Human family systems have been shaped by hundreds of millions of years of evolution.

Given the variable but always significant degree to which comfortably close relationships enhance an individual's well-being and functioning, it is not surprising that protracted disturbances in these relationships are prime generators of the chronic stress response. The importance of relationships to an individual's emotional well-being is captured in three questions all human beings worry about: "What do you think of me?", "Do you accept me?", and "What do you want me to do?" This understanding opens a doorway to diseases and diagnoses being considered symptoms of a disturbance of not only the patient's mind–body system but also of a disturbance in the patient's important relationship systems.

The human species is at a fork in the road. We can continue on a path that embraces the myth of emotional autonomy and fails to acknowledge the limits of the medical model, or we can choose a new path that recognizes human emotional interdependence and the need for a systems perspective to address the complex forces that govern health and disease. The many research interests and ideas of Bowen theorists contained in this volume will help its readers better understand that by applying systems thinking to human emotional functioning, options for problem solving in many arenas will expand exponentially.

Michael E. Kerr, MD
Director, Bowen Center for the Study of the Family
Washington, DC

References

Bowen, M. (1957, March). Treatment of family groups with a schizophrenic member. Paper presented at the Sessions on Current Familial Studies at the Annual Meeting of the American Orthopsychiatric Association, Chicago, IL.

McEwen, B. & Lasley, E. N. (2002). *The end of stress as we know it.* Washington, DC: Joseph Henry Press.

Sternberg, E. M. (2000). *The balance within: The science connecting health and emotions.* New York, NY: W.H. Freeman & Co.

Preface

The primary purpose behind *Bringing Systems Thinking to Life* is to provide readers who have a general interest in systems thinking or prior exposure to Bowen family systems theory with a single volume introducing them to a sample of essays that attempt to capture the breadth of systems thinking applications to human behavior by way of Bowen theory. A second or "metapurpose" of almost equal importance is to illustrate, through the breadth of applications represented in this volume, that Bowen family systems theory merits serious consideration as one of the 20th and current centuries' most significant and comprehensive social–behavioral theories. Although at first consideration the book's primary purpose may invite criticism that this is merely a "resource manual" for Bowen theory enthusiasts, I contend that classifying this volume solely as a resource book would be to understate its importance. There is no more compelling vehicle for driving this point home than the book's opening chapter by nonclinician Patricia A. Comella, JD. By outlining an approach to observing societal-level emotional process based on Bowen's research methodology, she effectively launches the book toward a goal of demonstrating the transcendent nature and versatility of Bowen theory–based social assessment and its extension into fields of study and practice far beyond the original psychiatric context in which it was first formulated by Bowen more than 50 years ago.

Because of the book's uniqueness as the first attempt in a single volume to document the extraordinary diversity and breadth of Bowen theory applications—applications that address human functioning in various relationship systems across a broad spectrum of professions, disciplines, cultures, and nations—it also simultaneously fulfills the book's second or metapurpose by providing ample evidence that Bowen theory has joined an elite class of theories that have enjoyed broad application to social phenomena (e.g., psychoanalytic theory, feminist theory, Marxism, evolutionary theory) and lends credibility to the claim that Bowen theory is one of the 20th and current centuries' most significant social–behavioral theories. And yet, if you ask any roomful of social science academics to name the great theories of the 20th and current centuries, few, if any, would include Bowen family systems theory on their list. With that backdrop, this book is much more than just a reference book for people who have had prior exposure to systems thinking, Bowen theory, or both; rather, this book has the potential to be an important work that helps puts a new great theory on the intellectual landscape.

If establishing Bowen theory as an elite social–behavioral theory by show-casing the emerging ways in which it is being used to address human function-ing across a broad spectrum of social contexts does not engender some social science interest in this volume beyond the Bowen theory network, then per-haps Dr. Michael E. Kerr's Foreword to this book, coupled with the chapters by LeAnn S. Howard, MSW, MA (Chapter 28, "Building Bridges to the Natural Sciences: Field Research on Harvester Ants") and Mary Greenberg, MSW, PhD (Chapter 29, "Social Behavior in Nonhuman Animals: A Behavioral Model of Proximate Mechanisms Based on Bowen Theory"), documenting their bidi-rectional bridge-building efforts between Bowen theory and the natural sci-ences, will generate interest in a different audience—the broader community of natural scientists who are making significant strides toward an authentic natural science of human behavior that is grounded in the facts of evolution and recognizes the human as subject to the same natural forces that govern the rest of life.

Fulfilling the metapurpose of this book—demonstrating that the extraor-dinary diversity and breadth of Bowen theory applications sets this theory apart from nearly all contemporary social science theories claiming to explain human behavior—would justify a closer examination of this theory in the nat-ural sciences and strengthen its standing as a potential candidate or contender for consideration, in whole or in part, for inclusion in a forthcoming natu-ral science of human behavior. Although having an extraordinary breadth of application is *a necessary* threshold for a theory to cross to maintain its viabil-ity for potential inclusion in such a science, in and of itself, this is not *the sufficient* criterion for a theory to make movement toward science. History is littered with theories and belief systems that enjoyed broad application and appeal but had little or no potential to become part of a science of human behavior. Tempting as it may be for me to put forth a rationale for why Bowen theory has potential to become science, a satisfactory treatment of that stance is beyond the scope of this preface and this book.

As for a second potential criticism of this book, that the volume's theory-extension goal and metapurpose are compromised by having too many chap-ters written by novice authors, I concede that although there are few seasoned academic or professional authors among the chapter author ranks, all of the chapters are written by nationally and internationally known Bowen theory practitioners, most of whom are recognized as the world's foremost authori-ties on the implementation of Bowen theory in their specific professional practice areas. This book is largely about real-world applications of systems thinking and Bowen theory, written by actual practitioners, not a collection of scholarly essays written in the abstract on how systems thinking or Bowen theory might be used in various practice domains. If only the "best authors" were selected to grace the pages of this volume—with secondary consideration given to the quality of those authors' understandings of Bowen theory and their actual implementations of the theory in practice—it would result in a shallow and uninspiring, albeit exceedingly well-written, book that would be swiftly rejected by the Bowen theory core audience. From previously edited books on the theory and its applications, that audience has come to expect that perseverance in sustained and challenging grassroots practice efforts coupled with theoretical precision will be the paramount considerations for such book chapters. Many communities of adherents to specific theoretical frameworks aspire to eventually produce quorums of dually skilled scholar–practitioners and practitioner–scholars, each possessing a curriculum vitae that features numerous authored articles published in refereed journals coupled with a plethora of consistently creative top-tier theory-infused practice innovations. I contend that although this is a standard for practitioner–scholastic performance, few theory-driven practice communities have achieved or could ever achieve it—with fewer still being able to produce 25 or so such dually skilled individuals to contribute to an edited volume.

A third potential criticism of this book may be that far too many chapters spend an excessive number of pages detailing authors' personal struggles and their efforts to acquire greater degrees of differentiation of self and that a couple dozen such chapters would quickly put a non–Bowen-theory-enthusiast reader, unfamiliar with the importance and transformative potential of differentiation of self, into a sound sleep. I acknowledge that many chapters do contain these author accounts of personal struggle and their differentiation-of-self efforts. What is largely absent in this criticism, however, is a recognition that being a successful systems-thinking pioneer or trailblazer—one who introduces a new way of thinking about human relationships to anxious and often recalcitrant social systems—requires an extraordinary degree of self-regulation, low-anxiety decision making, and principled leadership to realize lasting change in a system when faced with myriad considerable and entrenched counterforces dedicated to maintaining the status quo. I contend that, seen in this light, it is understandable that many chapter authors would include details from the personal journeys that made their pioneering works possible. To the degree to which the anticipated audience for this volume is made up of struggling systems-thinking pioneers who are actively attempting to use systems thinking, Bowen theory, or both in novel or challenging social settings and practice domains, the inclusion of authors' differentiation-of-self efforts could possibly be one of the most stimulating and inspiring aspects of this book rather than being a source of sedation for readers, as critics might predict.

Finally, what is also largely absent in the criticism that far too many chapters and pages are devoted to authors' personal struggles and differentiation of self efforts is a recognition of the often substantial professional costs that many—perhaps even all—of the chapter authors have endured as a result of maintaining their unwavering convictions about the potential and efficacy of Bowen theory for their personal lives and professional practices. A careful reading of the book's chapters may produce some partial answers as to what Bowen theory offers that elicits this type of loyalty and sacrifice from the chapter authors; however, there is likely an intangible quality to this for each author that cannot be easily articulated or explained. The extraordinary care and effort that Bowen put into developing this theory and maintaining its viability for potential inclusion in a future natural science of human behavior aside, there is something compelling—perhaps even *beautiful*—about this theory that is difficult to put into words and that nevertheless engenders a certain respect from those who come to understand this theory and begin to work with it in their personal and professional lives.

In his 1992 book, *Dreams of a Final Theory*, Steven Weinberg, the recipient of the 1979 Nobel Prize for Physics, shared some of his thinking on how certain theories come to be recognized as beautiful and attempted to explain the curious function of beauty as a means of evaluating the promise of certain theories in physics. Weinberg wrote,

> A physicist who says that a theory is beautiful does not mean quite the same thing that would be meant in saying that a particular painting or a piece of music or poetry is beautiful. It is not merely a personal expression of aesthetic pleasure; it is much closer to what a horse trainer means when he looks at a racehorse and says that it is a beautiful horse. The horse trainer is of course expressing a personal opinion, but it is an opinion about an objective fact: that, on the basis of judgments that the trainer could not easily put into words, this is the kind of horse that wins races. (p. 133)

I believe that the impressive systems thinking efforts detailed in the chapters that follow make a significant contribution to the ever-expanding body of work supporting the notion that Bowen theory is that "kind of horse that wins races."

At different times during my thus far 25-year journey with this theory, I have found myself pausing to wonder at, reflect on, and evaluate whether Bowen family systems theory will ultimately prove itself to be "a" or perhaps even "the" beautiful horse—possessing the endurance to go the distance and complete that arduous race toward a natural science of human behavior. One thing is certain: The principled and enduring commitments portrayed in this book to working with this theory over the course of long careers are clear indicators that the editors, chapter authors, and others associated with this book have made substantial odds-on wagers that this horse will complete, and perhaps even win, that race.

—**Charles M. White, MSW, March 2010**

My chapter was initially written for publication as an article. When discussing the manuscript with Charlie White, he indicated that he was considering putting together a book on the breadth and universality of Bowen theory. As a result of that conversation, we decided to coedit this book. A call for abstracts was sent out, and the response was overwhelming, representing a diverse range of prospective contributors from a variety of professions. Choosing from the wide pool of Bowen theorists, researchers, educators, and practitioners who submitted abstracts was daunting—and very instructive. This process revealed the number of people across the globe who were connected to Bowen theory in differing fields of specialization. Clearly, this book could attempt to capture the breadth of systems-thinking applications to human behavior by way of Bowen theory, as Charlie indicated earlier. It could also provide an opportunity for an exchange of ideas and applications among Bowen thinkers if contributors provided contact information and editors listed the various Bowen theory training centers. Of course, every contributor has a singular lens through which he or she views the theory, so each chapter represents its author's unique perspective or specific application, and each reader will obviously make sense of the material through his or her lens. Nevertheless, there is a universality about the theory that informs every chapter.

The years of reading and selecting abstracts and then reading chapters and connecting to the contributors led me to reflect on my own journey with this theory. Having been trained clinically during the 1950s in a psychodynamic framework, I struggled for many years with the sense that there were many missing pieces in my education about human behavior, but it was not until the late 1960s that I discovered the early family systems thinkers. After taking workshops with a number of the pioneers in family systems theory, and particularly listening to panels with all of them in dialogue with one another, I found that the presentations by Murray Bowen resonated with me. I wanted to know more. At the time, with limited funds and children at home, I could not manage getting to the Georgetown Family Center in Washington, DC, to train with him and had to settle for attending the occasional family center–sponsored conference. But my friend and colleague Margaret York was attending the commuter training program at the Center for Family Learning (CFL) in New Rochelle, New York, where, at the time, Dr. Bowen was a frequent trainer. With little coaxing, Margaret persuaded me to join her in this endeavor. So between 1972 and 1976, I participated in the CFL program, learning from and being challenged by Dr. Bowen, Phil Guerin, and Tom Fogarty. While Margaret and I were participating in the program at CFL, we also invited others back home to join us at weekly meetings after work. We read, studied the theory, and worked at using it to understand our own family systems and the family systems of our clients. For me, that adventure began what has become a lifelong journey.

In the mid-1970s, William McPeak secured a grant from the National Institute of Mental Health to initiate a family systems theory and therapy program within the clinical track at Syracuse University's School of Social Work. It became the most popular track at the school, and when the grant ended, the family mental health concentration became the single mental health track for many years, eventually quadrupling in size. Bowen theory was a solid piece of that track. During this time, there were many naysayers both within and outside the university. Critics suggested that the theory was antifeminist, disallowed feelings, and was at the very least just a fad. But it nevertheless remained a strong component of the family mental health concentration curriculum. After graduation, a select number of students would also seek coaching and supervision in Bowen theory. A Bowen theory component remains in the current curriculum alongside other systems theories, although it is not as central as in earlier years.

Today, it would be difficult to land a grant such as the one mentioned earlier. The field is moving toward evidence-based practice, and that is currently where funding is focused. Certainly, evidence is critical to the science of human behavior for which Bowen was striving. The question for me is, "What qualifies as evidence?" Self-reporting and short-term elimination of symptoms are not evidence of basic change. Focus on an individual can inform only one piece of the whole. A systems model studies the family unit over the generations, thereby presenting an enormous complexity for research. Not only are the many variables tracked, but consideration of how they interact must also be part of systems-based research endeavors. Observations focus on what people do instead of what they say they do. Moreover, research about humans will, at some point, have to be anchored in physiological markers. The chapters in this book provide examples of the variety of ways in which students of Bowen theory approach learning, practice, and research.

An area that has been particularly eye-opening for me involves the links between the behavior of other living organisms and that of humans. The scientists I have listened to at the Bowen Center for the Study of the Family Symposia and interdisciplinary dialogues, and the follow-up reading I have done, have helped me understand Bowen's concept of the emotional system. The first time I heard John Bonner (1980, 1988, 2009) present on the activity of slime molds as a system and listened to Frans de Waal (1982, 1988) discuss the relationships of chimpanzees, I was introduced to a new world of understanding systems. The chapters in this book presenting research with other species are examples of this type of work being done by people formally trained in Bowen theory.

Throughout my journey, there are many who have given me opportunities to learn. I gained a new understanding of the triangles in my family system from my work with Phil Guerin. And although Tom Fogarty did not see the relevance of the work with other species, his thinking about the individual in the system and emptiness and its relationship to closeness were very illuminating for me. The opportunities I had to interact with Dr. Bowen were humbling. He could say something to me that would reverberate for months, challenging any understanding I thought I had of myself. In a research seminar, when I was trying to understand variation in my clients' relationships with me, Kathy Kerr asked where I was in my relationship to Bowen theory and family during each time period—an insight that helped me connect this variation back to my own family relationships and systems-thinking development. Every interaction I have with a person who thinks within the framework of Bowen theory contributes to my own understanding of self and of systems concepts. It is my hope that this book will do the same for others. We have provided information about each contributor and an Appendix listing the network of Bowen theory training centers and contributor organizations throughout the country. We hope that these resources will encourage people to exchange their thinking about the theory, which may contribute to fostering its continued development.

This project has been a long and arduous but worthwhile journey, with much personal gain for me. Most valuable was the opportunity to learn more about the theory and myself as I moved through the editorial and publication process. Preparing this book provided an opportunity to continue observing self in relationship and, I hope, to make use of those observations.

—Ona Cohn Bregman, MSS, March 2010

References

Bonner, J. T. (1980). *The evolution of culture in animals*. Princeton, NJ: Princeton University Press.

Bonner, J. T. (1988). *The evolution of complexity by means of natural selection*. Princeton, NJ: Princeton University Press.

Bonner, J. T. (2009). *The social amoebae: The biology of cellular slime molds*. Princeton, NJ: Princeton University Press.

de Waal, F. B. M. (1982). *Chimpanzee politics: Power and sex among apes*. New York, NY: Harper & Row.

de Waal, F. B. M. (1988). *Peace-making among primates*. Cambridge, MA: Harvard University Press.

Weinberg, S. (1992). *Dreams of a final theory*. New York, NY: Pantheon.

Acknowledgments

It is difficult to know where to begin acknowledging those who have contributed to my connection to Bowen theory and, as a result, also contributed to enriching my life and my commitment to this book. It is with appreciation that I acknowledge the people who initially introduced me to Bowen theory in the early 1970s: a very special friend and colleague, Margaret York; Phil Guerin; Tom Fogarty; and Murray Bowen. Throughout the years since then, my students, clients, colleagues, friends, and others have contributed to my learning.

A person is who he or she is in relationships, and I have been fortunate to be in relationships with so many special people. I appreciate being part of a family system that over the generations has left room for each person to develop self and be able to remain connected throughout the ups, downs, and change. This has helped to pave the way for my journey with Bowen theory. The generations that follow me, my children Mark and Randi and grandchildren Brook, Sonja, and Carl, are an inspiration, and I thank them for being who they are. My husband of 53 years, Bernie, is always a support at the same time as he challenges me. I am grateful for his love and commitment. Because my family is honest in their feedback to me, they are a major source of my learning about myself. My 99½-year-old mother, Sylvia, who often asked when this project would be completed, did not live to see it finished. I hope that it will be one way to honor her memory.

Finally, this book would not exist if it were not for my coeditor, Charlie White, who gave birth to the idea. In addition, his talent for refining technical aspects, presentation, and language was an invaluable contribution. Working together gave me one more opportunity to observe self in relationship. In his acknowledgement, Charlie mentions my patience. Patience has never come easily to me, and the opportunity to practice it was a challenge and a gift.

I thank and value all those I have mentioned and those I may have missed.

—Ona Cohn Bregman, MSS, March 2010

As this project comes to a close, I find myself reflecting on the contributions of so many people—both personally and professionally—who were directly or indirectly involved in bringing this project to fruition. First and foremost, to my father and mother—the former, the first to coach me on hypothesizing about patterns of human behavior by taking me as a young child on archeological adventures to 100-year-old garbage dumps and abandoned settlements in search of old bottles and other relics. And the latter, whose 1950 college honors thesis, "Mathematics in Nature and Art," and whose interest in talking with me about these subjects influenced my topic selections on several primary and secondary school term papers and many of my high school and college photography subjects. May this book be an extension and a partial fulfillment of those interests and what you were trying to impart to me.

I am thankful for the years of thoughtful and principled engagement with my Bowen theory coaches and mentors, beginning with my first coach, Syracuse-area marriage and family therapist Mike Lynch, who in 1985 drew that first family diagram on a paper napkin at the Syracuse University Student Center Food Court and who, unbeknownst to either of us at the time, helped launch a struggling 22-year-old on a thus far 25-year quest to find out more about "that theory" that looks at relationship triangles, birth order, and those visually powerful family diagrams. A year later, as a newly minted college graduate in my first bachelor's-level social services job, I had the incredible fortune to cross paths with Tom Schur, who, at the time, was serving as a clinical consultant to my department at the social services agency. Many thanks to Tom for giving me a name for "that theory" and my first full introduction to Bowen family systems theory; he also, in the early 1990s, helped me sharpen my focus and solidify my interest in Bowen theory into a lifelong commitment by simultaneously serving as my social work internship supervisor and my "family systems theory," "therapist's own family," and "family mental health" professor, and, later, my coach.

In 1995, when I first heard Michael Kerr present and provide supervision to my fellow trainees and me during my first year in the Princeton Family Center's postgraduate training program, I knew that he was someone to whom I could present my best theory and family process thinking with a certain ease and get constructive feedback that motivated me to take ownership of the next steps of the work at hand. This extended throughout my remaining Princeton postgraduate training and my training years in the Special Postgraduate Program in Bowen Family Systems Theory and Its Applications at the Bowen Center for the Study of the Family, where I was fortunate enough to be able to continue my work with Mike as a member of his supervision group. As an important supplement to this work, I would be remiss not to mention the evening "beers and Bowen theory" discussions with my fellow trainee roommate, Michael Quinn. Finally, the relationships I have forged with several fellow participants in Dan Papero's Research Seminar have been invaluable to the development of my thinking in recent years—especially the dialogues with my frequent roommates Randy Frost and Phil Klever.

As for the book itself, a "perfect storm" of circumstances, with the requisite three or more elements coming together in close succession shortly after I finished my Master of Social Work studies in 1992, formed the impetus for this book. Peg Miller, director of field instruction at Syracuse University's School of Social Work, is to be thanked for sending me and my host agency social work interns who, over successive years, seemed to have progressively greater interests in wanting a formal means of learning the fundamentals of Bowen theory. It is with great appreciation for their desire to learn Bowen theory, and for the courage and budding Bowen theory interests of my friend and agency colleague, George Lufkin and my first agency client, Tom, whom I continued to work with as he was finishing up a human services degree at State University of New York Empire State College—and the director of this degree program, Thomas Hodgson, for giving me that first opportunity (and the conference room space) to design and facilitate a formal undergraduate- and graduate-level seminar on Bowen theory that was also consistent with the host agency's operating philosophy. My coeditor, Ona Cohn Bregman, is also to be thanked for her critical role in helping this seminar come about through her willingness to sponsor the social work interns' independent studies. For providing the final element in the perfect storm of circumstances, a special thank you goes out to my Family-of-Origin Response Survey (FORS) co-developer and research seminar colleague Selden Dunbar Illick, whom I first met and had a brief conversation with at the close of a Syracuse Family Center conference at which she was a keynote speaker. I walked away from that conversation with a conviction that there was a significant need for this book and a strengthened resolve to see this project through no matter how long it took.

Several of my fellow Bowen Center Special Postgraduate Program trainees are to be thanked for their short papers documenting their Bowen theory work in a broad array of venues and practice disciplines. Through listening to these papers and having follow-up meetings with these trainees, I was able to develop an initial list of potential chapters for this book. Cheryl Lester deserves special thanks in this regard not only for presenting a trainee paper that profoundly challenged me and other trainees not to limit our thinking about where and how Bowen theory could effectively be used but also for challenging me not to place emotional-process scripted limits on myself as to my capacities and, specifically, as to what roles I could assume in bringing this book to fruition. I am grateful to Paul Glasser, my first faculty advisor at Rutgers University, for allowing me to do a three-credit independent study to develop the book proposal and for suggesting that I contact George Zimmar, who, through a series of fortuitous circumstances, eventually became the book's publisher. I am most appreciative of Allison Zippay, director of the Social Work Doctoral Program at Rutgers University, who was, and continues to be, a source of constant encouragement to me in my scholastic pursuits, thereby simultaneously exemplifying the highest value in academia and social work—the right to self-determination. Finally, a sincere thanks to an early social science academic blind reviewer of the book proposal who, after being given detailed abstracts for every book chapter documenting the unprecedented breadth of Bowen theory application, reflexively cast aside as mere hyperbole my stance that this qualifies Bowen theory for serious consideration as one of the most significant social science theories of the 20th and current centuries. Nothing since has more reinvigorated my actions or conviction that an authentic natural science of human behavior could not be developed and disseminated soon enough.

As for my chapter, I extend my recognition and respect to my dual recovery intensive outpatient services (Dual Recovery IOS) colleagues, interns, and clients, who day after day brought their best thinking to the learning-for-self opportunities afforded by these services, thereby greatly enhancing the theory-grounding and differentiation-of-self potential of these opportunities for all participants, which simultaneously promoted the continual development of these services. Bob Leipholtz and Lee Gardner deserve special recognition in this regard, as does my supervisor, Walter Frankel, for giving me the opportunity to develop these services from the ground up and for having my back over more issues and time than either of us care to count or remember. Many thanks to Alan Lightfoot, whose "write a training manual" course assignment provided me with the initial and sustaining motivations to reflect on and document the nuanced developmental trajectory of the Dual Recovery IOS. Each of my social work Research Methods I and II sections and students deserve thanks for providing me with additional evidence that it is possible, although exceedingly difficult and sometimes perilous, to cultivate learning-for-self atmospheres around academic subjects over which students tend to have such to elevated anxiety that it often promotes scholastic underfunctioning, learned helplessness, and powerful emotional urges to be passive recipients of information. And finally, my greatest appreciation for Rutgers University evolutionary anthropologist and biologist Robert Trivers—whose "Natural Selection and Social Theory" joint undergraduate–graduate seminar course is the finest example of a cocreated learning-for-self opportunity and environment that I have ever encountered or participated in—for showing me by example that this can be done.

My talented wife of 20 years, Melanie, and our two wonderful daughters, Rebecca and Theresa, deserve my extra-special recognition and thanks—the former for bearing with me as I worked on this project for more than half our marriage and for lending her considerable creative abilities and skills to this project at critical times, and the latter for bringing a zest for life and an eagerness for learning that I find both inspiring and infectious. Also deserving of this level of thanks and appreciation is my coeditor, Ona Cohn Bregman, whose tenacity for staying on schedule and meeting deadlines coupled with her long-suffering patience with me as I juggled this project with parenting young children, is largely responsible for this book's making it to publication.

—**Charles M. White, MSW, March 2010**

Joint Acknowledgment

We consider it a rare privilege to have been able to engage the chapter authors over the details of their efforts to bring systems thinking to life and to have been able to work with all of the Bowen theorists who submitted initial abstracts for this book.

Michael E. Kerr deserves special thanks for his willingness to take time from his demanding schedule to contribute the Foreword to the book. Thanks also go to copy and chapter editor Diana Biro and APA-style editor William Aue for their work on the chapters, which significantly improved the style, quality, and uniformity of the book from cover to cover. The creative art-direction work of Melanie White is most appreciated for providing the book proposal design, formatting, and binding, and for developing the cover design, adding significantly to the appearance of both.

Mary Evans and Marlie Wasserman were invaluable to us at a critical stage in moving the project forward by giving us some much-needed validation on what we had accomplished thus far, constructive feedback on the initial book proposal, and several suggestions as to which commercial and academic presses to approach about potentially publishing the book.

Michael E. Kerr and Daniel V. Papero deserve recognition for being instrumental to our developing an initial list of contacts to approach for abstracts, providing us with the names of everyone they knew who were presenting the theory in some sort of practice context. Cheryl Lester is to be thanked for the vital role she played in this book's early development, as is Ruth Sagar for giving us permission to reprint two chapters from the book *Bowen Theory and Practice* (Sagar, 1997).

Peter Titelman is greatly appreciated by us for the constructive feedback he offered on our initial proposal and for making himself available for numerous consultations over the course of this project. Finally, Fred Coppersmith, developmental editor, and Marta Moldvai, senior editorial assistant at Routledge Mental Health, and Eve Malakoff-Klein, book project manager at Cadmus Communications, merit our sincere gratitude for their patience with our neophyte publishing questions and their unwavering support of us throughout this process.

Reference

Sagar, R. R. (Ed.). (1997). *Bowen theory and practice: Feature articles from the family center report 1979–1996*. Washington, DC: Georgetown Family Center.

Editors

Ona Cohn Bregman, MSS, retired from her position as associate professor of social work at Syracuse University in 2003 to devote herself to several writing and research projects related to Bowen family systems theory. She had been a faculty member at Syracuse University since 1985. Ms. Bregman was chair of the School of Social Work's Family Mental Health Concentration from 1991 to 1998, was selected Social Work Teacher of the Year by her colleagues in 1995, and served on the board of the Syracuse Family Center from 1991 to 2001. The Mental Health Association of Onondaga County, New York awarded Ms. Bregman its Lifetime Achievement Award in 2007. She received her BA from Goucher College in 1954 and her MSS in psychiatric social work from Syracuse University in 1958. Ms. Bregman participated in the commuter training program at the Center for Family Learning in New Rochelle, New York from 1972 to 1976 and has been studying Bowen family systems theory ever since. She has made numerous presentations over the past 34 years on aspects of Bowen theory and its applications at local, regional, and national conferences and to a variety of human service, religious, and civic organizations. Ms. Bregman continues to maintain a small private practice in systems psychotherapy, consultation, and supervision. Her primary research interests concern variations in human behavior and the neurobiology of emotion. The author of several newsletter essays, journal articles, and book chapters, Ms. Bregman's recent publications include an invited commentary on "Reframing Client Issues in Aging and Ability," and a case study on "Building Interventions in Cases Where Gender or Sexuality is at Issue" for *Social Work Practice With a Difference: A Literary Approach* (Lieberman & Lester, 2003) and the chapter "Triangles in the Academy" for *Triangles: Bowen Family Systems Theory Perspectives* (Titelman, 2008). Ms. Bregman lives in Syracuse, New York with her husband Bernard. They are the parents of two and the grandparents of three.

Charles M. White, MSW, is a social work field liaison with Rutgers University's School of Social Work (New Brunswick and Newark, New Jersey) and a doctoral student at Rutgers University's Graduate School—New Brunswick. He also maintains a Bowen theory–based psychotherapy, supervision, and training practice in Westfield, New Jersey. Since completing his Master of Social Work degree at Syracuse University in 1992, Mr. White has held several clinical, supervisory, research, and adjunct academic positions. A student of Bowen theory since 1985, he participated in postgraduate education and training in Bowen theory at the Syracuse Family Center and the Princeton Family Center for Education and in the Special Postgraduate Program in Bowen Family Systems Theory and Its Applications at the Bowen Center for the Study of the Family in Washington, DC. Since 2001, he has been a participant in Dr. Daniel V. Papero's Research Seminar at the Bowen Center for the Study of the Family. Mr. White is co-developer of a psychometric scale that attempts to measure emotional reactivity between parents and their adult offspring, the Family-of-Origin Response Survey (FORS), which is featured in the chapter, "Toward Understanding and Measuring Emotional Cutoff," in *Emotional Cutoff: Bowen Family Systems Theory Perspectives* (Titelman, 2003). Mr. White lives in Westfield, New Jersey, with his wife Melanie and their two young daughters, Rebecca and Theresa, with whom he has had the wonderful privilege and superb enjoyment of being on a rather unconventional adventure as their after-school and evening caregiving Daddy since their respective births.

References:

Bregman, O. (2003). Reframing client issues in aging and ability: Invited commentary. In Lieberman, A., & Lester, C. (Eds.), *Social work practice with a difference: A literary approach* (pp. 171–176). New York, NY: McGraw Hill.

Bregman, O. (2003). Building interventions in cases where gender or sexuality is at issue. Case study: Three women. In Lieberman, A., & Lester, C. (Eds.), *Social work practice with a difference: A literary approach* (pp. 210–218). New York, NY: McGraw Hill.

Bregman, O. C. (2008). Triangles in the academy. In P. Titelman (Ed.), *Triangles: Bowen family systems theory perspectives* (pp. 403–417). New York, NY: Haworth Press/ Taylor & Francis.

Ilick, S. D., Hilbert-McAllister, G., Jefferies, S. E., & White, C. M. (2003). Toward understanding and measuring emotional cutoff. In P. Titelman (Ed.), *Emotional cutoff: Bowen family systems theory perspectives* (pp. 199–218). Binghamton, NY: Haworth Clinical Practice Press.

Contributors

Katharine Gratwick Baker, PhD, is a clinician, business consultant, and trainer based in Northampton, Massachusetts. In addition to her training in Bowen theory, she received an MA in Russian Studies from New York University and a MSW and PhD from the Catholic University of America. She is a student of the Russian language and Russian history and has been presenting Bowen theory to Russian psychologists and social workers in Moscow from 1988 to 2005. She has published numerous articles and an edited book on Bowen theory in Russian for Russian clinicians. Dr. Baker has worked with family enterprises and closely held firms, providing executive and leadership coaching, strategic planning, time management seminars, and organizational learning services. She is especially tuned to the complexities of companies operating in the global marketplace and has a particular interest in working with family foundations and family philanthropies.

G. Mary Bourne, MSW, received her degree from the University of Minnesota in 1971, followed by 25 years of private clinical practice. From 1975 to 1978, Ms. Bourne studied in the Special Postgraduate Program in Bowen Family Systems Theory and Its Applications at the Georgetown Family Center (now the Bowen Center for the Study of the Family). In addition to individual and family therapy, she taught a series of Bowen theory workshops and a 10-session theory course for family therapists in Minneapolis. In 1980, she talked with Dr. Murray Bowen about starting a nonprofit training center in Minnesota, patterned directly after the Georgetown four-times-a-year program and with Dr. Bowen and Dr. Michael Kerr as its major facilitators. In 1981, Ms. Bourne became a founder and the director of that center, the Minnesota Institute of Family Dynamics (1981–1995). In July 1988, realizing the unique nature of the 8 years of Dr. Bowen's audiotaped sessions to date (1981–1988), she negotiated a contract with him that allowed her to edit and publish the collection. The transcripts and audiotapes will eventually be archived at the National Library of Medicine.

Jennifer A. Brown, MSc, is a clinical social worker and founder and director of the Family Systems Institute in Sydney, New South Wales, Australia. She works in the clinical program at the institute in addition to running training programs in Bowen theory for the Sydney region. She is currently a doctoral candidate at the University of New South Wales, where she is researching parents' interface with their adolescent's mental health treatment. Ms. Brown regularly presents at Australian family therapy and mental health conferences and has published in the *Australian and New Zealand Journal of Family Therapy* on applications of Bowen theory.

Patricia A. Comella, JD, has been on the faculty of the Bowen Center for the Study of the Family in Washington, DC, since 1993, where her primary focus has been on applications of Bowen theory to the study of emotional process in society. She received her undergraduate degree in mathematics from Hofstra University and her law degree from Georgetown University, and she has done additional graduate work in computer science and probability theory. Professionally, she applies her knowledge of Bowen theory to the formulation of public policy and the conduct of multiparty negotiations. Ms. Comella has had interdisciplinary experience, both in the United States and abroad, through public sector work (with NASA, the Nuclear Regulatory Commission, and the U.S. Department of State) and private sector legal, regulatory, and management consulting work in the area of nuclear energy law.

Mickie W. Crimone, MS, APRN, is a nurse psychotherapist in private practice in the Washington, DC, metropolitan area. She received a BSN from Georgetown University and an MS in psychiatric nursing from the University of Maryland Graduate School of Nursing, and she completed additional training in Bowen family systems theory at the Center for Family Learning in New Rochelle, New York. Ms. Crimone has coached hundreds of church, business, and health care leaders across the country. She is a cofounder of the Center for Family Process in Bethesda, Maryland, and was associated for 25 years with the late Rabbi Edwin Friedman, who pioneered the application of Bowen theory to leadership. As a leader, she has served as the director of a wide range of public and private organizations, and she conducts workshops and gives speeches on leadership and family systems theory nationwide.

John J. Engels, MA, is founder and president of Leadership Coaching, Inc., one of the longest running leadership development courses based on Bowen theory and natural systems research. Mr. Engels and his team of Bowen-trained consultants offer a comprehensive menu of services including individual leadership coaching, executive team development, and large group presentations on the science of leadership. He studied and has presented at the Bowen Center for the Study of the Family after an initial introduction to Bowen theory through Rabbi Edwin Friedman. Mr. Engels has worked with thousands of business leaders over 26 years, including business-owning families; global corporations; not-for-profit, government, and educational institutions; and nongovernmental service organizations based in Europe and Asia. He has appeared on ABC's *20/20* and has published many newspaper and magazine articles.

Priscilla J. Friesen, MSW, is on the faculty of the Bowen Center for the Study of the Family. She was the director of the Postgraduate Program in Bowen Family Systems Theory and Its Applications from 1990 to 2003. She administered the biofeedback clinical and training programs from 1979 to 1987. In 2005, she cofounded The Learning Space, which incorporates neurofeedback into consultation with families and organizations. The Learning Space offers learning forums for professional and community groups that highlight family, brain, and body interconnections.

Randall T. Frost, MDiv, is director of training and research at Living Systems in Vancouver, British Columbia, Canada. Living Systems is a pastoral counseling center that uses Bowen family systems theory as its primary clinical approach in counseling, education, training, and research. Rev. Frost is an ordained Presbyterian minister in the Presbyterian Church (USA). He was an assistant professor of pastoral studies at St. Meinrad School of Theology in St. Meinrad, Indiana, from 1978 to 1991. He regularly presents at conferences and symposia on such varied themes as the use of Bowen theory in pastoral ministry, the definition of key variables of Bowen theory including differentiation of self, the development of a model for outcome research of family therapy based on Bowen theory, the study of cases demonstrating societal emotional process and, most recently, the distinctive use of language by Bowen in defining the theory.

Mary Greenberg, PhD, is an animal behaviorist and an adjunct research associate in the School of Social Welfare at the University of Kansas. She recently finished her appointment and is developing an academic course on the impact of the natural sciences on culture. Dr. Greenberg is the first researcher to reformulate Bowen theory into an alternative structural framework to examine the possible complexity of social relationships in nonhuman animals. Her focus on interdisciplinary studies has resulted in advising students (Anthropology, Ecology and Evolutionary Biology, and English departments) interested in the foundations of evolution and animal social behavior. Dr. Greenberg is investigating research on social bonds in animals to identify contributions of the alternative framework that explain problems challenging traditional approaches, and biological mechanisms of social stress in humans as they affect disease processes in cancer.

C. Margaret Hall, PhD, is professor of sociology at Georgetown University. She has studied Bowen family theory since 1971 and is the author of *The Bowen Family Theory and Its Uses* (Jason Aronson, 1981). Dr. Hall specializes in theory construction in clinical sociology, with particular attention to social intelligence. She has strong research interests in the emotional bases of social intelligence in individual and social behavior. Dr. Hall has authored numerous scholarly articles, several books, and many book chapters.

David S. Hargrove, PhD, is Kulynych/Cline Distinguished Professor of Psychology at Appalachian State University, Boone, North Carolina. A former chairman of the Department of Psychology at the University of Mississippi, he studied Bowen family systems theory for many years at the Bowen Center for the Study of the Family. Dr. Hargrove's research and teaching interests include family systems theory and therapy, community psychology, serious mental illness, rural health, mental health, and literature and psychology. Dr. Hargrove is the author or coauthor of numerous journal articles and book chapters related to his research and teaching interests.

Victoria A. Harrison, MA, has a private practice in Houston, Texas, where she provides psychotherapy and self-regulation using biofeedback and neurofeedback based in Bowen theory. She directs the Center for the Study of Natural Systems and the Family in Houston and commutes to Washington, DC, to serve on the faculty of the Bowen Center for the Study of the Family. A focus of her clinical work, research, teaching, and writing is using Bowen theory and the sciences to understand human functioning, health, and reproduction.

Douglas Hester, DMin, is an ordained Lutheran pastor and a licensed marriage and family therapist. He is currently serving as counseling pastor at St. Andrew Lutheran Church in San Antonio, Texas. He leads family systems classes in the leadership ideas of Rabbi Edwin Friedman across Texas and Arkansas and is also a frequent presenter at regional and national Bowen theory conferences.

LeAnn S. Howard, MSW, MA, maintains a private practice based on Bowen family systems psychotherapy and supervision, the Kansas City Center for Family and Organizational Systems. She has conducted training of family systems therapists since 1980, and, since 2004, has been a field assistant to Dr. Deborah M. Gordon, professor of biology, Stanford University, in the long-term field research of harvester ant behavior. Ms. Howard is currently involved in writing and presenting regionally and nationally on Bowen theory's potential contributions to ecological research.

Michael E. Kerr, MD, has been a faculty member at the Georgetown Family Center (now the Bowen Center for the Study of the Family) since 1972. Dr. Kerr succeeded Dr. Murray Bowen as the director of the Georgetown Family Center in 1990 after a 20-year close association with Dr. Bowen. His primary research interests consider the relationship of Bowen theory to evolutionary theory; the relationship of physical, emotional, and social symptoms to family emotional process; and the process of differentiation of self in clinical work. Dr. Kerr frequently presents, on these and other topics related to Bowen theory, across the United States and abroad—at medical schools, universities, meetings of national organizations, and regional conferences. He is the featured lecturer for a new series of videos, *Bowen Family Systems Theory and Its Applications* (Bowen Center for the Study of the Family, 2004), and is the editor of *Family Systems: A Journal of Natural Systems Thinking in Psychiatry and the Sciences* (1994–present), which is published by the Bowen Center for the Study of the Family. Dr. Kerr has authored several articles, book chapters, and two books on Bowen theory and its applications: *One Family's Story: A*

Primer on Bowen Theory (Bowen Center for the Study of the Family, 2003) and *Family Evaluation: An Approach Based on Bowen Theory* (W. W. Norton, 1988), which he coauthored with Dr. Bowen.

Rita Butchko Kerr, PhD, RN, is Professor Emerita of Nursing at Capital University, Columbus, Ohio, where she taught for 36 years. Dr. Kerr's BSN, MS, and PhD degrees are from the Ohio State University. She was a past participant in the Postgraduate Program in Bowen Family Systems Theory and Its Applications at the Bowen Center for the Study of the Family. Dr. Kerr's areas of scholarship and research focus on family nursing and psychiatric–mental health nursing. Her clinical expertise includes psychiatric–mental health nursing; individual, marital, and family therapy; nursing research; transcultural nursing; and nursing leadership and management. The author of several book chapters and nursing journal articles, Dr. Kerr was a frequent presenter at national and international nursing educator conferences. The recipient of a Fund for the Improvement of Postsecondary Education Grant, Dr. Kerr also taught as part of an international consortium of three U.S. and three E.U. nursing graduate programs offering nursing graduate students a certificate in international, interdisciplinary, family-focused health care. She continues to serve as a team leader on the Commission on Collegiate Nursing Education evaluation teams for the American Association of Colleges of Nursing in Washington, DC.

Donna G. Knauth, PhD, RNC, is an advanced-practice maternal–child health nurse of more than 40 years. She held professorial appointments at Rutgers University, the University of Maryland, Georgetown University, and the Catholic University of America. Dr. Knauth began her studies in Bowen family systems theory during her doctoral studies at the University of Pennsylvania in the School of Nursing and, after graduation, continued her studies in the Postgraduate Program in Bowen Family Systems Theory and Its Applications at the Bowen Center for Study of the Family in Washington, DC. She is a consultant in family theory and uses Bowen theory as the theoretical framework for her research. She serves as a reviewer of research manuscripts for the national nursing journal *Nursing Research.*

Annette Kolski-Andreaco, MSW, MURP, provides management consultation and coaching to business customers as an account executive with LifeSolutions, an employee assistance program company. She also designs and presents training to employee groups and management on the intersection of work and personal functioning with an emphasis on health and wellness. Before joining LifeSolutions, she was the director of the Western Pennsylvania Family Center, where for 12 years she learned Bowen theory. She has been an executive director or senior leader in five human service or health care organizations. She maintains a private family therapy practice.

Cheryl B. Lester, PhD, is a faculty member in the Department of English and the American Studies Program at the University of Kansas and has served as director of American studies since 2006. She attended the Postgraduate Program in Bowen Family Systems Theory and Its Applications from 1997 to 2001, and she has attended the Postgraduate Seminar at the Kansas City Center for Family and Organizational Systems since 2006. Her research has primarily focused on the writings of William Faulkner as studies of the intransigence of one-sided thinking and its roots in human relationships; her own thinking has been enlarged over the past decade through extensive transnational research on her Jewish family of origin.

Michael J. Nel, DTh, is a Lutheran pastor with 19 years of parish experience in western Canada, a fellow of the American Association of Pastoral Counselors, and a registered clinical counselor in British Columbia. He was the director of consultation to clergy for the Lutheran Church in the Pacific Northwest (United States) from 2003 to 2009. Dr. Nel graduated from the University of Cape Town, South Africa, with a Bachelor of Arts degree and received Master of Divinity and Master of Sacred Theology degrees from the Lutheran Theological Seminary in Saskatoon, Saskatchewan, Canada. In 2008, he received a Doctor of Theology degree from the University of South Africa on completion of the dissertation *The Ancestors and Zulu Family Transitions: A Bowen Theory and a Practical Theological Interpretation* (University of South Africa, 2008).

JoAnne Norton, EdD, specializes in helping large multigenerational family businesses prosper across generations. An associate of the prestigious Family Business Consulting Group, she works with families to improve communication, to develop the next generation of leaders, and to coach nonfamily executives. Dr. Norton earned her doctorate in organizational leadership from Pepperdine University and did postgraduate work at the Georgetown Family Center (now the Bowen Center for the Study of the Family). In 2001, she founded the Family Business Dynamics course at California State University, Fullerton.

Daniel V. Papero, PhD, is a faculty member at the Bowen Center for the Study of the Family, a member of the board at the center, and a member of the editorial board for *Family Systems: The Journal of Natural Systems Thinking in Psychiatry and the Sciences*. In recent years, he has increasingly consulted with organizations across the United States in both the private and the public sectors about the impact of relationships on functioning and about the emotional process of organizations. He has authored one book, several articles, and several book chapters on various aspects of Bowen theory, family psychotherapy, and Bowen theory–based supervision and training. Dr. Papero maintains a consulting practice in Washington, DC.

Dennis A. Romig, PhD, is the chief executive officer of Side by Side, Inc., in Austin, Texas. Dr. Romig and his company have trained more than 10,000 leaders from industry (e.g., Texas Instruments, Shell, and IBM) and government. He is the author of the 2001 and 2002 *New York Times* bestselling book *Side by Side Leadership* (Performance Research Press, 2001), which also won the award as the Best Business and Career Book of 2002. Romig also authored *Breakthrough Teamwork: Achieving Outstanding Results Together* (Performance Research Press, 2000) and *Structured Synergy@: Outstanding Results Across Organizations* (Performance Research Press, in press). Romig has participated in and led Bowen family systems programs since 1995.

Thomas J. Schur, MSW, a systems therapist is a licensed Social Worker, a Marriage and Family Therapist, and an Approved Supervisor for the American Association for Marriage and Family Therapy. He maintains his private practice opened more than 35 years ago. As a member of the faculty at Syracuse University for more than 20 years, he continues to teach systems theory and practice courses in the School of Social Work and supervises interns in the Department of Marriage and Family Therapy. His thinking in all of this work has been grounded in Bowen theory since the 1970s.

Peter Titelman, PhD, maintains a private practice in clinical psychology specializing in Bowen family systems therapy, consultation, and professional education in Northampton, Massachusetts. He received his PhD from Duquesne University in Pittsburgh, Pennsylvania. Dr. Titelman has studied Bowen theory for 35 years and has edited four books on the theory and its applications. He has run a Bowen theory consultation group for more than 30 years and taught Bowen theory to Russian psychologists in Moscow from 1999 to 2005.

Anthony J. Wilgus, MSW, is an associate professor of social work at the University of Findlay in Ohio. Having taught in the undergraduate social work program since 1987, he has maintained a career-long interest in Bowen theory. In addition to presenting papers at the Bowen Center for the Study of the Family Annual Symposium, he has published chapters in edited books devoted to a review of the Bowen theory concepts of emotional cutoff and triangles.

Kathy Wiseman, MBA, teaches people to live, work, and govern their family businesses, foundations, and offices. Her expertise is in merging two tracks: business skills and Bowen family systems theory. She is a faculty member at the Bowen Center for the Study of the Family and adjunct faculty at the George Washington University School of Business, where she heads the Family Office Forum. She served as a dean of the Family Office Exchange Learning Academy, Chicago, IL, and president of the Family Firm Institute's Education and Research Foundation.

I

Theoretical Considerations in Learning Systems Thinking and Bowen Theory

Theorists in the future century, will move more rapidly toward a more factual theory, and ultimately toward science. The human is as scientific as all other cellular life on the planet. The human is also a feeling being, which is not scientific. Past theorists have found it impossible to connect the scientific with the nonscientific. Bowen Theory has conceptualized the human as a scientific creature, that also feels.

Murray Bowen, MD, August 6, 1989[1]

This section considers the theoretical foundation of Bowen family systems theory and explores the challenges and reciprocal aspects associated with the aptitude to learn and use systems thinking and theory, as well as the capacity to responsibly manage self in relationship systems. It also highlights the potential universality of Bowen theory and the requisite intellectual rigor, personal integrity, and authenticity needed to develop, sustain, and apply a systems perspective across life roles and circumstances.

---

[1] From *Commitment to Principles: The Letters of Murray Bowen, MD* (p. 22), compiled in 2007 by Clarence Boyd. This unpublished document reproduces a sampling of the letters of Dr. Murray Bowen that are archived at the National Library of Medicine in Bethesda, Maryland. To obtain a copy, contact Clarence Boyd at EscondidoFarm@aol.com

1
Observing Emotional Functioning in Human Relationship Systems: Lessons From Murray Bowen's Writings

PATRICIA A. COMELLA

This chapter provides a brief introduction to the eight interrelated concepts of Bowen family systems theory: *differentiation of self, nuclear family emotional system, family projection process, multigenerational transmission process, triangles, sibling position, emotional cutoff,* and *emotional process in society.* The theory facilitates observation of human behavior and functioning at multiple levels, including individuals in the context of the relationship systems to which they belong, the members in relationship to each other, and the systems overall. Learning and using Bowen theory effectively are correlated with the capacity to observe one's own emotional functioning in the relationship systems to which one belongs or is associated. All students of the human condition can benefit from improving their capacity for self-observation. The author discusses the process of building such capacity, particularly through consideration of Bowen's 1978 book, *Family Therapy in Clinical Practice,* and his 1988 epilogue, "An Odyssey Toward Science" in *Family Evaluation: An Approach Based on Bowen Theory* (Kerr & Bowen, 1988), coupled with a discussion based on the author's experience and thinking about the theory's application (see Comella, 1995, 1997, 2001, 2006, 2009).

Accurately observing and understanding human behavior and emotional functioning in the relationship systems to which humans belong require a systems frame of reference for making and interpreting observations of those systems and skill in applying that frame of reference. *Bowen theory,* a descriptive natural systems theory about emotional process in the human species, provides such a frame of reference for understanding how humans respond emotionally to the world in which they live. It broadens the observer's perspective from a focus on the behavior and functioning of individual people to a focus on the behavior and functioning of human relationship systems as a whole and of their members, in the context of mutual influencing from and mutual responding to relationship forces from within and outside of those systems in an ongoing, dynamic fashion.

Skill in using a natural systems frame of reference such as Bowen theory comes from the observers' continuing efforts over an extended period to increase their capacity for accurately observing their own emotional functioning in the relationship contexts in which the observations are taking place. People's capacity for accurate self-observation and their capacity to understand and apply Bowen theory are directly correlated. Learning Bowen theory and improving the capacity to observe one's own emotional functioning are inextricably interrelated. One cannot master Bowen theory without becoming a master of self-observation. Conversely, gaining mastery of Bowen theory, which requires a focus "on functional *facts* of relationships" (i.e., "on what happened, how it happened, and when and where it happened, insofar as these observations are based on fact"; M. Bowen, 1978, p. 261), assists in building the capacity for accurately observing emotional functioning in oneself. (For further discussion about functional facts of relationship systems, see M. Bowen, 1978, pp. 261–262, 359–360, 416–419; for a comprehensive index to Bowen, 1978, see Pemberton, 2006.)

Bowen's research demonstrated that there are challenges to accurate observation, but that with sustained effort challenges can be met and their effects mitigated or perhaps overcome. One challenge in the development of Bowen theory concerned appropriate criteria for deciding when to replace a frame of reference based on the observations. Another challenge concerned overcoming observational blindness in the observers. A third challenge concerned increasing the capacity to distinguish between emotional process within the observers in reaction to what they were observing and emotional process in the relationship systems under observation.

Bowen (1978) and the epilogue to Kerr & Bowen (1998) documented those challenges and the steps Bowen and his research team took to address them. Read chronologically according to their original dates of publication, the chapters of *Family Therapy in Clinical Practice* convey a sense of the stages through which Bowen and his research team progressed in accreting and interpreting accurate observations of human emotional functioning. A reader learns how the research team members came to understand how they were inadvertently and adversely contributing to increasing the intensity of the emotional process in the research families and were adversely affecting the team's capacity for accurate interpretation of the observations of the families. A reader also learns about the steps Bowen took to overcome this observational blindness challenge.

Observational blindness is a phenomenon about which all students of the human condition, be they mental health professionals, anthropologists, historians, lawyers, teachers, public policy makers, and so forth, need to be wary. Bowen's insight into the process of learning how to overcome observational blindness can be applied to developing competency in self-observation. The word *applied* cannot be overemphasized because only an ongoing action-based engagement works in an observational process. An effective engagement will include active self-observation and self-assessment of the observer's capacity to distinguish fact from nonfact, internal responses from the emotional reactivity of those under observation, and one's own contributions to the intensity of the emotional process being observed from the contributions of others. (For a discussion of the author's efforts to deal with observational blindness, see Comella, 2006.)

In developing the theory that bears his name, Bowen devoted more than 40 years to observing the human condition, developing the theory's concepts, integrating the concepts into a coherent theory, and testing the theory with hundreds of families. Bowen's quest for a science of human behavior took him (a) from operating theaters and recovery wards during World War II, where he observed the variation that soldiers exhibited in their recovery from the traumas of war; (b) to the Menninger Foundation in Topeka, Kansas (1946–1954), where he developed his first working hypotheses about the origins of schizophrenia in a mother–child symbiosis; (c) to the research ward of the National Institute of Mental Health (NIMH) in Bethesda, Maryland (1954–1959), where he recognized the family as an emotional unit (defined later in this chapter in the section on Bowen theory basics) and schizophrenia as a symptom of family functioning and where he described a continuum of human emotional functioning that included families in which an individual had schizophrenia, families exhibiting less severe symptoms, and "normal" families; and finally (d) to Georgetown University and the Georgetown Family Center (1959–1990), where he integrated the concepts into a coherent theory about human emotional functioning and tested the theory's validity again and again.

The therapeutic setting provided the immediate context for the development of Bowen theory, and the most highly developed application is, not surprisingly, the therapeutic. The original audience to which Bowen communicated his theory was mental health professionals. The language and examples that Bowen chose to use to express the theory reflect his efforts to communicate with that audience in a manner consistent with the facts of evolution and the human as part of life on Earth.

Bowen theory guided the development of therapy, and the observational insights gained in therapy regarding the adequacy of the operating assumptions or hypotheses guided further development of the theory. Although Bowen stated that the theory was "too intertwined with therapy to separate the two" (Kerr & Bowen, 1988, p. 339), out of the theory development process ultimately came a theory that applies to all human relationship systems, with applications going far beyond the therapeutic. Bowen "fashioned a natural systems theory, designed to fit precisely with principles of evolution and the human as an evolutionary being" (Kerr & Bowen, 1988, p. 360). Indeed, Bowen's writings provide the motivated observer of the human condition with an invaluable frame of reference through his focus on the preservation of Bowen theory for the future, emphasis on the use of language drawn from or inspired by biology wherever possible, and continued progress in broad applications of Bowen theory to understanding human relationship systems, coupled with growing confirmation of parallels in the behavior and functioning of members of human and nonhuman relationship systems.

In this chapter, the author explores the application of Bowen theory to accurate observation of human emotional functioning. This exploration begins with a discussion of Bowen theory basics, followed by a discussion of Bowen theory's research foundations, including the necessity for an observational frame of reference at the systems level, exploration of the scientific rigor of the research, and the successive frames of reference Bowen selected as the research progressed toward a systems theory of human emotional functioning. The challenges Bowen and his colleagues encountered in the research, especially the phenomenon of observational blindness, and how those challenges were met, are also discussed. The chapter concludes with an outline of a provisional approach to a frame of reference for observing emotional process in relationship systems at the societal level, by which the author means observing emotional process in relationships consisting, at least in part, of relationship systems other than the family.

Bowen Theory Basics

The research that led to the development of Bowen theory established the following:

1. Understanding individual behavior and emotional functioning requires understanding the relationship context in which the individual is functioning.

2. A person's basic level of emotional functioning is established in that person's nuclear family of origin, which constitutes a natural system of emotionally interdependent people functioning reciprocally in relationship to one another. That system is the appropriate unit for understanding individual functioning, especially a person's basic level of differentiation of self, described later in the section.

3. The founders of a nuclear family come out of a multigenerational family emotional process that shapes how the founders will in turn shape the behavior and functioning of the new generation, including offspring, adopted children, wards or other dependents, and even pets (see, e.g., Comella, 2001).

4. Emotional process shapes functioning in all human relationship systems, including nuclear and multigenerational family systems and nonfamily relationship systems such as the workplace, the larger community, and the general society. Appraisals of threat may take place out of awareness (see LeDoux, 1996), and what appears to be a threat that demands a response may actually be symptomatic of an underlying threat that was not ameliorated by the response.

5. Whatever the level of relationship system being observed, factors in the physical and external relationship environments that the members appraise to be threatening to the relationship system or its members must be taken into account as part of understanding the intensity of the emotional process around the appraised threats.

Emotional Process

Bowen theory describes emotional process in human relationship systems. *Emotional process* occurs automatically in a relationship context and involves the reciprocal responding of living organisms to each other and to the conditions of life to which they must adapt to survive or enjoy an acceptable level of well-being. Emotional process includes appraisals of those relationships and conditions of life and the internal states generated by such appraisals; it is seen in nonhuman species as well as in the human species. It appears to be a defining characteristic of life on Earth and essential to survival and well-being at both the individual and group levels. Without the capability to receive information from the environment, appraise threats as to the risks they pose to survival or well-being, and take appropriate action based on such appraisals, an organism's life would be short. Emotional process is essential to adapt to the conditions of life, to survive long enough to reproduce and rear the next generation, and to achieve an acceptable level of well-being in the relationship systems to which an organism belongs.

Emotional process regulates, and at times may govern, behavior and functioning, especially during times of imminent or potential threat to survival or well-being. Striking parallels are seen among species in patterns of emotional functioning, particularly under threat conditions. When useful, this chapter provides references to studies of functioning in the relationship systems of other species and among humans. For example, Dunbar (1988) examined why nonhuman primates formed social systems and why, within those systems, members make preferential relationship choices. Dunbar concluded that although nonhuman primates may form social systems to manage predation risk, they form special relationships within those systems to manage the stresses of living in groups.

Anxiety

In keeping with the relationship among theory development, its therapeutic application, and the first audiences for Bowen theory (i.e., mental health professionals), Bowen used the term *anxiety* to describe emotional process in response to threat. Threats are categorized as "real" (i.e., imminent and highly likely to materialize) or "imaginary" (i.e., not imminent but nonetheless enduring, irrespective of whether they will ever materialize). Response to a real threat is called *acute anxiety*. Response to an imaginary threat is called *chronic anxiety.* Bowen theory represents a particular effort to understand how anxiety (a) is present in human relationship systems, beginning with the human family; (b) may be contained within a relationship system and transmitted among other members of the same system; (c) may be transmitted from one relationship system to another; (d) may be transmitted from one generation to another over many generations; and (e) in the author's view, may be transmitted from one species to another (see Comella, 2001). Bowen theory may also offer insights into the transmission of anxiety in other species.

Eight Interrelated Concepts of Bowen Theory

Eight interrelated concepts currently make up Bowen theory:

1. Differentiation of self
2. Nuclear family emotional system
3. Family projection process
4. Multigenerational transmission process
5. Triangles and interlocking triangles
6. Sibling position
7. Emotional cutoff
8. Emotional process in society

New concepts were added to the theory as Bowen became satisfied that the weight of the evidence gleaned from the observations supported inclusion of a concept in the theory. Bowen regarded the triangle as the "glue" that integrated the concepts into a coherent systems theory that accurately describes human behavior and functioning. He added the last two concepts, *emotional cutoff* and *emotional process in society*, in 1975 but never regarded the theory as a necessarily complete description of human behavior and functioning. Bowen expected that as new facts and functional facts were discovered about the human as part of life on Earth, new concepts might be added to his theory or it might even be replaced.

The human species is an integral part of life on Earth, and emotional process is common to many if not all life forms. Emotional process in the relationship systems to which individual humans belong circumscribes their autonomy to make choices. *Emotional process, anxiety,* and some of the other terms Bowen used in presenting the theory, such as *emotional unit,* are not concepts of Bowen theory per se, but they are essential to its understanding and application, as are several assumptions and premises, including the premise that evolution of life on Earth is a fact. The basics of Bowen theory are summarized here.

Triangles and Adaptation The *triangle,* a three-party relationship system, is the smallest emotionally stable relationship system in which anxiety at a given level of intensity can be confined to the threesome. Within a triangle, the mechanisms for managing the stresses in the relationships among the three are entirely predictable. Should the intensity increase beyond what the threesome can manage, they will predictably "triangle" in another party and, if necessary, others, until the triangles and interlocking triangles defining the relationship system contain the anxiety. The relationship system that contains the anxiety is an emotional unit, which is described later in the section. Through triangles and interlocking triangles, anxiety may be transmitted from one relationship system to another. Bowen's research established the triangle as the basic building block of all human relationship systems. The triangle integrates the other concepts of Bowen theory into a coherent description of emotional process in human relationship systems. It appears that the triangle may also be a basic building block of nonhuman relationship systems (see, e.g., de Waal, 1988, 1989; Dunbar, 1984, 1988; Fossey, 1983; Lassiter, 2009; Strum, 1987). The relationship system into which a human is born, the nuclear family, is the most influential in shaping an individual's basic flexibility to adapt to life's challenges.

Differentiation of Self and Chronic Anxiety   Flexibility to distinguish between facts and speculations about the conditions of life to which members of a family system are responding, to distinguish the responses of other members to those conditions from one's own responses, to distinguish what one thinks from what one feels, and to appropriately adapt to the changing conditions of life varies from person to person within a family system, from family to family, and from generation to generation according to the intensity of the emotional process operating in the system. The differentiation of self concept captures this variation in people's emotional functioning and places the variation on a continuum related to their basic capacity to accurately perceive and appropriately respond to what is happening in the world around them, especially to challenges from the physical environment or from the relationship systems of which they are a part. Bowen called the capacity to maintain functioning when exposed to sustained levels of stress, or to recover functioning after a period of heightened stress, the *basic level of differentiation.* That capacity is formed in people's nuclear family in their early relationship with their parents (or primary caregivers), who, Bowen theory postulates, have similar levels of differentiation. Variation in emotional functioning is seen in nonfamily relationship systems, among family systems, and among relationship systems at the societal level.

People's flexibility to adapt is directly related to their level of chronic anxiety and the relationship systems to which they belong. Because threat focuses energy and resources to respond to the threat, the greater the level of chronic anxiety, the more likely it is that appraisals of threats and the adaptational choices based on those appraisals will be dominated by emotionally driven considerations, which automatically limit the range of choices. Bowen's research demonstrated that chronic anxiety affects functioning in both family and nonfamily relationship systems. Chronic anxiety within a multigenerational family system is transmitted to the next generation automatically through the primary triangle between an infant and the infant's parents or primary caregivers. The concept of nuclear family emotional system provides a description of emotional process in the nuclear family (see, e.g., M. Bowen, 1978, pp. 165–168, 203–205, 376–377, 475–477).

Emotional Process in the Nuclear Family Emotional System   In a nuclear family emotional system, two individuals, in particular the founding pair, function reciprocally in relation to each other. The pair adapts to stresses in their relationship when those stresses are within limits that are manageable for them. Those limits are related to their basic levels of differentiation. When those stresses exceed levels that the twosome can comfortably manage through the mechanisms of distance, conflict, reciprocal underfunctioning and overfunctioning, or some combination thereof, the pair will automatically focus on an emotionally vulnerable third party and automatically project the stress-related anxiety onto that third party. The threesome will then become an interdependent emotional system reciprocally functioning to manage the stresses in the three-party system.

The family projection process concept describes what automatically happens when the stresses in the relationship between the founding pair exceed the manageable limits and the vulnerable third is an offspring. The concept describes the factors that are likely to affect the pair's targeting of a particular offspring for managing the relationship stresses and how being selected affects the formation of the chosen offspring's basic level of differentiation. The family projection process is present in all families to some degree because of the degree of unresolved attachment, that is, "*fusion* ... between emotional and intellectual functioning" (M. Bowen, 1978, p. 362) or "undifferentiation" that each member of the founding pair brought into their relationship from their respective families of origin. The fusion (or undifferentiation) affects the degree to which threats affecting past generations of the respective families can be distinguished from real challenges to which the nuclear family must respond and, hence, the degree to which response to challenges in past generations have the potential to unduly influence or otherwise inappropriately compromise nuclear family response to present challenges. In other words, the degree of fusion and level of chronic anxiety transmitted through the multigenerational transmission process are correlated. In this manner, the emotional functioning of each member of a nuclear family emotional system is shaped through a multigenerational transmission process in which chronic anxiety from the previous generation is transmitted and mediated through the family projection process to the next generation. The multigenerational transmission process concept describes the changes that can occur over time in the average basic levels of differentiation of family members in the different family lines.

In a nuclear family emotional system, the founding partners must strike a balance between meeting their individual needs and meeting the emotional needs of one another and the other members of the family. The greater the degree to which the founding partners have had difficulty in separating emotionally from their own families of origin, the greater is the likelihood that they will experience difficulties in managing themselves in their relationship with each other and in striking an appropriate balance. The manner in which people begin their lives as adults is captured by the concept of *emotional cutoff*. The concept captures the physical and intrapsychic distancing mechanisms used by people as they try to function independently of significant others with whom they remain emotionally interdependent, in particular, their own parents.

Where there is extreme distancing (which Bowen termed *emotional divorce*) between the founding partners in trying to maintain separate identities in their relationship, a pattern of reciprocal functioning may emerge in which one partner chronically and automatically overfunctions and the other chronically and automatically underfunctions as part of managing the intensity of the marital relationship. Physical, emotional, or social symptoms may characterize the underfunctioning. With emotional divorce, there is increased likelihood that the founders will project their immaturities onto one or more of their offspring, in an effort to stabilize their own relationship. Bowen found emotional divorce between the founding partners and the emergence of schizophrenia in an offspring to be correlated.

Within a nuclear family, the intensity of the family projection process varies among offspring, according to several factors, including anxiety in the family system during the pregnancy and surrounding the birth. The research has established that birth order, gender, birth spacing, and the presence or absence of certain attributes or defects are among the factors that may affect selection of offspring for varying degrees of impairment through the projection process. On the basis of Toman's research, documented in *Family Constellation: Its Effects on Personality and Social Behavior* (Toman, 1976), the concept of sibling position established that, on average, the offspring of partners will exhibit predictable personality characteristics based on their birth order, gender, and birth spacing in relation to the birth order, gender, and birth spacing of their parents in their respective families of origin. The concept also established that deviations from the expected characteristics are indicative of heightened intensity of emotional process in the nuclear family at the time of the offspring's birth(s). The deviations may arise from internal or external factors. Although not addressed explicitly by Bowen, it would appear that the personality characteristics derived from considerations of sibling position are deeply rooted in nuclear family emotional process and probably the multigenerational transmission process.

Emotional Process in Society   Observations establishing how anxiety may be transmitted from the family to the larger society, and the converse, led to the addition, in 1975, of the concept of emotional process in society to Bowen theory. This concept describes chronic anxiety at the societal level and its effect on societal functioning over time. The concept explains the erosion of emotional functioning that happens to a family when subjected to sustained chronic stresses beyond that family's capacity to manage the intensity of the emotional process through containment of the anxiety within the nuclear family or extended family relationship system. The concept postulates that a parallel process can occur in relationship systems other than the family when such relationship systems are subjected to unrelieved stress exceeding those systems' carrying capacity (i.e., triangles serve the same function in non-family social systems as they do in nuclear family emotional systems). The observational data underlying this concept established a link between family emotional process and societal emotional process in the case of juvenile delinquency under circumstances in which the juvenile's social acting out had consequences that demanded the attention and resources of both family and societal-level relationship systems to constrain or respond to the acting out (M. Bowen, 1978, pp. 273–276).

An associated societal regression hypothesis, added at the same time, postulates that prolonged erosions of societal functioning (i.e., societal regressions) might have biological underpinnings rooted in the human's disharmony with the rest of nature. (For further discussion, see M. Bowen, 1978; Comella, 2009.)

Emotional Units   An *emotional unit* may be defined as the system of triangles and interlocking triangles that keeps the chronic anxiety contained and managed wholly within a nuclear family emotional system, an extended family emotional system, or a social system through the mechanisms of conflict, distancing, reciprocal underfunctioning and overfunctioning, and projection among members of that system. Emotional units have a specific environmental context, which includes influences from both the physical environment and the relationship factors external to the system. Should internal or external stresses increase the level of anxiety in the emotional unit such that the anxiety can no longer be contained in the system, the excess anxiety will be projected externally through triangles and interlocking triangles, thereby redefining the emotional unit. To accurately observe functioning within an emotional unit, one must be able to describe the external environment within which the emotional unit is functioning, understand functioning within the unit, and understand how the study unit and external environment interrelate and mutually influence each other.

Bowen's research established the nuclear family as the emotional unit for observing the functioning of a nuclear family member, with the founding partners' multigenerational families of origin providing one component of the specific environmental context. Bowen's research did not identify a generic emotional unit at the societal level, although the process between family and certain societal components in the case of juvenile delinquency, which provided the data for the emotional process in society concept, does describe a specific emotional unit.

In general, at the societal level the emotional unit must be "discovered" through an observational process that uses an appropriate frame of reference. In the section on observing human emotional functioning at the societal level (see "The 1975 Concepts of Emotional Cutoff and Emotional Process in Society," later in this chapter), a methodological approach to defining and applying a preliminary frame of reference to observations of societal emotional process is described. The approach is based on considerations of the study approach that Bowen used to establish the emotional process in society concept. It also reflects consideration of the societal regression hypothesis.

Research Foundations of Bowen Theory

Bowen's life goal was to move toward a rigorous science of human behavior. Scientific inquiry is a dynamic, open-ended process. Bowen characterized his inquiry in terms of movement (a) from an educated guess or assumption or notion (preliminary estimate); (b) to an educated guess about a tiny piece of the total puzzle (hypothesis); (c) to a larger piece of the total puzzle (concept); (d) to a logical fit of concepts into a larger explanation that represents a careful analysis of abstract principles and factual data (theory); and (e) to sufficient data, carefully guided by the rules for scientific research, to prove the accuracy of the theory, such that a theory is no longer necessary (scientific fact; Kerr & Bowen, 1988, pp. 349–352). In turn, preliminary estimates, hypotheses, and concepts provided the frames of reference that ultimately led to an integrated natural systems theory about human emotional functioning at the behavioral and psychological levels within a broader theoretical framework that considered the human as part of life on Earth and evolution as a fact: Bowen family systems theory.

At each step along the way, Bowen used the then-current frame of reference to make observations and choices about the observations. For example, were the observations discrepant with what would have been predicted from the frame of reference? If not discrepant, were the new observations consistent with previous observations that were also consistent with the frame of reference? If the observations were discrepant, were they a reflection of observational bias, flowing from an inadequate observational approach? Or were they new facts, pointing to the need to replace the frame of reference, consistent with the new facts? In sum, Bowen made progress toward a science of human behavior by using successive frames of reference, thereby bootstrapping his way to a natural systems theory of human emotional functioning at the behavioral and psychological levels grounded solidly in rigorous observation and interpretation. (For more on bootstrapping a natural systems theory, see Bates, 1990.)

The observational data on which Bowen based the concepts of the theory were gleaned during more than 10,000 hours of observing humans in the relationship systems to which they belonged. The observations extended over dozens of years and involved hundreds of people, multigenerational family systems, and relationship systems at the societal level, including work systems and the systems associated with problems of juvenile delinquency. Bowen theory is grounded in those observations, coupled with rigorous formulation and testing of hypotheses consistent with those observations. The developmental process was accompanied by "a comparative study of disciplines that dealt with the human," including "psychiatry, psychoanalysis, psychology, medicine, sociology, anthropology, ethology, physiology, biology, philosophy, social work, religion, mathematics, physics, botany, chemistry, evolution, systems theory, astronomy, [and] paleontology," with most of the disciplines including "a mixture of fact and feeling states" (Kerr & Bowen, 1988, pp. 359–360).

Bowen's odyssey toward a science of human behavior and functioning can be divided into three consecutive phases that roughly paralleled the progress of the research at the Menninger Foundation, NIMH, and Georgetown University/Georgetown Family Center. In the first phase, Bowen focused on the question of where Freudian theory lost science. In the second phase, Bowen addressed the questions of how a listener–observer in the therapeutic setting might separate feeling from fact and of how a listener–observer might define new ideas on the basis of fact without being disrespectful of different frames of reference or those who used them. In the third phase, Bowen focused on the question of how unverified ideas from Freudian theory might be replaced by scientific facts from evolution that could eventually be proven and validated.

Freudian theory provided the initial frame of reference for the research leading to the development of Bowen theory. As Bowen's odyssey toward science progressed, the weight of the evidence from the observations he was making led him to modify his initial framework to make it consistent with the observations. Ultimately, this bootstrapping, iterative process of observation, testing, and modification of the observational frame of reference resulted in the formulation of Bowen theory. Bowen ultimately came to believe that much of Freudian psychoanalytic theory was nonfactual, with foundations in literature rather than in science about human beings. However, Bowen believed that the transference and countertransference phenomena of Freudian theory (see Freud, 1939/1964) belonged in the realm of scientific facts and that these phenomena operated automatically in all significant human relationships, not merely in the psychoanalytic relationship (Kerr & Bowen, 1988, pp. 352–353).

Bowen recognized that the universality of automatically replicating and projecting into significant relationships one's early life experiences presented particular challenges to carrying out any descriptive research requiring the observation of emotional process and that those challenges had to be success-fully addressed. The author believes that Bowen's understanding of and experi-ence with the transference and countertransference phenomena assisted him in understanding the observational blindness phenomenon and devise research methods that avoided or mitigated the effects of observational blindness in himself, in the research staff, and in the research families themselves. Progress in devising appropriate research methods and achieving the theoretical under-standings went hand in hand with the effective management of the observational blindness phenomenon. The intertwining of therapy and theory development rendered management of the observational blindness phenomenon imperative.

The author surmises that Bowen applied his knowledge of transference and countertransference along the following lines: (a) Knowledge on the part of an observer of the transference and countertransference phenomena and some capacity to manage the countertransference increased the likelihood that the observations possessed the necessary factual quality to form an adequate basis for a descriptive theory about emotional process in human relationship systems and (b) specifically, this knowledge contributed to confidence that the observer could adequately distinguish between the feeling states of those being observed and the feeling states the observations were generating in the observer. In other words, a direct relationship existed between the capacity of the observer to manage the countertransference and the degree to which the observational data could be replicated.

Distinguishing facts and functional facts from nonfacts is a *sine qua non* of accurate observation of emotional process in human relationship systems, whether the context is one of research or the psychoanalytic or some other sig-nificant relationship. If researchers could avoid projecting their own expecta-tions from their own early life experiences onto the research families they were trying to observe, they could better distinguish among facts that the family members were relating, feeling states that the facts were arousing in the family members, and feeling states that the recitation was arousing in them. Should the researchers fail to avoid or only partially succeed in avoiding a counter-transference, there would be distortion of the observations as they were being filtered through the feeling states of the researchers' countertransferences. Thus, in the end, the validity of the observations being made hinged on the researchers' ability to manage their own reactivity to the content of what the family members were reporting and to discriminate fact from nonfact.

During his years at the Menninger Foundation (1946–1954), Bowen devel-oped preliminary ideas about the human emotional system, the human capac-ity for distinguishing between fact and feeling states, and the human's capacity to be an individual in a relationship system in which there is pressure from within the system to conform with the feelings of the moment and to the deal-ings of other members of the system. Bowen brought those ideas to NIMH and applied them in a research project (1954–1959) that ultimately included offspring with schizophrenia, their parents, and their siblings living together on a research ward under the observation of a research staff. Individual behavior and functioning came to be understood in the context of the families of which the individuals were a part.

To overcome observational distortions arising from observational blindness, Bowen wrote a "Rule Book" at NIMH that incorporated and reflected what was known about schizophrenia at the time. The Rule Book guided the therapy. Whenever there was a discrepancy between the predictions embodied in the Rule Book and the outcomes observed, the researchers went back to determine whether the fault lay in the rules or in the research staff's application of the rules. Over time, the predictions and outcomes matched better, and the discrepancies became attributable to misapplication of the rules.

In 1957, the research investigators in the NIMH research project were able to put "all families on a broad continuum" of emotional functioning (Kerr & Bowen, 1988, pp. 366–369). In 1959, Bowen moved to the Department of Psychiatry of the Georgetown University Medical Center in Washington, DC. Bowen modeled the Georgetown program on the NIMH developments and findings, which guided everything that transpired in the Georgetown program. The emerging theory "might be modified or extended by factual data from the emotional system or from the differentiation of self, but never by 'spur of the moment' feelings from the therapist or theoretician" (Kerr & Bowen, 1988, p. 373).

In its present form, the eight interrelated concepts of Bowen theory— differentiation of self, triangles, nuclear family emotional system, family projection process, multigenerational transmission process, sibling position, emotional cutoff, and emotional process in society—make up an integrated theory. The integration of the first six concepts of Bowen's theory occurred in the 1966 timeframe when he operationalized his understanding of the triangle in his own family of origin (Kerr & Bowen, 1988, p. 379). The addition in 1975 of the concepts of emotional cutoff and emotional process in society permitted new levels of integration. The societal regression hypothesis associated with the latter concept postulated biological underpinnings to at least some prolonged societal regressions, further extending theory development (see M. Bowen, 1978; Comella, 2009).

Table 1.1 highlights significant steps in the development and integration of Bowen theory through that period. By reviewing Table 1.1, it is possible to get a sense of how the frames of reference, improvements in the observational process, and concepts of Bowen theory developed in an orderly and integrated fashion. (The dates in Table 1.1 are approximate.)

Bowen theory was not born all at once, nor was it operationalized all at once. By 1957 (the dates are based on the original publication dates or on the first presentation of the research results), Bowen understood that the working hypothesis about the transfer of anxiety from the mother to her child

Table 1.1 Significant Steps in the Initial Development and Integration of Bowen Theory

Date published	Development reported in *Family Therapy in Clinical Practice* (M. Bowen, 1978)
1957	• Transfer of anxiety from mother to child with schizophrenia • Mother–child dyad as fragment of a larger family system

1959	• Primary threesome of mother, father, and child with schizophrenia described:
	  – Threesome as basic unit of interdependence
	  – Emotional divorce between the parents
	  – Functioning within the threesome and in external relationships
	  – Reciprocal functioning
	  – Overadequate or underadequate reciprocal functioning with equal degrees of immaturity

Presented 1959/published 1961	• Seeing shifts in behavior as relationship based • The "Rule Book" • Importance of the therapist's own functioning
1960	• Changes to hypotheses based on observations: from symptom in patient arising out of mother and a child with schizophrenia symbiosis to symptom in family manifested in patient • Shift in research orientation to family as single organism—an emotional unit and appropriate unit of observation • Multigenerational concept of schizophrenia's origin • Family emotional process in projection of anxiety in parents to child
1961	• Family as emotional unit captured in the term *undifferentiated family ego mass* • Functional helplessness within family • Opposing viewpoints in parents as way of maintaining separate identities • Separating a self from nuclear family emotional process through differentiation of self process
1965	• Efforts/challenges in communicating concept of family as an emotional unit • Observational blindness phenomenon • Family theory of emotional illness • Mature person defined

(continued)

Table 1.1 Significant Steps in the Initial Development and Integration of Bowen Theory (continued)

Date published	Development reported in *Family Therapy in Clinical Practice* (M. Bowen, 1978)
1966	• Spectrum of human adaptation presented • Emotional fusion • Differentiation of Self scale—variation in human emotional functioning • Family projection process in schizophrenia • An integrated theory of human emotional functioning • Centrality of triangle to integration of the theory

diagnosed with schizophrenia could not fully explain the research observations. By 1959, the research had extended the understanding of the relationship among the mother, the father, and the child with schizophrenia as being interdependent and had extended the understanding of the characteristics of the relationship between the mother and the father. The importance of the researcher's own functioning in what was occurring in the observational process with the research families and the need for a scientifically rigorous methodology for modifying a hypothesis were better understood. Out of that understanding came the Rule Book to guide the observational process and the modification of the working hypotheses.

By 1960, there was growing recognition of the family as the emotional unit for understanding individual functioning and of the family projection process as the mechanism for transferring anxiety in the parents to the symptomatic child. The hypothesis that the emergence of schizophrenia is the outcome of a multigenerational transmission process accompanied these insights. By 1961, there was increased understanding of the relationship forces operating within the nuclear family that influence its members' individual functioning and the development of a therapeutic approach whereby motivated family members could undertake a long-term process to take responsibility for their own functioning within the nuclear family emotional system, in the context of the larger multigenerational family emotional system. Such an effort could lead to a greater capacity for self-regulation *within* those systems, as well as *within* other relationship systems. The word *within* is emphasized because, throughout the differentiation of self process, the continuing objective is to remain in solid emotional contact with the anxiety in the nuclear family emotional system and with the other members of the emotional unit without absorbing the anxiety or further fueling the intensity of the process.

By 1965, it was clear that the members of a nuclear family emotional system formed an interdependent emotional unit and that there were challenges, captured by the term observational blindness, to accurately observing emotional process within that unit. It also became clear that the research discoveries about patterns of emotional functioning in the research families occurred in all family relationship systems, although the level of intensity and the intensity of the family projection process varied from system to system. By 1966, Bowen was able to operationalize his understanding of the triangle in his own family of origin and see its centrality to individual and family functioning. Bowen was then able to integrate the first six concepts into a coherent theory. Table 1.1 captures these developments, with the "Date published" column providing the year of original publication of the paper that reported the specific development, as documented in *Family Therapy in Clinical Practice* (M. Bowen, 1978).

The 1975 Concepts of Emotional Cutoff and Emotional Process in Society

Before its addition to Bowen theory in 1975, the concept of emotional cutoff had been, in Bowen's words:

> a poorly defined extension of other concepts for several years. It was accorded the status of a separate concept to include details not stated elsewhere and to have a separate concept for emotional process between the generations. The life pattern of cutoffs is determined by the way people handle their unresolved emotional attachments to their parents....The concept deals with the way people separate themselves from the past in order to start their lives in the present generation. Much thought went into the selection of a term to best describe this process of separation, isolation, withdrawal, running away or denying the importance of the parental family. However much *cutoff* may sound like informal slang, I could find no other term as accurate for describing the effort. The therapeutic effort is to convert the cutoff into an orderly differentiation of a self from the extended family. (M. Bowen, 1978, p. 382)

The concept promotes a new level of integration of facts and functional facts about what might be called the "emotional legacy" of chronic anxiety imported by the marital pair through their own undifferentiation into their newly formed nuclear family and the impact of that legacy on nuclear family emotional process. In an emotional cutoff, it is not possible to cut onself off from the chronic anxiety that has been transmitted multigenerationally through the projection process in each generation. However, there is cutoff from knowledge of the sources of the anxiety, which makes it more likely that efforts to transcend the anxiety will prove ineffectual. The chronic anxiety will continue to have a constraining effect on functioning. In the therapeutic application of Bowen theory, people can take on the effort of "bridging" the cutoff through contact with their living extended family and through acquiring facts about family functioning in the past. The knowledge acquired through this process can provide the basis for understanding the source of the chronic anxiety transmitted from the past, its past adaptiveness as a response to real threats or challenges, and its present maladaptiveness as an appropriate response to challenges facing the nuclear family headed by the marital pair. In sum, the process of bridging the cutoff, which also includes managing self in the moment in the presence of living members of the extended family, has the potential for diminishing the undifferentiation arising out of the unresolved emotional attachment. (For further discussion on the phenomenon of emotional cutoff and its intergenerational transmission, see Friesen, 2003, 2009.)

Bowen (1978, pp. 269–270) also added the emotional process in society concept to the theory in 1975, after having first defined it in 1972. Associated with the concept is a hypothesis about the biological underpinnings of at least some prolonged societal regressions (*societal regression hypothesis*). By establishing that triangles in societal-level relationship systems (*social systems*) operate the same as triangles in nuclear family emotional systems, the concept of emotional process in society extends Bowen theory to all human relationship systems. Moreover, the societal regression hypothesis postulates that drivers of prolonged societal regression may be related to the human's disharmony with the rest of nature. Considering the family as an economic unit of society as well as an emotional unit as defined in Bowen theory facilitates understanding of the reciprocal functioning between the family and the larger social systems of which the family is a part (see J. Bowen, 1990, 2009).

The process leading to articulation of the emotional process in society concept and the extension of Bowen theory to relationship systems at the societal level took place over an 18-year period. The impetus for Bowen to pull together his thinking and assemble the evidence that ultimately supported the addition of the emotional process in society concept to the theory came in 1972–1973 in response to an invitation from the Environmental Protection Agency (EPA) to do a paper on man's predictable response to crises (M. Bowen, 1978, pp. 269–270). *Crises* are inherently threatening to survival or well-being and demand an immediate response. They represent "a vitally important or decisive stage in the progress of anything," "a turning point," and a "state of affairs in which a decisive change for better or worse is imminent" (*The Oxford English Dictionary*, 1998). As an instinctual being, the human will respond to crises automatically, even if the underlying antecedents of a crisis are not fully within awareness or understood. Bowen took the opportunity of the EPA invitation to postulate a link between what he saw happening beginning in the 1960s and humans' overrunning of the planet.

According to the emotional process in society concept, sustained chronic anxiety is a necessary condition for a *societal regression*, which is a process that over time compromises a society's capacity for making intellectually determined choices. Choices increasingly become emotionally driven to allay the sustained chronic anxiety. The anxiety is an automatic, instinctual response to a sustained, underlying threat that is unknown, unacknowledged, unrecognized, or all of these at the societal level. This means that at the intellectual and cognitive levels, there is cutoff from knowledge of the threat, but at the emotional level, there is vague, undifferentiated awareness of the anxiety elicited by the threat. The felt anxiety is ready to be expressed in action—often action directed at resolving some issue around which societal conflict has erupted. The issue perceived to be stirring the conflict is seen as the cause of the sustained chronic anxiety. It is not. Therefore, the action is largely or wholly ineffectual at relieving the underlying anxiety because the underlying risk from the anxiety-triggering threat has not been sufficiently addressed, if at all. Bowen referred to the tendency in a societal regression for there to be "emotional band-aid legislation," which exacerbates the problem rather than fixes it. The ineffectuality of the response heightens the anxiety, and the regressive cycle repeats. As the societal regression progresses, the patterns of emotional functioning described by the other Bowen theory concepts intensify, and the flexibility to adapt to relationship stresses diminishes (see M. Bowen, 1978, p. 386; Comella, 2009). *Societal regression* is a process of erosion of functioning over time. At an earlier stage of the regression process, the functioning is less compromised. There is greater capacity for choice and action based on intellectually determined principles. In other words, the functioning level of differentiation at the societal level is higher on average at the beginning of a societal regression.

The concept does not include a scale of differentiation of societal functioning analogous to the scale of differentiation of individual and family functioning that is included in the differentiation of self concept. This lack of a baseline makes it difficult to judge the functioning level of differentiation of relationship systems at the societal level and whether the patterns of functioning observed indicate the presence or absence of regression. This is because anxiety can occur with change representing progression and with change representing regression, because each involves challenges and response to challenges and, hence, anxiety (M. Bowen, 1978, p. 271). However, with the use, where practicable, of comparative studies such as those carried out by Murray Bowen in establishing the foundation for the emotional process in society concept and such as those being used by Joanne Bowen in her studies of human subsistence systems, it may become possible to determine whether a process is regressive or progressive.

Despite the potential of Bowen theory to illuminate understanding of human behavior and functioning in all human relationship systems, application of the theory to understanding societal-level behavior and functioning remains underdeveloped, in part, the author believes, because application of the theory to societal-level questions is not straightforward. However, the theory's concepts about family functioning can be used to construct a research-oriented methodology and iterate frames of reference that consider how each might inform the study of emotional process in society and investigations involving the societal regression hypothesis.

Toward a Frame of Reference for Observing Human Emotional Functioning at the Societal Level

In this section, eight lessons gleaned from the research foundations of Bowen theory are described. They are based on consideration of the foundations of each of the theory's eight concepts and the societal regression hypothesis. Of particular importance methodologically is the comparative study on which the concept of emotional process in society is based. In the discussion that follows, the author uses the words *observer* and *researcher* interchangeably.

Lesson 1: Comparative Analysis of Societal and Family Emotional Functioning Where Possible

The elusive connecting facts that provided the foundation for the emotional process in society concept established that patterns of emotional functioning at the societal level parallel patterns of emotional functioning in the family under conditions of sustained chronic anxiety. The study that Bowen chose to underpin the emotional process in society concept was a comparative study. The author believes that this study, which is discussed in Bowen (1978), offers a methodological blueprint for systematically advancing the eventual application of Bowen theory to all human relationship systems. The study examined changes over time in family and societal functioning in response to adolescent acting out in delinquent actions in the context of broader societal functioning. (For further discussion of comparative studies involving families and the social systems of which they are a part, see J. Bowen, 1990, 2009.)

Lesson 2: Sources of Evidence About Emotional Functioning at the Societal Level

In brief, Bowen detailed changes over time in family response to juvenile delinquency. Bowen observed that under conditions of sustained chronic anxiety, family functioning regressed. The scale of differentiation provided a baseline that enabled Bowen to make the judgment that the emotional functioning he was observing constituted a regression. During the period of the study, Bowen determined that there were changes in functioning at the societal level. Bowen based his judgment on observations of changes in functioning at the local and national levels. At the local level, it could also be based on personal knowledge. Newspapers, magazines, and periodicals provided evidence of changes in functioning at the national level. In some instances, landmark court decisions also provided evidence when there were sufficient details about the functioning of key individuals (M. Bowen, 1978, p. 276). In her studies of subsistence, Joanne Bowen (1990, 2009) has used a variety of sources of factual data to discern interrelationships among changes in subsistence patterns; relationships within the extended family when considered as an economic unit involved in the production, procurement, and distribution of resources necessary for survival and well-being; and relationships between the extended family and its larger society. Sources include account books, genealogical texts, land and tax records, maps and family records, and faunal remains in the geographical areas of study. (See also Baker & Gippenreiter, 1996, and Krupnik, 2009, for further examples of sources and use of sources in societal-level studies.)

Lesson 1 (Revisited): Comparative Analysis of Societal
and Family Emotional Functioning Where Possible

Against the broad backdrop of societal functioning gleaned from the sources described in Lesson 2, Bowen then examined societal functioning over time around the issue of juvenile delinquency. Bowen conducted this study by examining shifts in the approaches used by those components of society that become involved in managing societal response to juvenile delinquency, including law enforcement agencies, the judicial system, schools, and social service agencies. Bowen saw that the functioning of such societal components and of the family exhibited parallel tracks. From this comparison, Bowen inferred a societal regression—that is, an erosion of societal functioning over time. More specifically, Bowen compared societal functioning over time to family functioning over time, and family functioning over time to the functioning levels described in the scale of differentiation. So one way of gaining experience in observing and understanding emotional process at the societal level is to examine issues in which both family and societal functioning can be studied.

Consideration of the implications of the societal regression hypothesis opens new investigative avenues. For example, the spring 2009 conference of the Georgetown University Department of Sociology and the Bowen Center for the Study of the Family, titled "Societies, Families, and Planet Earth: Exploring the Connections," began a synthesis of science about the reciprocal relationships that mutually influence human societies and families and the planet on which they sojourn and from which they derive the basic resources that sustain human societies in the interdependent ecological niches they occupy and share with other life forms. The synthesis is aimed at developing a body of knowledge that connects the behavioral and psychological levels of human functioning, where so much of human drama plays out and which Bowen theory purports to describe, to the biological factors that Bowen hypothesized are shaping and influencing that functioning even when the human is not aware of the process (Comella, 2009, p. 2).

Lesson 3: Distinguishing Among Threats

The societal regression hypothesis postulates that the chronic anxiety that drove some prolonged regressions, such as the one occurring in the post–World War II period, might be "the product of the population explosion, decreasing supplies of food and raw materials necessary to maintain man's way of life, and the pollution of the environment, which is slowly threatening the balance of life necessary for human survival" (M. Bowen, 1978, p. 386).

Bowen distinguished between the postulated underlying threat and the perceived threat related to issues around societal conflict, which provides a focus for the sustained chronic anxiety. An essential lesson to be drawn from the distinction is the importance of being clear about the nature of the perceived threat, the response to that threat, and its effectiveness in allaying anxiety in the societal unit under study. Having examined the effectiveness of the response, it might then be possible to begin to conjecture (and investigate) whether there might be some unknown, unrecognized, or unacknowledged underlying threat that might be the source of the sustained chronic anxiety in the system and offer evidence for that conjecture.

Lesson 4: Defining the Unit of Study

The research basis for Bowen theory established the nuclear family emotional system as the appropriate unit for studying and understanding individual functioning—in particular, the formation of a person's basic level of differentiation in responding to life's challenges. There is no such analogous "ready-made" unit for studying emotional functioning at the societal level. Identifying an appropriate unit analogous to the emotional unit of the nuclear family emotional system becomes the task of the observer. Drawing on Bowen's description of the emotional process in society concept, the observer infers that societal components involved in conflict around societal issues of interest to the observer form an appropriate and provisional starting point for identifying a unit of study analogous to the emotional unit of the nuclear family. From this beginning, other societal components can be added as the study progresses and the facts and functional facts warrant. Drawing on the societal regression hypothesis encourages consideration of whether deeper factors than those suggested by the presenting "symptoms" may be implicated. (In addition to the work of J. Bowen [1990, 2009] and Krupnik [2009], the work of Hillel [1992, 1994, 2006, 2008, 2009] and Outwater [1996, 2009] facilitates understanding of the human's reciprocal relationship with Earth and of the human's impact on resources essential to sustainment of life on Earth.)

The process of identifying the components of the unit for the study of functioning at the societal level and the context for functioning may be iterative. The goal, which may never be wholly reached, is to accurately include in the unit of study all of the interdependent relationship systems that appear to contain the chronic anxiety that is driving the intensity of emotional process around the particular questions or issues being studied and to accurately characterize the external or underlying factors that are influencing functioning within the unit. (Hillel's 1994 book, *Rivers of Eden: The Struggle for Water and the Quest for Peace in the Middle East*, presents in-depth case studies about possible paths to finding peace in the Middle East if the central issue of water is placed on the table and if all of the affected parties are brought to the negotiating table.)

Lesson 5: Assembling a Composite Picture
of Societal Functioning Over Time

The diversity of emotionally charged issues that may provide evidence of anxiety in relationship systems at the societal level is enormous. Through identifying the relationship systems or societal groups anxiously responding to those issues, detailing the facts and functional facts, and identifying patterns of functioning within and among these societal components, the beginnings of an overall picture of emotional functioning of the larger society of which the relationship systems or groups are a part can be put together. With sufficient sampling of issues, it might be possible to put together a composite picture of societal functioning at particular points in time and to begin to understand variation in functioning in the context of variation in circumstances and study units. Slowly, the approach might permit construction of a baseline for societal emotional functioning analogous to the scale of differentiation. Longitudinally, one might be able to draw inferences about progressive or regressive aspects of functioning.

Lesson 6: The Importance of Context—Describing External
Factors Influencing Functioning Within the Unit of Study

It is also clear from Bowen's description that any study of emotional functioning at the societal level must take into account the broader context for functioning within the unit of study. The societal regression hypothesis, which emphasizes the importance of ecological factors, reinforces this view, as does the theory's emphasis on the importance of multigenerational context for understanding nuclear family emotional functioning.

Lesson 7: The Role of Bowen Theory Concepts in Informing
the Study of Patterns of Functioning in the Unit of Study

Having provisionally identified the unit of study, the external factors influencing functioning around the issue or issues of interest, and the threats to which the societal elements composing the unit of study appear to be responding, the observer would use the facts and functional facts that have been gathered to try to examine and draw inferences about the patterns of emotional functioning observed within the unit of study. The patterns of functioning captured in the Bowen theory concepts would guide the examination. For example, drawing on the concepts of nuclear family emotional system and family projection process, the researcher would systematically try to understand and document whether and how the mechanisms of distancing, conflict, reciprocal underfunctioning and overfunctioning, and projection were being used to manage relationship stresses within the unit of study. The triangle concept (with interlocking triangles) would further inform understanding of the dynamic flow of anxiety within the study unit. Drawing on the multigenerational transmission process concept, the researcher might try to understand and document how anxiety has been built into the infrastructure of the laws, regulations, rules, and behavioral norms by which a society governs itself, particularly concerning the issues of interest in the study.

Drawing on the concept of emotional cutoff, the researcher might consider the manner in which facts and assumptions available to the components making up the unit of study about the issues of interest and the underlying threats were being used or not used to inform responses to the perceived threat. Also, the researcher could use the emotional cutoff concept to guide understanding of how transitions are effected, particularly in the occupation of key functioning positions in the unit of study. How transitions are effected would reflect the intensity of the emotional reactivity to unresolved differences between the new and the old occupants around the issues or problems of interest. Those differences would concern the facts and functional facts about the impact of the problems on the unit of study, the perceived adequacy of the old occupants' responses to the issues, and the degree to which the new occupants hold the previous generation responsible for perceived failures to find an adequate resolution to the problems. (Krupnik, 2009, provided an interesting discussion of the relationship between the generations among indigenous peoples of the Arctic in the face of climate change.) The study of transitions in nonhuman societies can assist in illuminating the reciprocal relationship processes involved in transitions. Interesting examples are found in Sherman, Jarvis, and Alexander (1991; naked mole rat societies); Dunbar (1984; gelada baboon harems); de Waal (1988, 1989); Goodall (1986; chimpanzee troops); Ito (1993; social wasps); and Thomas (2000; domestic dogs).

Drawing on the differentiation of self concept, the researcher might examine variation among the components of the unit in their capacity for making choices concerning the issues of interest on the basis of intellectually determined principles in contrast to emotionally driven choices. The most vulnerable components of the study unit would be expected to express their sense of vulnerability to the perceived threat in one of the several patterns described in the concepts of nuclear family emotional system, family projection process, and emotional cutoff. The level of intensity of anxiety that would trigger triangling and the projection process would also be expected to vary according to the functioning levels of differentiation of the components at any point in time and the particular circumstances at the time of the triangling. Variation in functioning between and among different study units might also be examined.

Drawing on the sibling position concept, the researcher might compare the functioning of study components, which may be individuals or relationship components, with functioning in other study units to gain insights into whether and how components occupying similar functioning positions in similar units of study would exhibit, under similar circumstances, similar and predictable patterns of functioning in those positions. On the basis of the sibling position concept, such patterns, seemingly associated with the occupants of the positions, would be expected to be a product of reciprocal relationship processes of mutual influencing and responding related to the study unit's responses to the physical and relationship environments. These reciprocal relationship processes and responses to the physical and relationship environments would be particularly evident under exigent circumstances perceived to be threatening to the survival of the unit or its members or significantly undermining their well-being or functioning. Deviations from the expected patterns would reflect some differences in the levels of threat presented or in the circumstances that triggered the response. An assumption is that similar study units, at similar functioning levels of differentiation responding to similar circumstances, would respond similarly and exhibit similar patterns of functioning.

Drawing directly on the emotional-process-in-society concept, the researcher might attempt to arrive at an overall assessment of whether the emotional functioning exhibited in the unit of study appears to be evidence of a regression, of an interruption or turnaround in a regression, or of no observable change. However, given the lack of a baseline for understanding variation in societal functioning, such assessments would more reliably be done in comparative studies requiring examination of both family and societal functioning around the study issues.

Drawing on the societal regression hypothesis, the researcher would give consideration to the question of whether the issues of focus under conditions of sustained chronic anxiety might not be surrogates for deeper, underlying processes linked to the human's disharmony with the rest of nature.

Lesson 8: Adequacy of the Frame of Reference Guiding the Study Process

Consistent with the research methodology Bowen used, the author believes it is critical to arrive at some judgment concerning the accuracy of the frame of reference used for the study and the accuracy of the observations. Otherwise, it is not possible to make adequate progress toward a science of human behavior. The key to arriving at that judgment would be the identification of any discrepancies between what the observer expected to see on the basis of the frame of reference and what the observer believes he or she observed. In doing so, the observer would also conduct a self-assessment of his or her own emotional functioning, particularly in relation to the presenting issues and the units of study.

To determine whether any discrepancies between the expected and the observed reveal new facts, thereby requiring adjustment of the frame of reference so as to make it consistent with all known facts, it would be necessary to consider whether observational blindness is influencing the process. The observational blindness that Bowen described can affect the postulation of the frame of reference, its application during the observational process, and its application in drawing inferences. This means that observers must be able to evaluate their own emotional functioning in relation to what they are observing. Thus, in ending this section, the author returns to her starting premise that accurate observation of human emotional functioning is grounded in accurate observation of one's own functioning in relationship to what is being observed.

Summary

Bowen theory offers a different, open-ended way of thinking about human relationship systems—specifically about emotional process within and among the components and members of such systems. Bowen theory grew with the addition of new concepts based on the discovery of new facts and functional facts about human emotional functioning. The observational process that produced the observations that form the scientific basis for Bowen theory as applied to family systems has implications for making observations about all other relationship systems of which the human is a part or associated, including relationship systems to which both humans and nonhumans belong and, the author believes, to nonhuman relationship systems as well.

One key to accurately observing emotional process in those systems is accurately observing one's own emotional functioning during the observational process. This requires a frame of reference grounded in facts and functional facts about human emotional functioning. Bowen theory provides such a frame of reference that is directly applicable to family systems. The concept of emotional process in society and the related societal regression hypothesis extend Bowen theory to relationship systems at the societal level under conditions of sustained chronic anxiety. However, the application of Bowen theory to relationship systems other than the family is not well developed.

In this chapter, the author outlined an approach to defining a preliminary frame of reference for observing emotional process at the societal level. Application of that frame of reference took, as a starting point, an issue or issues about which some societal components have expressed anxiety. From that starting point, the frame of reference offered lessons based on Bowen's research methodology that are intended to guide examination of emotional functioning around the presenting issues and to assist in identifying the societal components that should be included in the study unit. The chapter then returned to the necessary step of testing the adequacy of the frame of reference and the adequacy of the observational process and considering whether observational blindness may have distorted the observational process.

References

Baker, K. G., & Gippenreiter, J. B. (1996). The effects of Stalin's purge on three generations of Russian families. *Family Systems: The Journal of Natural Systems Thinking in Psychiatry and the Sciences, 3*, 5–35.

Bates, M. (1990). *The nature of natural history.* Princeton, NJ: Princeton University Press.

Bowen, J. (1990). *A study of seasonality and subsistence: Eighteenth-century Suffield, Connecticut* (Unpublished doctoral dissertation). Brown University, Providence, RI.

Bowen, J. (2009). Human subsistence systems: Family households as emotional and economic units. In Bowen Center for the Study of the Family (Producer), *Societies, families, and planet Earth: Exploring the connections* [DVD]. Available from http://www.thebowencenter.org

Bowen, M. (1978). *Family therapy in clinical practice.* New York, NY: Jason Aronson.

Comella, P. A. (1995). Natural selection, technology, and anxiety. *Family Systems: The Journal of Natural Systems Thinking in Psychiatry and the Sciences, 2,* 138–152.

Comella, P. A. (1997). Naturally constrained social systems. *Family Systems: The Journal of Natural Systems Thinking in Psychiatry and the Sciences, 4,* 19–33.

Comella, P. A. (2001). Triangles: The "glue" of Bowen family systems theory. *Family Systems: The Journal of Natural Systems Thinking in Psychiatry and the Sciences, 6,* 67–76.

Comella, P. A. (2006). A case study in observational blindness. *Family Systems: The Journal of Natural Systems Thinking in Psychiatry and the Sciences, 7,* 133–157.

Comella, P. A. (2009). Emotional process in society: The eighth concept of Bowen family systems theory. *Family Systems Forum, 11(2),* 1–2, 7–9.

de Waal, F. (1988). *Peace-making among primates.* Cambridge, MA: Harvard University Press.

de Waal, F. (1989). *Chimpanzee politics: Power and sex among apes.* Baltimore, MD: Johns Hopkins University Press. (Original work published 1982)

Dunbar, R. I. M. (1984). *Reproductive decisions: An economic analysis of gelada baboon social strategies.* Princeton, NJ: Princeton University Press.

Dunbar, R. I. M. (1988). *Primate social systems.* Ithaca, NY: Cornell University Press.

Fossey, D. (1983). *Gorillas in the mist.* Boston, MA: Houghton-Mifflin.

Freud, S. (1964). *Moses and monotheism, an outline of psychoanalysis, and other works (1937–1939).* In J. Strachey (Ed. & Trans.), *The standard edition of the complete psychological works of Sigmund Freud* (Vol. 23, pp. 139–208). New York, NY: W. W. Norton. (Original work published 1939)

Friesen, P. J. (2003). Emotional cutoff and the brain. In P. Titelman (Ed.), *Emotional cutoff: Bowen family systems perspectives* (pp. 83–108). New York, NY: Haworth Clinical Practice Press.

Friesen, P. J. (2009, July). *Exploring Bowen theory and technology.* Paper presented at the Two Roads Taken: Anxiety in Triangles & Differentiation and the Brain conference, Vermont Center for Family Studies, Essex Junction, VT.

Goodall, J. (1986). *The chimpanzees of Gombe: Patterns of behavior.* Cambridge, MA: Belknap Press.

Hillel, D. (1992). *Out of the earth: Civilization and the life of the soil.* Berkeley, CA: University of California Press.

Hillel, D. (1994). *Rivers of Eden: The struggle for water and the quest for peace in the Middle East.* New York, NY: Oxford University Press.

Hillel, D. (2006). *The natural history of the Bible: An environmental exploration of the Hebrew Bible.* New York, NY: Columbia University Press.

Hillel, D. (2008). *Soil in the environment: Crucible of terrestrial life.* Oxford, England: Elsevier.

Hillel, D. (2009). Influence of the physical environment in the development of the peoples and societies of the Middle East. In Bowen Center for the Study of the Family (Producer), *Societies, families, and planet Earth: Exploring the connections* [DVD]. Available from http://www.thebowencenter.org

Ito, Y. (1993). *Behavior and social evolution of wasps: The communal aggregation hypothesis.* New York, NY: Oxford University Press.

Kerr, M. E., & Bowen, M. (1988). *Family evaluation: An approach based on Bowen theory.* New York, NY: W. W. Norton.

Krupnik, I. (2009). Riding the tiger of climate change: Arctic people experience and interpret their changing environment. In Bowen Center for the Study of the Family (Producer), *Societies, families, and planet Earth: Exploring the connections* [DVD]. Available from http://www.thebowencenter.org

Lassiter, L. (2009). Are there basic characteristics of social groups to prolonged environmental stress? In Bowen Center for the Study of the Family (Producer), *Societies, families, and planet Earth: Exploring the connections* [DVD]. Available from http://www.thebowencenter.org

LeDoux, J. (1996). *The emotional brain: The mysterious underpinnings of emotional life.* New York, NY: Simon & Schuster.

Outwater, A. (1996). *Water: A natural history.* New York, NY: Basic Books.

Outwater, A. (2009). The interconnection of humans and non-humans in the health of water. In Bowen Center for the Study of the Family (Producer), *Societies, families, and planet Earth: Exploring the connections* [DVD]. Available from http://www.thebowencenter.org

The Oxford English dictionary (2nd ed.). (1998). Oxford, England: Oxford University Press.

Pemberton, D. (2006). *A new index to Murray Bowen's "Family therapy in clinical practice."* Washington, DC: Bowen Center for the Study of the Family/Georgetown Family Center.

Sherman, P. W., Jarvis, J. U. M., & Alexander, R. D. (1991). *The biology of the naked mole rat.* Princeton, NJ: Princeton University Press.

Strum, S. (1987). *Almost human: A journey into the world of baboons.* New York, NY: W. W. Norton.

Thomas, E. M. (2000). *The social lives of dogs: The grace of canine company.* New York, NY: Simon & Schuster.

Toman, W. (1976). *Family constellation: Its effects on personality and social behavior* (3rd ed.). New York, NY: Springer.

2
Various Theoretical Points People Miss: A Training Session by Dr. Murray Bowen at the Minnesota Institute of Family Dynamics

Edited by G. MARY BOURNE

Setting the Scene

The presentation that follows is part of a unique 10-year experiment in putting together a Bowen Training Center in the Midwest designed with Dr. Bowen as its central figure. I was a trainee myself, in the four-times-a-year program at the Georgetown Family Center, from 1975 to 1978. During that period, Dr. Bowen came to Minneapolis to participate in a series of Bowen theory workshops, and by 1978, I had a course under way which could, perhaps, be seen as the precursor to a full-blown training program. In the fall of 1979, during the Georgetown Symposium, I proposed to him a plan for a training center in Minneapolis, as similar as possible to the Georgetown four-times-a-year format. I suggested that Dr. Bowen come out four days a year, Dr. Michael Kerr a different four days, and that we also bring three supervisors out from the Georgetown faculty. He listened carefully to my proposal and then said, "It sounds consistent with our program here, and I pledge my support." He agreed to come to Minneapolis for two consecutive days, twice each year.

So, out of a two-person private practice, I set up a non-profit training center, together with Dan K. Myers, MSW, and about a dozen other people who agreed to help establish the non-profit and raise funds for it. The business of bringing in so many people from Georgetown required us to run beginning and advanced classes back-to-back. So the way we worked it out was that the stars (either Bowen or Kerr) would do one day of teaching, I would do one day, and the third day would be used for supervision. Dr. Kerr would cover theory and its application; I would deal with concepts, as well as something on comparative theories; and that would leave Dr. Bowen free to talk to us about his latest thinking. It turned out to be an exhausting schedule for all of us, but a very gratifying adventure, as well.

Audiotapes were made of Dr. Bowen's presentations, largely because of problems with his voice after his two surgeries[1] for aortic aneurysms in May of 1981 and the complication of a partially paralyzed vocal cord, which necessitated speaking into a microphone for even a small audience. But as we began to transcribe the tapes, we began to see something different about the characteristics of his presentations during those years, located as they were between the life-disrupting aneurysms in 1981 and his death in 1990. For one thing, his style took on an *immediacy* that I had not heard before—not really an urgency, but an immediacy in the sense that he used a somewhat more conversational style. He could be just as confrontational as ever, but there was a greater sense that he was listening more closely to his audience in order to hear where they were missing the point. There were, for example, more question and answer periods. Furthermore, he spent more time "going back to square one" to spell out the major points of theory. In the last few years of his life, he was more apt to say things like "that's part of my plan," as if focused not only on the far-distant future (50 to 200 years out), but also on the present generation of theorists and therapists, as well.

It is important—for whatever accidental reasons we audiotaped and transcribed these sessions—that the collection exists. For one thing, it represents the nine years he did those six-hour training sessions, with some of the same trainees continuing throughout. Also, it was, perhaps, the first time he did six-hour training sessions, since at Georgetown, Dr. Bowen led shorter presentations on each of the three days. And even more important is the fact that only a finite number of people ever got to experience such training sessions with Dr. Bowen, in person.

This particular day, which falls about a third of the way through the program, is one of the best organized, in my view. Perhaps it's because on the preceding day, with advanced trainees, he seemed unsure of the outcome. On this second day with beginning trainees, he mentions just briefly, "I was telling the class yesterday all these things I went through 40 years ago—as a background. And I was assuming everybody knew all this stuff. And then I find that people **don't** know it." This comment suggests to me that he seriously rethought his format overnight. It was typical for Dr. Bowen to end a morning session saying, "Most of the questions this morning were technique questions," and then upon returning after lunch, to say, as if to himself, "So, how do you make a point?" That's the sound of immediacy I'm referring to.

I came close to entitling this *A Day in the Life of a Training Program*, because this was the day (April 30, 1984) that lent itself best to a beginning-to-end presentation. In order to pare it down to chapter size, I had to reduce the content by about half. In doing so, I left out a good-sized segment about evolutionary time lines in the morning, and replaced it with a couple of much shorter references to evolution taken from other places. Those appear on pages 36 and 37,

---

[1] Bowen, M. (1981, Fall). My physical functioning. *The Family Center Report*, 3(1), 11.

blocked and dated. Also, I left out a fairly technical section about Symptom Formation in the afternoon. I tried to keep the focus as much as possible on Differentiation of Self, which Dr. Bowen said was also the theme of the video-tape he played. I took creative liberties with punctuation, particularly regarding dashes, italics and bold type, as a way to retain the cadence of his speech and his style of speaking. To the extent that it was possible, the content is verbatim, and people tell me "it sounds like Murray Bowen." I present this, then, as a single day of the Minneapolis training program—as it really happened—from start to finish.

—**G. Mary Bourne**
Editor

Dr. Bowen With Beginning Class of Trainees in Minneapolis, April 30, 1984

Dr. Bowen: I've got a total of about six hours with you today, and I'll do my best to convey as much in that time as possible. For the past three years my voice has been on the weak side, so why don't you move just as close to the front as you can. Otherwise I can't talk so it'll get to the back without a mike, and for a small group, I don't like to get too involved in trying to pull up my voice to the crowd.

I've brought a video tape with me. That'll run something like an hour and a half, after lunch. Then after the tape, we can get into whatever comments you have about it.

There is one major thing I wanted to do today. I wrote all this stuff 35 years ago and most people sift out big hunks of it. So, for the past two years I've been going back to square one with all of the theoretical stuff, and I've been trying to pick up the various points that people miss. Now, if you don't believe that people miss it, in the profession, you got another guess coming. How people can read something and leave out the major part of it—or how they can—see, you're always at the mercy of your own *thinking* system—which dictates your way through life. And you take in whatever your own thinking system permits you to take in, and all the rest of it remains a huge glob that you don't get. So that's what I've been trying to do, is to bring in the major variables that **most** people leave out. You see, every profession has its deficiencies, and leaving out variables is an individual thing—and it's a professional thing. In other words, certain professions leave out certain things that others don't. Every one of them leaves out something, and then beyond that it's an individual thing.

So I've tried to go back and pick up these things, and to say them over, in the hope people might hear. Over the years, I think people have been most inclined to associate my name with "systems theory," without much notion of where *systems* comes from—where does that come from? They do that without much notion about all of the other variables that get into it (laughs). Anyway that's one of the things I'll try to talk about today, as well as I can.

I think there is *one major difference* between my theoretical position and that of the other people in the field. And that is *a lifelong effort to define human functioning as a part of the earth and all living things and of the sciences.*

Back in the early days, I was concerned with why **psychiatry** was not a science like the rest of the sciences. And in my notion, it's a pseudo-science as are **most** things that have to do with human behavior. Not because the human is not a scientific organism, but because of the **heads** of people who think about the human—which makes it into a pseudo-science governed by the scientific method. And if it was a real science, you wouldn't have to have a scientific method. So the scientific method is a device designed to make those things scientific. As far as I was concerned, I didn't see that the scientific method would ever lead the behavioral sciences toward becoming real sciences. And now after another 40 years that's still my position. In other words, I think it has to do with **a basic way of thinking**, rather than what the human phenomenon is like.

So I've been going back to re-review and go back over all the things that I covered 40 years ago. And in that 40 years, it would be: Where did the scientific disciplines get to be the way they are? What is the bottom line for that—the thesis on which the scientific disciplines are based? And I doubted if I'd ever get very far with that. But at least that was my basic thinking—back then—still is!

Anyway—when you start thinking about human behavior from a pseudo-science, with a scientific method, toward becoming a real science, what do you do? Now most of the so-called theories of human adaptation are based on the working—on the basic notion—that the human is unique and different from all other forms of life, which continues to be a major operating premise of the total of society. So that's where the human has been since—for the past 2,000-plus years. And the human's made a pretty good record for himself on the planet, because the world acts almost as if the planet belongs to the human being. So how would you go about seeing the human being as part of **the total complex**, rather than the master of it?

I have absolutely no compunction that **some version of natural systems thinking** will eventually replace our conventional ways of thinking now. And that natural systems theory will, two or three centuries from now, be the basic way of thinking about

Homo sapiens. And I would say if **the human being** is a predictable form of life on earth, then **human behavior** is a science. It **can be** a science.

Now I'm not trying to sell a viewpoint. You're free in buying any viewpoint you want to buy. But remember any viewpoint that you buy, you make a choice. Maybe you've already made a choice—and if you've already made one then you're in good company (laughs). If you haven't made one, then maybe this will at least put in a variable or two to guide your thinking.

Anyway, those are some of the things that went into it. So in the beginning, I looked everywhere including the dictionary for definitions of terms. And the more mixed up society is, the more terms there are that will have a dozen definitions. And when you run into a word with a dozen different definitions, you can know that these are points about which society is not clear. And then you can pick out any definition you like. And there's no such thing as one **discipline** that knows the way, either—**absolutely none**. So when you keep your options open that's one of the things that gets into it (laughs). There ain't nothing making it easy for you. It's all just a simple matter of making decisions for yourself.

The big debate that goes on about that in society now—and that debate is as alive as it ever was—has to do generally with the notion of evolution versus—and the name that's been hooked to it is Darwinism. The other side of the argument gets to be the creationist's viewpoint, which would say that God created the heavens and the earth in a few days, exactly as it is now. And that argument is as alive and well now as it ever was and probably will continue to be. And why will it continue to be? Because for some reason the human brain is open to polarities—to opposing viewpoints. And the human struggle wants to argue these viewpoints, and media debates want to set up the polarities and get people to argue on them. So the human being is a set-up for arguing polarities. There is a never ending supply of polarities.

One of the big polarities right now would be men versus women. You can argue that 'til kingdom come—without answering it. So it gets to be an alive thing. It's alive in politics, which you know. People holding different viewpoints and people taking positions on these viewpoints. And a way of thinking which I would propose would be to get beyond the viewpoints—to get beyond the polarities. I would say that instead of getting **stuck** in the men versus women thing, you can say that men and women are both human beings and there are common denominators in human beings, and that can get you out of the differences.

The family field is absolutely **replete** with differences. The religious world is replete with differences. So all it takes to start a new church is develop a new way of thinking and develop a flock that believes in it. Now, that doesn't mean that this new way of thinking is **the** way of thinking—it is just different from something else.

Now, another one of those words you can look up is theory, and what does theory mean? There are so darn many definitions that you can start another argument about. You know, whose definition is the accurate one? And it has become such a thing to argue over the term evolution. But through the years I've used the term evolution as a way of thinking about the human as an evolving form of life. Well, that's OK, except in the dictionary there are all kinds of different definitions of what is evolution. So you can say that man is evolving, you can say that man's thinking is evolving, you can say that libraries are evolving, you can say the carpet is evolving—that means it's wearing out. So you can use evolving and you can be in pretty good company however you use it. So that evolution is another one of those terms with a lot of different definitions. You almost have to say what you mean by evolution.

I've been using the term *biological evolution*. That implies that when I talk about evolution I mean *the evolution of life*—rather than the aging of trees or the aging of a cell or the aging of mountains or what-have-you. So life appeared 500 million years—maybe 700 million years ago—make it whatever you want to, it don't make no difference. And if we take life and divide it into plant forms and animal forms—the only difference in them is that these move and these don't. They reproduce, they multiply the same confounded way. As far as I'm concerned, each reproduction is that living things reproduce themselves **almost** exactly, but not quite. *And the difference between one generation and the next and the next, and the next and the next is what I would call evolution.* So that everything is changing. And that has to do with *reproduction and the generations.* So generally when I use the word evolution, I've been using biological evolution and I put it that way to keep it away from just the aging process.

> The human phenomenon is a part of life that reproduces, and with each generation there is a *little* bit of change. That is part of genetics, that's how genetics gets into this thing. In other words, you don't reproduce exactly. A lot of things are exact, but a lot of things are different—a *little bit* of difference. And, if you take it over a long span of time, it represents change. That, to me, is evolution. (May 7, 1983)

I think it's absolutely amazing that man knew so much about evolution and he never did apply it to human behavior. And how did it take him so long to do that? Where was his head all the time? What was happening? (April 29, 1984)

—**Murray Bowen, MD**

Now the only difference when using **those** variables has to do with the presence of mobility. Animal forms are mobile. And what is characteristic of the mobility? That's called *a nervous system*. And in one-celled forms that was something that directed the animal form toward food and away from enemies, and all that sort of stuff that guided it. I've written about that—I wrote about that 20 years ago, would be a guess—that one-celled forms are directed by a biochemical process within the cell. In the more complex forms that becomes the beginnings of nervous tissue. And over the ages, nervous tissue has evolved from very simple things to the complexity of the human brain. So these forms are all alike, so that the brain of the human and the next subhuman, and sub, sub, sub, and it goes all the way down. And they all belong on a continuum. So that the major things had to do with *the mobility of animal forms, and a nervous system*. From the precursor of the nervous system to the complexity of the human brain—which is, as far as we know, the most complex version of the nervous system. So that's another one. And now it has even become a thing to debate what is a science? Even **that** is not fixed.

There was never a movement in any of the disciplines as big as Family Therapy. And you can say that it is a good thing. I tend to see it as an evolving thing. There are some good parts about it and there are some parts about it that's hideous. And if it keeps on going in the direction it's going, and something doesn't happen to change it, the hideous part of it is going to be a problem.

Another one of those words you can look up is theory. You know, over the years I believed that the term theory is lacking, unless it can be consistent with the universe, the earth, the tides, the seasons; and anything less than that is not worthy of the name theory. Because I think a theory has to be **that consistent**. Well, if you're thinking of the human being as part of the universe, then how do you go about it?

Now with that as a background, I was telling the class yesterday all these things I went through 40 years ago—as a background. And I was assuming everybody knew all this stuff. And then I find that people **don't** know it. And during those early years, I was in psychiatry and trying to find a way—is there a way to think about this to get us out of it? Which means you move ahead, with *a different way of thinking about the human*. So when I moved to family research, 30-plus years ago, I had a different view of the human than if you see the human as the master of the universe.

Now what I'm trying to say is that **this** view of man is what I have called "natural systems." In other words, he is a part of the universe, the earth, all life on earth. *Homo sapiens* is not separate from anything that has gone before or that comes after. He is part of it all.

Now, when it comes to family life, an important precursor was the Great Age of the Reptiles. It was a time when the earth, with the number of swamps and the vegetation supported a new form of life which literally dominated the earth. And as far as we know, all this started about 300 million years ago. It may have gone about a million years. The form of life that was greatest in that period was the dinosaur because it was biggest. And you can try to set out to classify all the dinosaurs—there were so many different species that you can't get them all classified. But as long as the earth provided the green stuff for them to eat, they flourished. And they flourished as animals that weighed up to 70 or 100 tons and they were over 100 feet long, some of them. And then they disappeared. Most of the big ones did. Maybe that says the reptile was not a very successful form of life. But there are actually more reptiles on earth right now—more species of reptiles—than there are mammals. So the reptiles are alive and well—after all this time.

There was one characteristic of the reptiles, they were **egg-layers**—mostly egg-layers. And toward the end of the reptilian period, the mammals developed. The mammal is a form of life in which the young grows inside the female. And there's enough evidence to suggest the family goes back to the beginning of mammalian life. So out of the reptilian age came the mammals, which as far as we know was the beginning of the family. So when you say that the family is going to pot—it's only been here for 200 million years—and it's alive and well. The family was beginning when it was necessary for the parents to take time in rearing the young until they could go on their own—200 million years ago.

Now from this standpoint I cannot see that you can separate human life from all the other forms of life on earth. I think human life—there's overwhelming evidence that human life evolved out of the distant past—and I put that up because this is a fast process. It's going so damn fast you can't keep up with it and it's still going on. So when I started doing family research, I already had a different view of the human. And the human has a specific time-table. I mean the period of gestation of the human and all other forms of life is down to *days*. All kinds of things that take place in the body are specific. The length of a life—everybody lives and dies—the length of one life. And you can go back to biblical times on that: three score and ten—and it hasn't been changed a hell of a lot. So there are all kinds of things in the human that are **absolutely precise**. Which go with the human being a part of nature. All other things are precise, including reproduction—that's one of the more precise ones.

Now let me put in one more, and then we'll take a break and come back. This would have to do with—what is the origin of general systems theory? And this is one which is so poorly understood, that anytime anybody says *systems*, people assume they mean general systems theory. I don't mean general systems theory at all. I mean the universe, the earth as a system, and all forms of life on it. That is a system that is **demonstrated** by nature and by the earth.

The general systems theory came out of the head of man. It's the same as mathematics. Mathematics wasn't here 'til man got here. Men cooked up this scheme. Men had another way of trying to define, to develop the notion of science—which is the way he applied his thinking plus his mathematical system to the scientific world. Which got to be science and from that—over the years he has developed mathematics to a pretty fine point. And other things that came out of mathematics was Einstein—relativity—all kinds of things which have to do with the great technology that came on during World War II. The thinking of Norbert Wiener, von Bertalanffy—which I would see as an extension of mathematics. And now the computer which in its existing state is an extension of math, which is all manufactured in man's head. *The model for general systems is not out there in the universe, but it came out of man's head. And natural systems—the model for that—came out of the universe.*

Let's take a short break and then we'll come back.

[BREAK]

Dr. Bowen Continues: This will give you some notion of where I was in this. It is that up until the time I got into this family research, the whole world was on Conventional Psychology—which is where Freud came from. Freud had a whole lot to do with developing that a century ago—which would see the *problem* as *within* the individual. A number of us got into studying families back in the 50s—and why this took so long to develop, who knows? But we could finally see *the relationship system* between people, which would be the main difference between a family orientation and an individual orientation. And from that standpoint, we were all describing a new world which hadn't been described in the literature before.

We all used different ways of thinking about it. So you can tell pretty much the researcher's way of thinking about it from his approach to family at the time. So that has resulted in the dozens and dozens of different kinds, or different approaches to family—which are basically based in the thinking of the individual who tried to describe it.

And that's not saying that my way is preferable than any of them. I would just say that I tried as well as I could to communicate where I was coming from, and then let you decide. But most of the ways of thinking about family is about the family as *a group of individuals*, so that most of the family therapy being practiced today derived itself originally from group therapy which went back to the early 30s. And that was a way of bringing a *group* of people together. That is not a natural thing. The group is a false thing brought together by the person in charge of it, or the clinic, or what-have-you. The group was not a natural thing to begin with. So that most approaches to family therapy were guru therapy, merely moved from the group over to the family, which sees the family as *a group of people*. Now my approach to that would be to see the family as *a natural phenomenon* and to devise a way of approaching that in a natural phenomenon way.

There was another one that has been misconstrued through the years, and that is what I would call **"getting detached from something."** Well, how do you go about getting detached? What the heck does that word *mean*? I would be attempting to look at the individual—or look at the family—as connected with the universe—me being part of that. You see, if you're thinking in terms of—that's why I put this time into thinking about this natural systems thing—if you think of yourself as a speck of cosmic dust then you're relatively unimportant in the scheme of things. If you think of the human as being master of the universe, that says something about *you*. That puts you in an omnipotent position. And when you get into an omnipotent position with your thinking—which depends on the way you see you—then it is a different ballgame. So if you can develop a way of thinking which puts you unimportant, and puts the human phenomenon just as an extension of something that has gone on for millions and millions of years in the past, you can see self and the world through different eyes. Or, you can see self as the master of the universe—which is where psychological theory as currently developed and practiced comes from. And that was developed mostly by Freud at the end of the 19th century. So you can go either way you want to.

But that's what I was trying to do. And from that early beginning, that was the major thing behind *detachment from.* The more you personalize your voyage on the earth, the more you will also personalize the family. And the more you personalize it, the more you cannot *see* the family as a phenomenon. So there's more to it than trying to be separate. I've had people over the years say, "I'm detached from my family." Well, *how* are you detached? "Well, I try to observe them." Observe *with what?* With your head, which is attached to you? And what do you do about getting your head back? So how can they be over there, and you can stay over here? (draws on blackboard) And how are you going to *see them over there* when you're *taking feeling sides* with what goes on over there? How do you get yourself *beyond* that?

And then, one of the things that I did with that—I thought this whole area of family is too new and too rich to develop it in a hurry. But I believed then, and I believe now, that sometime maybe a few centuries away, we will be thinking of the human as another form of life. And if that be so, then natural systems theory has quite a future. And if it's not so, we'll perish with all the other things. Anyway, that's all I tried to do.

You know, that has to do with all the things I've described in the various concepts. There's two major ones. Probably the most major one is **Differentiation of Self**, and I've tried to define that in the papers and in that book of papers[2] that goes back about six years. And another major one has to do with **Triangles**. Which I've described in some detail—where I would see the triangle as the basic building block of all human systems—not only human but subhuman, too. That last part of that has not been fully developed yet, but I'm sure that sometime it will be.

And then beyond that, this description—you would get to know the characteristics of **the Nuclear Family System**. And if you are precise enough in your observation and your description, you will have described it all in the nuclear family—which would be parents and children. And if you are accurate in having described the nuclear family, then all things being equal, the same process will have occurred in the generation beyond that, and beyond that and beyond that. See, you're not talking about great lengths of time— you're talking about 100 to 150 years, which is *a mere nothing* in

[2] Bowen, M. (1978). *Family therapy in clinical practice.* New York, NY: Jason Aronson.

terms of total time. Which is what paleontology does. In other words, if you really know what takes place in a nuclear family, then all things being equal, the same thing happened in the family beyond that, and beyond that and beyond that—back a reasonable distance. You don't get evolution into it in that time. But that's what paleontology has done.

How do you think you get a mock-up of what a dinosaur was like? I mean paleontologists have been able to define this little segment and this little piece, and this little piece. So that when you go through to develop what the total organism was like, a lot of that gets to be how do you take pieces and fit them together? And most of the notion of what it was like in the past is based on detailed knowledge from the present. So all I was saying by that is: If you really know what the nuclear family is like now, then you would also know the multigenerational past—all things being equal— although there may have been *some* differences. So that's what I've tried to do in defining the past.

There is another one in that, which has to do with the **Family Projection System**, and all that I tried to do is to define how a problem that exists between parents comes to exist in the next generation. How did it get there? So that's the theoretical concept—and that is merely a conceptual framework, an assumption about what happened—an assumption being the theory, a **concept** in the theory. So there's that one in it.

And then there is another notion about what happens with the **Family Projection Process over Multiple Generations**. In other words, if you know enough generations in the past, and this family projection process is taking place in every generation and involving somebody in it to some degree, then what is the predictable future of that? So that gets to be the multiple generational thing. All I was doing was taking—that is based on an *assumption* in the here and now—and if you know all the details about what happens in the here and now, then you'd have a pretty good guess what happened one generation back, two, three, four, five, and on back. With the changes that go with it. So that would be another part of the concept.

There was another major one in the theory, which has to do with **Sibling Position**. And I talk about that—how I incorporated Toman's work into it.[3] Because, I had almost gotten into doing Toman's work over again before I heard about it. And all that Toman said was something new in the world, because up until

---

[3] Toman, W. (1961). *Family constellation.* New York, NY: Springer.

that time it was believed—and you'd be amazed how much that is believed right now, and the amount of research that goes into it. It was believed that the individual is born as *a blank slate*, and the personality of that individual comes to be from the vicissitudes of living. In other words, that would be that the personality of the person is determined by the *situation* in which they grew up. This would be mostly the *bad things* that happen to them—there's precious little in there about the *good things* that happen to people.

And what Walter said was that a significant part of the personality of people is determined by *the family configuration* in which they grew up. And I would say the family configuration in which one grows up continues until the day he dies—all things being equal. That you would automatically live out the sibling position which you had in your family. So there's Walter with his sibling position, and it is remarkably accurate.

Now there are some ways to modify the characteristics that are present in everybody by the sibling position in which one grew up. These are hard to do, but it is modifiable—within limits. But all things being equal, most people will live the characteristics they developed in their families of origin. It is an unusual person that changes that.

So that, in essence, is where I was coming from in the definition of the eight concepts. [Those six, plus **Emotional Cutoff** and **Societal Regression**.] There were arguments about what is the difference between a concept and a theory. As far as I am concerned, and what I try to do is—a concept is a piece of a theory, and if put together with other concepts, it makes a total theory. There were arguments about this back 50 years ago, and that's where I stood on it, so that's why I call these *concepts*. In other words, **each concept is a piece of a total theory**—which I think is necessary for all of this. Anyway that's where I was and where I still am on that. **In other words, each concept describes a different segment of the family thing.** And all things being equal, it would apply to multiple generations in the past.

For this afternoon I brought along a video tape. I'm going to play just one hour of that. And you'll get some notion of what the therapy is about. Now, if you try to do therapy, I would say one of the greatest diseases of mankind is to try to change a fellow human being. And when you try to change your fellow human being, you are a malignancy. And how do you become something which is not a malignancy? And that also goes for parents. I would say one of the major problems of parents is to cause their kids to *be* something their parents want them to be. And I would say with all good intentions of parents, they often end up being malignant characters to their kids.

So how do you permit the world to be the way the world wants to be—to give it a choice? And how do you permit your own children to be the way they want to be, without trying to fashion them the way you want them to be? How do you go about giving them a choice? And the same damn thing applies to therapy. How do you permit that person, that family, to be what it wants to be without you trying to inflict yourself on it? And that is one of the things I call the malignancy of therapists.

And if you can see—and I believe this about the human phenomenon—is that most people want to do the most productive thing for themselves. And if there's one thing that you people can do, it is to help those people *be* as much as they can be within themselves and to keep yourself out of it. And the lower the level of maturity of a therapist, the more the therapist tries to inflict self on the other? And how in the world do you go about it? Without unwittingly trying to inflict yourself on the other? How do you go about permitting the other to be all they want to be, within themselves, without you developing a way of thinking which acts like God and which acts like you know the way? And there's another one that is pretty much par for the course with people that get into the mental health professions, is the more immature the person, the more that person acts like God. That's like they know something they don't know. And they do not have enough presence to know that they don't know it. So what do you do?

So that has to do with all this business that you call *therapy*. I don't even know what it is. So I would say when it comes to learning about them, if you're gonna act like the omnipotent one, they ain't gonna tell you very much about what's wrong with them. Because you already know what should be right. And if you know within you what you think is right, those people ain't gonna tell you very much.

So how do you go about getting your head clear so that you can really hear what's in the other without trying to inflict your miserable head on them? How do you go about hearing what's in them, without you becoming a preacher telling them what's good for them? Which I think is one of the terrible things about *all* of the helping professions. If people in the helping professions become a bunch of wiseacres that know the answer to everything, then they're not aware of *how little* they know about *anything*. So like immature parents, they pretend they know something they don't. And if there is anything you can spend the rest of your life doing, it's how do you remain *always* a student without becoming a professor that knows the answer to everything? Anyway, that one gets into this tape I'm gonna do today.

Let me hear some questions from you about where your heads are and what's going on inside you. That will help me with where I go next. How about questions that are inside you?

Trainee: You talked about being fixed in the family system. Is that the theory about the first born, the youngest and the middle child? Don't you need to be broader than that?

Dr. Bowen: Toman's work is different. You can go back and get Toman and know everything that I believed about it, but I don't have time to define differences here. I've tried to define them in the writings. And I would say everybody owes it to themselves to know Toman in detail. He has written up his work—he's now had about three editions of his book, which is *Family Constellation* by Walter Toman. He's the one who has done the most work about that and all of his stuff is remarkably consistent.

Trainee: We talked about triangles, and how we operate in our own families. How do you go about getting the same information about past generations?

Dr. Bowen: Well, it's all there—all things being equal. They didn't change that much. So if you go back to a family of origin, what you're trying to do is to follow a day by day, by day by day course. And—if you go back three generations there is all kinds of information that is available to you—that is available in records and family records and all kinds of things. And you know, all things being equal—say your grandparents were married on a certain day and from records you know a little bit about the families from which they came. And you know a little bit about the characteristics of each, when they were married, and you know where they lived when they were married and you know when their children were born—one by one, by one by one. You know what their relationship was like before they had children. You know how that relationship system *changed* when it *added one* to it.

When you take any group of two and you add another to it, you make a threesome and you change the characteristics of it. And they have a time when they are adapting to a three-person system, and then they add another one. And a three-person system becomes a four-person system, and then that becomes a new way of thinking about it. Then there are all kinds of variables that come in from the environment, which has to do with weather, and death and all kinds of catastrophic things, *and how they adapted* to each one of those.

So what you do is a day by day by day history, from the time that family was first started through as long as it was a family. And then you know something about how each kid turned out and that's pretty well written up in family records and that is available to you. You can find out if you're interested enough in it. And you know pretty well what each one of those kids tried to do with the future.

Dr. Bowen: You got another question? Where are the rest of your heads going?

Trainee: I'd be interested in how, in what you call symbiotic relationships, you try to separate out—to differentiate a self. Does that make any sense?

Dr. Bowen: Not exactly, but exactly. I would say that this has to do with reproduction. In reproduction, the human is a mammal, which means the human young grows inside the female. And that makes the female different from the male. So there's a big thing out there which says the man should be important in this. Well, what the hell? There are certain biological things that get into it too. Now the human will try to rearrange that, you know. And we'll try to say that the male influences the female, and female the male, and all that good stuff—which is so. Everybody is grinding an axe. So how do you get beyond the axe-grinding?

Anyway, I would say that every mother—if you just took it from the mother and you don't try to put fathers into this—that the mother will have a series of children. That is characteristic of mothers. There will be mothers who, after children are born, remain as feeling attached to one or another of the kids through the years as they were before the kid was born. That is what I have called *symbiosis*. And that is a thing—it's a variable that goes from here to there (draws on blackboard)—it is not a fixed thing at any one point. That is a variable.

So I would say that all mothers have certain kids that separate themselves from the mother—and they go through logical steps to become grown up, separate people. There are other kids who do not separate themselves—who remain emotionally attached to mother and they can *die* that way. And they are the people who are attached to mother. They are the people that I would call the deep level people. They are the people who will later get symptoms. And the people who later get symptoms are the people who have everything that you can think of, all the way from psychosis to neurosis, to the physical problems, to the social problems, to the legal problems and everything else. There are people who never separate themselves from their parents and—all things being equal—will remain attached forever. This I would see as a combination biological problem and a psychological problem.

There are certain things that can be done *about* this. There are certain things that *cannot* be done about it. But back in the 1950s I found one book—and I don't remember the name of it now, I'd have to go back and look again. It describes 37 different stages between parasitism and symbiosis. And a parasite is one form of life that appends itself to another form of life so its own life is dependent on the other form. Symbiosis is a form of life in which one form **complements** the other form. I picked up the term symbiosis because it was popular in the psychiatric literature back in the 30s. So when you talk about symbiosis—in **every** family—mothers are human beings, they ain't superhuman. And in every family there's gonna be some kids that are more attached than others.

So that's the human phenomenon—that's your family, that's my family, that's everybody's family. That ain't "them people out there." That belongs to you, and me—and everybody else. So it is a universal phenomenon. And people who get into the mental health professions fit into that total scheme—they ain't immune from it. But the more you can understand *you*, the better. And how do you go about getting honest with you? My experience with dealing with people, which applies to you and me and everybody else—is that you are inclined to over-estimate yourself or under-estimate yourself. The people who can be objective about themselves are in a minority. Most people on one side estimate themselves as being better than they are—which is a strict pretend—or being less good than they are, which is another side of the same pretend. So how do you go about being objective?

Dr. Bowen: What's the next question?

Trainee: When you talk about the biological aspects of emotional attachments, are you simply saying it happens in all of us, or are you saying something more than that?

Dr. Bowen: Damned if I know why it happens. What is biological—what does biological mean? Now is that something everybody assumes they know and they don't know? Biology has to do with a *life process*—present in everybody. So how would you go about defining what a **biological process** is?

What is a **psychological process**? Is a psychological process *in the individual* or was that in the head of Freud? How much of it is in people? How much of it does the *expert* assume is in people? In other words, there is a psychological *way of thinking*.

What is a **sociological** way of thinking? Where did sociology come from? Who started it? What's behind all this? What do sociologists say about it? Who anointed the sociologist? And I'd say that a sociological way of thinking has to do with **taking an**

average from society—to find out a societal attitude on something. I'd say the basis for most societal thinking is the public opinion poll. You're trying to find out what society thinks about something—it's a majority business. And that's sort of how sociology got into it. Then, how did psychology get into it? What's the basis for psychology?

These are all the kinds of things that I used to get into. What's the basis for **philosophy**? Where'd philosophy come from? Who started it? That's another beautiful one. For every philosophy there is a counter-philosophy. I don't care whose it is. And a philosophy at one time came out of the heads of men. And for every philosophy there is a counter-philosophy. People ask, "Well, what is your philosophy? What is your way of thinking?" I'd rather go back to *science* and not get into philosophy. Oh, philosophy can be real individual, but most philosophies have a counter-philosophy. They **all** do. There is no such thing as **one** philosophical viewpoint. Somewhere there is somebody that believes the opposite. Which is what I call a polarity. So what is a **mathematical** way of thinking? Where did that come from? What's a **scientific** way of thinking?

And then I'd say what is a **biological** way of thinking? Biology has to do with the life science of the various forms of life. In general, that's what it means. What are the principles that go into biology? How much does biology affect—involve—all of us? What is *genetics*? What's an *instinct*? Who defined instinct? Who accepts ownership for instincts?

That was one I got into a long time ago—when I was looking for a word that would describe instincts. I picked the word Emotional. Where does *emotional* come from? I was thinking in terms of the evolution of the nervous system—back in those years I was thinking of the nervous system, and the hind-brain, the mid-brain, the forebrain. And then over the years, Dr. Paul MacLean, who was at NIH when I was, and he's still there [1984], has worked on this.[4] I mean this concept of hind-brain, mid-brain, and forebrain had been there for centuries. And what Paul did was to work on it enough—he called it the Triune Brain—the brain with three parts to it. And he put in the idea of the R-complex, and that most of the time people live their lives according to feelings, rather than by principle as dictated by our frontal lobe. That's you and me and everybody else.

---

[4] MacLean, P. D. (1978). A mind of three minds: Educating the triune brain. In J. E. Chall & M. Murskey (Eds.), *Education and the brain* (pp. 308–342). Chicago, IL: University of Chicago Press.

I don't know how familiar you are with nervous systems, but all the nervous systems, including the human, have all kinds of centers in the spinal cord, and these are synapses. And they're the incoming nerves from here, and this has to do with righting reflexes, all kinds of reflexive things. So there's the incoming nerve that synapses with the outgoing nerve which has to do with the righting reflex, staying in balance, and all those things. And all of this is handled by nodes. It doesn't go to the brain. I mean this simple stuff doesn't come from the brain—it would have to go to the brain and get sorted out and then come back. But this don't go no farther than the spinal cord.

Back in the Age of the Reptiles, even the largest dinosaur had a very small brain. But these were huge animals, with all kinds of muscles and nerves that went everywhere. So the synapse system was much bigger than the brain. And as I understand the dinosaur, they had nervous synapses—far bigger than the brain—which was a hump in their back. And these would be the impulses that would come in from the extremities and then switch around and go back. They didn't have to go through the brain to get sorted out.

Now in the human, there's these things in the spinal cord that go up to the hind-brain—they go up to the mid-brain—and there are these automatic centers at work. And then there's a part called the forebrain, which is the frontal lobes which—all things being equal—are a little bit more cognitive than the others. The others are automatic. Paul MacLean has done this work in which he's talked about R-complex, the limbic system. The limbic system is mostly the mid-brain. R-complex is also mid-brain. So he's talked about the R-complex, that comes from reptilian. In other words, all the reptiles have these exchange centers—automatic exchange centers that operate without thinking—that still operate in everybody's autonomic nervous system. So anyway, I was looking for a term that would think of the human nervous system as a whole **complex** of these automatic things which don't even have to go to the brain. I was looking for a term to describe everything that would go from, say, the one-celled form that knows which way to go for food, you know, how to swim, all the way up to the complexity of the human form—and this would be the automatic nervous system. Which is also connected within the brain—*feelings* is a part of it. And I looked around for terms and I finally couldn't do any better than Darwin's writing about the emotional system. So I made a big distinction about the emotional system which I consider to be synonymous with instincts—and which also participates in feelings. And what do you call this? And I couldn't do any better than to go back to Darwin—where some of Darwin's writings are among the best on emotional systems—in which emotions would be *feelings plus motion*. Which is present in everybody. That's what acting out is. It's feeling converted into motion, into action.

So Darwin described this in great detail, had pictures in his writings, and that would be the animal that shows its teeth and feeling all in the same package. Which Darwin called "Emotional." And I used the same thing for Emotional—also, feelings included in it. And anywhere in my writing that I've used the term Emotional, that's where it got its beginning.

Now most of the people in the world use emotion as synonymous with feeling. I've never done that. So if people want to make emotion synonymous with feeling, then let them go back and redefine some of these other words—if you want to do it—a lot of the world does that. But there are three- and four-volume sets that have been written that are trying to define the difference between emotion and feeling. So if you go around using emotion when you mean feelings, you're going against a lot of stuff that's already been written ahead of you. I'd say you can do it, but it would be a good thing to go back and read it so you know it. And not just automatically assume that emotion and feeling are the same thing. So, I've used the term emotion as synonymous with *instinct*—and an instinct is a biological phenomenon which takes place automatically in the organism. And beyond that, who can define too much about it? But instinct applies to birds and animals, and the automatic self that governs the actions of people—all things being equal.

Trainee: You talked about taking the family history—three generations, maybe. I was wondering how you would do that.

Dr. Bowen: Well, that's duck soup. Ain't nothin' to that. Once you take a nuclear family, you take the day they met each other, the courtship, the day they were married, and then you take it day by day, by day by day, since then.

Trainee: Then how do you make it three-generational?

Dr. Bowen: Well, you go back to your grandparents since the day they were married and you take it day by day, by day by day. They might not know all the answers to the things, but within your head that's what you're trying to do. So all you do is put it together.

But you don't do it from a list. There ain't nothing like that. See, as soon as you try to detail what it is you're trying to do, now you've gone technique-ie. So if you write down that list and you check 'em off, that doesn't mean you did a damn thing. I mean you might check off every damn thing you had to do, but your model is still out there and you didn't achieve what you went after. So if you go at it with *a model in your head*, then you'll get some kind of a notion of whether you have succeeded yet or not. Most of the time, you will die before "yet" comes. So you'll just be working on it as long as you live.

Trainee: What are you actually doing with that model in your head?

Dr. Bowen: It's the nuclear family thing, extended. What the parents were doing with each other, how they were related to the past, and how they pulled off their own lives. That is your model and that's what I would call a day by day by day thing.

Somebody brought up this notion of a symbiosis. And somebody was asking about how do you go about characterizing the kids who are attached? How do you go about characterizing the kid who doesn't separate a self from mother? Well, there's the mother and she has one kid who is just a little bit separated, and there's another kid over here who does pretty well (draws on blackboard). And at the same time mother's always stuck to her husband, you know—we'll put him in there—and then mother was stuck to her own mother and then the husband was stuck to his mother so you got a mess of vipers. I talk about the family as a unit—that means people who are stuck together feeling-wise, emotionally. They're stuck together. And that's what I mean by family as a unit. OK, so what the hell you gonna do with that unit? If you're gonna try to help it? How do you know people don't want to be like that? They might like the great togetherness, you know.

Now, all these people would like some togetherness and they would like some separation. **In general**, what people do is—take this one, over here (draws on blackboard)—they can't stand that much togetherness, they've had too much of it. So they're gonna run away and run down here instead of up here [to the family]. And what they do is pull in another bunch of friends that **look** like this—and you got a new problem. So *you don't run away from anything.* If you have another relationship, that becomes a new clump. So what do you do with this?

And, in general, I would say that when you set it up as a group therapy thing—and a group therapy thing would be you bring in all them good people and put 'em in a room together, like this, and you get 'em all to talk to each other. And you just increase the clumpiness. So what do you do? I put in a word about that earlier. I would say *you don't decrease that clump with communication.* I heard one of those recently: "What you need to do when people have differences is to get them together and have them communicate with each other." *You don't separate a damn thing that way.* What you end up with is each person—well, people become clear on where they stand, but you don't decrease the distance between them. So what I would try to say is, "The way to do this is with *a way of thinking.*"

So what I've done with that is to say if you find one person in there—and I would look for the most dominant person, in terms of a family—and you try to help that person to become as much of a *self* as they can be. Then you will have a situation in which you'll have somebody at the *center* of that who'll be more separate from the others. And these people will **gradually** separate a little more. So it is not a big clump. *And that comes from one person who can define a self better.* But anything you try to do with this, as a group, is going to bring it together more and more and more. Now your group therapy is great for relieving *symptoms*, but it does **not** help people grow up. You can bring people together in a group, and for a day or week the symptoms are less, but they will come up again as soon as they leave. So there is no way to do that. But if one person can devote self to being *the best defined self they can be*, without trying to tell others what to be—you just go on and do it—then the whole family can do that. And this is the whole thing that I've talked about with Differentiation—which is above and beyond what you can do with group therapy.

That would be a pretty good notion of what I would call Differentiation. If that person can just stay on course, with what he believes in—there'll be all kinds of talk and opposition to it, but very slowly they'll build it up. I don't want to get off into that too much—which has to do with what you can do with your own family. You're not trying to influence your family to *be* anything. You are merely trying to live your own life according to some kind of principle. And there will be people who don't like it, who will be negative about it, but very slowly people will come to respect what you stand for and will be with you. That's what Differentiation is about.

And the more you try to take a clump like this (draws on blackboard)—see the whole damn family in that generation is clumped in one big clump—and it's still clumping. So what you're trying to do when you're trying to deal with it, is to pick out an individual in it and try to help that individual be all they can be. And when **they** can be that, then the group will gradually separate themselves. If you *try* to separate them, you get a thing like this. You get people who run away and then they form into clumps like this (draws on blackboard). So when you talk about the family as a unit, that's what the family as a unit is. So you're trying to help the people in that to separate themselves from that which they are stuck to. And how do you go about doing that? You don't have them separate themselves from their own family by bringing them together with their own family—which is fine for relieving symptoms if that be your goal—but you don't have people unclump themselves with group therapy.

[LUNCH BREAK—THEN VIDEOTAPE]

Dr. Bowen Continues: One reason I wanted to use this tape would be it presents a pretty good version of a fairly common problem, and somebody who is fairly conversant with it. If you could watch only one, I'd just as soon do this one as any other. Why don't we go on for a few minutes with questions? And then we'll take a break, and come back and use up the rest of the time. What kind of questions do you got?

Trainee: My understanding of what you were saying was, in order for her to de-triangle with her mother and daughter, her father needed to go back to his family and her mother needed to go back to her family. How is that done?

Dr. Bowen: I might have said that for the person on the tape, but I wouldn't say that for you. So I'll take that back. I have a simpler way of presenting that notion. What you are doing is you're asking for techniques to solve a complicated problem, and I would say get the *problem* in your head first and techniques will come later. If you start from the technique end, you're starting on a cookbook end. Does that make any sense to you?

Trainee: A little.

Dr. Bowen: You're asking, "How do you go about de-triangling?" and I'd say, "What is triangling?" I would say you need to get **that** in your head before you start asking "How do you go about de-triangling?" What I'm trying to convey is the notion of *a process*. And how do you relate to a process? If you're trying to relate, how do you deal with it? We don't even know what the process is yet. So if I was trying to answer your question, I would do the best I could to outline the process, which is mostly what that whole tape was about—was about process. In other words that is what my answer would be. It would be to direct your attention more and more to what is the process, and then will come the mechanisms by which you arrive at doing what you want to do with it. I don't know if that answers— does that answer what you're asking? Because when you asked—I said something about the parents in that. I will try to cover that briefly. But that whole notion was what I tried to talk about before noon today, and there's not time to talk about all of it. But that would be the family *as a unit*. The family as a bunch of grapes. And how far back do you go with it? Anyway, that's what I was trying to do, rather than talk about **how** you do it.

Trainee: I was thinking one of the goals for her in this session was to bring her to a deeper understanding of what's involved, rather than involve her in a process—trying to bring her to a deeper understanding—is that a goal?

Dr. Bowen: Yes [short pause] and No. I know she's been working on it for a long time. My view of it is she's been on it for a number of years, and still has a way to go. But the tape should convey the notion that this is not an instantaneous process—that this is one that goes for life. There are things that one can do. And that people can see the results of. She's made a lot of progress, but she still has a hell of a way to go. And that applies to your problem, and mine, and everybody else's. And there ain't no quick way to do nothing other than get rid of symptoms. There are ways you can get rid of symptoms in short-term therapy, but if you got a long-term thing, that depends on the individual getting the thing pretty well in mind and working on it—on and on, and on and on. And I thought this was a pretty good version of it, because you could see the intensity of it—because here would be things in which **one** action in this particular person (even though she's miles removed from her mother) would be resulting in a physiological reaction in the mother. It's almost on an ESP level, which I thought was a good part of this—and how do you go about stopping it?

Trainee: You're suggesting, too, that even without being in the presence of her parents she could have some sort of physiological reaction.

Dr. Bowen: She said it, didn't she? And that's not unusual at all. I mean there are all kinds of things that go on almost on an ESP level. How do you account for it? I would say that basically, it has to do with life styles of two people who live around each other for a long time, so they are familiar enough with each other that when something happens in one the opposite happens in the other.

Which is all of the stuff that I have tried to put under the general rubric of what I would call personality fusions and that sort of thing. And this is just a pure, old neurotic level problem. That ain't psychotic level stuff. When you get into psychotic level stuff it's many times more intense—but the same thing. The fact that it appears on this tape—she wouldn't have known how to talk about it, except she's put a lot of years in studying it. So she is more verbal about it. She puts things on tape that other people wouldn't know how to put on tape. But she's spent years working on it.

Trainee: Do you think there's a possibility of—it seems like other members of the family—other ancestors could have been psychotic or more seriously disturbed?

Dr. Bowen: I see no evidence of it.

Trainee: I thought the way you talked about her grandparents—

Dr. Bowen: That was mostly verbal on her part. She is verbal about things that other people would not have in their awareness. But I would see no evidence of a psychotic level thing anywhere in her family. If you've got somebody with psychotic problems, you would expect somebody to break out in a major symptom in response to something. Hers is mild stuff. She didn't have a psychotic breakdown, or wreck a car, or anything like that.

Trainee: I mean when she talked about her father's, father's sister or something like that, who she said was really kind of crazy—I thought that somewhere down the line, back in her ancestors, there might have been more severe reactions.

Dr. Bowen: There is no evidence anywhere in the line. But really your question has to do with an awful lot of what is communicated in mental health practices. I saw something—not more than a week ago—and this had to do with something on child abuse—that the child abuse could not have happened with a parent who has been reared by a mother who was a good parent. That it could not have happened in the mother who had been reared by a woman who had been a good mother. So that would be the assumption that child abuse in one person is directly related to the rearing practices of that person's mother. I don't buy that! And yet that appeared on TV. Now it might be a fact, but I don't even believe this.

See, the same thing happens in drinking problems. Personally, I have never been able to tell whether a symptom in a person, when it surfaces, is going to surface as a psychological problem, as a depression or something like that, in an acting out problem, in all kinds of law breaking, or in a physical problem. I have not been able to tell the difference. **The basic level of differentiation of a person would be the same**. But whether or not that symptom breaks out as a psychological problem, as a physical problem, or an acting out problem is dependent on something other than the basic level of differentiation. Because at that level of differentiation, any one of those three can develop.

Now this gets to be a part of a lot of research out there. But I have never been in agreement with that argument. It is that people will do a family diagram and seek out the drinking problems. So I don't know what you do with that, other than look at it and watch it the best you can. **But I do not see drinking as related to drinking.**

I would see the basic level of self as related to the basic level of self. And whether that surfaces as a drinking problem, as a purely psychological problem or a physical problem is something else. But I do know that there's a fair percentage of researchers who will go back and they'll make a big separation on it. And they would say if you're gonna do research on this, you should go back and check out the drinking problem. They find it speckled around in the family diagram, but I don't think drinking is any different than depression or acting out or all those other things. And whether a problem takes that direction or not depends on variables **other than ancestry**.

But anyway these are things that you have to struggle with over the years. And how do you keep your variables straight? You can predict basic level of differentiation, and you could say that level of differentiation can give rise to a spectrum of half a dozen different things. Now, which one of the half dozen it picks depends on variables other than the basic thing—I believe.

Trainee: I still don't know what you mean by differentiation of self.

Dr. Bowen: I don't know what you **understand** about differentiation of self.

Trainee: To be your own person—to (inaudible)

Dr. Bowen: That is a complex question. I wish I could communicate differentiation of self in a short period of time; but that is a very, very complex subject. And that would be under the rubric of: a mother can have two children that can grow up side by side, and one of these children—they can be identical twins, or fraternal twins even—and one of those two grows up to be a separate person and the other remains attached to the parents forever—a child forever. Now what in the world goes into one being a separate person, and the other being a child forever? What are the elements that go into that? And I would say that too much of the human phenomenon has gotten terribly simplistic, and they don't know the elements that go into it.

And then you could say there's another one which I called "functional levels." It's another tricky one, because this can happen to anybody. I mean you can wake up today and feel like staying in bed, and you say "I'm gonna get up, and I'm going to pretend to be grown up today." Well where did you get **that** notion of what pretend means? And I would say if you feel like being a dependent, house-bound thing and you're going to pretend to be going out—that gets to be at the pretend level. And I would say that most people do a heck of a lot of pretending in life. There's a lot of people who pretend to be something they are not. And how do you know what to pretend? Do you pretend out of something you want to be, or pretend out of something the other wants you to be?

Now all that goes into it. How much of life is a pretend? So when you start talking about what is differentiation of self, (laughs) all these things get into it. That and more, and more, and more. I do know that the world is very simplistic about the way they talk about it. I've heard people say things like, "I went home to visit my parents and I differentiated a self." What do you do with that? What kind of a pretend is that? (laughs). So it's a terribly complex subject.

[BREAK]

Trainee: (Inaudible question) probably about stress levels.

Dr. Bowen: That has to do with the level of anxiety. And then you go around and talk about stress when you don't know what stress means. So I'd rather talk about anxiety or some other notion that gives you the idea of increase in anxiety. Now I hesitate to use the word differentiation because I'm not communicating anything with that—but the degree to which somebody is a responsible person, or maybe when somebody is a contained self, or one who operates as an individual. These are all synonyms of a sort for what goes on in differentiation of self. So the lower the level of differentiation of self, the more vulnerable one would be. And the higher the level, the more you are free to govern your life by principles rather than what **feels** right.

So that's what it's all about. That's what the tape was about. I mean is your life governed by principles or by what feels right? That's a life-long struggle. Which also has to do with a thing I defined as a Societal Problem. Because the same thing happens in society. On one level society has a notion of what would be the profitable thing to do. But on another level it is hard to do the profitable thing while all the people out there **feel** the best way to do it is some other way. And very often you'll do things the way people want you to do them, so you can keep a good relationship with your friends.

That's what Congress does. Congress got its jobs by votes. And they are probably going to vote the way their constituents want them to vote. Not the way they think, but according to what their constituents—see, on the whole society is terribly responsive to the opinion polls. So you determine more of what you think based on what your friends think they should be. Or you determine more based on what your mother thinks she ought to be. Sometimes you're hard put to know the difference. But what I would say about principle—that comes pretty much out of one's own thinking. And what in the hell do you do when principle tells you to do the opposite of what your parents want? Are you being dictated by what your parents want in doing the opposites, or is that being dictated by your own thinking? Do you have a choice of either doing it the way they want you to do, or the opposite?

Trainee: This question is off base, but you talk so much about seeing human behavior as integrated with the whole of the animal world and the whole of nature. Are there any parallels in the animal world for stress reactions?

Dr. Bowen: I'm sure this will be proven in the next couple of centuries. You've seen all these movies recently [1984]—movies of animal life, all kinds of animals, which I think is a big plus. And then there's Jane Goodall. She's a fabulous character. She spent years observing this troop of chimps. And she's been doing some things with *National Geographic* articles and videotapes. She's reported some of the same kinds of adjustments. I'm sure Jane Goodall has never heard of the kind of stuff I did, in trying to point out the level of adjustment of each of the children in the long distant future, but she's done more than anybody in that direction.

Dr. Bowen: What other kinds of questions have we got?

Trainee: (Inaudible question) probably about symptoms in young children.

Dr. Bowen: In general, I would say when a symptom focuses in a young child that would be by now the entire family has the notion that the problem is in the child. So another way of thinking, or a way of thinking, would say that if you're thinking systems **the basic problem is in all the people around that child**. Now, conventional mental health practice would then have you to act as if the problem is in the child, which you can do. And lots of school systems, mental health clinics, act that out. And then they would like you to. The school would like the mental health clinic to treat it entirely as within the child and then they go about all this business of treating it that way. I've spent a lifetime on trying to redefine the problem as present in the entire family. Within limits, you can do that.

Now to be able to do it, you see, with a thing like that if you get parents and child together to try to redefine it over time, you might be able to do it. But in general if the family has already defined it as in the child and you see them all together you will end up with it still defined as in the child. I have been able, with parents, to appeal to the more mature side of the parents to treat the problem as if it is in them, or to accept their part in it. And to do something about it. And more mature parents will work their heads off on it. And I would say among the most motivated people I've ever seen would be the one in which the projection is largely in the mother, and the mother can put prodigious information on it. So if she can get it in her head that every time the problem comes up and she's seeing the problem in the child—that if she works on it—then a lot of these women will devote their whole damn lives to it. They will get it turned around.

Now a hell of a lot of people won't do it. They will continue to see the problem as in the child. And I don't think I've ever lost more than a handful of parents on that. I'm maintaining that position because when parents can see the difference, they are amazingly available and will devote their lives to it. And the successes in that are overwhelming. But the usual direction of the mental health places would be to accept the original verdict of the family and try to treat the problem as if it is in the child—which you can do. But I think that's a short-sighted way to do it. But that's one of the things that a family orientation will do. It will help you get it back on the family instead of on the symptomatic child.

Well, people, I didn't know what in the devil I was gonna take up when I came today and I still don't know what I took up. All I know is I gave it a shot. So I hope it's been worth something to you. I don't know whether it is or not. But it's 4:30 and we got to close up. And I got to go to the little old airport and catch a plane back to Washington. So maybe I'll see you again and maybe I won't. I guess I'll be back to Minneapolis sometime, but we gotta close up today.

3

An Obstacle to "Hearing" Bowen Theory[1]

MICHAEL E. KERR

My original intention in writing a piece for this issue of the *Family Center Report* was to reflect on the year since Murray Bowen's death [in 1990]. What has been the impact of his death on the Georgetown Family Center, on the vast network of people interested in Bowen theory, and on the overall family movement in mental health?

In reflecting on the question of the impact of Bowen's death, I decided I did not have any clear answers. Many people have wondered for years about this question, especially those who had some direct contact with Bowen. When you dealt with Bowen in person, you quickly realized the powerful force he was in the lives of those around him. It was natural to speculate about what people would do after he died. The only thing I am really clear about is that Bowen theory, despite the numerous misunderstandings that exist, continues to be important to many people, and the number is growing. Many of these people believe Bowen did as much as he could with the ideas, but there is a very great deal more to be done. People in many parts of the country are doing various kinds of research based on the theory. Conferences and seminars related to the theory are being conducted in many places, nationally and internationally.

What does all this activity portend for the 21st century? I do not know, but as my own sureness about the theoretical concepts grows, my conviction about the theory's future grows with it. Bowen was sure of where he stood theoretically. More than anything else, I think that sureness set him apart from others. He was sure because he did the work and the thinking to become sure.

I believe Bowen theory will gradually alter how psychiatry and all of medicine is practiced. The broader frame of reference will do it. Man tends to fight getting a broader frame of reference, but eventually facts force it on him. Once people have a broader frame of reference, they act on it. Decisions are just made differently. The theory's impact will even go beyond medicine and be seen to

---

[1] From Kerr, M. E., (1991), *Family Center Reports*, 12, 4, reprinted in Sagar, R. R. (Ed.), *Bowen theory and practice: feature articles from the Family Center Report 1979–1996*, Georgetown Family Center, Washington, DC, 1997. With permission.

have relevance to all manner of social problems. Problems are often unsolvable only because of the way they are thought about. Natural systems thinking will change the way a lot of things are thought about. Once we understood the physical forces in the universe, we could travel to the moon and beyond. Once we understand the emotional forces that govern life on this planet, then what becomes possible?

In any event, having commented on my original intention for this piece, I will get down to what I have actually done with it. I am going to talk about something very specific, namely, a common obstacle to people being able to "hear" Bowen theory. This obstacle was flourishing long before Bowen's death and, although I do not perceive it to be any more formidable than it ever was, it still seems as strong as ever. It is old stuff, but it is also current stuff. It has been discussed many times before. One could ask, "Is it useful to keep bringing up these matters?" I think it is because we are all so incredibly embedded in the emotional forces described by the theory that it is difficult to keep the influence of these forces in focus. The pull to lose perspective on the process is ever present. Murray Bowen was embedded in these forces too, but somehow got sufficiently "outside" them to describe them fairly objectively.

A concept that deserves repeated focus because it is so commonly misheard is *differentiation of self.* Much of my thinking about why many people have a difficult time "hearing" this concept has been influenced by having conducted numerous conferences on Bowen theory around the country. Some people "hear" this concept almost immediately. It simply makes sense to them. This does not mean that they totally grasp the concept, but they are attracted to elements of it that somehow ring true. Other people reject the concept almost immediately. Such people assume they understand what it means. They are uneasy. Something seems very "wrong" with the idea. Furthermore, since the idea is off base, then the person presenting it must be off base too. He probably has emotional problems of his own.

Outright rejection of the concept of differentiation of self certainly could reflect problems in the way the concept is presented. The presenter may be unsure of himself and unclear about the ideas. His unsureness may be manifested in a zealous approach. He tries to influence others instead of just stating what he thinks. His unsureness could also be manifested in criticism of other viewpoints, which turns people off. On the other hand, outright rejection of the concept can also occur when a presenter is very clear and not particularly invested in converting anyone. Negative responses to presentations of the concept of differentiation are to be understood, not bemoaned or decried. Such reactions are predictable, not aberrant.

Showing videotapes of clinical sessions done by therapists who have had a fairly good understanding of Bowen theory can be a superb means of eliciting people's negative reactions to the concept of differentiation. Oral and written presentations about the theory rarely have as much impact. People may be very positive about a lecture, but quite negative about what they see on a videotape of a clinical session.

Because negative reactions to clinical sessions are to be expected from a percentage of every audience, one could ask if it is worthwhile to show the sessions. I think it is for two reasons. First of all, an entire audience is never negative. Many people gain from hearing others talk about their efforts to think theoretically about their own lives and to act on the basis of that theoretical thinking. Second of all, the people who are negative, those who find the sessions disquieting, are stimulated to say what they think is wrong with therapy based on Bowen theory. Their responses highlight how this important concept is misheard and, as a consequence of being misheard, is either dismissed or pummeled into some unrecognizable form.

Most negative audience reactions to reasonably well done clinical sessions stem, I believe, from the feeling orientation of the viewer. A feeling orientation is not "good" or "bad," but it does carry with it certain expectations about what should transpire in a clinical session. People who have such an orientation get very concerned that something essential to the therapeutic process is missing in a session guided by Bowen theory.

The argument of a feeling-focused therapist goes like this. A therapist has a responsibility to sense and to elicit the feelings of the person being interviewed. The purpose of this approach is to help the "patient" become both more aware of his feelings and more capable of expressing his feelings. The inability to be aware of and to express feelings is seen as a prime cause of emotional problems. A therapeutic relationship by definition involves a "genuine" expression of feelings in clinical interview. The expression of feeling should come not only from the "patient" but also, to some extent, from the therapist. Feeling-focused therapists generally view a therapist's failure to elicit feelings in sessions as evidence that the therapist's theory is flawed and, more importantly, that the therapist has not dealt adequately with his own emotional problems.

Therapists with a feeling orientation are, of course, not all the same. Some can be relentless in their diagnosis of others. They do the same thing to the "patient" that the family did to the patient. They take the omniscient attitude that they *know* what the patient is or should be feeling and relate to the patient as if their viewpoint is factual. Such therapists are usually not malicious, just misguided. The more vulnerable patients give in to the therapist's pressure and accept his diagnosis to avoid upsetting the therapist. The patient may actually come to feel what the therapist thinks he should feel. This preserves the patient's comfortable relationship with the therapist, but the patient gives up self in the process. This is "family projection process 101" and occurs between a presenter and an audience as well as between a therapist and a patient. Of course, the process can work both ways: A patient can do it to the therapist and a presenter can do it to the audience. Generally, however, a therapist (by virtue of his status) and an audience (by virtue of its size and its potential for group process) occupy the "high ground" in the interaction, so the patient and the presenter are the most vulnerable.

A feeling orientation to therapy also represents a serious viewpoint in the mental health field. People gain something important from being more aware of their feelings and from having more ability to express them. A skilled therapist can be enormously valuable to his patients in this regard. There is nothing "wrong" with the feeling viewpoint, but differences in emotional functioning exist among the people who practice based on this viewpoint. Some feeling-focused practitioners respect "ego boundaries" far better than others. They do not exert emotional pressure on their patients to conform to their notions of what is "good" for people. These therapists simply try to represent the value they see in their point of view. However, even the therapists who are most thoughtful in their feeling-based approach are often disturbed by what they see in a clinical session guided by Bowen theory.

There are probably several ways to understand why feeling-oriented therapists are disturbed by sessions based on Bowen theory. Probably the most obvious way to understand it relates to the notion of the "therapeutic relationship." Feeling-oriented therapists frequently say they do not see any "therapy" in clinical sessions guided by Bowen theory. Some will acknowledge that the people being interviewed seem to be accomplishing something, but it is not at all clear what the therapist has had to do with their progress. Others will diagnose the people being interviewed as "intellectualizers," as not making any progress at all. They are viewed as talking about feelings, but not as "really" feeling.

The idea that a person can be helped in "talking therapy" without having to form an intense, feeling-based attachment to a therapist strongly conflicts with what is generally held about a "therapeutic relationship." A therapeutic relationship implies that therapy occurs largely within the boundaries of that relationship, so it must be fairly intense to achieve a therapeutic outcome. The idea of a therapist functioning in a way that minimizes the degree to which a person becomes emotionally focused on the therapist, and that *intrapsychic change is achievable based on such a relationship*, is foreign to a conventionally trained psychotherapist. So conventionally trained therapists not only see something missing in sessions based on Bowen theory, but the missing component is deemed essential to the therapeutic process.

Conventionally trained therapists tend to interpret what they see in therapy based on Bowen theory as the therapist and family member being emotionally distant from each other. In the absence of an alternative to a feeling-based frame of reference for conducting therapy, this relationship between therapist and family member almost has to be regarded as being dictated by an emotional problem, particularly a problem in the therapist. Why else would people act this way? An alternative frame of reference, of course, is differentiation of self.

Differentiation of self implies an ability to be in emotional contact with others while remaining "outside" the system. Two people can talk about the emotional process that can occur between them while only minimally activating that process. This is still an almost incomprehensible idea to most therapists. The point is to activate it, so the argument goes, so it can be examined and resolved. Without understanding contact with detachment, people interpret differentiation as emotional distance.

In a clinical session based on Bowen theory, the therapist is attempting to maintain differentiation in relationship to the family member. The therapist's effort stimulates the family member to do the same thing in relationship to the therapist. At its best, such a relationship permits the free exchange of thoughts and feelings on both sides. Because it is assumed that it is more productive for the family member to keep his emotional investment in existing relationships rather than in the relationship with the therapist, the therapy sessions look very different than conventionally based ones. The content of sessions includes some discussion of theory and considerable discussion of the relationship systems the family member is trying to understand and to become more differentiated in. There is not a rule against examining the therapist–family member relationship, but the goal is not to activate the family member's unresolved emotional attachments to others in the therapy session itself. *Intrapsychic change can occur through progress on intense relationships outside the therapy relationship.* Bowen theory, with its conceptualization of multiperson systems, makes it possible to work on self in the complex emotional arena of the real world.

Another way to understand the negative reactions to watching therapy based on Bowen theory may relate to a much broader issue, namely, the theory's conceptualization of the *emotional system*. The concept of the emotional system makes a distinction between emotion and feelings. Emotional process is considered synonymous with instinctual process, while feelings reflect the more superficial aspects of emotional functioning. This means that the feeling process is linked to the more basic emotional process.

The way people manage feelings is a reflection of forces operating in the emotionally governed relationship system. People are programmed to manage feelings in certain ways based on these forces. So although the awareness of and the ability to express feelings is important, its value is limited. There is much more to be seen and understood that governs human emotional functioning. So when the exchange between therapist and family member in a clinical session is influenced by the assumption that man, like other forms of life, is governed by an emotional system, an observer who does not hold that assumption will have great difficulty translating what he is seeing and hearing into something that makes sense to him. A collision of ways of thinking can trigger negative responses.

It took many centuries, but mankind, using its collective intellectual system, eventually defined fundamental forces and patterns in the solar system.

The mass of humanity, heavily influenced by one another, held onto imagined notions about the planets long, long after the facts were known. The togetherness process retards the progression of ideas. In spite of countervailing winds, pioneering individuals have and will continue boldly to plunge forward, unearthing new facts and thinking differently about old facts. Bowen, using his intellectual system, defined fundamental forces and patterns in living relationship systems. Mankind's collective intellectual system will eventually define these forces and patterns in intricate detail. The mass of humanity, again heavily influenced by one another, will likely hold onto imagined notions about human behavior long after these facts are known. The togetherness process is not "bad"; it serves important functions in sustaining life. It does have certain consequences, however. Perhaps people will "hear" more quickly in the 21st century than they have in the past. I am not sure about that. For now, the task is to understand how this process plays out and to avoid getting caught in the polarization that inevitably occurs about it.

4
Responsibility for Self[1]

DANIEL V. PAPERO

An increasingly common procedure in mental health practice today assigns several therapists to a family. A person may have an *individual therapist*, a married pair may have a *couples therapist*, a child may have a *child therapist*. Additional specialty therapists such as a biofeedback therapist, a hypnotherapist, or a psychiatrist may also be involved. A somewhat different version of the same phenomenon links several therapists to one person. In the arena of clinical supervision, a clinician may also have several clinical supervisors. An employer may require a supervisor within an agency, the clinician may select an additional supervisor in a particular area of interest, and may also see a therapist about some personal dilemma.

The likelihood is high that each of these therapists or supervisors has a different way of thinking about the nature of human behavior, of human problems, and of how best to approach them. Even with a common orientation, transferences may exist between family members and the various therapists (or between supervisor and supervisees), complicating each person's ability to be responsible for and to represent self. From the viewpoint of Bowen theory, all symptoms are a product of the family emotional unit, and to divide them into separate problems to be addressed by different practitioners confuses the situation and adds additional relationship variables and triangles, which can be extremely complex.

The main thrust of the effort to learn and apply Bowen theory occurs outside the clinical hour in the important relationships of the family, the work system, and the community. The learning occurs in each family member's efforts to become familiar with the emotional system of family, work, and community and to manage self differently within it. The effort to improve functional differentiation of self is continual. A person's or family's efforts may occur in spurts and may or may not involve a clinician.

Basic to the effort to learn and apply Bowen theory is the person's understanding of responsibility for self. On a simple level, responsibility for one's

---

[1] From Papero, D. V., (1992), *Family Center Reports,* 13, 2, reprinted in Sagar, R. R. (Ed.), *Bowen theory and practice: Feature articles from the Family Center Report 1979–1996,* Georgetown Family Center, Washington, DC, 1997. With permission.

life involves thinking through situations, making decisions, and accepting the consequences of those decisions. The process is more complex than it appears at first glance. How much thought and how much feeling should influence the decision-making process? And how do thought and feeling influence the acceptance of the consequences of decisions? Where do facts fit into the process? And what about relationships to other people? If a person and family understand and accept the notion of responsibility for self, multiple consultants provide no particular problem. But this is tricky territory indeed.

The general rationale for involving multiple clinicians in a family symptom generally includes the following arguments: (a) The individual/family is exposed to several viewpoints and ways of thinking about a problem. It is good to be exposed to several opinions and viewpoints. (b) Specialists may be particularly good at treating one kind of difficulty but not at another, and the patient benefits from the particular expert knowledge even if it is limited. The same arguments generally apply to retaining several supervisors and have merit.

Although rarely noted, the procedure may bring certain advantages to the therapists involved as well: (c) Each therapist may feel less anxious and less burdened if other therapists are involved. The patient may, in fact, benefit if the therapist is more relaxed. (d) The process fits better with the current medical model where specialists are frequently brought in to consult to the patient about a variety of problems. A team approach is highly regarded. To present oneself as a specialist and as a team player can lead to additional business, adding to experience and income. (e) Where multiple clinicians are involved, one has to accept responsibility only for one's own small piece of the dilemma, and someone else carries the burden of overall responsibility. These are also serious considerations, not to be dismissed lightly.

Multiple therapists/supervisors also present a number of dilemmas to the people involved. They can affect the therapists, but ultimately the individual/family comes to bear the outcome. Each of the common dilemmas has both subtle and overt forms, and resolution tends to be difficult. Central to all is the importance the person assigns to each therapist and each therapist to the other therapists or supervisors. In essence, the investment of life energy in another, whether by patient or therapist, is a major variable. The investment of life energy in others and the anxiety and reactivity that accompany it trigger the triangling process so familiar to students of the human family.

When a person or a family does not have a working understanding of responsibility for self, the involvement of others can compound the original problem. When anxiety is high, the varying viewpoints can confuse the person or family, intensifying helpless postures and reliance on outsiders to solve the problem. An anxious consultant can transfer anxiety to the person or family, disrupting a basic plan of action or reinforcing existing uncertainty.

The clinician can promise a family a result that he or she cannot deliver, and the family can act as if such a promise had been given.

Multiple clinical or supervisory relationships can impede the functioning of anyone involved, either clinician or patient. Tracing the difficulty is arduous and filled with blind alleys. A few of the more obvious examples follow. Many far more subtle dilemmas are also possible, each of which tends to disrupt a person's effort toward better functioning.

Therapists, even with a similar theoretical orientation, can become sensitive and reactive to the involvement of one another. This reactivity can be communicated in innumerable ways to the family or person being seen. When, for example, spouses each have a therapist, they may already be sensitive to the other's intense involvement with a therapist. The reactivity of the second therapist fits in with this sensitivity, confirming the person's mindset about the other's involvement. Often this occurs without any overt comment from either therapist about the other person's therapeutic involvement. One therapist's judgmental, critical reaction to another fuels the side-taking in the family.

The actual clinical approaches can collide with one another, and the family can choose sides as to whose therapist is right. One therapist may be pushing one person toward resolving internal conflicts and directly expressing feelings. The other may be coaching toward managing reactivity and ultimately differentiating a self. The more one expresses feelings, the more the other can become distant in imitation of self-management. The more the latter becomes distant, the more feelings are generated in the relationship for the other to express. Each can be encouraged by his or her therapist in this process, and the therapists can become sensitive and reactive to one another. The family can also maintain its relatively helpless attitude while the therapists work to solve the problem.

When transference has taken place, whether encouraged or not, the person's energy goes more into the therapy than into the family. The pouring of life energy into the therapeutic relationship can be as intense as an affair, and family members may react as if the patient were actually having an affair. This seems particularly common where a person sees a therapist for individual therapy, and the pair sees someone else for marital therapy. The one in individual therapy often sees the marital therapy as secondary and has little energy available for it. With more immature therapists, the individual therapist may advise the patient to do things that actually make the marital stalemate worse.

And finally, the therapists may actually take sides in the family dilemma, actively advocating for one against the other. This is akin to the alliance system of the great powers prior to the First World War. It provides at best an uneasy stalemate around the original problem and, in periods of heightened anxiety, can fuel a conflagration that might otherwise have been managed more thoughtfully and effectively.

In "From Couch to Coach" (Bowen, 1970), an unpublished abstract of a presentation given at the 1970 Annual Georgetown Family Center Symposium, Murray Bowen made the following observation about the efficacy of working out mature adult-to-adult relationships in one's own family. "From experience, any progress gained in the family of origin is automatically translated into the nuclear family" (Bowen, 1970, p. 1). He speculated on why this "method is more effective than the others" [psychoanalysis and family psychotherapy for husband and wife]:

> The format of the method requires the trainee to accept responsibility for his own life, and to accept the working proposition that he, through his own effort, can modify his own family system. It is the only one of the three methods of psychoanalysis, family psychotherapy for the clinician and his or her spouse, and the coaching process with the extended family in which the trainee is completely on his own, without a therapist during significant emotional reactions, that occur during his visits with his family. (Bowen, 1970, p. 1)

Although in this reference Bowen was talking about the training of family therapists, he highlights two important principles central to any effort to develop an application of Bowen theory: (1) the person accepts responsibility for his or her own life and (2) he or she accepts the working proposition that the family system can change in response to a change in self. As simple as these principles may sound, people do not seem to grasp them easily.

Bowen theory directs the person back to the original relationships or to their closest current approximation, downplaying the relationship to the coach. When the important relationships are activated, whether to a spouse, parent, or other significant emotional figure, and life energy is directed toward managing self in those relationships, the coach is effectively outside the transference, using knowledge of triangles to guide his or her behavior. The dilemma of transference can arise when seeing one person individually. To counter this possibility, Bowen refined the clinical skill which he called *staying outside the transference* (Bowen, 1978). He defined "staying out of the transference" as the clinician's ability to keep self emotionally disengaged. The clinician works to manage his or her sensitivity, interpretive mindset, and emotional reactivity to the other person.

The effort begins with initial contact with the family and the clinician's task of establishing the orientation of the theoretical–therapeutic system. Bowen describes his thinking in the following manner:

> Most families are referred with a diagnosis for the dysfunction. They think in terms of the medical model and expect that the therapist is going to change the diagnosed family member, or the parents may expect the

therapist to show or tell them how to change the child without understanding and modifying their part in the family system.... I persistently
oppose the tendency of the family to view me as a "therapist."... When
the therapist allows himself to become a "healer" or "repairman," the
family goes into dysfunction to wait for the therapist to accomplish his
work. (Bowen, 1978, pp. 157–158)

Many of the familiar techniques associated with family systems therapy
serve to accomplish this orienting task, including the basic idea of responsibility for self. This includes not diagnosing any family member, establishing the
clinician as a consultant for the initial sessions and as supervisor of the effort
if the process continues, and focusing on observation and research rather than
therapy. The family makes a research project of itself.

Another aspect concerns the clinician's defining him- or herself to the family. Bowen explains what he means in the following excerpt.

One of the most important processes in this method of psychotherapy
is the therapist's continuing attention to defining his "self" to the families. This begins from the first contact which defines this theoretical
and therapeutic system and its differences from others. It proceeds in
almost every session around all kinds of life issues. Of importance are
the "action" stands which have to do with "what I will do and will not
do." I believe a therapist is in poor position to ask a family to do something he does not do. (Bowen, 1978, p. 177)

The positions defined by the clinician are always presented in terms of what
he/she will or will not do, never in terms of what is best for the family.

Bowen sums up his basic notion of "staying out of the transference" in the
following paragraph.

The life style of this low level of differentiation is the investment of psy-
chic energy in the "self" of another. When this happens in therapy, it is
transference. A goal of this therapy is to help the other person make a
research project out of life. It is important to keep "self" contained with
the therapist as [with] the other spouse. If the person understands the
life-goal nature of the effort and that progress will slow down or stop
with energy invested in the "self" of the therapists he is in a better position to help keep the energy focused on the goal. (Bowen, 1978, p. 179)

To the degree that the clinician has been successful in functioning as
a coach rather than therapist and in staying out of the transference, the
dilemmas associated with the therapeutic relationship can generally be
avoided. Each clinician develops his or her way of presenting self and the

theoretical–therapeutic orientation to the family. Some elements are relatively common, including the respectful attitude of the clinician toward the family, the relative infrequency of appointments, often determined by the family, and the focus on learning more about the family rather than fixing the family problem.

Common relationship dilemmas between clinician and family generally indicate that the clinician has not defined him- or herself clearly enough to the family. The family's behavior may reflect the clinician's slipping from the role of coach to that of change agent, pressuring the family in the process to accept his or her interpretation of reality and to conduct themselves in the manner he or she deems appropriate. The clinician may not have defined his or her position adequately to the forces outside the clinical process itself, and his or her behavior may represent that blurred boundary. The clinician may reflect the anxiety of the agency, the court system, and the broader society in his or her approach to the family, which responds with its own anxiety. What is called resistance can also reflect the beginning of a person's effort toward differentiation within the family. That effort may not match the clinician's notion of what ought to occur, creating anxious discomfort in the therapist who defines the patient as resistant. In short, the coach works always to see and modify his or her part of an emotional process.

From the first contact, therefore, the clinician works to define self to a clinical family. The family is responsible for its own decisions, and the coach for his or hers. Each can end participation in the clinical process at any time for any reason. This is not a matter of technique but is built into the relationship between coach and family from the beginning. The ending of clinical contact can occur in innumerable ways. Typically the family decides when to begin and to end the contact. There is no concept of right timing, at least from the clinician. The family determines its priorities in much the same way it determines how often to see a personal physician, a banker, or any other sort of consultant. And the clinician determines how much he or she is willing to be seen. In short, the concept of termination applies to a different way of thinking about the relationship between clinician and family and a different focus and development of that relationship.

The involvement of several supervisors or consultants with the clinician incorporates all of the elements discussed above. The clinician can be expected to understand the impact of the triangling process and to conduct self with a respect for boundaries as an element of responsibility for self. When a person is aware of and has some ability to contain self within a relationship to a clinician or supervisor, and understands that he or she is alone in deciding how to conduct oneself in life situations, and when one accepts responsibility for the consequences of his or her decisions and actions, a person can employ multiple consultants advantageously.

As a supervisor or clinician, one also has the responsibility to understand the dilemma presented by multiple therapists to a patient, family, or consulting clinician and to recognize the indicators of difficulty for the family. Each clinician/supervisor has to think through his or her own way of monitoring the situation and communicating his or her thinking to the family. The clinician demonstrates responsibility for self in how he or she conducts self in the clinical or supervisory relationship. A clinician is in a poor position to ask another to do something that the clinician does not understand and does not do him- or herself.

References

Bowen, M. (1970, October). *From couch to coach* [Abstract]. Paper presented at the Sixth Annual Georgetown Family Center Symposium on Family Theory and Family Psychotherapy, Washington, DC.

Bowen, M. (1978). *Family therapy in clinical practice*. New York, NY: Jason Aronson.

5
Live Learning: Differentiation of Self as the Basis for Learning

VICTORIA A. HARRISON

Bowen family systems theory affords a new view of learning in both clinical and classroom settings. Bowen considered relationship reactions to be part of human evolution and part of the best and worst of human functioning. Before learning to talk, read, or write, infants are learning relationships, adapting to the family, and developing patterns of reacting and relating that fit within the family relationship system. Most of this learning occurs automatically, without awareness or planning, in the context of family relationships. In addition to relationship-based patterns, humans have an ability to think independently in the face of relationship reactions, to use the brain in new ways, to see reactions and change them, and to think for self. The capacity to develop and maintain one's own intellectual activity, somewhat separate from relationships that shape the brain, varies among individuals. Bowen (1978) called this variation in the counterbalance between emotional reactivity and intellectual activity *differentiation of self*. The *scale of differentiation of self*, as defined in Bowen's writings, addresses the variation in functioning among people that is associated with more or less emotional fusion between family members and with corresponding degrees of fusion between thinking and reacting in the human population.

How a person participates in an educational process is an outcome of his or her level of differentiation of self. Teachers and students with lower levels of differentiation of self invest more energy into relationships and react more to stress or anxiety arising from relationships in the family and in the educational setting. Those at higher levels are better able to think for themselves and engage the thinking of others in a wider range of circumstances. Bowen illustrated differences in levels of differentiation in one of his teaching tapes. A teacher describes one of her students: "He is just a little brain. All he wants to do is learn" (Bowen, 1970).

In "An Odyssey Toward Science," the epilogue to *Family Evaluation* (1988) by Kerr, Bowen distinguishes different ways people "hear" natural systems theory. The distinctions apply to learning other material as well:

The ability of people to "hear" is based more on the quality of early childhood relationships than in some vague chemical or genetic imbalance....It is harmonious with the concepts of "differentiation of self" and "societal regression." In any audience, lay or professional, there is a small percentage that either "hears" the presenter or asks pertinent questions. A much larger mid-scale group "hears" part of the presentation and is motivated to hear more. They hear best through what others think rather than from within themselves. They can slowly learn to think for themselves rather than depend on others. The other percentage is the most fixed. They are prisoners of the emotional system and teaching is slow and difficult. They hear very little and tend to be critical of the presenter, go to sleep, or otherwise absent themselves....Most people can become flexible in their ability to "hear." It merely requires longer for the more fixed people. The ability to "hear" does not appear to be significantly influenced by social class or formal education..... The presenter who assumes that all people are the same operates with a misassumption. (Kerr & Bowen, 1988, p. 349)

The basis for applying this knowledge is the practice of differentiation of self. Bowen's original papers, collected in *Family Therapy in Clinical Practice* (Bowen, 1978), best describe the many elements of working on differentiation of self (Pemberton, 2006). The process includes experiences that promote new learning: becoming a better observer of reactivity in self and in the family system; containing and managing one's own reactivity; defining operating principles for self in every area of life; acting on principles in the face of automatic reactions; and working to become more objective and thoughtful in relation to others and more responsible in one's own life. Steps toward differentiation include making and maintaining contact with every living family member, increasing factual knowledge about one's family and family history, being present at intense and anxious times in the family, and actively interacting with family to develop relationships in which thinking is engaged. The *live learning* in this process allows people to develop the ability to learn what they do not already know and almost always involves an element of surprise, if not awe. This chapter describes the author's observations about the live learning that occurs through work on differentiation of self in her own family, clinical practice, and educational settings and research that integrates knowledge from the sciences.

Live Learning: Differentiation of Self in One's Own Family

The author's family involved facts and factors that shaped her brain toward assuming responsibility for others and taking charge of a situation. Her mother developed type 1 brittle diabetes when the author was about 2 years old at a particularly challenging time in her family. In 1947, diabetes was quite difficult to manage, but the 23-year-old wife and mother adopted every medical direction and maintained tight control over her blood sugar. This left her vulnerable to frequent insulin reactions, which were equally dangerous and frightening. The young husband took the lion's share of responsibility for helping her, but he also traveled a great deal for work. He would recognize the onset of an insulin reaction and provided the orange juice or another source of sugar to prevent seizurelike attacks. Even as a 4-year-old, the daughter tried to look after her mother. Throughout childhood and adolescence, the daughter came home from school to check on her mother and often was the one to minister to her mother during an insulin reaction. The young wife and mother could not recognize the signs of low blood sugar, which could quickly become an emergency. She relied on her husband and daughter and other family members for their help.

By age 22, the author had borne a daughter, married and divorced, graduated college with honors, and cut off from her family. She experienced many physical and psychiatric symptoms but avoided doctors and psychiatrists, throwing herself into work and "changing the world." The habits of reacting that had been established in her family proved an advantage in the field of crisis intervention, where she first worked, but also involved a sustained level of nervous system activity that triggered her own symptoms and a style of leadership that often found her at odds with authority.

The author met Bowen in 1975 and began coaching and participating in the Postgraduate Program at the Georgetown Family Center. She began to visit her parents and extended family every 3 months. Her mother's complicated health problems would worsen around each visit, and the author became determined to understand the part her mother played played in her increased anxiety. She recognized the automatic sense of anxious responsibility for her mother that arose during each visit. One of her first memorable experiences of live learning was figuring out whether her mother could recognize the onset of a low-blood-sugar reaction and take steps to deal with it herself. The author made a plan to wait 2 or 3 minutes when her mother showed signs of low blood sugar and see whether her mother could see those signs as well. When the author noticed such symptoms, she watched the kitchen clock and, instead of pouring a glass of juice for her mother, asked, "Mother, I know you don't know when you are going to have a reaction ... but what do you think other people notice? What are the signs?" With slightly slurred speech, her mother said, "Well, people say that I start to talk really slow and space out a bit. I slur my words. And ... (a long pause) ... my tongue feels thick to me." That was about all of the experiment the author could tolerate. She said, "Mother, I think you may be having a reaction now. Do you want me to get your juice?" Her mother replied, "Please." And she did.

This was a small first step for the author in developing an awareness of the part that her own take-charge reactions played in sustaining an anxious dependence that operated in family triangles. As her mother began to take more responsibility (a) for recognizing her own blood sugar levels, and (b) for getting her own orange juice or food, the author's family reacted as though this was dangerous or irresponsible. Over time, the author was able to begin to learn the difference between telling others what to do and simply working on her own anxious reactions. She could see how quickly she became critical of others and had numerous opportunities to understand better the efforts others made to be helpful. Now, almost 30 years after the initial live learning, there are times when the author's mother, who is a lovely and capable 86-year-old woman, can recognize her own situation and take care of it and there are times when she cannot. She and her 88-year-old husband work together as a remarkable team, each relying on the other to be factual and knowledgeable about medical procedures and blood sugar levels. There is more flexibility in their appreciation of both independence and the necessity of help. A touching experience occurred a few years ago when the author joined her parents for a college football weekend. Her mother was tardy leaving the motel room, and her father was rushing her mother along. The author managed her tendency to take charge of the problem and trailed behind, listening to the conversation between her parents. Her father was worried: "Please, won't you just drink some juice now, so when we are late to lunch you will be OK?" Her mother responded, "I don't need any now." There were several rounds of this, and then her mother stopped and said, "OK. I'll drink some now for you." Her dad was obviously relieved and said, "I believe I will have some too." They laughed. It was a chance to see unexpected flexibility in the face of anxiety.

These and many other such opportunities in the family are central to the ability to suspend one's subjective assumptions, expand one's view of reactivity in the system and one's own anxious reactions, and formulate operating principles to apply in clinical practice, in teaching, or for live learning in other areas of life. Experiences of learning in one's own family such as these raise questions for research. What changes in the biology and behavior of family members accompany thinking for self and increased responsibility for self by any one family member? How does live learning in one's family transfer to other areas of life (Harrison, 2005, 2006)?

Steps Toward Differentiation of Self as the Basis for Learning: Clinical Example

The author served as the therapist for a small psychiatry department at a community hospital at which she inherited a few chronic patients from the previous therapist. One of these people was a 30-year-old man with multiple disabilities. Bob Harris was legally blind from birth, was seriously obese, and was considered mildly retarded. He had never learned to read. He behaved badly in public and became easily frustrated and agitated. Bob had a certain charm, however, and had married a woman with multiple sclerosis. They lived together in an apartment provided by social services. Neither he nor his wife worked, and they lived on disability payments. Mr. Harris had little contact with his three sisters or his parents, all of whom lived in town. He and his wife had Sunday dinner with his wife's mother on a regular basis.

Mr. Harris had been a patient at the community hospital for several years and was accustomed to meeting with a therapist once a week. He would routinely talk about his masturbation fantasies and complain about his wife. When the author became his therapist, she said that she would meet with him once a week, but she would not talk about sex or masturbation fantasies. He reluctantly agreed. The author remembered Bowen's examples of how much it is possible to learn from those who represent the more extreme versions of human problems. She prepared for each session with a multitude of who, what, where, when, and how questions about the Harris family. She practiced a few other principles in her work: she would work on developing genuine interest in this man and in his best thinking about life from the unique vantage point nature provided him. Within 6 months, Mr. Harris had reestablished contact with his older sisters. They began to include him in visits to their parents. The author will never forget the session, almost 9 months into their meetings, when Mr. Harris reported, "My father has lung problems. He must use oxygen now all of the time." He went on to say, with pride, "Dad wants me to carry his oxygen tank and go with him so he can visit his family and his friends. I've never spent so much time with my father." And he added, "You know, I can understand how disappointed my father must have been with me as his only son. He could not stand to be around me....But now, he wants me to be around, and I think that he is proud of me."

The changes that Mr. Harris brought about for himself in his family were a prelude to unexpected decisions related to reading and learning. He began to walk to the local library to listen to reading programs for children. An elderly retired librarian took an interest in him. She arranged for him to be fitted with very strong reading glasses and began to teach him to read. Mr. Harris began to bring large-print children's books to his sessions and read them aloud. He graduated quickly to large-print adult literature.

It was at this point that his wife joined him for therapy sessions. Mrs. Harris was anxious that her husband had become too independent and would "find another woman." Mr. and Mrs. Harris began to meet together and discuss the kinds of changes they might foresee in their life together. It was useful for Mrs. Harris to hear her husband talk about how he was functioning in his own family. She began to contact her siblings and extended family, who lived in Pennsylvania. During the 3rd year of therapy, Mr. Harris's father died. Mr. Harris served as one of his father's pallbearers and was included as a responsible and respected member of his family at the funeral and family gatherings. After this death, Mr. Harris and his wife established a plan to relocate to Pennsylvania, where they had found housing for handicapped people within walking distance of the zoo, a library, churches, and other community resources. Mrs. Harris's brother and his family also lived there. It took another year and persistence to overcome administrative hurdles, but Mr. and Mrs. Harris accomplished this move. They maintained contact for a time before Mr. Harris began to talk with a therapist in his new hometown.

It is not clear who learned the most in this clinical example, Mr. Harris or the author. The steps that Mr. Harris took in his own family were on his own initiative. The author simply focused her thinking on factual questions about family and worked toward neutrality and genuine interest in his thinking. Her respect for him and for his family grew.

This clinical experience raised/raises fascinating questions. What is the nature of differentiation of self? Is it a faculty or quality that operates independently of intelligence or of sensory capacity? In what way does establishing personal relationships with one's family and becoming an important, responsible family member have an impact on the ability to learn? What changes in the brain, in biology, and in behavior accompany such work on differentiation of self?

Relationships and Differentiation of Self in Classroom Education

Classroom education provides numerous opportunities for the live learning of work on differentiation of self. The author's observations are based primarily on teaching adults in the context of postgraduate programs at the Bowen Center for the Study of the Family in Washington, DC; in educational programs at the Center for the Study of Natural Systems and the Family in Texas; and at conferences and programs throughout the country. Bowen theory both provides the content and guides the process of education in these introductory and advanced levels of learning.

The level of differentiation of self that develops in the family emotional system affects learning and teaching in adult life. Teacher and student bring their levels of differentiation to the classroom. Behavior and process in the classroom provide clues to ordinary and innocent relationship reactions that play out there. One can observe variation in the investment of energy into relationships, in reactivity to relationships, and in the exercise of independent intellectual activity. The predictable uncertainty of where to sit, for example, activates varied reactions. One student walks into the classroom and looks for someone to ask where to sit; another takes a seat in front; another drags a chair to the back of the room to sit separate from the group; another takes off her shoes and stretches her legs, unaware that she is blocking the row.

Teachers may observe their own anxiety reactions and the impact of those reactions on the learning of others. Relationship triangles operate in- and outside the classroom between teachers and students. A teacher who is unsure of self may engage reassuring eye contact and favor students who defer to his or her expert opinion. An anxious teacher may come across as critical in her or his effort to distinguish one set of ideas from another. Students may speak critically of a teacher with each other or with other teachers. It is a challenge to elevate this predictable emotional process to the level of live thinking and thinking for self.

It is necessary not only to talk about the process of differentiation of self but also to practice it in the classroom. Differentiating of self in the classroom involves thinking through principles and operating principles about the myriad details around curriculum, methods, and relationships in ways that are consistent with Bowen theory; calmly stating one's convictions without debate or explanation; acting on principles and observing the reactivity stirred; and managing one's own reactivity in a responsible fashion.

The author would pose projects to work on patterns of emotional reactivity that she could observe in herself. How could she shift the "other-focus" that is part of educational process? How could she distinguish anxious functioning from the necessity to be responsible for classroom administration, that is, starting and stopping on time? How could she decrease her tendency to tell others what to do, on one hand, and fail to be responsible, on the other? One predictable opportunity to experiment would occur at the beginning of each class. The author tried many ways to interrupt the buzz of conversation to start the program. After about 2 years, she decided that the best way was with a factual focus: "The first lecture will begin now" or "There are 25 minutes for the next presentation" instead of "Please be seated" or ringing a cattle bell. A factual approach was most consistent with a principle she had defined to treat the class as adults responsible for organizing themselves.

It is possible to observe the reactions stirred, in self and in others, when one defines and uses principles that interrupt or alter the ordinary, predictable, and often polite relationship orientation. The responses to differentiation that Bowen (1978, p. 216) described for the family are also present in the classroom. "Change-back" reactions occur within self and from others, pulling teachers and students toward a level of togetherness that is comfortable, but with predictable consequences for learning. If a teacher can sustain ways to work on differentiating a self, in his or her own family and in the classroom, it is possible to evaluate the effects on learning.

Differences in how people approach learning and using Bowen theory to think for self are visible to some extent in the projects and presentations students pose for themselves. Most people will initially focus on how Bowen theory "fits" with what they already think or on similarities to theories they have adopted. Others will absorb a concept or idea from Bowen theory without recognizing the individual focus or cause-and-effect thinking that distorts the concept into a pathology focus. Over time, those who persist in the study of Bowen theory and work on differentiation of self will begin to examine the assumptions that operate in their thinking and find a way to recognize the value of facts (Harrison, 2008a).

Evaluation incorporates emotional process visible through the lens of Bowen theory and presents challenges for differentiation of self. How does one modify the other-focus that is conventional in evaluation and base evaluation on evaluating oneself? The author experiments with ways to shift from evaluating others to evaluating self in relation to her purposes and to the observations of process that are possible. One example is the design of program evaluation documents that ask individuals to identify their own objectives for learning and the extent to which those were met.

Classroom education, like work on differentiation of self in one's family and in clinical practice, has required defining criteria for anxiety or levels of anxiety; distinguishing intellectual activity from emotional reactivity; identifying indicators of togetherness and individuality; and using these criteria to evaluate self and the overall educational effort. Many questions raised are similar to those in clinical practice. How does work on differentiation produce change in the capacity to learn, to think for oneself? What part do relationships play in learning?

Bowen emphasized the importance of a research attitude and viable connections to science for learning. The author's work on differentiation in her own family, in clinical practice, and in educational settings provokes research projects that involve developing relationships with scientists, reading research from diverse fields in biology and neuroscience, and using biofeedback and neurofeedback instruments for observations about reactivity and intellectual activity (Harrison, 2003).

Relationships and Differentiation of Self: The Basis for Learning in the Brain

This last section on live learning reviews research in neuroscience and evolution that provides background for the study of relationships and differentiation of self in learning. Several fields converge to form a crazy quilt of research related to relationships and differentiation of self evident in brain functioning and biology. Although the implications may seem clear to those who study Bowen theory, education and other fields related to human behavior continue to operate with few connections to facts available in the research described here.

The past 30 years of neuroscience (neuroanatomy, neurochemistry, and pharmacology; electroencephalogram studies; oxygen and blood flow measures; and molecular research, as well as biofeedback and neurofeedback) provide a patchwork of studies indicating ways in which responsiveness to relationships and the ability to be a somewhat independent self are integral to biology and behavior. This diverse literature lacks the years of actual research that can integrate facts into a coherent body of knowledge. Although any effort to make use of knowledge from neuroscience is limited, one can use the conceptual framework provided by Bowen theory to identify relevant research and functional facts to observe in the process of addressing questions raised in clinical practice and education.

The ability to learn has its foundation in the connectedness with others. Flinn, a professor of anthropology at the University of Missouri, and colleagues put it this way:

> Throughout human evolutionary history, parents and close relatives provided calories, protection, and information necessary for survival, growth, health, social success, and eventual reproduction....Natural selection has designed our neurobiological mechanisms, in concert with our endocrine systems, to generate potent sensations in our interactions with the most evolutionary significant individuals. (Flinn, Ward, & Noone, 2004, pp. 559, 563)

MacLean's research, surveyed in his life's work *The Triune Brain in Evolution* (MacLean, 1990), studied how the human brain evolved to ensure survival of the individual while adding the limbic capacity for relationship responses that are the hallmark of mammals, along with an expanded prefrontal cortex affording the intelligence to learn about the universe and oneself as well.

Henry (J. P. Henry, personal communication, 1992; Henry & Stephens, 1977; Henry & Wang, 1998), an early student of MacLean's work, pursued his own research in stress, health, and the social environment to describe ways in which brain, biochemistry, and behavior are designed for reactivity in the service of both individual survival and relationships. He outlined research demonstrating the impact of threats to survival and to relationships on biochemistry, brain functioning, memory, concentration, and other behaviors associated with learning. Disturbances in the counterbalance and interaction between left brain activity, associated with individual survival, and right brain activity, associated with relationship orientation, affect both learning from others and learning for oneself.

Porges (2001, 2003, 2009), director of the Brain-Body Center at the University of Illinois at Chicago, presented a new "biobehavioral" view of human interactions and relationships. This perspective, his *polyvagal* theory, is based on the phylogenetic lineage of the nervous system and on how various brain structures regulate physiological state via the autonomic nervous system. According to the polyvagal theory, the human autonomic nervous system incorporates three different neural pathways that evolved in sequence. The oldest one is an unmyelinated vagal visceral pathway connecting the brain to the heart and gut. Behaviors associated with activation of this vagal pathway protect the organism from danger through immobilization and shut down. The second is characterized by the sympathetic nervous system, which evolved to increase metabolic output, inhibit the visceral vagus, and mobilize fight-or-flight responses. The third, and phylogenetically most recent, represents a "brain–heart–face" connection that involves the brain stem regulation of both the heart via a mammalian myelinated vagal pathway and the striated muscles of the face and head via cranial nerves. This system facilitates engagement and detachment from the social environment. Each autonomic pathway provides reactivity patterns that are associated with adaptation to anxiety and the social environment. Initial reactions to the environment and especially to people are through the brain–heart–face mammalian vagal system. This system relies on facial expression, voices, and information about relationships as a reference point. If relationships are absent or anxious, the sympathetic nervous system activation stirs mobilization to fight or flee. If stress continues or sympathetic strategies are ineffective, the "old" unmyelinated vagal visceral system, designed to immobilize or "play dead," is activated. An exquisite sensitivity to danger or safety in relationships regulates sensory experience and brain states associated with learning, social engagement behaviors, and basic defense strategies. Porges' (2005) interest in autism and learning problems has led him to develop methods that provide stability, through modifying sensory input and through verbal and nonverbal communication, when an individual may not be able to establish the sense of safety within himself or herself.

Mirror neuron research examines another basis for ways in which brains and behavior are shaped by relationships. What came to be called *mirror neurons* were observed in 1990 by Rizzolatti and Fadega at the University of Parma while studying visual perception and movement in macaque monkeys (Rizzolatti & Fadega, 1996). They found that neurons in the premotor cortex fired in a mirroring fashion when one monkey observed the behavior of another. For example, the neurons in one monkey fired as though he were reaching for a banana when he observed another monkey reaching for one. This area of the brain, which has been studied in chimpanzees and humans, is located where antlers might sprout if humans had them and integrates information from sight, sound, and movement, coordinating responses involved in feeding and in social interaction (Grazziano, 1999; Rizzolatti & Fadega, 1996). Scientists in this study observed that mirror neurons were particularly active in response to facial expression and were most active when individuals were in arms' reach and within eye contact of each other.

Scientists who study mirror neurons are quick to see their importance for learning and adaptation. Neuronal activity that mirrors facial expression, gestures, and movement of those nearby is part of adaptation to the social environment (Winerman, 2005). The mirroring process primes neuronal connections in young to fit into the social environment and synchronizes individuals to each other over the life course.

The ability to be a separate individual within the fabric of connectedness with others is also built into human biology and brain function. In "The Neurobiology of Self," Zimmer (2005) reviewed research demonstrating that the left hemisphere, particularly in the medial prefrontal cortex, is actively involved in maintaining the sense of who one is as an individual. Although research in neuroscience has yet to take advantage of Bowen theory, many studies have provided evidence for Bowen's observations about variation in the fusion between emotion and intellect and in the capacity for intellect to influence emotional reactivity. LeDoux (1996), known for his popular books on the brain and also for his rock group The Amygdaloids, has demonstrated variation in the number and functioning of neurons reaching downward from the prefrontal cortex into the limbic system. LeDoux has noted far more neuronal traffic from the limbic system and brain stem upward to the cortex, making the impact of emotion on intellect more available than the influence of intellect on emotionality.

The research of Allman (2005) provides a glimpse into ways in which variation in the interplay between intellect and emotion is built into people's brains. He investigated variation and functioning of spindle cells that form a bridge of neurons where the prefrontal cortex and the limbic system meet. Individuals vary in the number and strength of these neuronal connections, which are associated with perceiving and correcting errors and with learning from trial and error. Being anxious about making mistakes inhibits these connections and leaves one more under the influence of emotional reactions. Differences in brain functioning and behavior clearly affect how people learn. Bowen theory provides a conceptual framework for integrating facts from neuroscience and biology and can be used to better understand factors that affect how people learn. Differentiation of self would be central.

The author uses neurofeedback and biofeedback instruments in clinical practice to observe physiological and neural reactivity associated with anxiety and relationships and with changes that occur through work on differentiation of self. She has developed a baseline protocol for research and for clinical practice that involves taking a three-generation family history and asking a person to sit quietly while she measures skeletal muscle activity, digital skin temperature, skin sweat response, and electrical activity in brain waves. She has adapted this protocol to measure simultaneously the neural and physiological reactivity of three family members as they take turns talking to each other and sitting quietly (Harrison, 2007, 2008b).

Physiological measures indicate some activation of tension states or stress reactions for everyone while talking about family members. People at higher levels of differentiation show more flexibility and variability in reactions while talking about family members and particularly while sitting quietly. For example, skeletal muscle tension or sympathetic nervous system activity increases while a woman talks about her husband's heart attack. Those anxiety reactions decrease when she is talking about the family members who are in contact with her husband and while sitting quietly (Harrison, 1995).

Measures of the brain's electrical activity produce complex information about the ongoing, dynamic interaction between emotional reactivity and intellectual activity. Scientific certainty about the interpretation of measures is impossible without a lifetime of studies to correlate measures across methods and instruments that measure brain activity in different fashions. Science will likely confirm Bowen's observations about the variation in fusion and differentiation between patterns of emotional reactivity and intellectual activity and demonstrate the correspondence with patterns of relationships, both formative and ongoing, within the family.

Observations that emerge from working on differentiation of self within one's family, in the classroom, and in clinical practice raise similar questions. In what ways do the levels of differentiation of teacher and student interact in learning? How does one person's work on differentiation of self affect the learning of another? How does anxiety affect learning at various levels of differentiation? How does the family of teacher and student affect learning in the classroom? It would take a survey of the sciences and the development of research projects beyond the scope of this chapter to address the questions raised. Live learning awaits those who are able to pursue the study of learning, relationships, and differentiation of self.

References

Allman, J. M. (2005). The neurobiology of intuitive decision making. In Bowen Center for the Study of the Family (Producer), *The family and the brain: An integrated circuit* [DVD]. Available from http://www.thebowencenter.org

Bowen, M. (1970). Differentiation of the self or the "I" position. In Georgetown Family Center (Producer), *The basic series* [DVD]. Available from http://www.thebowen center.org

Bowen, M. (1978). *Family therapy in clinical practice.* New York, NY: Rowman & Littlefield.

Flinn, M. V., Ward, C. V., & Noone, R. (2004). Hormones and the human family. In D. Buss (Ed.), *Handbook of evolutionary psychology* (pp. 559, 563). New York, NY: Wiley.

Grazziano, M. (1999). Where is my arm? The relative role of vision and proprioception in the neuronal representation of limb position. *Proceedings of the National Academy of Sciences, USA, 96,* 10418–10421.

Harrison, V. (1995). [The study of family emotional process, reactivity, and patterns of ovulation]. Unpublished raw data.

Harrison, V. (2003). Bowen theory and the study of reproduction and evolution. *Family Systems Forum, 5*(3), 5–10.

Harrison, V. (2005). Family systems and learning Part 1: Teaching what one does not know. *Family Systems Forum, 7*(3), 3–7.

Harrison, V. (2006). Family systems and learning Part 2: Reading, writing, and relationships. *Family Systems Forum, 8*(2), 1–2, 8–12.

Harrison, V. (2007). Variation in physiological reactivity in parental triangle. In Bowen Center for the Study of the Family (Producer), *Triangles as regulators of social systems* [DVD]. Available from http://www.thebowencenter.org

Harrison, V. (2008a). Language and learning. *Family Systems Forum, 10*(2), 3–5.

Harrison, V. (2008b). Physiological reactivity and anxiety in nuclear family triangles. In Programs in Bowen Theory (Producer), *Theory, emotional process and the integration of self* [Video]. Available from Programs in Bowen Theory, 1076 Geneva Street, Livermore, CA 94550-5624.

Henry, J. P., & Stephens, P. M. (1977). *Stress, health and the social environment.* New York, NY: Springer-Verlag.

Henry, J., & Wang, S. (1998). Effects of early stress on adult affiliative behavior. *Psychoneuroendocrinology, 23,* 863–875.

Kerr, M. E., & Bowen, M. (1988). *Family evaluation: An approach based on Bowen theory.* New York, NY: W. W. Norton.

LeDoux, J. (1996). *The emotional brain.* New York, NY: Simon & Schuster.

MacLean, P. (1990). *The triune brain in evolution.* New York, NY: Plenum Press.

Pemberton, D. (2006). *A new index to Murray Bowen's family therapy in clinical practice.* Washington, DC: Bowen Center for the Study of the Family.

Porges, S. W. (2001). The polyvagal theory: Phylogenetic substrates of a social nervous system. *International Journal of Psychophysiology, 42,* 123–146.

Porges, S. W. (2003). Social engagement and attachment: A phylogenetic perspective. *Annals of the New York Academy of Sciences, 1008,* 31–47.

Porges, S. W. (2005). The role of social engagement in attachment and bonding: Insights from polyvagal theory. In Bowen Center for the Study of the Family (Producer), *The family and the brain: An integrated circuit* [DVD]. Available from http://www.thebowencenter.org

Porges, S. W. (2009). The polyvagal theory: New insights into adaptive reactions of the autonomic nervous system. *Cleveland Clinic Journal of Medicine, 76,* 86–90.

Rizzolatti, G., & Fadega, L. (1996). Mirror neurons. *Brain, 119,* 593–609.

Winerman, L. (2005, October). The mind's mirror. *Monitor on Psychology, 36*(9), 48.

Zimmer, C. (2005, November). The neurobiology of self. *Scientific American, 293*(5), 92–101.

6

A Systems View of the Training Program at the Bowen Center: Guiding Principles (1990–2003)

PRISCILLA J. FRIESEN and CHERYL B. LESTER[1]

This chapter was crafted from an interview of Priscilla J. Friesen conducted in 2001 by Cheryl B. Lester. The interview addresses four basic principles that guided Ms. Friesen's efforts as director of the postgraduate program. First is a belief that learning Bowen theory requires integrating the concepts of the theory with one's emotional self. Second is the assumption that the concept of differentiation of self, the key concept and the ideal aim of Bowen theory, guides the Postgraduate Program. Third is the idea that the Postgraduate Program should offer examples and models of learners working to integrate and apply Bowen theory rather than a set or sequence of concepts and techniques. Fourth is the goal of promoting differentiation of self in family, work systems, professional arenas, and the world of ideas.

Dr. Lester: Priscilla, Dr. Bowen developed the Postgraduate Training Program in 1969 at Georgetown University Medical Center and initiated a special Postgraduate Program in 1976 for people from outside the Washington, DC, area. What unique contribution do you believe you have made to the program as director since 1990?

Ms. Friesen: My understanding and thinking about the program have certainly become more sophisticated, particularly as I learned more about the brain and the role of the family system in emotional functioning. I have realized that what each of us brings to the training program is based on the way in which our perceptions, senses, memory, and history are shaped in our own families. In a room of 40 people, each person's perception and experience of the environment is based on his or her part in a multigenerational process. At

---

[1] The authors express their appreciation and gratitude to Michael Sweeney, Ph.D., Lecturer, University of Missouri at Kansas City, whose extraordinary curiosity, patience, and diligence contributed to a thoroughgoing revision and vastly improved version of the initial interview, which was conducted in 2001.

any given point in time, because of differences in individual capacities to integrate theory with what I am calling one's emotional self, different individuals may be more anxious and at different levels of exposure to and understanding of the ideas. All this is living in one room with individuals trying to access their broadest ability to take in information and to interact with a set of ideas that is colored, filtered, and flavored by each person's emotional experience.

What I mean by *emotional self,* from a learning perspective, is the level or degree to which ideas are integrated with perception and feeling-based experience as well as with cognitive experience. My thinking as director of the program has been focused on promoting the integration of the concepts of Bowen theory at the level of the emotional self. Learning at this level involves developing emotional neutrality about how you experience the world. Applying Bowen theory in one's life, at this level of experience, challenges fundamental emotional assumptions that one developed in the context of experience in the family of origin. Thus, for example, a person might question the emotional assumptions with which she vigorously defends the downtrodden and discover its roots in her position in the primary triangle. She can connect her automatic response to a lifelong habit of feeling sorry for and defending her mother from the poor treatment she received from her father. Rather than acting on the basis of early emotional habits of sympathy toward the mother and antipathy toward the father, which stem from her position in the primary triangle, she can respond to relationship patterns on the basis of a relaxed and enlarged repertoire of emotions and understanding.

Dr. Lester: Through your clinical practice, you have undertaken a prolonged study of hundreds of individuals' brains, by way of neurofeedback and other tools offering windows into the integrative capacities of the brain. This has led you to observe firsthand that how one learns and what one understands is optimized or constrained in the relationships of one's family. That learning process shapes what you are calling the emotional self. Can you speak further about how your understanding of the emotional self influences your view of learning at the emotional level in the program?

Ms. Friesen: The job of our brain is to receive information about the world through our senses, organize it, interpret it, and act. This capability is organized through a lifetime of adapting to the relationships that are essential for our lives. Given the length of the period of human development and dependency (lasting perhaps into one's 20s), humans spend more of their life spans than other species adapting to relationships with the previous generation(s). These adaptations, which show remarkable variation from individual to individual, then interact with the next generation(s) and so on. The variability of this multigenerational process for the nature of an individual is remarkable. Bowen theory describes the patterns by which our brains are organized over the generations through the interplay of development and the patterns of emotional interaction in the family.

The training program assumes individual variation among participants, even from day to day, and addresses this variation in individual capacity on two levels. On one level, the program presents Bowen theory as a set of concepts and offers presentations that demonstrate how the concepts provide a theory for interpreting and understanding actual family examples. On a second level, the program promotes the experience of interacting with the ideas as they apply to oneself. During the question-and-answer periods that follow didactic presentations within the larger group, individuals have a chance to think and exchange ideas with the presenter, and presenters have a chance to challenge the emotional assumptions in these exchanges. In consultation groups, individuals can apply the concepts directly to the family or to other systems in which they function and discover blind spots that are part of their everyday lives. Through the practical and personal application of the concepts, individuals make Bowen theory their own rather than accepting it on faith as a dogma or a belief system.

Fundamentally, the notion that it is possible to become more accurate in our way of experiencing, of seeing the world, is really the basis and the ideal goal of the training program. This ideal is the underpinning of the goal of developing the ability to function optimally for self *and* for the group. This ideal, moreover, assumes that the ability to see the world accurately is organized and limited by emotional process. The training program challenges the accuracy of one's experience of the world. To confront that challenge, it is necessary to learn more about how one has organized oneself. Key to this is self-observation and self-awareness, sophisticated brain functions that cannot even occur without developing a certain level of ability to override emotional experience. Bowen spoke a lot about being alert, being aware, setting up research projects to enable you to begin to see more. Learning involves the capacity to overcome emotional processes enough to see things to which you were previously blind.

Dr. Lester: How do you relate the idea of "blindness" and "emotional blindness" to the Bowen concept of emotional cutoff?

Ms. Friesen: I relate emotional blindness to the process of emotional cutoff in the family. By *emotional cutoff,* I am talking about the way in which one "leaves home," the steps it takes to move from the dependence on one's parents to making a life for oneself. Emotionally and physically, this process of leave-taking can occur as a smooth transition in higher functioning families, or it can be very intense. The process can be observed not only in how far away a person "chooses" to live from his or her family or how often there is contact with family but also in the ways in which there is an emotional dismissal of the importance of parental relationships. One hears it, for example, when people say such things as "My family is toxic. I have chosen a healthier family."

There is a correlation between emotional cutoff in the family and the emotional blindness that impinges on perception and experience. In a general sense, the more emotional cutoff from the family, the more intense the feeling states, and the more polarized the perspective on emotional relationships. Going back to my earlier example, I would argue that a person who habitually champions the rights of children and seeks to protect them from "bad" parents is constrained by an intense, polarized reaction to her own history and is governed by this reactivity in her life. Acting from a polarized perspective to help children is different from working with families without taking sides (as one did in one's own family) to help them function at an optimal level.

Emotional blindness includes not only having difficulty entertaining an idea but often even perceiving it. This means that one's perceptual ability, literally the way in which information is taken in through the senses of hearing and sight—something that is organized in the development in the family—may be interrupted and impaired.

The learning environment in this training program assumes that learners are to greater or lesser extents emotionally blind to their own limitations, not only as individual learners in the program but also as actors in the group of learners, in their families, in their professions, and so forth. Because this emotional blindness emerges over time through constraints in the emotional process within their own families, individuals in the program need to acquire learning methods for becoming aware of these constraints and the way they affect one's ability to function effectively in all walks of life. Learning about emotional cutoff as an intellectual concept often opens a doorway to these "blind spots" in perception. Emotional cutoff is a powerful concept to see in one's own family and a starting point for appreciating the impact that emotional process in the family has exerted on one's life.

Dr. Lester: Would you say that work on one's family of origin is a fundamental method for learners to become aware of emotional blindness and emotional cutoff?

Ms. Friesen: Yes, definitely. It is the cornerstone for learning. Bowen theory suggests that there is a relationship between an individual's ability to function in the world and the constraints that impinge on his or her emotional relationship functioning. Reentering these relationship triangles through the family-of-origin work is the royal road in Bowen theory for learning to observe and recognize the emotional patterns that constrain his or her experience. I have observed that this road seems longer and more arduous where there is more emotional cutoff. Emotional cutoff may emerge in reaction to an intense emotional process and may help one generation cope with this intensity; however, it constrains subsequent generations in their ability to perceive the world accurately.

Dr. Lester: Can you speak further about your observation that learners with more emotional cutoff in their family of origin take longer to become aware of themselves and the constraints on their perception of others and of the world?

Ms. Friesen: There is a lot of variability among learners, but I have observed that the greater the cutoff, the more challenging it is to integrate Bowen theory. Yet those who are most emotionally cut off may also be precisely the people most motivated to learn Bowen theory. Some people understand and perceive the richness of the theory as they become increasingly aware of what they do not know and of what stirs anxiety in them. Certain parts of the theory make sense and become useful for some individuals, and other parts remain hidden from them and out of reach. In my case, it took a long time before I could see triangles. From learning more about how the brain works, I can say that the ability to understand oneself accurately in an emotional grouping and to adopt some way of acting based on that information is a complex and sophisticated brain function. One is blind to one's part in the world to the extent that one's functioning is muted, distorted, or affected by emotional forces, forces that limit one's own functioning. These limits affect one's professional functioning and one's ability to understand Bowen theory. In the past 10 years, I have acquired an appreciation of how much time is required for people to integrate the information at an emotional level.

This, to me, gets back to the brain. When you begin to move into the relationships that are a part of your own history, you develop new neural pathways. Those pathways are fundamental in the brain, just as fundamental as those early relationships can be. The brain moves beyond what one initially experienced as the arenas in which one would operate, moving, in fact, into very different arenas than one would have predicted. I think those changes occur in the brain and body. That is what integration is about. When you start bridging cutoff, as difficult as it is initially, it sets changes in motion and expands your horizons. You can't really anticipate these transformations, which are quite enriching and as infinite as they are hard won. You can continue bridging cutoffs for the rest of your life. As you begin to develop trust in the process and in its rewards, you move more willingly toward unfamiliar relationships and ideas. You come to accept the fact that there will be benefits.[2]

Dr. Lester: Are some of these processes triggered as participants leave home and work and travel to the arena of the program?

Ms. Friesen: I think it's an advantage for the program to meet only four times a year and for people to have to leave their habitual worlds to enter into another one, composed of people who do not live or work in the same environment all year long. People willing to remove themselves from their emotional systems and commit the resources of time and money to do so are highly motivated. In some cases, the emotional forces at home are so strong that it is a challenge to get away. For some, just developing the ability to get themselves emotionally out of their home environment to come here can be very disruptive to others in their family. Given the difficulty of leaving, it also takes some time to get settled down and to gain enough autonomy to learn. Alternatively, coming here for themselves can be very disorienting, being disconnected from the physical proximity of their emotional unit at home.

On the other hand, coming to the program does put people together in a clump with predictable and challenging group processes. People may stay at the same hotel or share rooms, creating triangles that live outside the actual classroom space. These group processes, which are primarily anxiety based, can lead to simple problems, such as people failing to respect the confidentiality of the supervision group. Such problems are part and parcel of what people are learning to bring to a level of conscious awareness.

Dr. Lester: How is the structure of the training program deliberately designed to help participants manage group emotional process?

---

[2] In her article "Emotional Cutoff and the Brain," Friesen (2003) described the concept of emotional cutoff in relation to what is known about the brain and human development. Using neurofeedback and biofeedback, she was able to document changes in the brain that occurred as one individual bridged cutoff by expanding her relationships through the generations.

Ms. Friesen: The training program makes a deliberate effort to structure a physical social arrangement that downplays togetherness while at the same time placing people together in large and small groups, for example, in consultation. The goal is to promote the ability for people to have enough physical and emotional space to observe and reflect on their own experience while remaining in contact with others. This effort encourages people to develop awareness of their own anxiety or emotional reactivity in their interactions with others and of the ways that these emotional forces constrain their freedom and ability to act.

To promote this ability in each participant, the program downplays the social aspects of the meetings, doesn't prepare nametags, for example. Some people describe the environment as unfriendly, but the social behaviors that are part of group process—the eye contact, graciousness, being friendly, the social stuff—they are there. They are there, but they are downplayed. Although some learning settings promote the relationship aspect of connecting to a group, this program promotes an environment that focuses on the exchange of ideas.

Often, the ideas in Bowen theory activate emotional reactivity in the learner. The goal is to develop the ability to observe an emotionally reactive response to ideas and to manage oneself in relation to that reactivity to ideas that are challenging or threatening. As I said earlier, this ability allows a person the freedom to speak about his or her experience or viewpoint as distinct from other experiences or points of view. Becoming aware that there may be another way to think of something is not only an intellectual but also an emotional learning process, which can be threatening and disorienting.

I want to emphasize the relationship component of that process. Learning is fundamentally a relationship process; even learning from a book involves a relationship process. In didactic presentations, the faculty or presenter serves as a model of the ability, to a greater or lesser degree, to entertain ideas and exchange responses in the context of that relationship component. The ability to manage oneself is a step toward awareness of the learning environment as influenced by relationship process. The expression of differentiation occurs in every exchange of ideas. The training program is organized to help people experience a set of ideas through a process that helps them become aware of what constrains their ability to learn and to see the world more accurately.

Dr. Lester: Bowen theory assumes that learning is affected by relationship processes, not just the relationships among participants and faculty in the program, but by the patterns that individuals bring to relationships without awareness or knowledge that these patterns constrain learning. How does the training program try to relax these constraints?

Ms. Friesen: The training program tries to minimize the constraints of relationship process at a number of levels. It sets the tone based on an appreciation for the structure and the emotional assumptions present in the training facility. It sets an example by the ways in which boundaries are defined, the ways in which everyone takes responsibility for setting boundaries, from the staff to the supervisors. It communicates an environment that is clear and that allows people to experience less ambiguity and to be freer from emotion, from what I would say are relationship issues. I pay attention and listen in the hallways to assess the relationship content of conversation. I observe who has connected with whom. I don't focus on it, but I keep track of it, and I look for emotionality where the alliances have coalesced. When things are working well, the alliances are less visible.

Dr. Lester: As director, what do you see as your role in helping participants become more aware of these emotional processes and the ongoing effort that is necessary to define self in the context of emotional fields?

Ms. Friesen: As director of the program, my responsibility is to represent what it means to define or differentiate self to faculty, staff, and program participants. I do this by maintaining a learning environment structured to promote individuality; by staying alert to the emotional processes and triangles in the training group, faculty, and staff; and by trying to demonstrate what it means to differentiate a self in the context of those triangles. Indeed, because relationships are essential for learning, all the individuals responsible for program administration, consultation, and presenting the theory in the program are vehicles for the participants to learn Bowen theory. For all associated with it, the aim of the program is on "learning for self"—an aim that is reinforced through a focus on learning in its own right rather than on gaining licenses, certifications, or academic credit.

Key to coordinating the program is an awareness of the process of anxiety that affects everyone, faculty included. People further down the road have enough experience to predict anxiety and to know what threat and fear look like; they can take it less seriously and proceed through it. In any case, the process of integrating Bowen theory generates anxiety. At an intellectual level, the anxiety may be related to whether ideas make sense and are consistent with one's own upbringing. At an emotional level, the anxiety may have more to do with the experience of looking at emotional perceptions in one's own family. Either way, developing more facility in the face of anxiety enhances the brain's ability to experience information differently and experience the world differently. For this reason, I don't worry so much about varying the content of the program every year. Even if we could offer exactly the same material from one year to the next, people's experience and level of integration would be different over time. I think that is the way the brain works, the way learning works, through this integration process.

Dr. Lester: Unlike many training programs, which separate novices from more experienced learners, this training program combines learners of all levels in the same environment and presents all of them with the same material. Would it be reasonable to say that the emphasis of this training program is on the participant's development of a greater capacity for learning rather than on the communication and mastery of information about the basic concepts of Bowen theory?

Ms. Friesen: Since I became director of the program, I've increasingly thought that it offers a format for learning that is useful to people throughout their entire lives and at all stages of their learning curve. Individuals can come for the initial training and then return after a year or more to refresh and sharpen their understanding of the basic concepts and theory. The passage of time enables them to articulate and vocalize their progress in the context of an ongoing effort. It's unlike a "training and then you're done" kind of idea. This type of learning takes a certain amount of time. The 1st year is kind of a "get used to it" year. The 2nd year, people seem ready and able to take on relationship challenges, particularly cutoff, that seemed unapproachable and made them squeamish during the 1st year. The 3rd year, the anxiety is a little lower, and the ideas are a little more available. It's almost as if the learning does not begin until some initial groundwork has been addressed, probably in relation to cutoff, and a new emotional threshold has been reached. For many, it takes longer to reach this threshold and get steady. At different levels of differentiation, particularly at high levels of cutoff, it is harder to develop the ability to enter arenas with a lower level of anxiety and a higher level of learning. This may explain why many participants return to the program after they have developed a greater capacity for learning. With time and integration, the program may offer a richer and more productive learning environment.

Dr. Lester: I have noticed that my reception of the very same ideas seems to be quite different from 1 year to the next. At times, the content of a video, for example, has been completely inaccessible to me because of my own anxiety or because of some heightened emotional process in myself or in the group. For that reason, I have been grateful when the same videos were shown repeatedly.

Ms. Friesen: I intentionally show videos repeatedly for the very reason that people experience information differently over time. Dr. Bowen's book and videotaped sessions take on a very different character every time they are consulted or viewed. Say you have a life experience that really changes your point of view; this affects what you learn from his book or from the tapes. Parents die, people get married, life events happen that contribute to changing one's perspective. As individuals develop more theoretical awareness, more integration of the theory with the emotional self, and more differentiation of self, they have more access to ideas. Viewing a video for the second or third time highlights that development and continues to teach you in different ways.

As for the Bowen tapes in particular, I think it's important to experience and be exposed to Dr. Bowen himself in the videos and to gain a familiarity with how he communicated ideas. The videos show that there was a difference in what he was relating and how he was communicating over time, from the "chalk talks," to the discussion tapes, to the tapes that were made toward the end of his life. I believe there is value in viewing the difference between the first and the last fruits of Bowen theory and in recognizing that there was a trajectory in the development of Bowen theory.

Dr. Lester: Are you making the point that individuals, including Dr. Bowen himself, never stop working on the ideas and on defining a self? Would you say that supervision and the relationship with the faculty supervisor serve as models of this ongoing process of developing greater theoretical awareness, emotional integration, and differentiation of self? The faculty supervisor in the training program is not presumed to have mastered Bowen theory or its integration with his or her emotional self or to have reached the ideal level of differentiation of self. Rather, he or she is someone whose experience with the challenges of learning Bowen theory and defining self can be helpful to participants. Would you agree?

Ms. Friesen: It's probably more consistent with Bowen theory to think of the supervision group as a consultation group, in which individuals seek integration of the knowledge by examining and presenting on efforts in their own arenas. Primarily, these arenas are their own family and work setting, other social or political groups, or their relationship with the ideas themselves. The consultation group and the relationship with the consultant are key to the goal of developing and maintaining an ongoing relationship that will enable one to challenge his or her own emotional functioning. It is assumed that the consultant, too, is working on his or her own emotional functioning, so that the focus in consultation is not on a group process but rather toward promoting an optimally differentiated relationship between the consultant and each participant.

Actually, the term *supervision* reflects the mental health history of the training program, but I think that the use of the term does not adequately convey the working hypothesis here, which is that someone's effort clinically can profit from the assistance of someone with experience. Unlike some mental health supervision groups, the focus of the small-group work at the Bowen Center is not to encourage participants to share their experience with others but rather to take on and reflect on their own experience. The presentation of individual efforts offers others in the group a chance to relate these efforts to their own functioning and to their own lives.

The consultation group, which usually consists of four to six people in addition to a consultation leader, is aimed at differentiation itself by working to downplay the emotional process present in that group. The environment of the consultation group minimizes interaction among the participants to allow individuals to observe and reflect on their own functioning in the context of the ideas of Bowen theory and their own emotional life. That is where the rubber hits the road.

The person who is taking on the ideas of Bowen theory in the context of his or her own family works with a consultant, sometimes called a coach, who is walking alongside with some knowledge of what it takes to make this effort in a family and what is needed to take on one's own emotional functioning. As a complement to the more content-oriented training that occurs in the didactic presentations, which of course generates its own emotional reactivity, the consultation group highlights the more up-close-and-personal challenges of learning and integrating the content of Bowen theory.

Dr. Lester: Consultation is not limited to the group meetings that occur in the program. Participants consult with their coach between meetings. What is the role of that relationship in the context of the larger effort at learning to observe and define self?

Ms. Friesen: Individuals do have one-on-one individual consultation with the coach between training sessions, about once a month. People use the individual and the group time differently. Individual time provides personal contact outside the triangles in the group and has a different quality, even when the triangles are pretty benign in the group. Generally, in the training program, one consultant continues with the same person over time. It means hanging in there with someone, whether it's the consultant or the participant, and allowing the relationship to develop over time. When you've been around a long time with someone, you have a different level of experience and, just as in families, a different level of commitment, both on the part of the faculty and on the part of the participant.

Dr. Lester: I see how consultation and the relationship with the consultant provide avenues for learning how relationship process both enhances and constrains learning, but what do the didactic presentations by Dr. Michael Kerr and other faculty contribute to this path of learning?

Ms. Friesen: The didactic presentations provide windows into the relationship process that goes into presenting and managing oneself both as a presenter and as an audience member. In organizing the program for the year, I ask faculty to present their cutting-edge thinking in a particular content area or to explore something new. I want to feature presenters who are active learners, not presenting content that they have mastered or from which they have disengaged. My goal is to demonstrate that the process of learning how ideas fit into this thinking about developing a self is an ongoing process.

Dr. Lester: How do the didactic presentations serve to demonstrate this learning process?

Ms. Friesen: The didactic sessions and the question-and-answer periods follow the model established by Dr. Bowen in clinical conferences. The purpose of the setup is to allow individuals to relate to the presenter rather than to each other. The discussion is conducted as a one-on-one exchange between the faculty presenter and individuals in the audience. Even if a person is interested in responding to a former participant's response, this is done directly with the presenter. The idea is to minimize the emotional process and the anxiety that gets transmitted in a group of learners, many of whom are emotionally reactive to an idea. If a comment or idea can ping off of others—which can occur very quickly to the extent that there is eye contact, personal address, turning around in a seat and looking backward—that diverts the ability of others to stay steady in the effort to think for themselves. The challenge, certainly for the presenter, is to relate to a group with anxiety in it. That is a challenge, and that challenge is part of the learning experience for faculty presenters. Learning to be an effective presenter and respond in a way that's productive also makes one a more effective supervisor, coach, or consultant. It is a task or function that you have to work at.

Dr. Lester: I would think that managing this process is especially difficult when it comes to the presentations by participants, many of whom are in the rudimentary stages of learning to manage emotional reactivity in themselves and in others. Did you design the structure of presentations by participants to help manage emotional reactivity?

Ms. Friesen: I changed the setup for question-and-answer sessions in presentations by participants after I found myself in a challenging triangle between faculty and participants. The challenge was to provide a format for faculty to hear what participants are thinking about and to give participants a chance to respond. A lot of emotionality was entering into the process, either as people directed questions or comments directly to a presenter, or as presenters, without being skilled at managing the reactivity, attempted to respond. To optimize the learning in that situation, I decided to designate faculty members as respondents with the responsibility to take the time to organize their thoughts. I would field further comments from the group and direct them to the responders. By channeling and directing group process, the anxiety [was] reduced and [it] gave people more room to think.

I watch for signs of emotionality in a group. I can see where people shut down, are unable to talk, become sleepy, start to complain, and so forth, and the emotional process inhibits lively discussion. Although there may be a number of other reasons, the absence of lively discussion usually offers a clue that the level of emotionality is high. I keep track of what might be the factors in the emotional process that runs through the group in the room. My goal is to take responsibility for directing the transmission of information so that people can be as free as possible to focus on their ideas rather than be caught in the crossfire of emotionality. When group process is running great, people have little idea that emotionality is even present. When it's not running great, everyone knows it.

Dr. Lester: Absolutely! As participants, we marvel at the skills of many presenters who are on the faculty of the Bowen Center. Could you speak further about the qualities that make someone skilled at presenting ideas and managing the emotionality of a group?

Ms. Friesen: First of all, a skillful presenter is also learning. He or she has the ability to provide an open forum for discussion, to ask good questions, and to challenge assumptions. In addition, a good presenter is able to manage self emotionally and to appreciate the emotional processes involved in the formulation and communication of ideas. A skillful presenter is a person who is also able to be at his or her best, neutral, enjoyable, enthusiastic self. Of course, on a bad day, not everyone can hit that. One's ability to manage self is certainly communicated to others, and others can respond in turn by being aggressive, antagonistic, challenging, or overly solicitous. Yet these interactions are indicators of emotional process rather than thoughtfulness, and they offer a clue that something is off kilter. From an emotional point of view, a key factor is a presenter's ability to exchange ideas with others without preventing others from preserving their own thoughts and without relinquishing his or her own ideas. An optimal presenter should be able to appreciate what a comment is about. He or she demonstrates a subtle way of getting at what's behind the question or what's emotionally driving the comment itself.

The ability to be more savvy as a presenter, fielding questions and comments from others, is a skill that translates readily to efforts in other arenas, such as the family and professional organizations. Knowing the lay of the land and managing yourself well in emotionally reactive triangles enables you to be more effective. A relatively nonanxious presenter who is genuinely interested in what he or she is learning is compelling. He or she permits others freedom to be themselves in that world of ideas.

Dr. Lester: The training program offers a kind of introduction to the challenges of differentiating a self. What challenges do participants in the training program face when they try to promote differentiation of self in other spheres of life, namely, in family, work systems, professional arenas, and in the world of ideas?

Ms. Friesen: The training program is really an exposure to Bowen theory at a particular moment in time. People enter at different stages of life and learning, some after quite a bit of exposure to Bowen theory. The challenge is to persist in the serious effort of integrating the ideas of Bowen theory into all the arenas of our lives. Over time, the focus of learning moves to all arenas of one's life—from the intimate arena of one's nuclear and extended family to the arenas of work and community—each arena informing the others. Some make the ideas of Bowen theory their life's work and communicate their efforts to study and understand their part of the world as it is informed by Bowen theory to all who want to learn.

Reference

Friesen, P. J. (2003). Emotional cutoff and the brain. In P. Titelman (Ed.), *Emotional cutoff: Bowen family systems theory perspective* (pp. 83–108). New York, NY: Haworth Clinical Practice Press.

7
Managing Self in Emotional Fields When Presenting Bowen Theory

ONA COHN BREGMAN

Bowen family systems theory describes patterns of emotional process as they occur in the nuclear family and over multiple generations of a family, as well as in larger systems and in society (Bowen, 1978; Kerr & Bowen, 1988). The ability to feel and become aware of instinctive emotional reactions (the *feeling system*) is described by Bowen (1978) as being a function of the connection between the emotional (instinctual) system and the thinking system. This connection provides humans with an opportunity to observe their own emotional functioning, which is at the foundation of all behavior.

People's ability to grasp new ideas can be compromised by the automatic responses of the emotional system. Those who present the ideas may not be aware of this emotional reactivity, and the value of the presentation may then be compromised by the presenter's emotional system. This chapter describes some of the research findings elucidating the role that relationship processes play in neurological development and functioning, and how the nature of this functioning can support or impede the brain's capacity to learn and to organize sensory input. The author also draws a connection between Bowen theory and data from neuroscience that appear to support the theory and consider how these findings inform our understanding of presenting the theory to others.

As Michael Kerr (1984) stated, "While lectures and reading contribute something, *learning to think systems in relationship to human behavior is dependent on emotional changes occurring within the learner*" (p. 17, emphasis in original). While working at being grounded in Bowen theory and presenting it to others over many years, the author has become acutely aware of how influential emotions are in the process of learning. Building on recent neuroscience research, the author discusses the importance of being aware of this functioning and using this awareness to manage self when presenting Bowen concepts to others. Observations and examples of emotional process focus on the relationships of instructor–student, supervisor–trainee, and clinician–client.

Brain Organization and the Learning Process

Research has demonstrated that it is becoming increasingly difficult to separate emotional and intellectual structures and functions in the brain. John Allman (1999), Fritjof Capra (1996), Terrance W. Deacon (1997), Gerald Huether (1996), and Joseph LeDoux (1998, 2002) are among those exploring the complexity of the brain, how it develops, and how it is organized. Advances in neuroscience may help inform and expand our understanding of Bowen's concept of the link between cognitive and emotional processes in living beings.

Recent Advances in Neuroscience

In *Evolving Brains*, John Allman (1999) explored how the human brain developed in relation to other species and in response to environmental challenges. While noting that complex behavior is evident even in many simple organisms, he pointed out that the human brain has evolved to a larger size with an even more complex blueprint. Researchers now have a better understanding of the brain's relationship to many parts of our biology and environment, as well as of the connection between humans and the survival systems of simpler organisms that preceded humans on the phylogenetic scale. In fact, Allman observed that other species do some things better than humans and that this is one of the costs humans bear as part of their evolutionary development. An example of this trade-off is the sophisticated fear response that humans possess, which produces anxiety. Allman discussed the tremendous effort it takes for a person to use his or her consciousness to take control of such fear or anxiety. Such discoveries in the neurosciences can further inform the relationship between the emotional and the thinking systems that Bowen posited. Allman also considered the need for extended family in humans. He attributed success at survival to the extended family and suggested that the development of our larger brain is the result of this need. It is no wonder that the family emotional system has so powerful a relationship to each family member's functioning.

Incorporating Santiago theory as developed by Humberto R. Maturana and Francisco J. Varela, Fritjof Capra (1996) expanded the concept of thinking in humans by suggesting that conceptual thinking is distinguished from perception and instinctive understanding or sensing, which he called "knowing." Santiago theory proposes that even simple organisms perceive, interact with, and respond to environmental changes and thus are capable of cognition. The expanded view of cognition put forth in Santiago theory asserts that

> the process of knowing is thus much broader than that of thinking. It involves perception, emotion, and action—the entire process of life. In the human realm, cognition also includes language, conceptual thinking, and all the other attributes of human consciousness. (Capra, 1996, p. 175)

Not surprisingly, there are areas in which other species do a better job of knowing certain things than do humans. Capra's thoughts on the difference between thinking and knowing suggest that emotions contribute to a human's perceptions and instincts and that these processes compete with the thinking of the neocortex. This concept helps explain those times when a thoughtful, principled decision has been reached by a person who then moves on to act in contradiction to that position. At the conclusion of a discussion on recent developments in the cognitive sciences, Capra (1996) stated, "Moreover, neuroscientists have discovered strong evidence that human intelligence, human memory, and human decisions are never completely rational but are always colored by emotions, as we all know from experience" (p. 68). This idea clearly supports Bowen theory.

Neuroscientist Terrence Deacon, in his 1997 book *The Symbolic Species*, proposed that the human's large brain, which includes the prefrontal cortex, evolved to handle the cognitive and communicative tasks associated with the use of symbolic language. Deacon asserted that symbolic language is distinct from iconic and indexical forms of communication. Although icons are recognizable representations of things, and indexes allow correlational connections to be made between things, symbolic language involves sophisticated socially agreed-on inferences. Symbolic language became necessary as human societies began to engage in reciprocal behavior and live in cooperative groups. According to Deacon, social and biological processes interacted in evolution and influenced the development of the human brain. He further suggested that the brain and language coevolved, enabling the establishment of social contracts among humans. These contracts, and the rituals that grew out of them, fostered the evolution of the extended family as we know it, and Deacon implied that language was essential to this process. Language in this sense is not simply communication but rather a biological process that allows humans to be conscious of self and the connection of self to others. In his view, brain development and the family are connected.

Neurobiologist Gerald Huether (1996) discussed the stress reaction consequences of organisms as they appear on the phylogenetic scale. Distinguishing between the physical stress that is usually examined in animal experiments and the psychosocial stresses experienced by human beings, Huether detailed the kinds of adaptations triggered by differing stress experiences in humans. He suggested that psychosocial conflict is a frequent and regular source of stress in humans (and in other social mammals). According to Huether, human infants are born with both differing sensitivity to stress and differing levels of intensity in their response to stress: Those with more extreme sensitivity and response intensity are more likely to adapt in a less functional manner. This degree of sensitivity and response intensity contribute significantly to how a person is able to adapt to stress later in life. Another factor that affects later adaptability is the repertoire for dealing with stress during the earliest life stages (often called *resilience*). As a human develops, it is important that the person be able to handle the feeling of not being in control. In Huether's (1996) words,

> The experience of stress, of the right quality, of the right intensity, in the right context and at the right age is a prerequisite of normal development. If stress is experienced in modes, in intensities, in contexts and at ages which prevent the acquisition and facilitation of ample coping strategies, it may disrupt normal development. (p. 603)

Huether further noted that when the experience of stress is inconsistent with the norms stated earlier, the stress and inability to deal with it creatively can lead to changes in the structure and function of the brain. Family systems clearly have a significant role in this process.

In *The Emotional Brain*, Joseph LeDoux (1998) pointed out that it is possible to have emotional memories without involving the cerebral cortex. He considered emotions to be biological functions that can be tracked across different species, including those without a cerebral cortex. An example of a precortical emotional memory would be an organism's automatic emotional response to a perceived threat. Specifically, the amygdala works to handle responses to fear with more speed than other areas of the brain, thus enhancing the organism's survival. According to LeDoux, a neuroscientist, such responses have been shaped by evolution, and only in the later phases of evolution has the human been able to develop awareness of these emotional responses. His research is directed toward gaining more understanding of how one's brain learns and manages fear. LeDoux discussed both natural triggers and learned triggers, each of which can initiate emotional responses. The learned trigger response is particularly relevant to this discussion. The ability of a trigger to predict danger is critical to survival but is accompanied by increased anxiety in humans that, in the extreme, can manifest itself in the form of an emotional disorder. He observed:

> It is well known that the connections from the cortical areas to the amygdala are far weaker than the connections from the amygdala to the cortex. This may explain why it is so easy for emotional information to invade our conscious thoughts, but so hard for us to gain conscious control over our emotions. (LeDoux, 1998, p. 265)

LeDoux developed these ideas further in a later book, *Synaptic Self* (LeDoux, 2002). In it, he suggested that the human brain has an ongoing process that is often out of people's conscious awareness yet constantly remembered. Periodically, a person becomes aware of what is happening as this awareness is built into brain neural circuits. In LeDoux's words, "Much of what we humans do is also influenced by processes that percolate along outside of awareness. Consciousness is important, but so are the underlying cognitive, emotional and motivational processes that work unconsciously" (p. 259). These ideas can inform Bowen's (1978) ideas about emotional functioning, which include "the automatic force that biology defines as instinct, reproduction, the automatic activity controlled by the automatic nervous system, subjective emotional and feeling states, and the forces that govern relationship systems" (p. 305). Anxiety goes up as one feels threatened. According to Bowen, the degree of anxiety and how it is managed affect differentiation of self.

Emotion and Relationship Systems

In summary, current neuroscience research appears to provide support for the critical role emotions and family systems play in our understanding of all human processes. This research is also discovering that people's brains are plastic and can be shaped by their experiences, which supports Bowen's thinking about the relationship of thinking and feeling and the family projection process. In this context, the author believes that there is a strong connection between emotional process and the challenge of new learning and change.

Challenges in Presenting Bowen Theory

The process of assimilating systems ideas and applying these ideas to human behavior ultimately requires more than an ability to let go of cause-and-effect thinking. It involves an emotional shift that is often accompanied by a period of significant cognitive and emotional dissonance and anxiety as the brain works to accommodate new systems ideas, which may even change the brain structurally and functionally. Moreover, despite this arduous accommodation work, the brain's host is unable to get totally beyond his or her own subjectivity, which can be driven by family emotional process. It makes sense that Bowen theory is both difficult to learn and frequently misunderstood, which often manifests itself in blind acceptance or a critique based on erroneous interpretations. Both positions frequently represent emotionally reactive stances. People who struggle steadfastly to understand the theory and make it their own usually find it an ongoing task.

Most teaching, supervising, and therapy takes place in the context of focusing on the "other," that is, outside of oneself. When presenting Bowen theory, whether as an educator, supervisor, or coach (*Bowen therapist*), much of the focus moves to self, taking responsibility for what one says and does. Once one has experienced the emotional shift involved in systems thinking, it is more difficult to close one's mind to a systems framework. Previously held beliefs and opinions may be rooted in political or social ideals that the person has a strong investment in maintaining, but a person's beliefs and opinions are also grounded in family emotional process. The task of separating a reasoned and principled position from an emotionally invested stand is challenging.

When the presenter of theory is overly zealous about "selling" the theory, it can fuel reactivity in others, which may spark more reactivity in the presenter and result in a loss of focus on self. What is important here is not the content of the exchange but the emotional process driving it. Bowen's theoretical concepts challenge a person's place in a relationship system and that person's perception of the system and of self, which may play out in the formation of triangles.

Triangles in the Learning Environment

Bowen (1978) hypothesized the *triangle* to be the basic building block of an emotional system. With a triangle or interlocking triangles, there are more relationship conduits for emotionality to travel through. Some brief examples of emotional process in the context of learning follow.

In the university setting, the instructor has a relationship with each student in a class, and many of the students have relationships with one another. Tensions in a student–instructor dyad may occur during and after examinations, when written assignments are submitted for grading, or both. At such times, it is a near certainty that some students will be dissatisfied with an instructor's evaluation of their academic performance. In such situations, some students may handle their discomfort by forming alliances with other students, leaving the instructor in the outside position of these newly created triangles. Another common contributor to tension in a student–instructor dyad is an unfavorable evaluation of the instructor submitted by the student. In such situations, an instructor may handle the discomfort by seeking to recruit other faculty members, administrators, or both into a triangle as allies. The student is typically in the outside position of this triangle. With both of these triangles, it is likely that the alliances formed are infused with emotional reactivity and the behaviors that follow will be reactive and subjective (Bregman, 2008, pp. 404–405).

There is also potential for triangles to emerge in supervisory relationships. For example, the anxiety of the supervisee related to doing some task "right" can attract a supervisor's need to provide instruction on the right way to do the task. A triangle is then formed involving the client, the supervisor, and the supervisee. The client is deprived of the opportunity to discover and develop self, and the supervisor and supervisee are able to avoid self by focusing on the other (the client). Supervisor and supervisee form an alliance to "fix" the client to reduce their own anxiety. Family members may form various alliances as interlocking triangles are formed. An anxious supervisee may act to keep the client or the client's family happy, and the client may act to please the supervisee. The process of defining a self gets lost in the blur of these triangles.

Training programs presenting Bowen theory offer another venue in which potential triangles can erupt and interrupt a genuine person-to-person relationship. Papero (1988) discussed the mutuality and interaction between teacher and learner in a training situation. "Training is seen essentially as a person-to-person effort, with the instructor having as much to learn as the learner. In a sense the training process becomes a dialogue between engaged minds, at least when it is occurring most efficiently" (p. 71). Both trainee and trainer can avoid engaging their minds either deliberately or naïvely, without conscious awareness, by involving other parties to dilute or avoid a personal relationship. But a true engagement of minds—without triangling—produces neither clones nor devotees. Rather, the dyadic relationship contributes to a creative process in which each person adds to his or her own understanding and use of Bowen theory.

When an educator, supervisor, or coach can maintain person-to-person contact with all triangle participants, hold others accountable, and take responsibility for decreasing the degree of emotional reactivity associated with his or her own participation in unavoidable triangles, then the other person in the dyad has more opportunity to take responsibility for his or her own behavior and accept the consequences of his or her choices. Because triangles are common in the relationships arising both in clinical practice and at the university or training center, the educator or clinician must stay vigilant about tuning into the anxiety that fuels triangling.

Responsibility for Managing Self

The person in the position of presenting the theory makes a critical contribution to the nature of the experience. Presenting Bowen theory is not an exercise in didactic instruction but is rather putting forward one's own understanding and operating principles, that is, a presentation of self. By providing the space and climate for the learner to explore and discover self, the one who presents theory provides an opportunity to learn without getting in the way of that learning. The most valuable contribution to others' learning Bowen theory is to present a principled self with as much neutrality as possible and with a lack of investment in persuading others. It is then up to the other person to interface and find a fit with the theory or not.

Any attempt to present the theory necessitates being able to think systems and be aware of and able to observe self. This requires commitment and discipline as one takes responsibility for his or her piece of the relationship. Each person must clarify and define his or her thinking and position in relationship to the other as part of a reciprocal learning process. Consistent with Bowen theory, how this proceeds will be influenced by one's family emotional process, degree of anxiety, and level of differentiation because this learning happens in the context of interpersonal relationships.

In the author's experience, many other approaches to teaching, supervision, and clinical work are more focused on the other person as a totally separate individual or on the person as part of a group rather than as an individual who is both separate from and, to varying degrees, part of, larger systems.

Other approaches may view the learner as the passive recipient of information or as one who will process new information if he or she is motivated and if the information is presented properly. In Bowen theory, the learner and presenter are both actively involved. No matter what the theoretical framework, however, the role of the emotional system and emotional reciprocity in the relationship is typically not attended to. Clearly, changing established patterns is no simple task, and neither is new learning. As the means by which human beings receive new information and come to understand it is further explored, the role of relationships in the neurology of emotional process will merit further scientific and clinical consideration.

Summary of Observations From Interviews

This section summarizes three interviews with Bowen theory learners: a client, a recently graduated social work student, and a supervisee. The author was the presenter of theory in each of the learning contexts. The purpose of these interview segments is to illustrate the subjective experience of the interviewees through anecdotal testimony. Although well aware of LeDoux's (1998) caution—"We have to be very careful when we use verbal reports based on introspective analyses of one's own mind as scientific data" (p. 32)—the author nevertheless found value in the feedback presented here.

The following questions were asked:

1. How were you introduced to Bowen theory?
2. What was your initial response to this introduction?
3. What was your response to the focus on self emphasized in this theory?
4. Did you encounter stumbling blocks as you became acquainted with the theory?
5. What questions have been raised for you as you became acquainted with the theory?
6. How did your relationship with the coach or instructor influence your learning?
7. Describe specific ways the coach or instructor got in the way of learning the theory.
8. Were you aware of an emotional shift at any point? If so, describe the experience.

Papero (1988, p. 73) formulated four areas to use as a general framework for evaluating the work of a learner. These items were converted to questions and concluded the interview.

1. What have you observed about yourself and your family since your introduction to Bowen theory?
2. Have you developed any new person-to-person relationships in the family? If so, with whom?

3. Have you increased your ability to control emotional reactivity to the family?
4. Are you able to remain neutral or "detriangled" while relating to the emotional issues of the family?

The student, who was learning many theoretical frameworks through her master's in social work (MSW) coursework, initially had the most difficult time understanding the relevance of Bowen theory to anything personal. The academic year was almost over before she found herself engaging with the theory when a situation arose in her family of origin. Although the supervisee was an earlier graduate of the same university and degree program as the student, she did not have the same struggle with seeing the relevance of Bowen theory to her personal life. The difference may be that the supervisee had been exposed to the theory before entering the MSW program. When the client returned to the author in recent years for more coaching, she knew she was returning to something that made sense to her and stood in contrast to her other therapy experiences. A common denominator for all three interviewees was a developmental process that was activated as each interviewee attempted to "learn" Bowen theory. As evidenced through the interviewee responses, this is an ongoing process that takes a gigantic effort.

The two interviewees who were "studying" Bowen theory were positive about the focus on self, as opposed to the client, who was in pain and who initially just wanted others to make the pain go away. Nevertheless, the client spoke of working to develop her capacities to focus on self, recognizing the benefits when she was able to do this. A common theme regarding a stumbling block to learning Bowen theory was identified by all three interviewees: namely, the anxiety that accompanies the challenge that systems thinking represents. They found it difficult to reconcile systems thinking with their established ways of thinking. When this conflict occurs, people tend to move toward what they are used to and more comfortable with.

All three interviewees pointed to the relationship with the author as a significant factor in their learning Bowen theory. The attempt of the coach–instructor–supervisor was to present self in a fashion consistent with principles of Bowen theory and personal values. The responses to the question about the influence of the coach or instructor raised for the author the question of her presentation. Had she actually presented herself with the degree of neutrality she had assumed? Feedback frequently confirms that the Bowen presenter, who is also a learner, is not as far along as she or he thought.

It is important to recognize that each of the three interviewees began at a different level of functioning and at a different level of familiarity with Bowen theory. All three had made significant observations, to varying degrees, about themselves in relation to their families. Each reported having done some work on developing person-to-person relationships in their families, although the bridging of cutoffs was most notable with the supervisee, who had the longest exposure to Bowen theory. When asked about increased ability to control emotional reactivity to the family, the client primarily focused on her relationships with the members of her family of procreation, whereas the student focused primarily on her relationship with her mother. Of the three interviewees, the supervisee appeared to have the broadest perspective with respect to her own emotional reactivity.

When asked about being able to remain neutral or manage self in triangles, the client had the most limited response, whereas the supervisee's response was the most comprehensive. Does the variability in these two responses represent a function of time with Bowen theory, the level of differentiation of self of the interviewee, or a combination of these and other factors? The answer is that all these factors likely contribute to the differences among the respondents. In contrast, none of the interviewees understood the question about experiencing an emotional shift: All of them interpreted this shift on a superficial feeling level rather than Bowen's concept of a deeper emotional and cognitive way of perceiving oneself and the world.

Conclusion

The role of emotional process appears to be central to understanding how people move toward an understanding of Bowen theory. This observation has several implications for further study. Of particular interest to the author is the influence of emotional reactivity in the relationship between the person presenting the theory and the person hearing it. The student mentioned the instructor's enthusiasm for Bowen theory as the single most important thing that kept her engaged in learning the theory. Was this an overinvestment on the part of the instructor? How might a more neutral stance by the author toward the theory have influenced the learning process? Could it be that the student's connection to the theory was more a function of the instructor's enthusiasm than of the theory itself?

Perhaps the neuroscience research cited earlier could offer some ideas and direction for assessing specifically how humans learn Bowen theory and, more broadly, any new material that contradicts their established positions. Such research could contribute to an understanding of the learning process in general and whether an emotionally reactive response on the part of the learner involves a reaction to the subject matter; an overinvestment on the part of the instructor; intellectual factors, emotional factors, or both; differences of opinion; a variety of other factors; or all of these. As Oscar Wilde observed, "Education is an admirable thing, but it is well to remember from time to time that nothing that is worth knowing can be taught" (as quoted in Pinker, 1994, p. 19).

One can anticipate that neuroscience will discover even more complexities as a new generation develops a brain with a different structure. In a *New*

York Times book review of *Reading in the Brain* by Stanislas Dehaene, Gopnik (2010) stated,

> We are seeing a new generation of plastic baby brains reshaped by the new digital environment....There is every reason to think that [this digital-age generation's] brains will be as strikingly different as the reading brain is from the illiterate one. (p. 15)

How this neurological rewiring will influence emotional process has yet to be discovered.

Emotional process as we know it now can present an obstacle to learning how to apply systems thinking to human behavior. The author believes that too little attention is paid to this issue. In the literal sense, it is unlikely that Bowen theory can be taught, which presents an enormously complex situation and a serious challenge to the Bowen educator, supervisor, and coach. Subject to the same emotional process as the learner, the Bowen theory presenter must also be a learner. It can be difficult not to be critical of other theories and approaches to human behavior. It is equally as difficult to take a step away from subjectivity and refrain from becoming emotionally invested in what seems to the author to be a very useful way of thinking.

References

Allman, J. M. (1999). *Evolving brains.* New York, NY: Scientific American Library.

Bowen, M. (1978). *Family therapy in clinical practice.* New York, NY: Jason Aronson.

Bregman, O. C. (2008). Triangles in the academy. In P. Titelman (Ed.), *Triangles: Bowen family systems theory perspectives* (pp. 403–417). New York, NY: Haworth Press/ Taylor & Francis.

Capra, F. (1996). *The web of life.* New York, NY: Anchor Books.

Deacon, T. W. (1997). *The symbolic species.* New York, NY: W. W. Norton.

Gopnik, A. (2010, January 3). Mind reading. [Review of the book *Reading in the brain,* by S. Dehaene]. *The New York Times Sunday Book Review,* BR15. Available http:// www.nytimes.com/2010/01/03/books/review/Gopnik-t.html

Huether, G. (1996). The central adaptation syndrome: Psychosocial stress as a trigger for adaptive modifications of brain structure and brain function. *Progress in Neurobiology, 48,* 569–612.

Kerr, M. E. (1984). Theoretical base for differentiation of self in one's family of origin. In C. E. Munson (Ed.), *Family of origin applications in clinical supervision* (pp. 13–36). New York, NY: Haworth Press.

Kerr, M. E., & Bowen, M. (1988). *Family evaluation: An approach based on Bowen theory.* New York, NY: W. W. Norton.

LeDoux, J. (1998). *The emotional brain: The mysterious underpinnings of emotional life.* New York, NY: Touchstone.

LeDoux, J. (2002). *Synaptic self: How our brains become who we are.* New York, NY: Viking.

Papero, D. V. (1988). Training in Bowen theory. In H. A. Liddle, D. C. Breunlin, & R. C. Schwartz (Eds.), *Handbook of family therapy training and supervision* (pp. 62–77). New York, NY: Guilford Press.

Pinker, S. (1994). *The language instinct.* New York, NY: William Morrow.

II
Established Domains for Systems Thinking and Bowen Theory

The therapy movement is a big thing these days. All I do know is that people in the professions rush in and start doing family therapy. And they're more interested in how you do it. They're more interested in developing a cookbook way of doing it than developing a way of *thinking* about it. I believe this has to do with a human characteristic. I think the human is on the reluctant side to learn something that does not have some immediate usefulness, and that's called "therapy." Now your ability as a family therapist, and this comes from my own experience, will be many times better if you can think of this in *theoretical* terms, rather than cookbook, gun-barrel terms.

Murray Bowen, MD, October 1984
Minnesota Institute of Family Dynamics, Minneapolis, MN

Murray Bowen had an unrelenting conviction that theory was the most important foundation for psychiatry, family therapy, and other practice areas. Therefore, absent some theoretical rationale, he would reject technique-based, how-to, and recipe approaches to practice in favor of a thoughtful, theory-grounded, open-systems perspective on the human condition and the process of change. This section presents a sample of applications in professional practice areas in which Bowen family systems theory has been used for decades—mental health, social services education, faith communities, business, and leadership development.

8

Learners Without Teachers: The Simultaneous Learning About Self-Functioning and Bowen Theory by Supervisor, Staff, Interns, and Clients in an Outpatient Program

CHARLES M. WHITE

This chapter details how the author's consistent focus on *learning for self* served as the creative force behind a 4-year effort to develop two mental health–substance abuse outpatient programs based on Bowen family systems theory—a 27-hour-per-week day program and a 12-hour-per-week evening program. The author, who served as the program coordinator and supervisor, illustrates how aspects of his own *differentiation of self* trajectory were represented in program components and protocols. Principles of Bowen theory were infused into the program components in which the supervisor and all staff, interns, and clients participated. When these Bowen theory principles were consistently lived and emphasized by the supervisor and the staff, they functioned as catalysts for creating an emotional atmosphere in which simultaneous and reciprocal learning could occur for all program participants (i.e., supervisor, staff, interns, and clients) regardless of their place or role in the agency or program hierarchies.

One specific principle that was consistently lived and that permeated all aspects of the program was that each staff person, intern, and client assume complete responsibility for his or her own life, learning, symptoms, and behavior. From the program's onset, the supervisor and the staff shared the observation that the staff, interns, and clients who adopted this "assume-responsibility-for-self" behavioral stance often reported developing more objective and factual understandings of their multigenerational family emotional process and tended to engage in more thoughtful actions aimed at increasing their degrees of differentiation of self. They also reported greater overall success in symptom, behavior, and life management.

Agency Context for the Simultaneous Learning Curriculum

Bowen theory places considerable emphasis on individuals, including supervisors and coaches, engaging in a continuous effort to increase their own levels of differentiation of self in their nuclear and extended families of origin. For serious students of the theory, this effort is deemed an essential prerequisite and corequisite to any attempt to communicate Bowen theory to others. The curriculum for learning about self-functioning and Bowen theory detailed in this chapter incorporates this emphasis by having the supervisor's continuous effort to increase his level of differentiation of self as the principal function behind the learning-for-self curriculum.

The department and agency context for this curriculum was the outpatient department of a Community Mental Health Center in central New Jersey. The programmatic contexts for the curriculum were two intensive outpatient programs (called *intensive outpatient services,* or IOS): a three-phase, 18- to 22-week day service and a three-phase, 18- to 22-week evening service. Descriptive flyers detailing service hours and components were provided to all clients and client referral sources. Service clients were coping with or recovering from both substance use and mental health-related symptoms, hence the name *dual-recovery IOS.*

Clients physiologically dependent on one or more substances (typically daily substance users who had developed clinically significant tolerances to those substances) first completed medically supervised inpatient substance detoxification before referral to the day or evening dual-recovery IOS. Clients who were actively psychotic, suicidal, homicidal, severely depressed, manic, or anxious typically completed short-term voluntary or involuntary inpatient psychiatric hospitalizations before their referral. Clients discharged from detoxification or hospitalizations on psychotropic medications were immediately referred to the Community Mental Health Center's Medication Clinic for consults and medication monitoring from a staff psychiatrist or clinical nurse practitioner at the onset of their service participation.

A continuous rotation of five 2nd-year clinical master of social work (MSW) or master of arts (MA) in psychology graduate student interns was essential to the day-to-day service operations. Beginning at two different times during the year—MSWs in September and psychology MAs in March—the internships lasted approximately 7 months, with the first and last 2 internship weeks devoted to being trained by outgoing interns and training incoming interns in various service responsibilities and protocols. The supervisor, whose agency title of coordinator made him the dual-recovery IOS's functional leader, designed and facilitated the services with a focus on learning for self—not on trying to impart or teach anything to the staff, interns, or clients. In contrast to this learning-for-self agenda, the agency's agenda was to pay the author (as coordinator) a salary based on his output to others: providing treatment to dual-recovery IOS clients, supervising staff, and teaching interns. Although these agendas may appear incompatible, the author contends that this apparent incompatibility can be resolved when the supervisor's theoretical and practice orientation is Bowen theory.

The author's experience with Bowen theory over 25 years has convinced him that his differentiation of self effort is (a) absolutely essential to his becoming a progressively more effective supervisor and coach with staff, interns, and clients and (b) qualitatively the same as that in which staff, interns, and clients engage as they seek to increase their levels of differentiation of self in their nuclear and extended families. One result of combining the perspectives of learning for self and qualitatively-the-same differentiation efforts was that the supervisor would naturally and routinely use his own family diagram and refer to his own family emotional process during his interactions with service participants. Although the intent behind these family references was to facilitate the supervisor developing a more objective and factual understanding of his family emotional process and self-functioning in a multigenerational context (not to teach anything), these family references did have a useful by-product—providing the staff, interns, and clients with a perpetual case study that simultaneously facilitated the recognition and understanding of family emotional processes while illustrating aspects of Bowen theory.

In addition, the supervisor was continually reading the prevailing emotional atmospheres for the staff, intern, and client relationship systems. His intent in maintaining awareness of these emotional climates was not to facilitate changes in the dual-recovery IOS components or structures, but rather to provide another vehicle for his effort to become more objective and factual about his multigenerational family emotional process and self-functioning. The link between the supervisor's monitoring the agency's emotional climates and his effort to become a more differentiated self in relation to his family played out as follows: (a) Emotional storms among the staff, intern, and client systems were usually indicators that the supervisor had not been clearly defining self in areas critical to service operations; (b) the supervisor's lack of clear stances typically resulted in an observable increase in confusion and indecisiveness among the staff and interns coupled with a decrease in morale; followed by (c) the clients responding in a manner similar to that of the staff and intern systems, often coupled with an observable increase in acting out, substance use relapse, or other reactive behaviors directed toward self, other clients, interns, staff, supervisor, or service structures and guidelines.

These reactive system responses usually motivated the supervisor to focus on developing clearer, more consistent, less ambivalent, and less reactive stances from which to lead and supervise the services, which eventually brought him back to examining unclear stances in the context of his functioning in his nuclear and extended families. This process led him to greater objectivity about his functioning in his family and ultimately moved him to adopt clearer, more defined leadership positions from which to oversee the service programming and personnel. The staff, intern, and client system emotional storms often subsided as the supervisor successfully implemented these more clearly defined leadership stances.

The services afforded the supervisor, staff, interns, and clients with several learning-for-self opportunities each week through a curriculum loosely organized under two developmental domains: (a) grounding self in Bowen theory, and (b) understanding one's family emotional process and self-functioning in a multigenerational context. Many of these learning-for-self experiences were embedded in the service weekly schedules and involved the supevisor, staff, interns, and clients. Other learning-for-self experiences, such as the 2.5-hours-per-week Supervisor, Staff, and Intern Family-of-Origin Exploration Supervision and the 1.5-hours-per-week Clinical Team Meeting, involved the supervisor and one, some, or all of the staff and interns; such meetings were usually held at times when the services were not in session.

Grounding Self in Bowen Theory

General Resources for Learning Bowen Theory

The author finds continually grounding himself in Bowen theory basics instrumental to his developing a more objective and factual understanding of his multigenerational family emotional process and his effort to increase his level of differentiation of self in his nuclear and extended families of origin. His more concentrated Bowen theory learning experiences have included participating in postgraduate training programs, symposia, seminars, conferences, and workshops at the Princeton Family Center for Education in Princeton, New Jersey, and at the Bowen Center for the Study of the Family in Washington, DC; giving presentations on Bowen theory at universities and to the community at large; and using his PhD coursework opportunities to research and write about aspects of Bowen theory (e.g., writing this chapter).

The author also engages in more routine activities to ground himself in Bowen theory basics, such as investing time in reading and rereading the primary texts on Bowen theory, supplemental texts and book chapters that synopsize or focus on specific aspects or applications of Bowen theory, and journal and magazine articles that summarize Bowen theory or explore its relationship to natural systems thinking. In recent years, the author has used a few Internet resources: The Bowen Center for the Study of the Family (http://www.thebowencenter.org/) and the Western Pennsylvania Family Center (http://www.wpfc.net/) Web sites, in particular, offer extensive resources and Web-based opportunities.

Family Systems Theory Education Presentations

Most of the supervisor's regular Bowen theory–grounding experiences were embedded in the dual-recovery IOS weekly schedules. The most substantial of these experiences was the audience-participatory Family Systems Theory Education Presentation (1–1.5 hours per session) that he or a senior staff person facilitated one to three times a week uninterrupted for almost 4 years. The presentation curriculum covered the theory's eight basic concepts and foundational postulates through a 10-presentation series. Staff members, interns, clients, family members, and friends attending the presentations each received a packet of readings and excerpts from central Bowen theory works to enhance their knowledge of the 10 presentation topics.

By choice, facilitators used no presentation notes or outlines, although key points were illustrated through overhead transparencies (e.g., Bowen theory quotes, family diagrams, cartoons, artwork photographs, and nature photographs with animal researcher captions), a three-generation "family mobile," and occasionally short video segments. Not using written notes or outlines thoroughly exercised the facilitators' abilities to draw on their internalized knowledge of Bowen theory while simultaneously honing their capacity to use conversational language to talk about the theory. The advantage to facilitators in using simple transparencies, family mobiles, video segments, and unscripted conversational language to provide a synopsis each week of a specific theory topic was that it tended to stimulate audience participation. The barrage of questions and comments from the audience of staff, interns, clients, family, and friends greatly enhanced the potency and theory-grounding potential of these presentations for the facilitators.

Ideally, the 10 presentations were conducted over a 10-week span so that clients graduating from service Phase 2 (typically 8–10 weeks) had the opportunity to hear most or all of them and participate in the discussions. The occasional to-be-announced presentation had a more in-depth participant discussion with additional illustrative video segments about the previous week's topic. Because each service ran 18–22 weeks, a client's family and friends had the opportunity to participate in approximately two complete cycles of the 10 presentations if invited by the client to the once-a-week evening programming for the entire time that the client was in either service.

Bowen Family Systems Theory Video and Seminar Series

A second substantial Bowen theory–grounding experience for the supervisor, which simultaneously exposed staff and interns to the theory, was the Bowen Family Systems Theory Video and Seminar Series. For the video part, half-hour video segments detailing aspects of Bowen theory or using case studies to illustrate the theory were followed by supervisor-facilitated half-hour discussions with the staff and intern participants. Held weekly year-round, the videos were organized to capitalize on thematic similarities between each week's segment topic and the Family Systems Theory Education Presentation topic. The thematic similarities promoted more robust dialogue among participants in both the series and the education discussions, increasing the theory-grounding potential of both weekly discussions for the supervisor.

Starting in September and again in March, the series featured foundational Bowen theory DVDs and videotapes from Bowen's *The Basic Series* (Georgetown Family Center, 1980) and Kerr's *Bowen Family Systems Theory and Its Applications* series (Bowen Center for the Study of the Family, 2004). These videos provided participants with an introduction to the theory's postulates and eight basic concepts. Showing these videos in the fall and spring provided incoming interns with a Bowen theory overview at the outset of their internships, and this early exposure to theory basics promoted more focused and thoughtful exchanges among the supervisor, staff, and interns during series discussions, with this dialogue quality typically lasting for the duration of the students' internships. For the supervisor, one benefit in re-viewing these foundational videos was having his basic understanding of Bowen theory recalibrated through repeat exposure to some of Bowen's and Kerr's thinking on the theory's central concepts. Many of these foundational videos were also shown in 1-hour segments to the day Phase 1 (typically 4–5 weeks) clients during their once-weekly Family Systems Theory Video.

After the foundational Bowen theory videos, advanced theory clarification DVDs and videotapes were shown during the early winter and summer months. Used for this sequence were selections from the *Bowen/Kerr Interview Series* (Georgetown Family Center, 1987), which features Kerr interviewing Bowen on aspects of the theory that many people find difficult to understand. After these advanced theory segments, the final few winter and summer weeks featured a sequence of illustrative case study DVDs and videotapes. Segments were selected from a number of sources: clinically oriented client interviews with commentaries, animal research and nature films, documentaries and independent short films, select episodes from television series, illustrative feature film segments, and even short animation films.

By viewing these illustrative case studies after the foundational and advanced theory segments, series participants could then observe the case studies through the theoretical lenses they had constructed from the Bowen theory knowledge they had acquired in part through the preceding theory segments. Thus, the discussion sessions became a venue for participants to hone their theoretical lenses and learn how to synthesize and integrate their Bowen theory knowledge with their family emotional process observations. Taking family emotional process markers displayed in the case studies, participants proceeded to formulate, articulate, and evaluate systemic hypotheses based on those observations and Bowen theory. Many of these illustrative case study videos were also shown to the evening service clients during the extra half hour scheduled for that service's Family Systems Theory Education Presentation, affording the supervisor an additional opportunity each week to further hone his theoretical lens.

For the seminar part of the series, the bimonthly full-day Princeton Family Center for Education seminars and annual conferences provided the supervisor, staff, and interns with a more concentrated and in-depth exposure to Bowen theory, as presented by some of the theory's foremost experts. For the supervisor, the principal Bowen theory–grounding benefit gleaned from these expert-facilitated, theoretically precise seminars and conferences was that they served to further recalibrate his basic understanding of Bowen theory. A secondary benefit to the supervisor, which came through the staff and interns attending these seminars and conferences, was a sustained increase in the overall quality of thoughtful, Bowen theory–based dialogue offered by the supervisor, staff, and interns during both the weekly series and the education discussions. This increased quality in the theoretical exchanges served to greatly enhance the Bowen theory–grounding potential of both weekly discussions for the author.

Family Emotional Process Video and Case Studies Forum
(Fridays and Mondays)

The illustrative case study videos mentioned earlier were all shown in 1-hour segments to the day service Phase 1 and 2 clients (typically 8–10 weeks) during their twice-weekly Family Emotional Process Video. When an edited-for-length feature film was used as an illustrative case study, the first half of the movie was shown on Friday morning and the second half was shown on the ensuing Monday morning. All participants at both morning sessions received photocopies of a family diagram detailing what was known of the case study's nuclear and extended families and a page of open-ended questions (e.g., who, what, when, where, and how questions) formulated from a careful case study viewing and designed to stimulate participants' factual understandings of the family while promoting family emotional process pattern recognition.

The case studies were also sequenced to create a thematic match between each Friday's Family Emotional Process Video and the Family Systems Theory Education Presentation topic. This thematic matching greatly enriched the education discussions by encouraging the participants to rapidly formulate, articulate, and evaluate systemic hypotheses generated from their newly acquired Bowen theory topical knowledge and their case study family emotional process observations from earlier in the day. This discussion enrichment then surged through the rest of the Friday service day, promoting thoughtful, integrative, and energetic Bowen theory–based exchanges among the supervisor, staff, interns, and client participants of the accompanying half-hour Family Emotional Process Case Studies Forum.

These supervisor- or staff-facilitated twice-weekly forums provided the supervisor, staff, interns, and day service clients with a venue in which to vigorously discuss the Friday–Monday illustrative case study. The case study family diagram and open-ended questions became the forum discussions fodder, providing participants with opportunities to recognize what was objectively known about the case study family from the video segments and family diagram and to identify observable family emotional process markers. With their growing knowledge of Bowen theory, forum participants proceeded to formulate, articulate, and evaluate systemic hypotheses based on the family facts, observations, and Bowen theory. The supervisor found facilitating the forum discussion quite challenging in that it tested his capacity to (a) synthesize family facts and Bowen theory in real-time, and (b) build on the open-ended questions in a way that further exposed the family emotional process displayed in the case study segments. In essence, the forum provided participants with more opportunities to hone their theoretical lenses and further integrate their knowledge of Bowen theory and family emotional process.

Understanding One's Family Emotional Process and Self-Functioning in a Multigenerational Context

To implement the second developmental domain, understanding self-functioning in a multigenerational family emotional process context, the author finds having regular opportunities to present his family facts and current understanding of the family emotional process associated with those facts to be instrumental to his developing a more objective understanding of his family. The author has used several means to enhance his understanding of his multigenerational family emotional process. The more focused opportunities have included compiling vast amounts of current and historical family data on a 17-generation family diagram for a graduate school Family-of-Origin presentation; constructing detailed five-generation family diagrams and providing extensive answers to family-exploratory essay questions for the Princeton Family Center for Education and Bowen Center for the Study of the Family postgraduate training program applications; presenting his family diagram during training program supervision sessions; and engaging in three courses of nuclear and multigenerational family systems–focused individual coaching with seasoned Bowen theory coaches.

Similar to the service-associated Bowen theory–grounding learning-for-self experiences detailed earlier, most of the supervisor's regular opportunities to present his family facts and family emotional process associated with those facts were embedded in the service weekly schedules or happened at meetings with staff and interns at the conclusion of specific service days. The most substantial of these service-associated learning-for-self opportunities were the day and evening Family-of-Origin Interview and Discussion sessions and the Supervisor, Staff, and Intern Family-of-Origin Exploration Supervision.

Family-of-Origin Interview and Discussion

The supervisor, staff, interns, and clients all participated in the day and evening Family-of-Origin Interview and Discussion sessions. Like the other curriculum components, the focus for the supervisor as he participated in these sessions was on learning for self—not on trying to impart or teach anything to the staff, interns, or clients. The four concentrated session hours each week gave the supervisor time to reflect on or present his family facts and his current understanding of the family emotional process associated with those facts, with the aim being to develop a more objective understanding of his family and perhaps increase his level of differentiation of self. As noted earlier, a by-product of this effort was that the author became a progressively more effective service supervisor while his family references provided participants with an ongoing case study that could simultaneously facilitate a recognition and understanding of family emotional processes while illustrating aspects of Bowen theory.

Modeled to an extent after the supervisor's postgraduate trainee supervision sessions, a set of roles and tasks associated with these interview and discussion sessions were assigned to the supervisor, staff, and interns according to hierarchical rotational sequences based on participants' depth of knowledge and proficiency with Bowen theory. When thoughtfully performed, these assigned roles and tasks created a synergistic effect that produced one of the most stimulating and rewarding venues for reflecting on and articulating his understanding of his own multigenerational family emotional process that the supervisor has ever experienced.

If it was a client's first interview for the Family-of-Origin Interview and Discussion session, then the assigned Diagramming Assistance intern (15 minutes) began by asking the client a series of open-ended, fact-seeking questions concerning the anatomy of the client's immediate, extended, and multigenerational families. These questions addressed the names, number, gender, ages, and order of siblings in each diagrammed family; dates of birth, death, marriage, separations, divorce, and remarriage; and level of education, occupation, and places of residence. The intern then organized, assembled, and illustrated these family facts on a multigenerational family diagram that he or she drew on a large whiteboard in a dual-recovery IOS service room. As additional family facts emerged during the interview, this intern was also responsible for immediately amending and modifying the whiteboard family diagram so that at any moment it was the most accurate and factual representation of the client's immediate, extended, and multigenerational families. At the session's end, a digital photograph of the most current multigenerational family diagram on the whiteboard would be taken and presented to the client in hardcopy and overhead transparency forms before the end of the service day.

For a client interviewed in a previous session, the client drew his or her own family diagram on the whiteboard while the assigned intern offered diagramming assistance only in response to client solicitation. Most clients would use their previous hard-copy family diagrams as the basis for their current family diagram drawings. Client family diagram hard copies were also provided to the supervisor, the client's agency record, and the staff person or intern who was responsible for providing that client with individual or couples Bowen theory–oriented coaching sessions. This staff person or intern was also provided with an overhead transparency copy for use in other service-related learning-for-self experiences such as Supervisor, Staff, and Intern Family-of-Origin Exploration Supervision and Clinical Team Meetings.

During the Clinical Team Meeting, a staff person or intern presenting an assessment of a client's progress was expected to project that client's family diagram transparency onto an overhead screen and present the assessment in the context of that client's current and historical functioning in his or her immediate, extended, and multigenerational families. Furthermore, whenever any client was discussed at that meeting, it was expected that his or her family diagram transparency would be projected as a visual reminder to all meeting participants that there was always a larger family context for understanding any client's functioning and a multigenerational emotional process legacy that was influencing his or her progress in the service.

The first task for the supervisor, the staff person, or the intern assigned Introductory Questioning and Recruit for Next Week (15 minutes) was to recruit client volunteers to be interviewed during the following week's Family-of-Origin Interview and Discussion sessions. The rationale for recruiting interviewees a week in advance was to give client volunteers time to gather initial or additional family facts for their multigenerational family diagrams and reflect on the family emotional process that accompanies their family facts. The advance scheduling also gave the supervisor, staff, and interns time to adjust the clinical team task assignments so that, if possible, a client volunteer was interviewed by the staff person or intern who provided him or her with coaching. Assignment changes were made only if a client volunteer's coach was scheduled to perform another role or task during that interview and discussion session.

The second and primary task for the questioner and recruiter was to engage the client volunteer and other session participants in a semiscripted sequence of questions concerning the purpose and value in drawing and being interviewed about his or her multigenerational family diagram and family emotional process. The questioner sat with his or her back to the client's whiteboard family diagram and facing the interviewer and client volunteer, who were seated in the center front of the room. The questioner began the discussion by asking the client volunteer what he or she thought was the purpose and value of looking at and being interviewed about the facts of one's family diagram.

Respectfully listening to the client volunteer's response, he or she simultaneously listened for a specific key theme in the client's response: an acknowledgment that by looking at the facts of one's family diagram, one could identify common and persistent patterns of behavior in the various family members across the generations.

If a client volunteer did not identify the multigenerational behavioral patterns theme in his or her response, the questioner then posed the same question in succession: first to the other client participants, then to the interns, and finally to the staff and supervisor until the key response theme was verbalized. Throughout the sequence of questions, the succession up the participant hierarchy always stopped at the level of Bowen theory proficiency needed to satisfactorily articulate the response theme. On hearing that response theme, the questioner always returned to the client volunteer to pose the next question in the sequence. The sequence of questions and corresponding key response themes were as follows:

1. What do you see as the purpose and value of looking at and being interviewed about the facts of one's family diagram? *Key response theme:* Through looking at the facts of one's family diagram, one can identify common and persistent patterns of behavior in the various family members across the generations.
2. How is it useful to be able to identify the common and persistent patterns of behavior in various family members across the generations? *Key response theme:* Identifying the patterns of behavior across the generations allows one to see these patterns as being facts of the family that have histories and influence that precede and transcend the history and influence of any one family member.
3. How is it useful to be able to see these behavioral patterns as being facts of the family that have histories and influence that precede and transcend the history and influence of any one family member? *Key response theme:* It allows one to develop more objective understandings of these behavioral patterns, family members, and the parts that self and other family members play in creating and perpetuating these behavioral patterns.
4. What can happen when one becomes more objective in one's understandings of the behavioral patterns, family members, and parts that self and other family members play in creating and perpetuating these behavioral patterns? *Key response theme:* One can become more neutral and less reactive toward those family patterns, family members, and oneself.
5. What can happen as one becomes progressively more neutral and less reactive toward family patterns, family members, and oneself? *Key response theme:* This can lead to less blaming and more acceptance

of self and other family members for the patterns in the family while simultaneously encouraging one to assume responsibility for the part that self plays in creating and maintaining these patterns.

6. What can less blaming and more acceptance of self and other family members free one up to do? *Key response theme:* With less time and emotional energy being invested in blaming self and other family members, one has more time and emotional energy available to invest in pursuing one's own life changes, goals, and aspirations.

7. What will be different about one's investment and pursuit of these life changes, goals, and aspirations? *Key response theme:* Unlike one's previous goal pursuits and attempts at change that were impulsive and driven by emotions, one can pursue these new life changes, goals, and aspirations in a more thoughtful, less reactive manner.

8. Finally, when one's life changes, goals, and aspirations are more thoughtfully and less reactively attained, what does that permit one to do? *Key response theme:* Because these life changes, goals, and aspirations were more thoughtfully and less emotionally determined, one will likely have greater success at being able to sustain these changes when the family puts pressure on one to "change back."

On successful completion of this sequence of questions through the articulation of the corresponding key response themes, the questioner's final tasks were to (a) encourage the other participants to reflect on their own multigenerational family behavioral patterns and emotional process as they listen to the client volunteer be interviewed about his or her own family behavioral patterns and emotional process, (b) invite all participants to consider the universal aspects of this emotional process and behavioral patterns across all families, and (c) inform the participants that one or two emergent family patterns or emotional process themes from the interview would be the topics of a Discussion (15 or 30 minutes) that was open to all clients, interns, and staff, providing them with opportunities to share how they saw aspects of these family patterns or emotional process themes in their own families.

By choice, the supervisor used no question or key response theme notes or outlines as he performed this questioner and recruiter primary task. Similarly to how he facilitated the Family Systems Theory Education Presentations, the supervisor found that not using written notes or outlines when posing the sequence of questions or identifying key response themes thoroughly exercised his ability to draw on his internalized knowledge of Bowen theory and the theory's conceptualization of the process of change (i.e., differentiation of self). Not working from notes or outlines also honed his ability to use conversational language to pose these questions, identify key response themes, and describe differentiation of self. The advantage for the supervisor in using conversational language to accomplish these tasks was that it tended to stimulate quantitative and qualitative increases in client, intern, and staff participation in the questioning sequence and during the subsequent discussion segment. These enrichments in client, intern, and staff participation also ultimately benefited the supervisor in his efforts to develop a more experience-based understanding of differentiation of self and a more objective and factual understanding of his own multigenerational family emotional process.

As mentioned earlier, whenever possible the Interviewer (45 minutes) role was reserved for the staff person or intern who provided the client volunteer with coaching sessions from the onset of that client's service participation. During service Phases 1 and 2, the advance recruitment and scheduling of client interviewees usually made adjustments to the clinical team task assignments possible so that clients could be interviewed by their coaches. However, during Phase 3 (12 weeks minimum), the same two service personnel (staff person and intern) cofacilitated this phase each week, with the intern conducting all Phase 3 Family-of-Origin Interview and Discussion sessions. Phase 3 was 3 hours per week on one evening. Having the same person and intern cofacilitating it each week promoted continuity for all of the Phase 3 participants and facilitators. The supervisor decided that staffing continuity was a higher priority than attempting to have Phase 3 clients be interviewed by their regular coaches because, given Phase 3's length and census (6–15 clients), clients were typically interviewed only one to three times during that phase.

As with anything participants gleaned about their own family emotional process through their participation in the interview and discussion session, all were encouraged by the introductory questioner, interviewer, and discussion facilitators to bring these insights and discoveries back into their coaching or supervision sessions. At the Clinical Team Meeting, the staff and interns who provided coaching to Phase 3 clients reported that the quality of this coaching and their clients' work on differentiation of self were enhanced by the insights and discoveries their clients gained from being Phase 3 family-of-origin interviewees and discussion session participants.

The Family-of-Origin Interview (45 minutes) was divided into two subsessions—a Dialogue (30 minutes) between the client and interviewer over the facts and emotional process evident in the client's immediate, extended, and multigenerational families; and a Panel (15 minutes) in which the supervisor, staff, and intern participants posed an assortment of follow-up and clarification questions to the interviewer, who then selected two or three of the most thoughtful, process-oriented questions to then re-present to the client during the remaining minutes of the interview. The Dialogue subsession was modeled after the theory-driven approach to interviewing exemplified in *Family Evaluation: An Approach Based on Bowen Theory* (Kerr & Bowen, 1988). Readers are encouraged to review this requisite text for a detailed account of questions to ask and topics to cover during a comprehensive family facts and multigenerational emotional process coaching interview.

The Panel subsession bore some procedural similarities to the audience participation segments from a Bowen Center for the Study of the Family Clinical Conference and the supervisor's postgraduate program trainee supervision sessions. Panel follow-up and clarification questions were first written by panel participants and then verbalized to the interviewer. Before the first panel question was read, the interviewer instructed the interviewee not to respond to any of the questions posed but rather to listen carefully to all questions and note any thoughts regarding his or her family emotional process stimulated by these questions.

The function of having all questions directed toward the interviewer was twofold: (a) It gave the client the freedom to think about the questions and his or her family emotional process without feeling pressured or obligated to craft responses to any of the questions, and (b) it allowed the interviewer to serve as a buffer for the client, assisting the client in maintaining his or her thoughtful and reflective posture by filtering out and setting aside any questions that may be laced with the emotional reactivity or lack of neutrality or objectivity of the participant questioners. During the Phase 3 interview panels, this buffer function took on particular importance in that the interviewee's fellow clients were full panel participants in that phase—allowed to pose follow-up and clarification questions to the interviewer just as the supervisor, staff, and interns were permitted during the Phase 1 and 2 interview panels. As each interview and discussion session ended, panel participants gave all of their written questions to the interviewer for possible reintroduction into the interviewed client's subsequent coaching sessions.

Finally, as a technical aside, during all interviews, dialogues, and panels, laser pointers were extensively used to identify areas of interest on multigenerational family diagrams by the interviewer, client volunteer, and all panel participants. Laser pointers were particularly useful because participants could quickly and visually identify precise areas of interest on family diagrams from any place in a service room without having to leave their seats. A required purchase for interns and staff, laser pointers were routinely used in every service-related learning-for-self experience that involved whiteboard-drawn or overhead-projected family diagrams.

Only the supervisor and senior staff, having considerable prior exposure to and training in Bowen theory, could serve as the Interviewer's Coach (45 minutes). Working concurrently with the Family-of-Origin Interview, the interviewer's coach sat against the service room's back wall facing the whiteboard family diagram on the front wall, with the interviewer and client interviewee seated in the center front of the room also facing the whiteboard with their backs to the interviewer's coach. The selective staffing of the interviewer's coach role was to (a) ensure that the interview was conducted in accordance with Bowen theory protocols and (b) guide the interviewer as to which family facts and emotional process themes to further explore or focus on during the interview. The interviewer's proficiency in using Bowen theory to guide the interview was the primary factor in determining the frequency with which the interviewer's coach interrupted the interview to redirect the interviewer.

For example, interns serving as interviewers early in their internships, when they have a limited understanding of Bowen theory, will tend to receive frequent coach interview interruptions with redirections often focused on such basics as (a) assisting interns in rephrasing their interview questions in a more open-ended, exploratory, objective, or neutral manner; (b) making sure interns confirm all known family facts on whiteboard family diagrams before focusing their attention on common or persistent behavior patterns in specific family members across generations; and (c) guiding interns' initial forays into identifying aspects of family emotional process (e.g., triangles, over- or underfunctioning reciprocity, family projection process) that are supported by family facts. Over the course of a student's internship, as he or she developed a basic understanding of Bowen theory and a proficiency in using the theory to guide client interviews, the frequency and extent of the coach's interview interruptions and redirections would extensively decrease. The inverse relationship between increased knowledge of and proficiency in using Bowen theory and decreased coach interruptions and redirections became so consistent that interns often used the latter as an indicator of progress on the former.

Lest the reader think that interns were the only service personnel subjected to interruptions and redirections from the interviewer's coach, there were plenty of interviews in which the supervisor or staff interviewers were subjected to repeated and extensive coach interventions. In part, this was because of the broader perspective on the family diagram and family emotional process that the interviewer's coach was afforded from sitting in the back of the room during the interview, coupled with not having to actively think of the next exploratory question to ask the client to illuminate the client's multigenerational family emotional process. The methodical, Bowen theory–grounded approach to interviewing and exploring family emotional process often left interviewers vulnerable to becoming too narrowly focused on a few family facts during the interview, resulting in a loss of perspective on how those facts related to the larger multigenerational family emotional process evident in the family system. This vulnerability to narrow focus was effectively addressed through the active interventions of the interviewer's coach, who challenged interviewers to broaden their perspectives to see specific family facts in larger multigenerational contexts. Idiomatically, if interviewers were stuck "seeing only trees," then the interviewer's coach would redirect interviewers so clients, interviewers, and other session participants might be able to "see the forest" as well.

For the supervisor, staff person, or intern facilitating the Discussion (15 or 30 minutes), the first task was to have carefully listened during the family-of-origin interview and to the interviewer's coach interventions. From that interview and intervention content, the discussion facilitator identified one or two family emotional process themes that were (a) depicted on the interviewee's family diagram and (b) explicitly addressed through one or more Bowen theory concepts (e.g., triangles, family projection process, emotional cutoff) and through particular patterns or variations in family emotional process described in those concepts (e.g., marital conflict, dysfunction in one spouse, impairment of one or more children, emotional distance).

The facilitator's second task was to lead a 15- or 30-minute participant discussion centered on the one or two identified family emotional process themes. The facilitator would sit in front of the service room facing the other session participants, who were seated around the perimeter of the room. The interviewer and interviewee were no longer seated in the center front of the room but rather had taken seats around the room's perimeter with the other participants. The facilitator then stated four procedural rules to the participants for the ensuing discussion: (a) keep the focus on themselves and how the identified themes are represented in their own family emotional process, (b) speak from the "I" position (e.g., I think…; My belief is…) as they talk about their own families or the personal relevance of the identified themes, (c) refrain from introducing the interviewee's family or family diagram as a discussion topic, and (d) direct all questions and statements to the facilitator, not to the interviewee, interviewer, or other session participants.

The discussion usually began with the facilitator speaking on how the theme was illustrated in his or her own family and how it was addressed through one or more Bowen theory concepts and through particular patterns or variations in family emotional process described in that concept or concepts. The facilitator then opened the discussion up to the other participants with an invitation to share if and how they saw the theme reflected in their own family emotional process. As participants voiced observations about their own family emotional process as these observations related to the theme, the facilitator routinely asked these participants open-ended follow-up questions aimed at clarifying if and how these observations were examples of the family emotional process pattern that was addressed in Bowen theory. If 30 minutes were allotted for the session, then with approximately 15 minutes remaining, the facilitator would repeat the discussion procedures with a second theme. The discussion concluded with the facilitator encouraging participants to (a) continue thinking about their own family emotional process as it related to the identified theme or themes and (b) resume the dialogue during Self-Status Reports (a daily forum in which clients articulate their efforts to define self in relationship systems) and during their coaching or supervision sessions.

Supervisor, Staff, and Intern Family-of-Origin Exploration Supervision

The second substantial service-associated learning-for-self opportunity—Supervisor, Staff, and Intern Family-of-Origin Exploration Supervision (2.5 hours per week)—afforded the supervisor with another venue in which to present the facts of his family and his current understanding of the family emotional process associated with those facts. Using a rotating presentation schedule, the supervisor, a senior staff person, and all interns participated in this supervision. The supervisor and the senior staff person always interviewed each other and alternated as the interviewer for the scheduled intern presentations. The format for this supervision was modeled after the supervisor's and the senior staff person's postgraduate program trainee supervision.

The construction of an interviewee's first multigenerational family diagram before his or her first family-of-origin exploration interview closely resembled the Diagramming Assistance procedures for the Family-of-Origin Interview and Discussion sessions detailed earlier. Similar to how those family diagrams were archived, the supervisor or the senior staff person would digitally photograph the whiteboard family diagram and present this to the interviewee in hard-copy and overhead transparency forms at the end of the session. This family diagram transparency was then used during that interviewee's future supervision interviews. If participants found it necessary to update their family diagrams, they would either make modifications to their initial family diagram transparencies using fine-point transparency markers or redraw their updated family diagrams on the whiteboard, take new digital photographs, and make updated hard-copy and transparency versions. The supervisor and the senior staff person were also given family diagram hard-copies on which to take notes during subsequent interviews with an interviewee.

An interviewee's first family-of-origin supervision interview used two Supervision Slots (35 minutes each) and was essentially identical in format and methodology to a client's first family-of-origin interview detailed earlier. The rationale for the supervisee and client interviews being indistinguishable was that Bowen theory makes no distinction between supervision and coaching in that both have the same focus and aim: an opportunity to develop a more objective understanding of one's multigenerational family emotional process and consequently choose to behave in ways with family that may result in increases in one's level of differentiation of self.

Regarding format, the first supervision interview was also divided into two subsessions—a Dialogue (45 minutes) between the interviewer and the supervisee over the facts and emotional process evident in the supervisee's immediate, extended, and multigenerational families and a Panel (25 minutes) in which the other participants pose follow-up and clarification questions to the interviewer, who then selects a few of the most thoughtful process-oriented questions to then re-present to the supervisee during the remaining minutes of the interview. For methodology, similar to the client interview dialogues, this dialogue was also modeled after the approach to interviewing exemplified in *Family Evaluation: An Approach Based on Bowen Theory* (Kerr & Bowen, 1988), whereas the panel was procedurally similar to the client interview panels described earlier, the audience participation segments from a Bowen Center for the Study of the Family Clinical Conference, and the supervisor's postgraduate program supervision sessions.

Similar to the client interview panels, before the first panel question was verbalized, the interviewer instructed the supervisee not to respond to any of the questions posed but rather to listen carefully to all questions and note any thoughts regarding his or her family emotional process stimulated by these questions. The same two reasons put forth earlier in the client panel description for having all questions directed to the interviewer instead of the interviewee applied for this panel as well. Also, the interviewer's buffer function was important to the same extent during supervisees panels as it was during the Phase 3 panels in that the interns were full panel participants—allowed to pose follow-up and clarification questions to the interviewer about the intern, supervisor, or senior staff person interviewee's family facts and family emotional process to the same degree as the supervisor or senior staff person. A final area of similarity between the client and supervisee family-of-origin interviews involved the extensive use of laser pointers by all dialogue and panel participants to precisely identify areas of interest on client and supervisee family diagrams.

The only differences between the client and supervisee family-of-origin interviews were that (a) the follow-up and clarification panel questions were written and verbalized for the client interview panels, whereas the questions were only verbalized for the supervisee panels, and (b) during subsequent Supervision Slot (35 minutes) interviews, supervisees were expected to simultaneously project two transparencies on the overhead screen (one above the other): their own family diagrams and the family diagrams of clients toward whom they were having repetitive positive or negative emotional reactions. For the Dialogue (20 minutes) portion of a subsequent supervision slot interview, the interviewer started by asking a supervisee to briefly describe the client behaviors to which he or she is repeatedly reactive to and the type of reactions that he or she is having toward that client and those behaviors.

Next, the interviewer asked the supervisee to provide an overview of the client's family facts and family emotional process, with a special emphasis on describing the emotional process that appears to contribute to the client behaviors to which the supervisee is reactive. The interviewer then asked the supervisee to provide an overview of his or her own family facts and family emotional process and highlight the family emotional process that appears to be contributing to the repetitive emotional reactions toward the client and the client behaviors detailed earlier. The interview progressed with the supervisee and interviewer alternating their attention between the supervisee and client family diagrams in an attempt to place the supervisee's reactivity to the client's behaviors in factual family emotional process contexts that were congruent with both the supervisee and the client family facts. As the alternating between the two family diagrams continued for the remainder of the dialogue and into the Panel (15 minutes) subsession, the interviewer and panel questions inevitably shifted to a near-exclusive focus on the supervisee's multigenerational family facts and emotional process. The shift in focus occurred because, with few exceptions, a supervisee's reactions to a client's behaviors have origins in the family emotional process of that supervisee's family.

Similar to other service-associated opportunities, the family-of-origin exploration supervision sessions afforded the supervisor with a concentrated time each week to focus solely on learning for self and absent any instructional agenda toward his fellow supervisees. Provided with this setting in which to reflect on and articulate his thoughts on his own family emotional process and family facts, the supervisor's primary concern was on developing a more objective understanding of his family with the goal of increasing his level of differentiation of self in relation to his family of origin. It bears repeating a final time that an important by-product of this, and the other service-associated learning for self opportunities, was that the author became a progressively more effective service supervisor and his family references provided participants with a recurring case study that could facilitate an understanding of family emotional process while illustrating aspects of Bowen theory.

Summary

The purpose of this chapter was to detail how the author's consistent focus on learning for self served as the creative force behind his effort to develop two mental health–substance abuse outpatient services grounded in Bowen theory. Examples of the operationalization of this learning-for-self orientation were provided throughout the chapter to illustrate the interaction between this orientation and the evolution of the dual-recovery IOS components and protocols. The supervisor demonstrated how aspects of his own differentiation-of-self trajectory were represented in several service components. Specifically, details were provided on how the service-associated learning-for-self curriculum afforded the supervisor, staff, interns, and clients with several opportunities each week to (a) further ground their thinking in Bowen theory and (b) further their understanding of how their multigenerational family emotional processes influenced their self and family functioning. Principles from Bowen theory were infused in the service components, and when these principles were consistently lived and emphasized by the supervisor and staff, they functioned as catalysts for creating an emotional atmosphere in which simultaneous and reciprocal learning could occur for all service participants regardless of their place or role in the agency or service hierarchies.

References

Bowen Center for the Study of the Family. (Producer). (2004). *Bowen family systems theory and its applications: Lectures series by Dr. Kerr* [DVD]. Available from http://www.thebowencenter.org

Georgetown Family Center. (Producer). (1980). *The basic series* [DVD]. Available from http://www.thebowencenter.org

Georgetown Family Center. (Producer). (1987). *Bowen/Kerr interview series* [DVD]. Available from http://www.thebowencenter.org

Kerr, M. E., & Bowen, M. (1988). *Family evaluation: An approach based on Bowen theory.* New York, NY: W. W. Norton.

9

Clarifying Principles for Investing in Self

LEANN S. HOWARD

In November 1979, the Menninger Foundation, a psychoanalytic institution located in Topeka, Kansas, invited this author to establish the first branch office of Menninger outside the main campus. The new office, located in Kansas City, was begun with this sole director, an office administrator, one telephone, and refurbished chairs from Menninger in Topeka. It was an office begun on a shoestring budget by an institution that had no history of "outposts." Within months of the opening of this outpost, the Menninger Foundation Marriage and Family Therapy Training Program for Community Practitioners was founded. The early program reflected the influence of a psychoanalytic institution on the world of family therapy. It also reflected a lack of clarity in this young director regarding theory and therapy. It was, however, a beginning effort to establish an autonomous community program for mental health practitioners in the burgeoning field of marriage and family therapy. This author was was joined by Steven Lerner, a talented psychologist from Menninger, to teach and supervise the first training classes in Kansas City.

A new way of thinking had been quietly emerging within the main campus of Menninger for several years before the opening of the Kansas City office. Arthur Mandelbaum, director of social work at Menninger, along with Steven Jones, Marianne Riche, and Katherine Kent, had been meeting privately to study the new field of marriage and family therapy. Their efforts led to the development of a training program in Topeka.

This author had also participated as a member of the training faculty in the Menninger program in Topeka before taking the helm in Kansas City. While this author was still a participating faculty member in Topeka, Donald Shoulberg, a Bowen family systems therapist, was invited to be a guest presenter for an end-of-year presentation to students and faculty. Shoulberg introduced Bowen theory by presenting the emotional (automatic responsiveness) process in his own multigenerational family system. The response to his presentation was immediate. Several members of the training faculty began consulting with Shoulberg. In time, many individuals within the Menninger system became interested in viewing their own families through the lens of Bowen theory. It seems fitting to this author that Bowen theory would emerge in the setting in which his early work originated.

By January 1981, the new office in Kansas City was operating in the black and ready for expansion. This author made the decision to leave the position as director of Menninger and of the Menninger training program to have more time to devote to raising her young family. She recommended Donald Shoulberg to take her place as the new director and remained a part of the growing faculty. Shoulberg slowly introduced a new way of thinking, based on Bowen theory, that challenged the individual model on which psychoanalytic theory was based. Over considerable time and careful reflection, this author determined for herself that a family systems model was a more accurate lens for understanding human behavior and the emergence of symptoms within the family. (Each person who enters the broad field of mental health has a similar task of determining for his- or herself which model or models are most accurate and useful in the therapeutic context.) This process cannot be underestimated because it requires rethinking fundamental assumptions and theoretical concepts. This therapist developed the conviction about the accuracy of this new lens.

By 1983, the Kansas City Menninger Family Therapy Training Program for Community Practitioners, based on Bowen theory, emerged as a clearly defined program for mental health professionals. The program in Kansas City was distinguished from the program in Topeka because it was based entirely on Bowen theory. In 1983 Carroll Hoskins joined the faculty, and in 1987 Margaret Donley came on board. Donley became the final faculty member to complete the emerging program. Lerner continued his practice based on Bowen theory but left the Kansas City office in 1986. Shoulberg continued to direct the program until 1998, at which time Hoskins became the director until the program ended in June 2000 and Menninger moved its base of operation to Baylor College of Medicine in Houston, TX. Over the 20 years of the program, several hundred social workers, psychologists, psychiatrists, and ministers completed a minimum of 2 years of training. Many individuals also completed a 3rd year of study.

Theory and science are at the heart of the study of Bowen theory, and efforts to think broadly and factually through a natural systems lens are continuous (Bowen, 1978; Kerr & Bowen, 1988). All efforts toward training in Bowen theory reflect a long-term focus on theory and guiding principles for self-functioning in the presence of others making a similar effort. This chapter describes the author's efforts to apply the theory in her own family, in the training program, and in her contributions to the Kansas City community. Summarized here are the principles by which this author strives to live.

A Theoretical View of Self and Family

The effort to engage Bowen theory is potentially life changing and very difficult. The first principle identifies a distinction between Bowen theory and all other theoretical lenses on which training in family theory and therapy is based. The process of defining a self (*differentiation of self*) concerns the effort to understand on a factual and emotional level one's undifferentiation arising from the multigenerational process of the family, or a process in which one contributes one's own full share of immaturity to the functioning of the unit. In his chapter on training family systems therapists, Papero (1990) wrote,

> Because Bowen family systems theory is a theory about the human and human functioning, a member of the faculty is expected not only to talk about theory but to embody it. At the heart of Bowen family systems theory lies the concept of differentiation of self. A faculty member can never address him- or herself sufficiently to the concept of differentiation, not only in what he or she says but in how he or she functions. On a broad level differentiation takes up the manner in which organisms differ from one another in terms of sensitivity and automatic or instinctual response to the environment. An important direction in training involves the effort to learn about one's own sensitivity and automatic responsiveness. The learner also aims to develop a degree of control over the automatic nature of the response. (p. 101)

The effort to learn Bowen theory becomes, for the serious student, a lifelong process in which gaps between intellectual knowledge of the theory and actual functioning are continually addressed. Acquiring a detailed, factual understanding of the lack of differentiation of self and engaging in efforts to improve functioning within the multigenerational family represent an ongoing and significant goal.

Obstacles to defining a self can be many. Each person who engages in the effort has the task of identifying obstacles to progress. This author has encountered many obstacles along the way, and with each passing year she identifies new obstacles and revisits old ones. The presence of strong feeling states is one example of an obstacle to forward movement. Although feelings are always present, to some degree, more and more intense feeling states alter the capacity to observe objectively, reflect carefully, and choose behavior. The presence of high levels of subjectivity regarding self and other is another. Many individuals see what they have been taught to see even when facts do not fit the emotionally colored observations. Efforts to grapple with an understanding of the emotional system, central to an understanding of Bowen theory, are beneficial in stepping back from the automatic process. Often, many years of effort are required to be able to observe and choose behavior within the crucible of the family relationship system.

Basic to an understanding of the concept of differentiation of self is the fundamental relationship to each parent. All individuals have some unresolved level of attachment to parents and other important members of the multigenerational family system. The level of unresolved emotional attachment varies, however, and reflects the level of differentiation. Many variables contribute. The degree to which each parent was able to separate from his or her own parents, facts of the family at the time of one's birth, parents' capacity to adapt to the addition of each child, and the number of anxious events arising within the life of the family are examples of fundamental interacting variables. No one variable and no one person is the cause of undifferentiation. Instead, many players contribute to the atmosphere of the unit.

Although no person can be credited or blamed for the level of differentiation acquired through the emotional process, an ongoing and persistent effort to differentiate a self is a central principle in the training of Bowen family systems therapists. Unlike training programs that are focused on techniques for changing families, a family systems training program focuses on theory and the effort to change self. A well-defined family systems therapist, seeking to maintain differentiation in the face of a clinical family presenting with a symptom, is central to the clinical effort. No matter what level of symptom is presented, the clinician seeks to maintain a well-defined self. Faculty and students alike are engaged in the same complex process of defining a self and maintaining a clear theoretical lens to guide the process.

Growing Sureness in Self About Theory

In 1985, this author began the Postgraduate Program in Bowen Family Systems Theory and Its Applications, directed by Bowen, while continuing to participate as a faculty member and clinician in the Kansas City Menninger office. From 1985 through 1990, she attended 3 years of the training program followed by 2 years in a small study group. Each year since completing formal training, she has attended a yearly meeting in Washington, DC, sponsored by the Bowen Center. Efforts to live the theory have been a daily challenge. Progress is slow, but sustained effort, through time, gradually leads to increased sureness in self about the theory and greater capacity to use principle and theory as a guide during times of stress and major life transitions. A seminar titled "Female Functioning" was established in 1987. It was this author's first step in functioning as a more separate self within the Menninger system through the establishment of a unique seminar for women seeking to define a self in their own families. The seminar continued throughout her years at Menninger and continues today in her ongoing work outside of the Menninger system.

Thinking for Self in the Presence of Others

The growing sureness in self regarding theory emerged in the seminar and in the formal training program. Early meetings in which this author taught concepts of the theory were replaced by efforts of all students in the study group or the formal training program to study the theory and natural systems for self. Each is responsible for conducting his or her study of the theory and efforts to engage science, particularly the natural sciences and evolution. Each member works to think on his or her own in the reciprocal dialogue, with others seeking to do the same.

The uniqueness of this form of teaching cannot be underestimated. The effort to learn a new skill such as playing classical piano (a long-term interest of this author) begins with a teacher who has mastered the scales and the musical works of Beethoven, Bach, Brahms, and Mozart, for example, and who meticulously guides the student to develop the technical skills needed. Mastery of classical piano takes many years of repetitive practice and execution of specific technical maneuvers.

Mastery of Bowen theory is both similar and different. A similarity is that the teacher of Bowen theory has spent years in the effort to define a self in his or her own family and to modify thinking from an individually oriented, cause-and-effect model to a way of thinking that includes emotional fields, the life forces of individuality and togetherness, and reciprocal processes to which each family member contributes. The teacher of Bowen theory, unlike the piano teacher, however, cannot direct technical maneuvers to a student of theory or a clinical family if differentiation of self is the long-term goal. The development of the self of the teacher and of the student is the primary goal of the process. Efforts by the teacher to change the other, or to place new ways of thinking into the other, slow or block the process entirely. Bowen often referred to the effort to differentiate a self as almost a do-it-yourself theory.

An unsure teacher can block the development of a student of the theory through efforts to represent him- or herself as more or less knowledgeable and more immature or mature than is actually so and the theory as more complete than it is. A broad theoretical lens that moves toward science requires the capacity of each to think for self and to engage the other in a reciprocal exchange of ideas. For this author, it has been particularly difficult to stand alone and speak when her view is out of step with what others may approve. A more highly differentiated person finds this an easier task. The effort to do so, through the years, has been among one of the most important in her efforts to develop a self.

In the context of the Menninger program, enhancing the understanding of the theory occurred most often through reciprocal exchanges with fellow faculty and program participants. Formal presentations by faculty and students served to facilitate the process. Faculty worked to develop a curriculum in which each would present on an area of theory of interest. At times, faculty would present the emotional process in their own multigenerational family unit. Such efforts increase the capacity for objectivity and emotional neutrality. Such presentations also reflect the view that all humans are subject to the forces of the emotional process. Supervisory sessions included student presentations of clinical work, efforts to define a self in their own families, and study of other natural systems of interest. (A fundamental assumption governing the study of other natural systems is that human behavior is governed by the same or similar life forces as those found in older forms of life.)

Clarity of thinking is not guaranteed through years of training or study. Long-term efforts to modify self in family while studying theory tend to increase this capacity, however. Central to the ability to think for self is the ability to tolerate and deal with disapproval and difference. Seeking agreement and avoiding difference are at the heart of undifferentiation, and an effort to gain approval from another slows or stops the effort entirely. This is not to imply that an effort for self implies automatic disagreement. A focus on self is at the heart of the learning process. The effort is not done to please another but to increase maturity in the learner.

Leadership

This author demonstrated leadership, the fourth basic principle, in the training program as she initiated making contributions to the broader body of knowledge and research associated with Bowen theory. Several years into the study of Bowen theory, participation as a member of the Menninger faculty, and efforts to regulate self within the original family, this author determined that it would be important to step forward and accept more responsibility for leadership in the broader community.

In 1987, this author founded the Kansas City Forum, along with Margaret Donley, to promote the theoretical exchange of ideas between individuals engaged in the long-term study of Bowen theory. She presented her own thinking regularly at the annual meetings. In addition, local scientists were invited to present their research. The efforts to establish contact with the sciences through the meeting was one of the first of its kind in the Midwest. In 1996, this author stepped down from the leadership position to more actively engage the sciences, and Kathleen Riordan took over leadership of the meeting until its conclusion in 1999. By that time, other programs were emerging throughout the country and the Midwest.

The success of the Menninger program led to contributions by former students in the program who went on to years of study through the Bowen Center. A complete list of individual leaders is too long to include in this brief chapter, but the efforts of a few stand out through their contributions to training over the past decade. Margaret Otto, director of the Kansas City Center for Family and Organizational Systems, and Kathleen Riordan, associate director of the center, have provided Bowen family systems training since 1997. Tamara Hawk, director of the Prairie Center, has been a major contributor to training programs in Manhattan, Kansas; Carroll Hoskins and Margaret Donley have continued to lead through an ongoing seminar held in Prairie Village, Kansas.

This author has also worked to increase her contributions by teaching Bowen theory in universities in the region, local and national presentations, recent participation as member of the staff faculty of the Kansas City Center, and her own efforts to engage the sciences. That effort did not cease when the Menninger program ended.

Making Contact With the Natural Sciences

It was many years into the study of the Bowen theory before this author fully grasped that the theory is based in evolution and natural systems and that it is an open body of knowledge. Moves into the natural sciences occurred while this author was a part of the training faculty at Menninger and continue to this day.

In 1987, this author took a first course in biology at the University of Missouri, Kansas City. Several years of coursework in the biological sciences at the University of Kansas followed. She took one course at a time while continuing to teach and maintain a clinical practice. (See Chapter 28 for a more complete exploration of the process of moving into science.) Years of biological fieldwork research ensued.

Although the specifics of this effort are unique to this author, it is not unusual for serious students of Bowen theory to spend years in the effort to define a self, to gain theoretical understanding, to make contact with the natural sciences, to contribute to the broader community, and to function on the basis of life principles.

Representing Bowen Theory Within a Psychoanalytic Institution: Defining a Self During a Period of Rapid Social and Institutional Change

In this last section, the author reviews the history and challenges associated with representing this unique theory at an institution that had a long prior history of being identified with psychoanalytic theory and through the years of rapid change in the delivery of clinical services to families.

Beginning in the late 1980s, rapid shifts began occurring within the broad field of mental health. Many companies across the country started to offer a mental health managed care benefit to their employees. On the upside of this rapidly shifting climate, individuals who had previously been unable to afford mental health care services had the opportunity to see a mental health professional, usually for the first time. On the downside, the managed care model promised a quick fix for human dilemmas that often reflected the outcome of complex, long-term processes. The promise confused the field and continues to confuse it to this day.

Another outcome of the advent of managed care was that funding for psychiatric hospitals was reduced. Menninger was struggling to survive in this environment, and many psychiatrists, psychologists, and social workers lost their jobs in the new climate. Before this time, the branch office of Menninger in Kansas City had autonomy to conduct operations mostly free of the psychoanalytic perspective. Once survival was at stake, the Kansas City office, a profitable operation, became less autonomous as a full-scale clinic moved into the setting.

Anxiety, a huge factor in human emotional functioning, began to rise. Pressures to conform to the new environment grew, and survival fears rose.

This author remained a part of the Menninger Family Therapy Training Program while moving her practice away from the Menninger site. This decision had pluses and minuses, but it was made with the belief that the capacity to say no to managed care or no to pressures of conventional thinking would be more possible in a separate setting. One outcome of the decision was that income went down. In time, it became clear that it would be important to respect the reality of the new conditions and learn to operate within them while holding on to convictions regarding theory and therapy. A societal atmosphere that required individual diagnosis for reimbursement, reduced the number of sessions that would be covered, and asked therapists to reduce complex human difficulties to simple and quick fixes would need to be respected, and principles would remain in the driver's seat. The family therapy training program also became more difficult to preserve in the new environment. Therapists were struggling in their own settings to survive the societal shifts, and money to pay for training became less available as well. Faculty remained focused on theory, careful articulation of the Bowen theory, and principled operation of the training program, and the program remained clearly defined in spite of the reduced numbers of individuals seeking training. The effort to maintain a clear focus on theory and principle in the face of societal pressures can be significant. At the heart of the struggle is responsibility as a clinician. For example:

> It is not uncommon for a parent to contact a therapist seeking help for a symptomatic offspring. Theoretical clarity that the presence of a symptom in a child reflects an underlying division between the parents guides the therapy structure. Agreeing to focus on the child contributes to cementing the family problem within the child. With the entire family emotional unit as the focus of the process, this therapist began to let families know that parents would need to be included in the process. (Often offspring are left out of appointments for parents to focus on their own contribution to symptoms in a child.) At times, parents would decide to select another therapist. Many respected the clarity and proceeded.

> Frequently, couples would seek therapy hoping the therapist would see their mate as the problematic one. A therapist who is unable to see the reciprocity in the relationship process can unwittingly contribute to the marital problem by subtly taking sides with one member of the pair. Neutrality in the therapist is not a technical maneuver but an outcome of a differentiating effort. Any change in the person of the therapist toward increased separateness, objectivity, and neutrality in his or her original family is translated into the therapy process. In addition, conviction regarding theory increases the likelihood that theory rather than feeling states in the therapist will guide the process.

Conclusion

In the latter years of his life, Bowen talked about the erosion of theory. A significant aspect of erosion concerns the tendency to append a few concepts of Bowen theory onto more conventional theory based on cause-and-effect thinking. Considerable effort is required not to contribute to the erosion process. The long-term goal of those seeking to advance Bowen theory is to maintain the new natural systems theory in the face of strong headwinds that dilute and modify the lens. The effort to maintain viable contact with accepted sciences has been an important part of the effort. Through meetings and research that establish contact with many scientific disciplines, Bowen theorists seek to ground theory in principles of the natural world and the human as an evolved form of life on the planet.

At the time of this writing, societal regression has reached a significant peak. One indication of the regression can be seen in the near collapse of U.S. financial systems and those throughout the world. The capacity for self-regulation, a hallmark of differentiation, has been on the decline. A family system lens, grounded in the natural sciences and evolution, will be important in the years ahead.

The Menninger Family Therapy Training Program for Community Practitioners has played a part in the long-term development and dissemination of Bowen theory. The relocation of Menninger in 2000 did not end the continuing contribution of Bowen theory. In fact, the four original Menninger faculty have continued to contribute to the theory, and regional training programs in Bowen theory outside of Washington, DC, have emerged. Two of the programs are located in the Midwest and directed by former students in the Menninger program who went on to years of serious study at the Bowen Center. Bowen often spoke of the lag time in articulation and acceptance of a new systems theory of human emotional functioning. But the theory will continue to guide those interested in defining a self in family, clinical process, and society.

References

Bowen, M. (1978). *Family therapy in clinical practice*. New York, NY: Jason Aronson.

Kerr, M. E., & Bowen, M. (1988). *Family evaluation: An approach based on Bowen theory*. New York, NY: W. W. Norton.

Papero, D. (1990). *Bowen family systems theory*. Boston, MA: Allyn & Bacon.

10
Can Undergraduates Learn Bowen Theory?

C. MARGARET HALL

I was appointed assistant professor of sociology at Georgetown University (GU) in 1970 and have taught Bowen family systems theory to undergraduate students at GU since 1971. The chair of the Department of Sociology asked me to teach the only GU College of Arts and Sciences class about families in 1970. Although I had heard about Bowen's research on families in the mid-1960s, it was not until I was scheduled to teach a families and society sociology course that I began to attend Bowen's weekly family systems theory seminars for GU and local mental health professionals. I also enrolled in Bowen's 2-year postgraduate course on family psychotherapy in the fall semester of 1971.

When I discussed including Bowen theory in my families and society sociology course with Bowen, he was discouraging. He did not think undergraduate students would understand his family systems theory, and he pointed out that undergraduates were neither sufficiently mature nor sufficiently economically independent to differentiate self by using his theory. Bowen's views influenced my decision making and prepared me for the complex teaching tasks ahead. Consequently, in my first families and society course, I presented Bowen theory only in addition to sociological research on families. However, in 1973, I developed a family interaction undergraduate course in which Bowen theory became my primary theoretical base for teaching and learning research.

My family interaction course was reviewed by the GU Department of Sociology curriculum committee largely because students had shown genuine interest in the Bowen frame of reference and wanted to use Bowen theory to understand their own families more fully. My new course description specified that the family interaction course would be based on Bowen theory and would be a more advanced research course than the families and society course, which was later taught by adjunct sociology faculty from time to time as well as by me.

Bowen was ambivalent when he heard about my second, more specialized family course based on Bowen theory. He advised me not to present his theory in a positive light because this would predictably stir up opposition among my colleagues and students. I still use this sage counsel today, even though my job security increased through the years by achieving tenure and promotions to associate professor and professor. I also chaired the Sociology Department for 10 years, 1976–1980 and 1983–1989.

During my early years at GU, I focused on learning Bowen theory for myself. For example, I started to write *The Bowen Family Theory and Its Uses* (1981) with supervision from Bowen. In addition to the Bowen theory seminars for mental health professionals and the postgraduate program on Bowen theory psychotherapy, I had biweekly writing consultations with Bowen. These one-on-one meetings also yielded opportunities to discuss with him teaching Bowen theory to undergraduates.

In spite of his criticism of the appropriateness of teaching his family systems theory to undergraduates, Bowen congratulated me on securing a teaching position at GU and encouraged me to continue teaching undergraduates. Even though he still considered that teaching his theory to undergraduates might turn out to be a waste of time, he thought there was some value in discussing family concepts with members of the younger generation. Bowen's sighs and frowns were frequent, however, and he again warned me not to show enthusiasm about his family systems theory during my didactic presentations to undergraduates. He told me that being more objective would help my students to hear what I was saying and encourage my colleagues to be more accepting of my professional work in family therapy and clinical research.

The students who choose to enroll in the family interaction sociology courses over the years function well in the academically demanding GU community and complex social settings. However, they also tend to conform to the expectations of other students, GU faculty, and their own families rather than assert their independence or innovate. Although some students have already survived extremely challenging family emotional situations and severe restrictions in financial circumstances before they arrive at GU, those who sign up for family interaction often come from protective large families who take considerable pride in their children's achievements and capacities to meet family expectations. Undoubtedly, the Roman Catholic Jesuit heritage of GU supports these intergenerational patterns of behavior, which also reflect the largely upper middle-class cultures of GU's international student body.

Qualitative Research Methods

The family interaction classes are given throughout a 13-week semester. I use the two weekly class meetings to create a field study of Bowen theory in which students conduct longitudinal research about families with a minimum of three generations of detailed data on family interactions. Given this context, I use selected qualitative social science research methods to clarify the extent to which students learn and make use of Bowen theory in class and their own lives.

Although this report is not a formal research project, I used qualitative research methods to interpret the most marked results of teaching Bowen theory to undergraduates for almost 40 years. For example, qualitative research methodologies increase my objectivity in evaluating my descriptions and explanations of Bowen theory in my family interaction classes. These assessments reflect the degrees of success I have in meeting my learning objectives for students: my effectiveness in presenting Bowen theory, students' skills in systems thinking, and students' applications to self. The three learning objectives are discussed in the next four sections of my report.

The qualitative research methods I use most when teaching Bowen theory to undergraduates include observations of students' participation in class discussions about families; content analyses of students' narratives about the families they are researching—their own families or families from whom they collected three generations of data; content analyses of students' questions about the families they are researching; and content analyses of students' narratives when presenting different stages of their research on families. For example, I evaluate questions that students ask family members about patterns of interaction around sensitive family issues such as significant deaths, family leaders, religious beliefs, and emotional cutoffs.

I also assess my own communications with students to understand my varied successes and failures in teaching Bowen theory. However, because I am the only person who is a continuing influence in my observations and assessments, the patterns I find may not represent changes in students' understanding of Bowen theory so much as my increasing ease in teaching it, the primary subject matter of my family interaction courses. For example, I am more successful today in meeting my learning objectives about Bowen theory than I was in earlier years because of my firmer grasp of the theory rather than because of changes in students' responses to Bowen concepts in recent family classes.

The qualitative research methodologies I find most conducive to analyzing substantive data about my family courses are

- Observations and content analyses of students' views of families in societies
- Observations and content analyses of students' views of the families they are researching
- Content analyses of students' narratives about their positions in their families' emotional systems when they choose to research their own families
- Content analyses of students' questions about the families they are researching

- Observations of students' indicators of emotional processes in the families they research
- Observations of patterns in classroom exchanges

Applying qualitative research methodologies in my family interaction classes makes me more aware of how students think and react as they learn Bowen theory. Even though I did not accept Bowen's advice not to teach his family theory to undergraduates, I consider it both wise and practical to continue to assess the impacts Bowen theory has on my teaching family classes at GU. Also, because Bowen theory is so different from theories in my other course offerings, I need to understand my nuanced interactions with students more fully in my family interaction classes, especially when students are researching their own families.

Learning Objectives

The first assessment of my teaching effectiveness in presenting Bowen theory involves examining my course objectives of learning about the principles of Bowen theory, systems thinking, and self. Next, I consider advantageous aspects of my learning objectives, as well as some consequences of not accomplishing these objectives.

Curriculum policies in GU's Department of Sociology require undergraduate coursework to reflect principles of the discipline of sociology and to promote mastery in applying sociological theory and research methods to social topics such as family interaction. My family interaction course was no exception to this rule, so colleagues asked me to present the substance of Bowen theory in relation to sociological knowledge. Because Bowen considered family systems to be unique and interdisciplinary, I traced some affinities between sociology and Bowen theory, especially because Bowen stated publicly that he did not consider social sciences to be sciences and did not think that societies could be understood scientifically. At best, I anchored family interactions within sociological traditions of research that provided broad social contexts for Bowen theory, without limiting the theory's scope or uniqueness.

The most meaningful common denominator between Bowen theory and sociological theories is Bowen's concept of family systems. As a substantive focus, which leads to understanding patterns in emotional interdependence, and as a methodological approach, which includes tracking patterns in family processes, family systems bases lead to thoughtful analyses. Similarly, Bowen's emphasis on cultivating objectivity about families, through examining family facts, furthers possibilities for social science analyses of families.

Writing up my Bowen theory course syllabus for a family interaction class required me to select which particular aspects of Bowen theory I would focus on as learning objectives, so that students would learn the most. I gave priority to three substantive goals: learning about Bowen theory, systems thinking, and self. My first learning objective gives students sufficient working knowledge of Bowen theory as a whole by examining each of Bowen's eight basic family systems concepts: *differentiation of self, nuclear family emotional system, sibling position, triangles, family projection process, multigenerational transmission process, cutoff,* and *societal emotional process.* My second learning objective builds on students' knowledge of Bowen theory by strengthening their capacities to think in terms of family systems and social systems. For example, once students understand relationships in families as significant emotional systems, they begin to identify patterns in interdependence and triangles in both families and social systems. My third learning objective focuses on Bowen's concept of self. This idea helps students to apply their knowledge of Bowen theory to themselves and their own families, whether or not they choose to research their own families as a family interaction class option. Questions about differentiation of self inevitably arise in describing and explaining self, even though undergraduate students are more able to make functional shifts in self during the one-semester course than they are to attempt to differentiate self.

I describe these three learning objectives in greater detail in the next three sections of this chapter because they reflect the substantive core of teaching Bowen theory to undergraduates. Although variations have occurred among these learning objectives during the time I have taught family interaction courses, substantive emphases on Bowen theory, systems thinking, and self have effectively anchored my family interaction class presentations through the years. However, students' particular issues and interests consistently focus class discussions on any one or more of the eight basic family systems concepts. For example, students are frequently curious about Bowen's concepts of cutoff and family projection process in relation to their own families.

The GU Department of Sociology reviewed and approved my family interaction Bowen theory course syllabus. The department sees this course as specialized family studies based on my research in developing Bowen theory, which explains substantive links among individuals, families, and societies.

Bowen Theory

When teaching Bowen theory in family interaction classes, which is my first learning objective, I necessarily deal with students' resistance to abstractions and theoretical analyses. Although this resistance is also evoked by sociological theories, it applies especially to Bowen theory because of students' difficulties in understanding family systems concepts and their connections to each other. Some immediate reactions of students include "Why is this theory so difficult to learn?" "Is Bowen theory up to date?" "What is the significance of squares and circles?" and "How can Bowen theory apply to all families?"

I usually respond by asking students to put their judgments about Bowen theory aside until after the midterm exam, which requires students to demonstrate a working knowledge of the theory. However, in spite of agreeing to do this, distinctions between "believers" and "nonbelievers" of Bowen theory often develop from the beginning of my family interaction classes. Also, the student culture of wanting to do the minimum amount of work to get through courses is at odds with signing up for the family interaction course. For example, many students' attitude is that because they already know a great deal about family interaction, the course should be easy.

If I am deft in fielding criticisms of Bowen theory, students soon settle down to learn substantive meanings and applications of the eight basic family systems concepts of differentiation of self, nuclear family emotional system, sibling position, triangles, family projection process, multigenerational transmission process, cutoff, and societal emotional process. Although this sequence of concepts is different from the historical development of Bowen theory, it addresses some of students' strongest interests. For example, because we live in times when nuclear families are increasingly separated from their extended kin, students are more familiar with patterns of family interactions in their nuclear families. From the Bowen theory perspective, nuclear families are best described and explained by the five basic concepts of differentiation of self, nuclear family emotional system, sibling position, triangles, and family projection process. I then emphasize that one of the major strengths of Bowen theory is that it connects people's experiences and understanding of nuclear families with broad kin networks. The remaining three basic concepts of Bowen theory, together with sibling position, explain this. For example, the concepts of multigenerational transmission process, cutoff, and societal emotional process define how people are connected to or separated from their broad kin networks.

So far, so good; GU students tend to absorb information presented to them didactically. However, criticisms of Bowen theory arise in class discussions, in spite of students' avowed willingness to put their judgments aside for a while. In general, students take Bowen theory seriously because it is complex and because they usually find something that rings true among different aspects of the eight basic concepts.

Although sibling position is a well-received concept of Bowen theory, students are conventional individual thinkers. For example, they do not readily consider substantive connections between behavioral expectations for particular sibling positions and differences in the functioning of siblings produced by family projection processes. Nor do they appreciate how family projection may be sufficiently powerful to impair a child's behavior for a lifetime. Another Bowen concept that students find fascinating is triangles. At the beginning of a semester, I often ask students to observe triangles in families and everyday settings. Thus, triangles introduce undergraduates to new ways of thinking about interactions in a variety of family and social settings.

Mapping out family diagrams of three generations of family members is the most effective way for students to understand relationships between two and three generations of relatives, as well as the systemness of interactions among several generations. For example, even if students merely ponder national or international migrations in their families, including cutoffs, intergenerational perspectives show the rootedness of patterns in family interactions. Considering family histories and the major turning points in family histories—Bowen's "nodal events"—also increases students' awareness of family processes and family emotional systems.

Although Bowen advised me against presenting his whole theory in one sitting, keeping several Bowen theory concepts in mind helps students to clarify the significance of particular patterns of family interaction. It reminds students of the emotional fields of different nuclear families in any kin group, for example, and shows the influences of parents' original sibling positions on their current parenting behavior. The eight basic concepts of family systems also prepare students to think in terms of systems, which Bowen considered to be one of the most valuable goals of learning his family systems theory.

Systems Thinking

Once students have learned something sufficiently distinctive and accurate about all eight of Bowen's theory concepts, they understand more fully the basic definition of *family* as an emotional system. Cultivating students' abilities to think in terms of systems is my second learning objective. Even though students may agree that families can be characterized by intense emotional reactivity, with some students suggesting appropriate indicators of emotional intensity in the families they are researching, contrasts among varied degrees of interdependence in families are not always easy to identify or understand.

It is often only fairly late in the semester that a few students find meaningful connections among all eight basic concepts of Bowen theory. At least one third of the students in my family classes—currently, each family interaction class has 15 students—refer to individuals and relatively unrelated concepts when using the Bowen frame of reference. Also, at earlier stages of teaching Bowen theory, for example 1971 to 2001, when my class size was 25 to 30 students, the proportions of those who "heard" or "did not hear" the systemness of Bowen theory were about the same as those in my later small classes. This gap in students' understanding of Bowen theory occurs because making sense of family facts requires students to examine at least three generations of connections between self and family emotional dependencies, linking concepts such as family projection and multigenerational transmission within the same family systems. When these complex patterns in family functioning become clear, students identify additional family system characteristics and experience family systems at deeper levels of understanding. Making these substantive connections moves students from recognizing Bowen's basic family concepts as individual outcomes to thinking systems about families.

Systems thinking is particularly complex and difficult for undergraduate students because it challenges conventional thinking. Systems thinking requires students to relinquish their individual cause–effect thinking and at the same time reduces their needs to label or diagnose family problems. The goal of Bowen theory is to observe and interpret the complexities and power of emotional dependencies in families, which is a more daunting and difficult task than characterizing the behavior problems of individual family members. For example, Bowen urges the use of systems principles to look beyond family troublemakers so that it can be seen how systems conditions precipitate these patterns of emotional reactivity. Students' diagrams of their researched families help them to appreciate the timing of significant events in these families and at the same time make it possible to break out of linear thinking about events precipitated by family dependencies and to think systems. For example, collecting family facts and mapping them throughout different generations of families helps them to use more Bowen family systems concepts to understand families.

It usually takes at least half a semester to teach undergraduates the eight basic concepts of Bowen theory. Students' midterm exams are tangible evidence of how they think about families in light of Bowen's family systems concepts. However, there are considerable contrasts in students' capacities to apply Bowen theory to given situations in families, as posed by the midterm essay exam questions. Although teaching Bowen family systems concepts does not stop until the last day of classes, the focus of the second half of the semester of the family interaction course is on understanding one family in detail by applying Bowen theory. Students are required to write a research paper that analyzes a topic of interest in this family. Five pages of family diagrams are included in the 20-page research paper assignment, which is further evidence of the extent to which students now think systems about the families they are researching.

From time to time, students like to think systems in relation to friendships and other social situations such as GU dormitories, religious communities, political groups, and workplaces. These systems applications often increase students' appreciation of the versatility and power of Bowen theory. For example, applying systems thinking to the tasks involved in completing degrees at GU, or to social changes produced by current political shifts, enables students to make more sense out of their stressful worlds.

Self

The last of my learning objectives in family interaction classes is an emphasis on self. I focus on self partly to sustain students' attention and enthusiasm and partly to be true to Bowen theory. Although I may begin discussions on how to apply the theory to self by referring to concepts such as *differentiation of self, overfunctioning, underfunctioning, basic self, pseudoself,* and *responsible I,* I eventually encourage students to understand self more fully by focusing on their own positions and interactions in their families. Bowen suggested that people operate more effectively in all areas of their lives when they understand how they function in their own families. I use this principle with my students, and they choose how to apply Bowen theory to self. However, by the time students are ready to accept this challenge, some may have already decided that Bowen theory is not useful to them because of their unique family situations.

I also encourage students to focus on self through commentaries about my own family experiences. For example, I report that I use Bowen theory to deal with stresses such as parenting or work–family balance. Moreover, I resolve some of these issues more effectively now because I have developed useful ways to keep my cool in challenging situations. Through these years of teaching Bowen theory and applying it to my personal and professional experiences, I have become more relaxed about discussing real-life examples. Giving information about myself to students enables them to think more deeply about who they are in their families and other social situations. These experiences also substantiate, refute, or critique Bowen theory from the point of view of self.

When students diagram their own family emotional systems, I require them to asterisk their positions in their family networks. I also ask them to use one or more Bowen concepts to describe and explain dominant patterns of interaction in their families, as well as their own parts in these repetitions. For example, students try to situate themselves in multigenerational transmissions over at least three generations. Staying focused on the facts of family interactions increases students' objectivity in these explorations of self and limits any unproductive sentimentality about family togetherness.

Many GU undergraduates are impatient to assume personal and professional responsibilities. They say they like the family interaction class because it gives them tools to understand themselves better amid the pressures of their demanding social worlds. They not only learn about the emotional roots of their present family situations, but they also find guidance for managing their futures. Some of the best compliments I receive from students in my course are given after they graduate from GU. For example, students have told me that they remember their family interaction class better than their other classes or that they still apply Bowen ideas to themselves and their families. Several former students have reported that they have bonded with members of their grandparents' generation who live in distant countries. Students also tell me that they continue to diagram their ongoing family histories, or they send me photographs of themselves and their new families.

Another aspect of self in assessing my learning objective to understand self is the fact that any success I have in communicating Bowen theory to undergraduates is probably more a result of my maturation of self over the years than of any particular approach to teaching family interaction courses. A real test of Bowen theory is whether a person can use family systems concepts to understand self and live more fully. Being a family member is a leveling experience, and there are important similarities among people that do not depend solely on culture, customs, race, ethnicity, religion, gender, and social class.

Furthermore, all benefit from developing self in relation to family systems because this deepens their realization of the pervasiveness of emotional interdependence in their daily lives.

Findings

My 40-year journey in describing, explaining, and applying Bowen theory to families in the context of an undergraduate class has sharpened and strengthened my sense of self and my awareness about how best to communicate the main strengths and weaknesses of Bowen theory to young adults. Even though I have a more relaxed way of presenting family systems knowledge to students now, the pedagogical methods I use in the family interaction classes have remained fairly constant throughout this period.

In part, such stability was achieved because I consulted with Bowen frequently about the best ways to communicate his theory. These conversations usually occurred while he advised me about writing my book on his theory, *The Bowen Family Theory and Its Uses.* Although Bowen continued to see my teaching his family theory to undergraduates as largely foolhardy or a waste of time, given the financial dependence and lack of emotional maturity of many students, he continued to give me invaluable pointers on how to deal with significant teaching issues, such as my need to neutralize aggressive questions from students about Bowen theory and how to use humor to reduce anxiety in discussing families.

Bowen's familiarity with GU's institutional structures made him a superior mentor in commenting on my teaching family interaction to undergraduates. For example, he pointed out emotional systems in classroom exchanges within the broader GU institutional emotional system, especially during the 10 years that I chaired the Department of Sociology. Thus, Bowen's know-how helped me to be more discerning about professional priorities that met my most important teaching, scholarly, and administrative responsibilities.

Overall, Bowen theory provides students with important life lessons, which are surprisingly difficult to find in institutions of higher learning. These life lessons derive from applying Bowen's family emotional systems concepts to everyday exchanges in families and other social settings. For example, when people understand the extent to which they are interdependent social beings, especially in families, they find similar patterns of interdependence in a wide variety of small and large groups, as well as in local, societal, and global social conditions. People also see that whatever they decide to do on a daily basis affects others. Being responsible includes recognizing the effects of one's interactions, so that people make wiser choices about how to accomplish their preferred long-term goals before they act.

One of my first impressions of Bowen when I met him in 1971 was his capacity to move between different levels of abstraction in linking his family systems theory to everyday social realities. This is a strong example to follow in teaching undergraduates. When I can meaningfully link Bowen theory to a variety of lived experiences, my teaching comes alive and has relevance for students' decision making.

Bowen's use of humor—particularly to lower anxiety about critical family issues—was another useful model to follow in my family interaction classes. Bowen did not laugh at people; rather, he tried to break through their overseriousness about coping with family issues. His rationale was that humor makes people more objective and less anxious, so that they stay relatively outside families' emotional fields.

Bowen also recommended that I stay outside the emotional field of GU collegial exchanges about my family interaction classes. For example, if colleagues react negatively to the family interaction course content of Bowen theory, it is best to acquiesce by acknowledging that Bowen theory is a controversial social science theory rather than emphasize Bowen's national and international contributions to clinical family research. In fact, Bowen advised me to be mildly critical of his family systems theory at all times.

Conclusions

My students and I learned many life lessons in my family interaction classes. My fondest hope is that students remember and use Bowen family systems concepts in their families, work, and everyday lives. In many respects, the power of Bowen theory lies in the difference it makes to problem solving in people's families, jobs, and other social settings. However, I was not always successful in teaching Bowen theory to undergraduates. For example, the fact that students who enroll in the family interaction classes tend to be deeply interested in their own families has some disadvantages and advantages. When students are intensely immersed in their families, they sometimes become unteachable, in part because these students are often closed to considering common denominators among all families. When people are too invested in their own families' ways of doing things, they cannot see the weaknesses and the strengths of their family emotional systems.

Furthermore, because most students feel strongly about some aspects of their families, they often protest academic assessments of their family research. Consequently, some of the more mundane aspects of my teaching responsibilities—such as grading—are often more problematic in my family interaction classes than in other classes. This difficulty occurs because students think they know a great deal about their families before they start to study Bowen theory. For example, they may prematurely reject Bowen's professional contributions because they think his theory is not sufficiently familiar in relation to their own experiences or not scientific enough.

The specific conclusions listed below about teaching Bowen theory to undergraduates support my overall conclusion that teaching Bowen theory to undergraduates is worthwhile.

1. Students appreciate knowing that some patterns of family interaction tend to be predictable because of their emotional content.
2. Students see that they are integral parts of their families' problems and that changes happen when they act more responsibly.
3. Students question their comfort with the status quo of their families.
4. Students become better prepared to deal with the resistance of family members who maintain the status quo in their families.
5. I no longer urge students to learn Bowen theory beyond their minimal course requirements.
6. I do not belabor explanations of Bowen theory and do not dispute alternative interpretations, but rather stay calm in my own understanding of Bowen theory.
7. I am responsive to students who are highly motivated to know more about their families.
8. Being available to students who are interested in questioning and discussing Bowen theory is a high priority.
9. We need to reach out to young adults by communicating clearly about how to build strong, healthy families for the future.
10. Bowen theory helps students to realize that a penalty of not interacting differently in their families may be that they get trapped by their families for decades or more.
11. Bowen theory guides students to observe and assess their responsibilities in families and other social situations.
12. Students use Bowen theory to distinguish among being responsible, overresponsible, and underresponsible in their families.
13. Bowen theory makes students more aware of their kin groups and of emotional systems in communities, in societies, and globally.
14. Students understand more fully how they get drawn into unproductive emotional issues in their families and other social settings.
15. Students become more immune to others' reactivity when they ground their actions in Bowen theory principles.
16. Students realize that they benefit from continuing to research their family histories, sometimes with goals of understanding differentiation of self, nuclear family emotional system, sibling position, triangles, family projection process, multigenerational transmission process, cutoff, and social-emotional process.

Reference

Hall, C. M. (1981). *The Bowen family theory and its uses*. New York, NY: Jason Aronson.

11
Incorporating Bowen Theory Into an Undergraduate Social Work Curriculum: An Exercise in the Responsible Management of Self

ANTHONY J. WILGUS

As a profession, social work is ambitious in its breadth and scope:

> The primary mission of the social work profession is to enhance human well-being and help meet the basic human needs of all people, with particular attention to the needs and empowerment of people who are vulnerable, oppressed, and living in poverty. (National Association of Social Workers, 1996, paragraph 1)

Implicit in this broad mission is an understanding of human behavior and a grasp of the factors that contribute to both the deterioration and enhancement of human functioning. Preparing social work students at both the undergraduate and the graduate level for this work is no small endeavor. The Council on Social Work Education has carefully delineated a curriculum designed to equip students with the prerequisite knowledge, values and ethics, and skills required for this noble task. Coursework in human behavior and social work practice with individuals and families is an integral part of the training of future social workers as they embark on the process of striving to comprehend the human condition and, it is hoped, alleviate human suffering.

The initial section of this chapter highlights the conventional placement of Bowen family systems theory in social work programs and a potential rationale for this decision while presenting a case for the theory's inclusion primarily in two undergraduate courses. The second section of the chapter describes the evolution of the author's thinking, culminating in the development of some guiding pedagogical principles derived from participating in an ongoing reciprocal learning process spanning more than 2 decades. Next, the author outlines several working principles used in this process orientation, including the effort to regulate his own reactivity and to manage himself in a clearly defined manner. Subsequently, the author elucidates several strategies for incorporating Bowen theory into undergraduate social work courses, followed by a description of the challenges associated with this approach. A sampling of student responses over the years concludes the chapter.

Exposed to Bowen theory in a graduate program in social work and trained further in Bowen theory in a postgraduate training program at the Georgetown Family Center, I have made a concerted attempt over 22 years to incorporate this theory into an undergraduate social work program. Although typically relegated to graduate programs in advanced family therapy courses, Bowen theory has relevance for all levels of social work education. In this chapter, the author posits that Bowen theory is relevant to all social work students interested in developing a more comprehensive understanding of human behavior, regardless of whether they are engaged in undergraduate- or graduate-level social work education. The theory, then, is a lens through which to view human behavior rather than simply another social work practice model or technique.

Why Bowen Theory?

Not surprisingly, challenges abound in this venture. Unlike the natural science of biology, which has a unifying theory of evolution, the field of social work has no such framework, as Turner (1986) noted:

> The cry has been frequently raised that social work practice does not have an adequate theoretical base. Clearly, like all other professions practicing in the area of human adjustment, we do lack a sufficiently comprehensive and integrated body of theory necessary to understand and explain the myriad of situations we are called upon to assess. (pp. xxvii–xxviii)

Although a plethora of studies in the past 20 years have added to the body of knowledge, the status of theory development remains expansive: "Theories of and research about human behavior are nearly boundless and constantly growing" (Hutchison, 2008, p. 29). Adding to this maelstrom is the obvious subjectivity inherent in such diversity: "There is no one theory that all practitioners universally accept; each theory has its dedicated adherents and its impassioned critics" (Pillari, 1998, p. 10). This apparent edifice of Babel can offer both stimulation and confusion.

An academician faces some daunting tasks, including the choice of theories for examination and the degree of depth required for informed consideration. Pragmatism dictates action, however. Because the theories are indeed boundless and instructional time is finite, a faculty member, not unlike the social work practitioner, makes choices: textbooks (replete with their own selection of theories and practice models), assignments, assorted readings, lecture material, classroom exercises, and the like.

The human behavior curriculum in social work entails a developmental overview of the human, covering infancy through adulthood from a biopsychosocial perspective along with a macro view situating humans in the context of families, groups, organizations, communities, and society. If textbooks on human behavior in the social environment do mention Bowen theory, they typically highlight the concepts of differentiation and triangles and depict the often-used genogram (Bowen's *family diagram*) as a tool for gathering multigenerational facts of the family (Ashford, LeCroy, & Lortie, 1997; Dale, Smith, Norlin, & Chess, 2009; Hutchison, 2008; van Wormer, 2007; Zastrow & Kirst-Ashman, 2010).

A generalist model in social work entails multiple theories and practice models, including problem solving, ecological systems, cognitive-based theories, crisis intervention, and strength-based approaches (Johnson & Yanca, 2007). In the midst of this panoply of theories and practice models, this author held to the view that Bowen theory was far more than a form of therapy or a specific technique used with certain families. In the same way that Darwin discovered an entirely new way of looking at all life on this planet, Bowen theory is a bold attempt to understand the human condition in the broadest sense. Confining the theory to graduate-level courses in clinical social work or advanced family therapy approaches fails to appreciate the theory's magnitude. As an effort to move the study of the human more toward science, Bowen theory retains relevance for any practitioner striving to more fully understand the behavior of the species. With an undergraduate degree, social workers interact with clientele in the most anxious of scenarios: homelessness, domestic violence, child abuse and neglect, and so forth. These students can benefit from exposure to a uniquely different way of thinking about the world.

Toward this effort, the author includes the 1988 seminal work of Kerr and Bowen, *Family Evaluation*, as a required text for both the initial human behavior in the social environment course and the social work practice with individuals and families course in addition to some of the standard texts in the profession. Rather than restricting discussion of Bowen theory to a segment in either of the courses, the instructor integrate concepts and readings from the theory throughout the duration of the academic term. Students gain full exposure to the eclectic theoretical and practice approaches of the social work profession and also receive a concomitant familiarity with the entirety of Bowen theory. Because the practice course focuses on some of the techniques of social work practice, students read a work on family diagrams (McGoldrick, Gerson, & Petry, 2008) and additional readings on Bowen theory.

As a result, students receive not only the standard, eclectic orientation typified in the profession of social work but also become familiar with a more singular and unique approach to the study of human behavior. Part of the theory's uniqueness is that it is not a patchwork of concepts from other orientations. It is holistic in the sense that much like evolutionary theory, it provides a comprehensive explanation for the human condition. Scholars agree with Bowen's pioneering contribution: "Bowen's own theory is among the most carefully worked out and influential of family systems" (Nichols, 1984, p. 349). Far more than a therapeutic approach or even a branch of family systems theories, then, it behooves students interested in becoming more knowledgeable about human functioning to be conversant with the theory. Undergraduate social work majors can benefit from a thoughtful exposure to this way of thinking about the world.

In the course of a 2-decade effort to integrate Bowen theory into an undergraduate social work curriculum, the author's thinking as a faculty member has evolved. Like some neophytes, this author struggled with the notion that Bowen theory was "the truth" at the outset of his teaching career. Bowen himself predicted this outcome among people who heard him:

> From the beginning I have been concerned about people who become disciples and who accept the theory without thinking for themselves .... One variable is the degree to which my theory, or any theory, is a closed belief system.... There is a considerable danger that my theory will also become a closed system of beliefs. (Bowen, 1978, p. 390)

Dogmatism, then, manifested itself in a number of subtle and not-so-subtle ways. For instance, as a faculty member, the author would present other theories and models of practice while consistently denigrating their accuracy, and under the guise of pseudo-objectivity, would offer the theory as the correct way to think. This discipleship led the author to skew data and discussions because he was intent on having students learn the "right way" to think. Paralleling this stance was a heavy focus on stuffing as much content as possible into the perceived empty brains of the students.

Swimming in data, students would respond in ways that, in hindsight, suggested this heavy-handed style of teaching. There were always those students adept at deciphering exactly what the instructor wanted in papers, exams, and class discussion. Or there were those who rebelled and dismissed the teaching content, complied on the surface, or argued vociferously. By whatever measure used, the instructor clearly invested in teaching students what to think rather than how to think. Paradoxically, this very process runs counter to a central precept in the theory, namely differentiation of self. This orientation was actually a reflection of the author's level of differentiation.

Over time, an awareness of this dogmatism within the instructor and the impact on the reciprocal learning process with students became gradually more apparent. Instead of a preoccupation with the amount of content that in any course is quite voluminous, the focus shifted ever so slightly to the task of creating a climate for student and instructor alike in which the thinking of all parties would find space to flourish. This orientation necessitated encouragement of student thinking for self while clarity of position for the faculty without defense or counterattack became paramount. A burgeoning sensitivity to the difficulties of this effort yielded the development of some basic pedagogical principles.

Pedagogical Principles

In the attempt to alter the terrain from content to process and from dogmatism to more thoughtful inquiry, the author defined a set of principles that offer some guidance in the incorporation of this material into the undergraduate social work curriculum. At this juncture, they include the following, with an understanding that there is room for additional maneuvering.

1. Bowen theory provides a way of thinking about human behavior that transcends the commonly found undergraduate- and graduate-level dichotomies within social work, and it is relevant for the undergraduate social worker who encounters the vast range of human functioning.

If Bowen theory consisted of a set of discrepant concepts and therapy techniques used with certain clinical families, it would understandably be the province of the advanced graduate student in social work. If it were a branch or school of family therapy as typically categorized in many compendia, then graduate students would be the appropriate audience. Students training for the master of social work degree prepare precisely for these tasks and can select a clinical or family concentration in their respective universities.

If, however, Bowen theory transcends technique and therapy as Bowen steadfastly maintained (Bowen, 1978; Kerr & Bowen, 1988), then it holds a place along with the other theories of human behavior (e.g., Freudian theory, cognitive theories, and behavioral theories). Historically, undergraduates in social science cover these theorists in a cross-section of courses in psychology and social work. Inclusion of this material is a prerequisite to developing an appreciation for the various ways in which major theorists attempt to explain the human phenomenon. Aware that students are not clinicians, faculty develop these curricula as legitimate exposure to the ideas of those who attempted to move the study of human behavior more toward science. Situating Bowen's contributions in this context allows for incorporating his theory into this sequence. It is important that students become familiar with the wide range of approaches to the study of the human. Bowen's work fits well into this schema.

As the author reviews the activity of undergraduate social work majors engaged in their initial and final field placement experience in just the past year, he notes that students encounter the following situations: intense conflict between couples (domestic violence shelters and custody mediation); emotional and behavioral problems in children and adolescents (family service agencies); psychiatric and substance abuse issues (mental health clinic); physiological illnesses and conditions (hospice, hospitals, nursing homes); removal of children from biological parents for physical and sexual abuse and neglect (child welfare agencies); violence and criminal behavior (correctional institutions and criminal courts); extreme poverty and isolation (neighbor-hood community centers and homeless shelters); and sexual trafficking (group home). This is a partial list. What is most evident is the fact that students at an undergraduate level in social work face the entire spectrum of human func-tioning. Daily, they come face to face with a whole host of biological, psycho-logical, and social symptoms. There are competing ways to think about each and every situation. There are diverse views on appropriate social work prac-tice with these problems and populations, and there are benefits to exposing students who encounter the most anxious human conditions to an accepted way of thinking about how those situations came to be. Bowen theory proffers this lens to these future social work practitioners.

2. Bowen theory is merely one of a variety of ways of thinking to which students will gain exposure, and it is important that they begin to move in the direction of thinking for self on matters of theory and practice.

Because the profession of social work borrows from many disciplines, undergraduates take a variety of courses in the social sciences and elsewhere. Introductory and upper-level courses in psychology, sociology, political sci-ence, and economics offer diverse conceptualizations about how the human behaves and explanations for this behavior. In these areas, students gain famil-iarity with competing views of human functioning and the challenges inher-ent in the diversity of ideas. Although some of these courses are introductory and cursory in nature, the upper-level coursework does provide more depth. For instance, students often enroll in abnormal psychology and the funda-mentals of counseling as well as in another course in the use of the fourth edi-tion of the *Diagnostic and Statistical Manual of Mental Disorders* (American Psychiatric Association, 2000).

The social work course on human behavior in the social environment is the initial major theory course for students. After being admitted to the major, stu-dents begin their practice sequence with social work practice with individuals and families. Each course requires multiple texts, representing the eclectic nature of the social work profession. Adhering to the person-in-environment framework and the generalist model of preparing social work undergraduates to work at the entry level with individuals, families, groups, organizations, and communities, the author immerses students in the profession's conventional knowledge base. Hence, students receive a biopsychosocial life span approach in human behavior and a generalist, problem-solving overview in the practice course.

A social worker once told the author of a jury trial in which psychiatric and psychological experts fundamentally disagreed on the defendant's sanity, causing a juror to exclaim, "If the experts cannot agree, then what is a layper-son to think when presented with this evidence?" For social work students, the burgeoning realization that there are radically different ways to think about human behavior is a major intellectual hurdle. By reviewing some of the major theories over time, they come to see that not all views carry the same weight. For example, the instructor highlights some of the major explanations of and treatments for mental illness, noting that the physician who pioneered the use of the lobotomy received the Nobel Prize for Medicine (Valenstein, 1986, 1998). At the same time, they come to understand that there may be some fact in a particular theory. Freud's concepts of transference and countertransference have merit, whereas other parts of his theory fail closer empirical analysis.

In the midst of so many explanations of human behavior, how does a student begin to move in the direction of studying or adopting a theoretical framework for practice? Although perplexity may result from an array of queries provided by the instructor, students slowly realize that they do have some responsibility for developing their own thinking. Of course, some students may choose to blindly embrace the theories and models of their mentors, including that of their sometimes dogmatic instructor. Still others opt to pursue the more arduous path of thinking for themselves with an awareness of the limitations of the knowledge base within the discipline and their own personal frailties in that venture.

3. It is incumbent on the faculty member to acknowledge his or her own biases while respecting the student's capacity to think for self.

During the early years of integrating Bowen theory into the curriculum, the author, as instructor, adopted a posture of purported objectivity, often an admirable trait in the academic world. Despite claims to neutrality, students read beyond the verbiage and responded to the dogmatic style in the presentation of Bowen theory and other views of human behavior. Again, some students chose to humor the instructor, regurgitating the "right" way of thinking. Others argued more in response to the instructor's emotionality than to cohesively present a competing view. The actual impact of this pseudo-objective stance coupled with the sometimes persuasive yet feeling-laden presentation of Bowen theory actually impeded the students' ability to think for themselves.

With a small measure of seasoning and recognition of the fruitlessness of objectivity pronouncements, the instructor altered his stance. Rather than pretending to be neutral or objective, he not only stated the theory that made the most sense to him but also explained the trajectory by which he arrived at that place. Fortunately, he had mentors who allowed him to think for himself, and he saw the wisdom in creating a similar opportunity for students. This slight shift in attitude resulted in the redesigning of lectures, course content, exams, and written assignments. Central to this process was an emphasis on student choice combined with rigorous thinking. The effort here was to move students in the direction of pursuing some of their own interests while substantiating their positions with as much research and fact as possible.

Concurrent with all of these principles is the instructor's effort to focus on his own functioning, to be aware of and manage his own reactivity, and to adhere to these defined pedagogical and theoretical principles. To realize a little more of these goals, with the assistance of a coach the instructor continued a long-term differentiating effort relative to his immediate family and his family of origin. Intrinsic to this strategy is the notion that the ability to become a more clearly defined self with one's most important relationships transfers into other significant relationships. This capacity dampens dogmatism and inculcates a greater tolerance for different ways of thinking. A more differentiated certainty of position contributes to a greater respect for others' point of view without defending one's own position or attacking that of others. In the reciprocal learning process between faculty and students in which students thinking for themselves is desirable, then, this work is critical.

Accompanying this effort is the ever-present attempt to consider the part that one plays in any relationship system. A faculty member is certainly ripe for transference issues because a percentage of students quite typically gravitate toward approval or disapproval. Part of this phenomenon is the idealization (or demonization) of the faculty member and the tendency to accept (or reject) whatever material he or she disseminates. Less mature faculty members can feed this deification of his or her persona. Thus, a stellar student receives an A but does not learn to think for her- or himself. An ongoing effort to demythologize the self of the faculty member manifests some awareness of the role that he or she plays in the mutual learning process. Unwittingly, professors can get in the way of students' developing their own thinking.

Pedagogical Methods for Incorporating Theory and Practice

Incorporating Bowen theory into human behavior and practice courses entails more than affixing readings to the syllabus. The instructor synopsizes each chapter of *Family Evaluation* (Kerr & Bowen, 1988), giving this material to students in hard copy. These handouts elicit much positive feedback. PowerPoint explanations also facilitate review and discussion of the theory content during class. Including Walter Toman's (1974) descriptions of the 10 basic sibling profiles and the multiple and middle sibling constellations adds to one of the theory's key concepts. Also, Bowen's (1978) seminal article, "The Family Reaction to Death," complements material on the final stage of the life cycle in the human behavior course. Writings from Dr. Roberta Gilbert (1999, 2004) serve to amplify lecture material on the theory.

To support ongoing thinking, students maintain a weekly journal submitted to the instructor. At that time, they do not spew back the material read but instead give their thoughts, observations, critiques, and questions. This vehicle presents a unique opportunity for instructor and student dialogue. More often than not, students are skillful in reflecting on many aspects of theory as they begin to think a little differently about human behavior. For example, they speak of anxiety in self and others and its contagion, along with the impact of calm under stressful situations. Sibling position always generates much commentary along with the challenge of understanding differentiation. Parenthetically, students comment on all of their readings, including the standard social work texts and articles.

Rather than having in-class exams that often test students' memory capacity, not necessarily their critical thinking abilities, the instructor uses take-home exams that are open book and open note. In these exams, students apply cases from their own experiences (field instruction, friendship, family, and acquaintance network) to the concepts from the theory. Translation of the material into realistic human conditions, however tedious and time consuming, does seem to provide an integration of some very complex concepts. Moreover, each exam is quite different, serving to keep the instructor alert and always intrigued. In a practice exam, students write about how they might go about selecting a practice model of social work, what those models of practice might be, the rationale for that selection, and their plans to pursue further knowledge about the model or models.

In each course, students write two papers that emphasize student choice. Selecting a symptom that is biological, psychological, or social for the human behavior course, students go into detail about the nature and manifestations of that condition coupled with the attempts by a theory or theories to explain it. The paper for social work practice requires students to pick a particularly attractive practice model and research the history, concept, and application of that approach. Additionally, students complete a family-of-origin paper for the practice sequence in which they provide a family diagram and a beginning interpretation of some of the Bowen theory concepts in their own history.

A host of other methods elucidates theory. Using the Web site of the Bowen Center for the Study of the Family (http://www.thebowencenter.org) gives students a chance to review the basic concepts and how they apply to a particular family. Video clips from a variety of sources offer insight into theory relevance. For instance, an interview with Wanda Kaczynski, the mother of Unabomber Ted Kaczynski, yields rich information on family process. A presentation of the parents of Amy Biehl, a Rhodes scholar slain in South Africa, offers a fascinating portrait of levels of differentiation.

Role-plays in class engage students in a different way. Descriptions of sibling position by physically spacing students out in class and having them reflect on how that influences their functioning is not only informative but also fun. Giving students the chance to act out triangles in front of their classmates adds levity and understanding to the entire group. Again, the instructor marvels at students' creativity in this regard. These kinds of techniques or methods are a reminder that humans are mammals and that mammals learn much through play. And learning can be fun. In that regard, the instructor received a gracious invitation from the staff at the Bowen Center for the Study of the Family to bring students to the annual symposium in the early 1990s. Since then, two to nine students have traveled to Washington and assisted with tasks during the 2-day stint. This is a marvelous opportunity to personally witness theory explication and application.

Challenges Facing the Faculty Member

Of course, this long-term effort is replete with past, present, and future challenges. In addition to voluminous content for both courses, the multiplicity of approaches, and the propensity toward dogmatism mentioned earlier, there is a complexity to Bowen theory's just standing on its own merits. Exposing students to some conventional and novel ways of thinking about the human in one or two semesters leaves little time for the percolation of ideas that any theory requires. Students grasp some concepts more readily (e.g., sibling position). Situating the human within an evolutionary framework is more difficult. With limited knowledge of evolutionary theory, students often reel when facing a chapter on natural systems thinking (e.g., Kerr & Bowen, 1988, Chapter 1). Some students make an immediate connection with aspects of the theory, and others take more time to process the concepts. Juxtaposing Bowen theory with the eclectic nature of social work is quite a dizzying experience for most, if not all, students.

There are challenges external to the classroom, also. Students taking these courses complete a field placement in a human service agency in their sophomore or junior year, often at the same time as the human behavior course. When interrogating the professional staff about their theory orientation, students hear comments about the disconnect between theory and practice, a few concepts from discrepant theories (often unknown to the practitioner), or an agencywide orientation. These practitioners call their practice eclectic in nature, tailored to the particular family or clientele with whom they interact: Some individuals benefit from a cognitive-based model, and others need crisis theory. The arbiter, of course, is the practitioner. Inferred from these responses, then, is the slant that techniques matter. This sometimes dismissive view of theory in the practice world is a reality facing both the student and the faculty member.

Maintaining awareness of the reciprocity that occurs between instructor and student is another ongoing effort. Given the hierarchical nature of this relationship (the faculty member does grade the student), there is a built-in tendency to conform. Students' determining what they perceive the teacher wants is an oft-perceived route to a good grade. Although this togetherness intensity may flatter the instructor, it is also a red flag that learning is not taking place—namely, students thinking "like" the professor does not imply learning. At the same time, slipping into defending Bowen theory with students who are more critical is also less than helpful in assisting the student to think for self. For this faculty member, this is an ever-present challenge.

Student Response

At the completion of each course, the faculty member requests feedback that is more comprehensive than the standard evaluation form used by the university.

Students respond in a narrative form with assurances that their commentaries are valuable. As an aggregate, the major themes of these evaluations fall into four categories: (a) the amount of content covered in the courses, (b) the complexity of the material, (c) the degree of critical thinking required for the courses, and (d) the application of the concepts and theories in students' daily lives. An arbitrarily selected array of student commentaries makes up the final segment of this chapter.

In general, students typically speak to the tremendous volume of information in the courses and the complexity of the material with the resulting sense of being overwhelmed. One student commented, "Sometimes [you] gave out too much information. I got all confused"; another concurred, "Covered way too much to really be able to grasp all the information." Still others put it this way: "I have loved and hated human behaviors. The class is so very interesting, but there is so much work involved with it that it is overwhelming at times." And some students used a wonderful sense of humor in responding, for example, "I honestly leave your class with my brain hurting, but I like it."

Students have described course complexity in a number of ways: "This class, I would have to say, has challenged me more than any other class I have taken." "This class has probably been the most difficult course I've ever taken. However, it has been very influential in challenging my thinking and creating a stronger desire to learn about others." In the latter case, then, the material piqued their curiosity, leaving them eager to pursue the journey of exploring human behavior in more detail. And for some, this complexity has some merit; as one student stated, "I love learning about the way humans act and reasons for functioning. I am now able to reflect back on the concept of sibling position, chronic anxiety, differentiation, and various other theories." Complexity in and of itself is not necessarily perceived negatively.

The exposure to multiple ways of accounting for human behavior and the varied ways to potentially intervene with those experiencing problems contributes to a more discriminatory orientation. One student explained it this way:

> It forced me to use critical thinking in evaluating the information and research. It also expanded my thinking by removing and forcing me to think and analyze outside of the parameters I was familiar with. I have a better understanding and appreciation for individuals and their behavior.

Another student spoke to both the all-consuming nature of the course and how the content and complexity contributed to a personally more discerning view of the world around her: "I love the idea that the more I learn, the more I want to know, the more questions I have. This class truly developed my critical thinking skills."

An unintended consequence of presenting this information to students contributes to a capacity and eagerness for many to find ways to concretely apply concepts, parts of theory, and even theory itself, as one student noted: "I also started to work on myself and what I need and related the material covered with my own experiences." Another student put it this way: "I constantly find myself applying concepts from class and the research from various authors we studied to real-life situations." Students can begin to grasp the link between theory and practice.

There are always a startling number of students who begin to make connections with their families and other relationship networks. "This course has allowed me to assess and understand more about myself and my own family dynamics," one student maintained. The concept of triangles strikes a chord with many students: "I have found myself analyzing triangles in my personal life, especially between my sister, my mother, and me," and another claimed, "I have some very visible triangles happening in my own life, along with many more that I have not analyzed yet." Evidently, some of the methods of role-playing various scenarios in which students perceive triangles take root in their thinking.

Even more intimately, a student may find fodder that gives pause for reflection, as this comment manifests so strikingly:

> I have realized through class that I adapted in my marriage in order to preserve harmony. … I have been so close to him [her son] probably because I didn't feel close to my husband. Now it is time to readjust. I want to be his mom without fixing his problem. … But even though I know I need to do this, it is a daily struggle, and I have to be very conscious of everything I do and say when it involves him.

Even with so much information, a student may sometimes appropriate the information that is unique to her or him and yet quite consistent with a particular concept or theoretical approach.

Sibling position, differentiation, anxiety, emotional cutoff, multigenerational emotional process, and triangles become real to younger and older students. Some of them are clearly able and motivated to not only hear the theory but to practice the theory in their own lives. The instructor underscores the fact, however, that at no time during the course does he suggest anything prescriptive to the students. These observations, insights, and efforts flow from hearing some different ways of thinking about the world. They are the translators. Therein lies the value of creating a climate in which students can tap their innate curiosity about the world around them and slowly begin to think for themselves.

Conclusion

Bowen theory is a stand-alone theory that contributes to moving the study of human behavior into the scientific realm. Open to the influx of information emanating from the natural sciences and rooted in evolutionary theory, this perspective has value for those who wish to better comprehend the functioning of *Homo sapiens*. Social workers at the undergraduate level encounter every kind of biological, clinical, and social impairment. Competing explanations for the etiology of these phenomena exist and proliferate. Inasmuch as these future practitioners hope to not only understand the human predicament but also alleviate suffering in some way, an exposure to this elegant explanation is beneficial. For the student, this is exhausting. For the faculty member, it is demanding. Learning to think for self is not for the timid. As the author's father loved to say when describing how he maintained himself in a 62-year marriage, "It's not easy. But it's worth it." Wise words, indeed.

References

American Psychiatric Association. (2000). *The diagnostic and statistical manual of mental disorders* (4th ed.) (Text revision). Washington, DC: Author.

Ashford, J. B., LeCroy, C. W., & Lortie, K. L. (1997). *Human behavior in the social environment: A multidimensional perspective*. Pacific Grove, CA: Brooks/Cole.

Bowen, M. (1978). *Family therapy in clinical practice*. New York, NY: Jason Aronson.

Dale, O., Smith, R., Norlin, J. M., & Chess, W. A. (2009). *Human behavior and the social environment: Social systems theory* (6th ed.). Boston, MA: Pearson Education.

Gilbert, R. (1999). *Connecting with our children: Guiding principles for parents in a troubled world*. Hoboken, NJ: Wiley.

Gilbert, R. (2004). *The eight concepts of Bowen theory*. Falls Church, VA: Leading Systems Press.

Hutchison, E. D. (2008). *Dimensions of human behavior: Person and environment* (3rd ed.). Thousand Oaks, CA: Sage.

Johnson, L. C., & Yanca, S. J. (2007). *Social work practice: A generalist approach* (9th ed.). Boston, MA: Pearson Education.

Kerr, M. E., & Bowen, M. (1988). *Family evaluation: An approach based on Bowen theory*. New York, NY: W. W. Norton.

McGoldrick, M., Gerson, R., & Petry, S. (2008). *Genograms: Assessment and intervention* (3rd ed.). New York, NY: W. W. Norton.

National Association of Social Workers. (1996). *Code of ethics*. Retrieved from http://www.socialworkers.org/pubs/code/code.asp

Nichols, M. P. (1984). *Family therapy: Concepts and methods*. New York, NY: Gardner Press.

Pillari, V. (1998). *Human behavior in the social environment: The developing person in a holistic context* (2nd ed.). Pacific Grove, CA: Brooks/Cole.

Toman, W. (1974). *Family constellation: Its effects on personality and social behavior* (3rd ed.). New York, NY: Springer.

Turner, F. J. (Ed.). (1986). *Social work treatment: Interlocking theoretical approaches* (3rd ed.). New York, NY: Free Press.

Valenstein, E. (1986). *Great and desperate cures*. New York, NY: Basic Books.

Valenstein, E. (1998). *Blaming the brain: The truth about drugs and mental health*. New York, NY: Free Press.

van Wormer, K. (2007). *Human behavior and the social environment, micro level: Individuals and families*. Oxford, England: Oxford University Press.

Zastrow, C. H., & Kirst-Ashman, K. K. (2010). *Understanding human behavior and the social environment* (8th ed.) Belmont, CA: Brooks/Cole.

12
Bowen Theory in Undergraduate and Graduate Nursing Education

RITA BUTCHKO KERR

Unlike in other health professions, nurses bear the responsibility for providing care for families in inpatient settings 24 hours a day. Nurses are often the primary caregivers for families on an outpatient basis in clinics and at home. Obstetrical nurses witness families in transition as they add a new member. Medical–surgical nurses see health and illness at every stage of the family life span, and nurses are often primary caregivers at the end of life, in either intensive care units or hospice. Nurses not only function as the most visible and ongoing caregivers, but they are also the family's bridge to other health care professionals involved in patient care through their observations and accurate reporting.

The purpose of this chapter is to show how Bowen family systems theory (Bowen, 1978; Kerr, 2004; Kerr & Bowen, 1988; Papero, 1990; see also Chapter 1) can provide a framework for nurses working with families in any kind of setting—inpatient, outpatient, or community. The adventures of a nursing professor presenting Bowen theory to undergraduate and graduate nursing students over the past several years at a small liberal arts university provide the context for the development and transmission of this framework. Objectives for students at both the undergraduate and graduate levels are discussed, as well as the specific expectations for students at each level. Both undergraduate courses (human development through the life span, nursing of families and children [traditionally referred to as *pediatric and obstetrical nursing*], psychiatric–mental health nursing, and community nursing) and graduate courses (family nursing and community nursing) include family theory. Both psychiatric–mental health nursing and family nursing, the specific foci of this chapter, begin with a historical perspective about how families have changed over the centuries.

A Historical Perspective on the Treatment of Families

Family treatment appears to date back many generations in southern and western Africa. Africa has a tradition of oral history, so it is difficult to say how far back family treatment occurred. One can only say that family treatment began as far back as any tribal member can remember and as far back as the generation who talked about the tradition (Ebigbo, 1990; Janzen, 1978; Kiev, 1990; Nzewi, 1990; Romme, 1990).

According to Bourguignon (1990), many African cultures conceptualized the individual as intimately tied to the group—the living, ancestors, and perhaps the unborn. Concepts of illness were often considered far more social than biological (Lambo, 1964), and any treatment for an ill individual needed to include both the family and the tribe. Nzewi (1990) found that in Nigeria, regardless of diagnosis, persons were considered ill to the degree to which their illness interfered with human relationships, their role in the family, their social and economic activities, or all of these. The traditional healer conducted interviews with family and friends of the patient to determine the degree of family responsibility for the patient's illness in terms of interpersonal relationships, especially relationships in polygamous families. When illness lasted a long time, family members took turns joining the individual for treatment because the ill individual was never left alone. In addition, when there were issues between the family and the tribe, these issues were settled as a strategy to improve the individual's health. Kiev (1990), also working in Nigeria, found that the goal was change rather than treating the patient's specific illness, and for change to occur, family participation was critical.

In Zaire (previously the Belgian Congo and now the Congo), diseases were divided into diseases of God and man, the specific category being designated by the patient and family. Diseases of God were treated with herbs and Western medicine. Diseases of man, however, were characterized by some sort of family or tribal dysfunction. The family or tribe was gathered together to receive therapy from a shaman. The focus was both on the present and on the behavior of ancestors (Janzen, 1978). Although these beliefs may sound primitive from a Western scientific medicine perspective, they provided the context for looking at health and illness beyond the concept of the individual. Such health care practices were important in areas in which the individual was explicitly tied to the social group, which included family and tribe. Health care practitioners are wise to remember that Western scientific medicine is only one of multiple medical systems throughout the world in which people live and die. It appears that a broad level of systems thinking about health and illness might have been more possible before the introduction of scientific medicine, which tends to focus primarily on biology.

Family systems thinking started in the United States in the 1950s with the pioneering work of Bowen, as well as that of many others working in different settings across the country (Bowen, 1978). Bowen's focus, however, was on the family as a natural system (Kerr & Bowen, 1988). Although the conceptualizations of these early family systems pioneers took many directions, Bowen theory and its focus on the family as a natural system has proven useful not only to the profession of psychiatry in which it was developed, but also to many other health care and service professions.

Use of Bowen Theory in Nursing Practice

It is the author's stance that Bowen theory is very applicable to nursing practice if nurses are willing and able to think beyond the individual patient and the medical system in which patients participate. Nurses need to learn to view patients as part of family systems and themselves as part of health care systems. Such changes in thinking require a tremendous amount of unlearning and relearning, but to the extent to which nurses are willing to relearn, new options for decision making, patient–family interventions, and participation in the health care team become available to them.

Developmental Stage of Traditional Undergraduate Students

Nursing students typically enter undergraduate education while in the throes of moving away from their families of origin. At one end of the continuum are students for whom this transition stage may go quite smoothly, and at the other end of the continuum are others for whom the process may be fraught with family conflict, ambivalence, and symptom development of varying degrees depending on the challenges in their family systems. While students are trying to learn nursing knowledge, problem-solving skills, and patient care techniques in a nursing curriculum, it is the author's assessment that the most important issue in these students' lives seems to be the quality of their relationships. These students appear to be very aware of the quality of their peer relationships, and those relationships seem to occupy a substantial amount of their thinking and emotional time. However, their family relationships also often take a larger portion of their thinking and emotional time than some students are willing to admit. They appear to want relationships with peers and with their siblings and parents, although they are less likely to admit to the latter. It is during this stage of personal transition that Bowen theory is presented in the nursing curriculum.

Undergraduate Curriculum

Undergraduate nursing students complete a curriculum that prepares them to be generalists in the profession. As part of their curriculum, these students care for adults and children in a variety of inpatient and outpatient settings, including medical–surgical nursing, pediatrics, maternal–child health, psychiatric nursing, and community health nursing. Family nursing, a relatively new construct in the profession over the past few decades, has been conceptualized in a variety of nursing frameworks and theories (Friedemann, 1995; Friedman, 1998; Gillis, 1991; Wright & Leahey, 2005). Although concepts about family are taught in pediatrics, maternal–child health, and community health nursing, the author uses Bowen theory as a primary theoretical framework to conceptualize family nursing within the context of the undergraduate psychiatric mental health nursing curriculum. The goal of this endeavor is for nursing students to see family as an integral context for patient care. The author presents her understanding of family nursing by exposing students to the history of the modern family (Stone, 1977), Carter and McGoldrick's (1980) family life cycle, and Bowen (1978) theory concepts, and suggests relationships among family developmental concepts, Bowen theory concepts, and all areas of nursing care. In addition, the author asks students to relate these concepts to both nursing and their own family lives, as well as to life in the university setting—in terms of both hierarchical faculty–student relationships and peer interactions. As the author presents Bowen theory to students, she highlights the difference between reactive and reflective thinking. Her focus is on how both nurses and families manifest reactive behaviors and how nurses' efforts to become more reflective before acting may not only serve to modify their own behaviors, but may also have a positive influence on the thinking and health care decisions of the families to whom they provide care.

In the undergraduate nursing curriculum, students focus on theory related to development of the therapeutic use of self in relationships with patients and their families in a psychiatric setting. The course syllabus states that at the completion of this course of study, students will

1. Demonstrate increasing awareness of themselves and how their behavior influences their interactions with others
2. Demonstrate use of self with individuals and families
3. Use theoretical concepts from Bowen theory as the basis for nursing assessment, intervention, and evaluation
4. Evaluate the social and economic impact of mental illness on individuals and families

History of the Modern Family

Classes in family nursing at the graduate level and in psychiatric mental health nursing at the undergraduate level start with a brief historical overview of the Western family from agrarian 16th-century Western Europe to the present, with a focus on how the Western family developed to its present form, including a historical analysis of the rise of individualism (Stone, 1990). Throughout the 16th and 17th centuries, children in Western families were seen as miniature adults, not as individuals. For example, artwork from this century depicts children in adult clothing. Children from poor families were often sent to work from the ages of 5 or 6. Also, because many children did not survive to adulthood, if parents wanted a name to survive, more than one child might be given that name. Children and women of the household were deemed the father's and husband's property, respectively. The 18th century brought the notion of romantic love, the recognition of childhood as different from adulthood, and the freedom to select one's spouse. The 19th century brought self-expression in the form of diaries, love letters, and novels; the notion that each man and woman is master over him- or herself versus being owned or dominated by another; antipathy to physical cruelty; and the recognition of adolescence as a stage of development. The 20th century saw a rise in the taste for luxury, decreased kinship in which nuclear families were separated from families of origin because of allegiance to the corporation, increased self-interest, the use of conscience versus organized religious doctrine, recognition of young adulthood as a separate life stage, and significant increases in the rates of cohabitation outside of marriage (Carter & McGoldrick, 1980).

Family Life Cycle

A second topic introduced to students in their family or psychiatric mental health nursing course is Carter and McGoldrick's (1980) *family life cycle*. The family life cycle expands students' notions about how family members over three to four generations develop in relation to each other. This perspective on family development is typically new to students, but it is also understandable. They can begin to understand how the life cycle expands and contracts among economic classes, race, and ethnicity. For example, women from some cultural, ethnic, and socioeconomic status groups may become parents in their teens and grandparents in their late 30s or 40s, whereas women from other backgrounds may not experience their first pregnancy until after 40. Because Carter and McGoldrick's family life cycle starts with the single young adult, it provides nursing students with opportunities to discuss the family emotional processes that occur when young people leave home and to reflect on and assess the students' own and their families' reactions to this family life cycle event. Most important, students become conscious of the reality and effects of their own economic dependency because most of them continue to be supported, at least to some degree, by their parents.

The parents' and grandparents' generations are also discussed in terms of length of marriages. At the beginning of the 20th century, statistically, the first parent died within 2 years of the last child leaving home. At present, an increasing numbers of adults in their 60s and 70s are still caring for an elderly parent. Students whose parents have been involved with caring for chronically ill grandparents know the impact on the daily lives of everyone involved, including their own. The older generations are also discussed with respect to their facing multiple losses in their lives, including the loss of a spouse and possibly the loss of their health and home.

Another area of discussion is the contribution of cultural rituals related to how families begin, develop, and grow old. For example, it would be unusual to have a leader older than 80 in Western cultures, whereas in Eastern cultures, it would be unusual to have a leader younger than 80. As students become aware of the emotional processes that can occur during transition times in the family life cycle, they begin to understand how life cycle transitions as a variable can be one of many factors that influence health and illness (Carter & McGoldrick, 1980, 1989; Kerr & Bowen, 1988).

Equipped with a basic understanding of the stages of the family life cycle, students can then consider the relative influence of normative (expected) and paranormative (unexpected) events in family life (Carter & McGoldrick, 1980). Some of the early research of Angell (1936), who studied family behavior during the depression, and Hill (1949), who studied family behavior after a husband went off to World War II, is presented. Students then begin to see how disruption of families' lives influences them in terms of their ability or inability to meet the challenges as they transition through expected versus unexpected events. Some families may become chaotic and lose their ability to function in terms of appropriate decision making, whereas others will be able to meet the unexpected challenges.

Bowen Theory in the Undergraduate Nursing Curriculum

Classroom discussion of Bowen theory is initiated through the use of several prompts from the instructor in an attempt to facilitate students thinking more broadly about individuals, families, and the health care settings in which they work. The first prompt is an adapted prologue from Bradt and Moynihan (1972):

> Who is sicker
> Mrs. Sicker or Mr. Sicker or
> Mr. and Mrs. Sicker's child?
> The child is just a little sicker! (p. 23)

Several questions are then used to prompt ongoing class discussions:

- When someone in a family is ill, who hurts?
- If everyone hurts when a family member is ill, to whom should care be given?
- What is happening in the family system that may influence symptoms to present at any one point in time?
- When an individual gets any kind of a diagnosis from schizophrenia to diabetes to Parkinson's disease to cancer, why now (Kerr & Bowen, 1988)? Why not last month, last year, or 2 or 3 months or years from now?

Such questions are often new to students, and over time, they begin to understand that these questions might represent a different way of approaching and thinking about not only what kind of nursing care they are giving but also who might be the legitimate recipients of that care and how symptoms and diagnoses may be handled in a more constructive manner.

Differentiation of Self

Class discussions continue with the introduction of the following Bowen theory constructs: *anxiety, chronic anxiety,* and the forces for togetherness and individuality that occur within every family (Bowen, 1978; Kerr & Bowen, 1988). The Bowen theory concept of *differentiation of self,* the most difficult of all the course concepts for students to digest, is presented in terms of maturity–immaturity, solid self versus pseudoself, fusion, and the ability to separate thoughts and emotions. Growing up in a culture that has encouraged and equated the expression of feelings with being "in touch with self," the author finds that these undergraduate students often have difficulty thinking about the notion of separating their thoughts from their feelings and knowing when the expression of each is appropriate. How does one become a separate self, responsible for one's own thinking, feeling, and behaviors? And how can one keep from participating in the immaturity or irresponsibility of others? The author has found these to be very difficult abstractions for her older adolescent–young adult students to grasp, particularly because they are just beginning to find their way in the world on their own. A few more questions are then posed:

- For what do differentiated people stand?
- With whom do they compromise?
- Whom do they hurt in the process of stating what they stand for?
- How do they treat those around them?

As students begin to understand the Bowen theory concept of differentiation of self, the question then becomes, "What does the opposite end of the continuum look like, that is, low differentiation of self?" Such concepts as being overwhelmed and directed by one's emotions, lack of knowledge of self, and lack of principles for functioning are discussed. Students begin to recognize the reactivity in many of their psychiatric patients and the difficulty in getting very reactive patients to think about the decisions they need to make to proceed with their lives.

Subsequent questions then focus on

- What do behaviors look like in most people who have a moderate level of differentiation of self?
- How might people's maturity or immaturity manifest itself in their daily behaviors?

The students, most of whom graduated from high school within the past 4 years, can begin to gain some insight about how they are maturing if they can see positive changes in their behaviors during college life. For students who have used college as a way of embellishing their immaturity, insight regarding their current behaviors is more difficult, if not improbable.

Family Projection Process

The Bowen theory concepts that address multigenerational and nuclear family projection processes are a mystery to students until they start discussing how their parents talk about their extended family members and how they themselves took on similar attitudes toward those same family members. Follow-up questions for these discussions often include

- Who was seen as successful?
- Who was seen as not so successful?
- Who was seen as harboring most of the family's problems?
- Why would one family member inherit more family problems than other members?

These questions are easier for students to think about in their parents' generation than in their own generation. Just the small amount of emotional distance students have from their parents' generation is useful in allowing them to see the emotional family issues in which their parents were involved.

Emotional Triangles

The Bowen theory concept of the *emotional triangle* is also a conceptual stretch for most students, and the ensuing classroom discussions on the topic are approached with the following set of questions:

- What do you do if you have an issue with another person? Do you always discuss the issue directly?
- If you do not discuss the issue directly, with whom do you discuss it? Hence, the birth of an emotional triangle!
- Does discussing the issue with a third person solve the problem or prolong it?
- What happens to marriages when important issues are not discussed over many years?
- How else might issues between twosomes be avoided? Students suggest the use of golf courses, basements, going home to mother, alignment of one of the parents with a child, and extramarital affairs as possible examples.

The concept of the triangle, with its potential to spawn and maintain interlocking triangles over generations, is then applied to families, college campuses, doctor–patient–nurse relationships, and nurse–patient–family relationships. Can students imagine a college president and provost not dealing with the issues between them and displacing the problems onto the deans, who eventually take the problems out on faculty in whom the dysfunctional behaviors progress to the point where students are unhappy on campus and with each other and no one can explain why? This is a scenario to which many students can relate.

What happens when nurses are caught between the wishes of a physician and the wishes of a patient or family? This is a second scenario to which some nursing students can relate. How can such problems be solved? When is it appropriate to advocate for a patient, and when is it not appropriate? How can students tell when a patient is thinking clearly versus being reactive? How can students tell when they themselves are thinking clearly versus being reactive? Finally, what kinds of traits would they like to see in a family member with whom they would want to work if a patient were unconscious?

All of these questions are probed and answered in class, and clinical discussions after the concepts are presented until students begin to gain confidence about who they are as professionals and how they can enact their professional roles responsibly. All of these issues are discussed in terms of level of anxiety, clarity of thought, and emotional reactivity and in the context of the triangle-rich emotional systems that influence level of anxiety, clarity of thought, and emotional reactivity.

Sibling Position

Students have fun with the Bowen theory concept of *sibling position* and go from disbelieving its relevance, significance, or both to some understanding about how one's sibling position contributes not only to one's behavior but also to one's understanding of the larger world. Students are put into small groups according to whether they are oldest, middle, youngest, or only children. Although the subtle nuanced findings from Toman's (1974) sibling position research are not captured in such groups, students in similar sibling positions begin to see their commonalities with each other as they discuss the advantages and disadvantages of their sibling position. The relationship systems effects of sibling position are then considered for parent–child relationships, relationships among roommates, and professional relationships.

Developmental Stages of Graduate Students

Generally, one third of undergraduate nursing students go on to graduate school, but the time lapse between their undergraduate degree and when they return to graduate school varies greatly—often, and without exaggeration, spanning from 1 to 40 years. Motivations vary for delaying and returning to graduate school. A few students know early in their career that they want leadership positions, but most will use their undergraduate degrees until they have opened all the doors that those degrees can open. Others begin to age and know that the energy they need for giving direct patient care 40-plus hours per week cannot go on forever. Others delight in new knowledge and the notion of doors opening to jobs they could not even have imagined being qualified for while practicing at the undergraduate level. A few are even finishing their graduate degrees after they have retired. If they have remained in the same city, one of their undergraduate peers may even be teaching in their graduate program. All of these motives and life circumstances result in nurses being at many stages of development on their return to graduate school. If there could be an average profile for a nursing graduate student, it would be of a woman 30 to 50 years old, married with children of various ages, and holding down a full-time job. Common variations in the profile include being divorced and a single parent or being a grandparent.

Bowen Theory in the Graduate Nursing Curriculum

In the university's graduate nursing program, the author defines her thinking in two areas of study: (a) family theory and research, and (b) interdisciplinary family-focused health care across cultures. Family theory and research is taught to graduate students on campus. Interdisciplinary family-focused health care across cultures is taught through Web-based Blackboard technology to students from three universities in the United States and three in Europe. Family content is identical in both courses. Modules on culture were developed for the latter course. During nursing graduate studies, the Bowen theory theoretical framework and family developmental content are presented throughout both courses versus devoting only a few hours to it in the entire undergraduate curriculum. Introductions to both graduate course syllabi are as follows:

> Families, like balloons, crayons, and automobiles, come in all shapes, sizes, and colors. We are born into a family, and, at some point in early adulthood, many of us choose to participate in creating and parenting in another family. We may, at various times, love our families, hate them, or leave them, but we never escape them. Studying about families is both a challenge and an adventure, full of the same kinds of emotions that consume life in general—joy, humor, challenge, tediousness, and, at times, pain. As we learn about families, we learn about self and the people whom we love and care for, perhaps in ways we have not thought about before. Come join me in this quest. Proceed with awe and reverence. The behaviors you see in your own families and in the families for whom you care professionally are the outcomes of family members doing the best they can over many generations. All families have multiple strengths even though these strengths are sometimes difficult to observe.

Purpose and Objectives   The major purpose of both graduate courses is the study of the family as client. Students are encouraged to examine Bowen theory and then use it to develop personal and professional ways of intervening with families that may enhance, challenge, or modify their current nursing practices. This course includes learning and applying family theory to clinical practice. Objectives in both courses specific to Bowen theory include

- Examine the historical development of families.
- Develop a working definition of family.
- Identify and define the basic concepts of Bowen theory.
- Use Bowen theory as the basis for the nursing process: assessment, diagnosis, outcomes, planning, intervention, and evaluation.

Faculty and Student Expectations   The family theory and research course meets 3 hours a week over a 15-week semester. The interdisciplinary family-focused health care across cultures course meets online, with students from each country contributing. In both courses, the instructor is responsible for the first 5 weeks, presenting Bowen theory concepts in much the same format that is used with the undergraduate students because this is often the first time that the graduate students have heard of Bowen theory. Once these students are exposed to Bowen theory concepts, they are then expected to view the family system as the unit of assessment, intervention, and evaluation. During the second class session, the instructor presents self as part of a four-generation family, using family diagrams and looking at some relationships within the system. In general, students are fascinated with this approach. They have never "met" an instructor in this manner, and many become intrigued with the approach. As Bowen theory content is presented during the next 3 weeks, the instructor can then refer to the family diagrams for both visual cues and explanations. For the remaining 10 weeks of the course, class discussions consider Bowen theory concepts as seen through the lens of Carter and McGoldrick's (1999) family life cycle developmental framework detailed earlier in this chapter, that is, how families develop over time. During the final weeks of the course, students are also required to present to the class either their own family or a clinical family. They are encouraged to use a family diagram and to try to maintain objectivity as they lead the class through a discussion of what they consider to be their significant relationships over time using the evaluation approach found in Kerr and Bowen (1988). To date, 75% of the students have chosen to present their own families, with many of the students spending much more time on this assignment than they ever would have believed. After several class sessions devoted to hearing their classmates use a Bowen theory lens to present their own or clinical families to the class, the students engage in a final class discussion to consider the proposition that Bowen theory concepts transcend race, culture, and ethnicity.

Evaluating Students' Learning   The courses' final examination is a take-home exercise that includes two major assignments. For the first assignment, students are asked to develop a family assessment tool based on Bowen theory that is appropriate for their clinical setting. One of the most interesting family assessment tools was submitted by an exchange graduate student from Italy.

He was an officer in the Italian Air Force, and the instructor had expected him to ask for an alternate assignment because he did not have a clinical practice. When he turned in the assignment, he explained that although the Italian government had not been at war for many years, Italian soldiers are often sent into other countries as peacekeepers. During such deployments, a health care area is established for use by the peacekeepers. However, many displaced refugee families also frequent the peacekeepers' health care facility, and it was for these families that the student developed his family assessment tool. The first question the student posed to each member of these refugee families was "Are you afraid of me?" And so began one of the most sensitive family-focused assessment tools ever written for the course. Once an initial level of trust was achieved with each refugee family, the student went on to ask targeted Bowen theory–directed questions to one or more adults as the peacekeepers attempted to meet each family's shelter and health care needs. Questions included "Are all members of your family here?" "Who is missing?" "Do you know where they are?" "Have you made plans for communicating with them?" "Whose idea was it to leave your village?" "Did you have a choice?" and "Is anyone else in the family upset with your choice?"

For the final examination's second assignment, students are asked to take two Bowen theory concepts and apply them to their own lives and to their clinical work. The instructor has found this to be an excellent means to assess what students have and have not learned from the course, and this part of the examination provides an opportunity to offer students a final round of feedback. For example, one student, who selected and reflected on the Bowen theory concept of the emotional triangle, ended her paper by writing that she had now invested in caller ID because every time she answered the phone when a family member called, she found herself in yet another triangle. Offering feedback, the instructor discussed with the student the possibility of answering the phone and attempting to stay neutral about what family members were saying, at least some of the time, rather than not answering the phone at all.

Conclusion

Presenting Bowen theory in both undergraduate and graduate nursing curricula has been a formidable challenge that has become synchronous with the author continuing to learn and use the theory in both her family and professional relationships. Finding ways to live and present Bowen theory remains a never-ending endeavor, full of the same kinds of intellectual and emotional hurdles that constitute family life in general—problem solving, joy, humor, sadness, tediousness, puzzlement, and, at times, pain. The most productive learning tends to take place when students and faculty join each other in learning about self, their own families, and families for whom they care. An essential part of this learning process involves the author attempting to diligently keep her own passion for learning Bowen theory out of her students' way.

Throughout their family theory coursework, both undergraduate and graduate students are invited to adopt those aspects of Bowen theory that they find useful to their personal and professional lives. Students are encouraged to regard concepts they do not find useful personally, professionally, or both as general information that other scholars have found helpful. The author also encourages students to consider behaviors they observe in their own families, and in the families for whom they care professionally, as outcomes of family emotional process that have developed over many generations. Another principle the author conveys to students is that all families have strengths, even though these strengths might be difficult to recognize. Focusing on families' strengths appears to be a good method of counteracting the mindset of the "dysfunctional" family, a construct that labels a family negatively and assists both students and professionals to perceive a family as hopeless. It is much easier for students and professionals to engage with families when they can identify a family's strengths.

Interactions with these nursing students serve to enhance the author's efforts at learning Bowen theory in much the same way that her own family-of-origin work continues to inform her understanding of the theory. Students routinely challenge the author, the theory, and, most important, the clarity of the author's thinking. Through this reciprocal learning between the author and successive classes of students, she has developed several principled stances over time for engaging with students that include (a) keeping issues clear in one's head, (b) focusing on maintaining curiosity about relationships, (c) controlling anxiety about what students learn and do not learn, and (d) defining self in terms of where the responsibility for student learning resides. A portion of an unsolicited e-mail from a former graduate student reads as follows: "[The course coordinator] said I am the first instructor she has worked with who knows and understands family theory! See what you did for me!" Not all students emerge from their nursing programs with a similar attitude, but the students who are interested can learn and find that an understanding of Bowen theory can be useful in their careers for both teaching and caring for patients and families.

References

Angell, R. (1936). *The family encounters the depression.* New York, NY: Scribner.

Bourguignon, E. (1990). Competition and complementarity in the utilization of health resources in Africa. In K. Peltzer & O. Ebigbo (Eds.), *Clinical psychology in Africa* (pp. 107–115). Uwani-Enugu, Nigeria: Chuka Printing.

Bowen, M. (1978). *Family therapy in clinical practice.* New York, NY: Jason Aronson.

Bradt, J., & Moynihan, C. (1972). *Systems therapy: Selected papers: Theory, technique, research.* Washington, DC: Groome Child Guidance Center.

Carter, B., & McGoldrick, M. (1980). *The family life cycle: A framework for family therapy.* New York, NY: Gardner Press.

Carter, B. & McGoldrick, M. (1999). *The expanded family life cycle: Individual, family and social perspectives.* Boston, MA: Allyn and Bacon.

Ebigbo, P. (1990). The practice of family therapy in the University of Nigeria Teaching Hospital. In K. Peltzer & O. Ebigbo (Eds.), *Clinical psychology in Africa* (pp. 551–574). Uwani-Enugu, Nigeria: Chuka Printing.

Friedemann, M.-L. (1995). *The framework of systemic organization: A conceptual approach to families and nursing.* Thousand Oaks, CA: Sage.

Friedman, M. (1998). *Family nursing: Theory, research and practice.* Norwalk, CT: Appleton & Lange.

Gillis, C. (1991). Family nursing research theory and practice. *Image: Journal of Nursing Scholarship, 23,* 19–22.

Hill, R. (1949). *Families under stress.* New York, NY: Harper.

Janzen, J. (1978). *The quest for therapy in Lower Zaire.* Berkeley, CA: University of California Press.

Kerr, M. (2004). *One family's story: A primer on Bowen theory.* Washington, DC: Bowen Center for the Study of the Family/Georgetown Family Center.

Kerr, M. E., & Bowen, M. (1988). *Family evaluation: An approach based on Bowen theory.* New York, NY: W. W. Norton.

Kiev, A. (1990). Some psycho-therapeutic factors in traditional forms of healing. In K. Peltzer & O. Ebigbo (Eds.), *Clinical psychology in Africa* (pp. 437–444). Uwani-Enugu, Nigeria: Chuka Printing.

Lambo, T. (1964). Patterns of psychiatric care in developing African countries. In A. Kiev (Ed.), *Magic, faith, and healing* (pp. 443–453). New York, NY: Free Press of Glencoe.

Nzewi, E. (1990). Cultural factors in the classification of psychopathology in Nigeria. In K. Peltzer & O. Ebigbo (Eds.), *Clinical psychology in Africa* (pp. 208–216). Uwani-Enugu, Nigeria: Chuka Printing.

Papero, D. (1990). *Bowen family systems theory.* Boston, MA: Allyn & Bacon.

Romme, M. (1990). Culture and psychosocial disorder in Zimbabwe. In K. Peltzer & O. Ebigbo (Eds.), *Clinical psychology in Africa* (pp. 56–67). Uwani-Enugu, Nigeria: Chuka Printing.

Stone, L. (1990). *Family, sex, and marriage in England, 1500-1800.* New York, NY: HarperCollins.

Toman, W. (1974). *Family constellation: Its effects on personality and behavior.* New York, NY: Springer.

Wright, L., & Leahey, M. (2005). *A guide to family assessment and intervention.* Philadelphia, PA: F. A. Davis.

13
Thinking Systems in Pastoral Training

RANDALL T. FROST

Pastoral care and counseling have always borrowed from secular wisdom. Clebsch and Jaekle (1964), in their classic study *Pastoral Care in Historical Perspective*, wrote, "In every historical epoch, pastoring has utilized—and by utilizing has helped to advance and transform—the psychology or psychologies current in that epoch" (pp. 68–69). They went on to say, "Openness to new psychological theories and notions in fact represents and continues a powerful trend found in every age of pastoring" (p. 79). This author believe that Bowen family systems theory offers an especially cogent resource that can inform every type of ministry in our age.

Bowen (1978) wrote, "Family systems theory as I have defined it is a specific theory about human relationship functioning" (p. 359). The emphasis on relationship functioning sets Bowen theory apart from psychological theories that focus on the individual. Conceptualizing how patterns of relationships determine the functioning of individuals fits well with the religious heritage of Christians and Jews. Right relationship with God and neighbor lies at the heart of the Christian and Hebraic tradition. A theory built on facts of human functioning in relationships is far more consistent with that tradition than with theories that abstract individuals from the web of relationships in which they live. This chapter describes the author's approach to thinking (relationship) systems in the training of clergy, religious, and laity for pastoral ministry.

For more than 30 years, the author has presented Bowen theory to numerous audiences in a variety of pastoral settings. Whether the setting is a 1-day workshop, an academic course in a theological seminary, or a multiyear training program in a pastoral counseling center, the author attempts to provide as thorough and accurate an introduction to Bowen theory as possible. If students are going to consider using Bowen theory to inform their ministry, at a minimum they need an accurate intellectual understanding of the theory. Equally important to any effort to understand the theory is the effort to know the theory experientially. How does one foster a learning environment in which a student can begin to move from individual thinking toward systems thinking?[1]

---

[1] The phrase "toward systems thinking" is intended to reflect Bowen's view of the difficulty in moving from conventional thinking to systems thinking. He was not sure any of us can ever shift all the way to thinking systems about our own behavior (Bowen, 1978, p. 415).

One way to begin to think toward systems is for trainees to read Bowen's (1978) early clinical descriptions of the families who lived on the research ward of the hospital at the National Institute of Mental Health. These observations of how family members related to one another provided the impetus for Bowen to begin thinking about the family as an emotional unit. Anxiety was not simply a property of individual members of the family, but was transferred from one family member to another. Moreover, the patterns by which anxiety was transferred were predictable. Often, one member's anxiety went down as the anxiety he or she was experiencing was transferred to another member of the family, whose anxiety then went up. The intensity of the emotional attachments between family members stood out as well. The intensity of the attachment between mothers and young adult schizophrenic offspring was influenced by the shifting character of the relationship between the parents and the functioning of nonsymptomatic siblings. The fluidity of the transfer of anxiety among family members and the way in which the intensity of attachments among family members was influenced by the larger family unit helped Bowen to reconceptualize schizophrenia as a process in the family as a whole that came to manifest itself as schizophrenic symptoms in one member of the family.

In longer programs, students follow the gradual development of the theory as it grew out of the initial observations of the actual functioning of the research families (Bowen, 1978). Linking research observations with the subsequent development of theoretical concepts is another way for trainees to develop a more accurate understanding of theory. Because the initial observations were supplemented by studies of families with less severe problems and then with families without diagnosable symptoms, Bowen defined multiple variables to account for the variation in how different family units function under stress. The eight concepts of the theory interlock with each other such that each concept influences and is influenced by the others. For example, the functional level of differentiation of a family cannot be estimated apart from the level of anxiety in the family, the degree of emotional cutoff from the family of origin, or the intensity of the triangling process. The author endeavors to convey how each concept of the theory interlocks with each of the other concepts by writing each concept on a whiteboard, explaining not only the concept but also the way in which its variables reciprocally influence the variables that make up each of the other concepts of the theory. To think systems about the family as an emotional unit requires an ability to keep all the variables in mind at once.

The central concept of Bowen theory is *differentiation of self.* Bowen (1978) wrote, "The core of my theory has to do with the degree to which people are able to distinguish between the feeling process and the intellectual process" (p. 355). Early in the research, Bowen's team found "that the parents of schizophrenic people, who appear on the surface to function well, have difficulty distinguishing between the subjective feeling process and the more objective thinking process" (p. 355), especially in a close relationship. Learning to recognize variation in the degree to which feelings and intellect are either fused with or more differentiated from each other is a crucial distinction for trainees to be able to make. One way the author tries to get at this distinction is to ask students to define the differences between someone who is

Principled............and someone who is .... rigid
Flexible ....and someone who is .... wishy-washy
Responsive ....and someone who is .... reactive
Committed...........and someone who is .... dependent
Objective ....and someone who is .... cold[2]

People usually describe the term on the left as representing the capacity to be more thoughtful and entailing a degree of choice in how one responds. Terms on the left also capture characteristics of people who appear less governed by emotional pressure from others, whereas terms on the right describe people whose functioning is more influenced by others. Students can also recognize that when any of us is more anxious, we tend to veer toward the set of terms on the right. This exercise demonstrates that the core of the concept of differentiation is embedded in everyday language and experience. Every aspect of training requires ongoing grappling with this essential distinction between the thinking and the feeling processes.

Learning about the distinction between the feeling process and the intellectual process is far more than an intellectual exercise. Critical to any effort to understand the theory is the effort to know the theory experientially. The author has found that the most valuable learning in this regard takes place when trainees begin to work on their own differentiation of self in their families of origin. When trainees begin to make more contact with their original family and begin to observe their own ability to separate the thinking and feeling processes while relating to members of their family, theory comes alive. Now trainees begin to experience the difference between being "in it" emotionally and being more "outside" the family's emotional field. They can begin to see how triangles operate and their own participation in taking sides in the family's emotional triangles. Trainees also experience the influence of anxiety on their ability to be more of a defined self while in active contact with family members. Theoretical concepts take on flesh and blood as trainees attempt to learn more about their own family and work to become more responsible people in their family's emotional field. Learning more facts about the multigenerational history of the family is part of the

---

[2] These terms came to the author's attention from a videotape of a workshop conducted by Rabbi Edwin Friedman at St. Elizabeth's Hospital Protestant Chaplains Section, Washington, DC, in 1973.

effort toward a better level of differentiation. The author always presents his own family and highlights of his own effort toward differentiation before asking students to present their family diagram and their initial efforts toward a better understanding of emotional process in their own families. Trainees are expected to relate to their families of origin whenever possible in ways guided by theory. Trainees report on their efforts toward differentiation in both individual and group supervision.

Trainees also experience differentiation through how the trainer manages self with them. The trainer assumes responsibility for designing the program and for the quality of his or her own teaching and supervising. Interns and students are expected to assume responsibility for their own learning. In the 1st year of the training program in marriage and family therapy and pastoral counseling that the author directs, trainees read most of Bowen's (1978) book *Family Therapy in Clinical Practice* and Kerr and Bowen's (1988) *Family Evaluation*. In the 2nd year, they typically read Daniel Papero's (1990) *Bowen Family Systems Theory*, among other books and articles. The author prepares a set of study questions for each reading assignment that helps to focus discussion of the assigned chapters. Students are expected to come prepared with their answers to the study questions along with any other comments or questions stirred by the reading. The author seeks to minimize group process by asking each trainee to interact with him while the others listen. This method of teaching and supervising parallels the way a systems therapist works with a couple or family. Each family member converses with the therapist while the other family members listen. Adopting the same structure for teaching and supervising in a group uses the triangle constructively to promote a more thoughtful process of teaching and learning. When the trainer and a trainee interact with each other, the rest of the group is in the outside position of the triangle. This structure helps to create a calmer environment in which each person can listen more carefully to what others are saying before putting in his or her own thinking. The emphasis is on trainees contributing their best thinking. If a trainee goes after the emotional side of an issue, it can provide an opportunity for learning by the entire group if the trainer–supervisor shifts back to a more objective thinking process. This approach is quite in contrast to some forms of clinical pastoral training that intentionally accentuate group process and actively promote a more intense feeling process in the group.

Another way in which the author fosters the process of differentiation is by assigning short papers in which trainees define what they believe regarding a matter of importance to them. The trainees are asked to reflect on the origin of the belief and to what extent the belief is based on fact. How much has the trainee uncritically accepted the opinions of family, friends, church, or society without thinking the belief through for self? After examining how they arrived at the belief and how much the belief is based on fact, trainees are asked to write what they now believe after having thought it through separately from what they are "supposed" to believe.[3] This process occurs again and again as a person works on differentiation. Trainees have found that this exercise can represent a useful first step in their individual efforts to define self more clearly. The next step toward differentiation is taking action that is consistent with the better-defined belief in their important relationships.

The author encourages trainees to question any aspect of Bowen theory based on their own thinking and whatever factual information they can adduce for alternative ways of thinking about human behavior. Bowen theory is not dogma. The questioning process is healthy for the student, the trainer–supervisor, and ultimately the theory itself. Bowen was asked to serve on the Curriculum Committee at the Georgetown University School of Medicine when he first joined the faculty there. The committee was supposed to evaluate the curriculum for possible revision. Bowen suggested they reorganize the curriculum around what the faculty did not know instead of around what they thought they knew. By clarifying the boundary between what is known and what is not known, Bowen thought the students would learn more. By questioning and challenging the theory, students learn the theory more accurately.

A major paper at the end of each year of training is required in which trainees report on their efforts to investigate any question or topic they wish in relation to Bowen theory. The papers are then presented to the entire group of trainees and clinicians at the center. During the year, each student is also asked to choose a concept from the theory, write a short paper on it, and then teach the concept to the training group, including the implications for family therapy or pastoral ministry. Papers, class presentations, and discussions challenge the trainees to do their own thinking about what they are learning. When the trainer–supervisor can respect the self of each trainee while presenting his or her own thinking as clearly as possible, trainer and trainee engage in a reciprocal process of learning that benefits both. As the trainer–supervisor focuses on managing self according to systems thinking and theory, he or she helps to foster an experiential awareness of differentiation through the educational process itself.

Bowen strove to think toward the biological life sciences.[4] He chose terms in his theory that are also used in the biological sciences (e.g., *differentiation* and *fusion*) to facilitate a process of making conceptual contact with the life sciences. Ultimately, his goal was to contribute to the development of a

---

[3] This assignment is modeled after "belief papers" that Bowen assigned when the author was in the advanced special postgraduate training program at the Georgetown University Family Center from 1980 to 1981.

[4] The phrase "think toward the biological sciences" reflects Bowen's view that to think in the direction of the biological sciences represents a long-term process that will extend indefinitely into the future.

science of human behavior. Accordingly, trainees are assigned readings in areas of the natural sciences that bear on the concepts of the theory. Trainees read authors such as Robert Sapolsky and Bruce McEwen, who study the stress response in humans and other creatures. Much of the very valuable research on the response to stress has centered on the physiology of the individual. Family systems theory, with its focus on the family as an emotional unit, describes how the unit functions to determine which member or members of the family end up carrying more of the physiological response to stressors. From a systems perspective, the intensity and duration of the stress response for each individual is heavily influenced by how family members interact within the triangles of the unit. For pastors, this awareness can be invaluable in how they think about and minister to families in which one member or one relationship appears to be carrying a disproportionate level of the anxiety in the unit.

Trainees have also been assigned readings by neuroscientists such as Paul MacLean, Jaak Panksepp, and Joseph LeDoux, whose work lends broad support to Bowen's idea that the human brain must integrate emotional and intellectual functioning. Bowen, with his concept of differentiation, went further to suggest that individual humans vary in the degree to which intellectual centers of the brain can retain relative autonomy from emotional centers in periods of heightened tension. This line of research on the natural sciences and Bowen theory raises intriguing questions about how ministries of religious education, homiletics, and pastoral care and counseling may contribute to parishioners' thinking through for themselves what they believe. When clergy and laity more clearly define a set of life principles on which to act, even in situations of high anxiety and duress, they may gradually raise their functioning level of differentiation and enhance their ability to live out their faith.

In pastoral settings, the author provides trainees with opportunities to think theologically about Bowen theory and about pastoral ministry that is informed by Bowen theory. This presents a challenge for the author and for trainees because Bowen, as noted earlier, was thinking toward the natural sciences as he conceptualized the theory, not toward theology. Recognizing this, the author makes an effort to think from the theory toward theology without distorting either Bowen theory or theology. Typically, this means acknowledging both points of overlap and points of discontinuity between theology and Bowen theory.

The work of theologian and ethicist Richard Niebuhr provides one example of overlap between theology and Bowen theory. Niebuhr (1963) suggested that the most recent symbol that has emerged to organize discussion of ethical behavior has been the image of the responsible self. "The image of responsibility," said Niebuhr (1963, pp. 60–61), "asks in every moment of decision, 'What is going on?'" and then seeks the "fitting response," the action that "fits into a total [pattern] of interaction as response and as anticipation of further response." Bowen theory contributes to a better understanding of responsibility through its careful discrimination between emotional and intellectual functioning in relationship systems. Responsibility suggests the ability to respond. To be able to respond, one has to be able to step back from the ebb and flow of events and think. Responsibility has a considered, deliberative quality. However, it also requires some accuracy about what is really going on in human relationship systems.

Systems thinking offers a way to think about human behavior that seeks to minimize subjectivity, the human tendency to generate explanations out of our heads that may have little to do with what is going on. By focusing on what happens, and how, when, and where it happens, systems thinkers strive to separate fact from opinion. Keeping a focus on what people do rather than on a verbal explanation about why they do what they do brings thinking closer to fact. The more thinking takes into account facts of human functioning, the more the response of the human can fit with the way things are in the situation at hand. The more objective our thinking, the more considered the response can be. The quality of thinking affects the quality of the response.

Systems thinking can help pastors avoid the mistake of "blaming" a person with a symptom for the whole of the problem. If the family is an emotional system in which every important member plays a part in a problem, then careful attention to the patterns of relationships in the family can contribute to each person coming to a better understanding of the part self plays. Parents of an acting-out teenager often contribute to the teen's behavior with an anxious focus on the problem. A pastoral minister can help parents look at ways in which their behavior exacerbates the problem. This exacerbation can include patterns of emotional distance in the marriage and emotional cutoff from the family of origin. There is an important difference between taking responsibility for the part self plays in a problem and blaming self or other. Blaming is an emotional reaction. Taking responsibility for self is a cognitive effort to identify the part self plays and to control it. Knowing the difference between the thinking process that goes into taking responsibility for self and the feeling process that goes into taking the blame is an example of what Bowen meant by *differentiation of self*. Members of a church or synagogue can set good goals for themselves, their family, and their community of faith, and they can clarify worthy principles to live by, but anxious emotional process will subvert the best of goals and undermine the most worthy of principles. The responsible self is only responsible to the degree that self can learn to respond instead of react.

Bowen himself provided a bridge from the concept of differentiation to an important theme of Christian piety when he presented a paper in 1987 at a conference on theology. In his paper, Bowen stated, "A major quality in the differentiation-of-self is complete selflessness in which 'doing for others' replaces personal selfish goals. Jesus Christ has been a model for total selfless-ness" (Carolin, 1990, p. 14). He went on to say:

> A well differentiated self in families has to get beyond the selfish pro-motion of self. One has always to be aware of "the other". To slavishly duplicate another, without due consideration of self, is a "no self." Automatically to oppose the other, without thought, is another "no self" trap that involves many. A self is assembled in relation to others, par-ticularly around emotional reactivity with the other. A model based on the lives of others can be a guide if the model is always a model and is never divorced from thinking. When selflessness is motivated by the feeling process, it can create predictable complications. When selfless-ness becomes a thinking model, largely separate from the feeling pro-cess, it can become a vehicle for a special form of differentiation. With that orientation, true selflessness, devoid of selfishness, can become part of the differentiation itself. (Carolin, 1990, p. 15)

Piety can be described as "that which unifies the specific acts and atti-tudes of the Christian life. A person's piety is a pattern of being and doing that arises out of a specific interpretation of the gospel" (Farley, 1966, p. 17). Sometimes, religious piety can emphasize the importance of doing for others at the expense of one's own perceived self-interest. Such efforts to do for others that are dictated by feelings of guilt, anxiety, or religious obligation will often make matters worse, both for others and for self. When one feels driven to act by a feeling process, choice is lost, and one can lose self in the process of trying to help others. A more thoughtful effort to lend a hand and to "be on the side of the other doing well" (M. Bowen, personal communication, March 17, 1985) can become a "special form of differentiation," according to Bowen. When people choose selflessness on the basis of carefully considered beliefs or prin-ciples and a reasonably objective assessment of the situation, they can become more solid as people and genuinely contribute to the well-being of others.

One of the discontinuities between Bowen theory and theology is the ques-tion of God. Theology assumes the existence of God. Bowen theory does not. At a broad level, Bowen theory can be said to be neutral about the existence or nonexistence of God. As an effort toward science, the theory per se does not take a position on the existence of God one way or the other. What the theory does provide is a rich opportunity for students to rethink what it means to live out one's faith. For example, all students gather facts about their multi-generational families and draw a family diagram based on nodal events. Some interns have taken it further and pursued a religious history of their family, noting important religious events and the possible impact of ancestors' reli-gious beliefs on family emotional process. Thinking through one's religious beliefs in the context of current family emotional process is another way to think systems. Some interns have worked to bridge emotional cutoffs in their family or invited the black sheep to family events, in part out of religious conviction. Other interns take theory and use it to analyze current congregational "landmines of anxiety" based on the congregation's history. Churches, like families, have a multigenerational history that can illuminate present troubles. One pastor required all of her lay leaders to take two courses taught by her, one on the Bible and the other on family systems theory. She said family systems training gave the leaders a common language to talk about emotional process in the church and a different way to think about their own part in it.

Bowen's effort to think toward the natural sciences has a number of important implications for thinking systems in pastoral training. His ability to see humans on a continuum with all of life introduces a breadth of thinking that keeps the theory open to new knowledge. An unintended by-product of Bowen's effort is that it can also broaden a theological understanding of human behavior beyond the contributions of conventional social science research. By focusing on common biological roots of human behavior, Bowen theory provides an ecumenical approach that transcends culture. As one example, interns from widely disparate cultures have found Bowen theory concepts applicable to their own families and the families of people from their cultures. Finally, the focus on science has led to the development of a research component for the internship program. Interns are encouraged to do research projects using Bowen theory to generate hypotheses and methodology that are consistent with systems thinking. The effort to think toward science and toward theology in pastoral settings seeks to evoke a sense of responsibility in interns to contribute to, as well as receive, knowledge about human behavior from a systems perspective.

References

Bowen, M. (1978). *Family therapy in clinical practice.* Northvale, NJ: Jason Aronson.

Carolin, J. (1990). The theoretical structure of the Catholic church. In J. Carolin (Ed.), *Systems and spirituality: Bowen family systems theory, faith, and theology* (pp. 10–15). Available from J. Carolin, Box 201, South Mountain, PA 17261.

Clebsch, W., & Jaekle, C. (1964). *Pastoral care in historical perspective.* Englewood Cliffs, NJ: Prentice-Hall.

Farley, E. (1966). *Requiem for a lost piety: The contemporary search for the Christian life.* Philadelphia, PA: Westminster Press.

Kerr, M. E., & Bowen, M. (1988). *Family evaluation: An approach based on Bowen theory.* New York, NY: W. W. Norton.

Niebuhr, H. R. (1963). *The responsible self: An essay in Christian moral philosophy.* San Francisco, CA: Harper & Row.

Papero, D. (1990). *Bowen family systems theory.* Boston, MA: Allyn & Bacon.

14
Across the Generations: The Training of Clergy and Congregations

MICKIE W. CRIMONE and DOUGLAS HESTER

The word *leadership* is often overused in the organizational literature. Yet, without a doubt, there is a crisis in most of our current institutions. Churches, mosques, temples, or synagogues are not an exception. Clergy of all denominations can have a profound effect on the health and welfare of their congregants. Clergy frequently believe it is their job to "save" congregants. They are often the focus of intense anxiety generated by the congregation. Like many leaders, clergy find themselves trying harder with little success. Their focus is on the parishioner rather than on defining a self, which can lead to a continuing cycle of burnout in the clergy.

Bowen family systems theory postulates that emotional process in families crosses and is passed on from one generation to the next. The work done by any member of a family to define a self may have a positive effect not only on the individual but also on the larger family system. Edwin Friedman, DD, was a pulpit rabbi in the Washington, DC, area. Like most clergy, he watched families grow and change while ministering to them across the life cycle. Clergy participate in their congregants' birth, coming-of-age, marriage, and death rituals. Friedman's interest in the functioning of his congregation led him to study Bowen theory.

Many of Friedman's clients were pastors with similar experiences regarding family functioning with their congregations. To avoid using more jargon, Friedman tended to use *self-definition* or *self-regulation* as a synonym for Bowen's term *differentiation of self.* He postulated that clergy need to define a self in their congregations and in their own families if they are to be successful leaders. Friedman built on Bowen theory to focus on leadership through self-differentiation. He argued that how a leader functions has a profound influence on the system, much more than any expertise or technique (Friedman, 1985, p. 229). Leaders lead by the nature of their presence—who they are, not what they do. No leader, moreover, dwells in a single system. Emotional process is the same in families and organizations, and issues in one system can trigger symptoms in another. Friedman taught that leaders must constantly monitor both their family and organizational systems.

Mickie W. Crimone originally learned systems theory from Philip Guerin, Thomas Fogerty, and Ann Cain, all early trainees of Bowen and each having a unique approach to the theory. She began coaching with Friedman in the early 1970s and eventually began teaching in his clergy seminars. She continues today as faculty at the Center for Family Process and coaches clergy of many denominations from across the country. It was equally as important for her to work on the issues in her family of origin as she coached the clergy to define a self in their families and churches. With Friedman first as a coach and then as a colleague, Crimone learned as much as she taught clergy participants. As a Christian layperson learning from a rabbi and teaching various clergy and other professionals, she found the universality of systems thinking striking. The various denominations can be thought of as a cultural lens affecting how an individual views the world. Each denomination has unique beliefs, yet the relationships among the clergy, their families, the congregants, and the faith communities remain the same.

The consultant-to-clergy, clergy-to-congregation families process illustrates how systems thinking is transmitted by means of a ripple effect from person to person and system to system across several generations of Bowen theory learners. This transmission of a new way of thinking across generations of learners has similarities to the Bowen theory concept of *multigenerational transmission process* in families in that emotional processes are passed along from one generation of learners to the next. To the extent to which the authors are able to keep their own families in their heads and work on their own differentiation of self while working with clergy consultees, the process of learning extends into the congregations and its members.

Clergy often have an uncanny interest in and ability to learn systems thinking and Bowen theory because they (a) know and work with multiple generations of many families across these families' life cycles, (b) are involved in numerous facets of their congregants' family lives, (c) interact with families during times of high stress—both joyous and sad, and (d) learn about their own family interactions and emotional process through what they observe in their congregant families (Friedman, 1985, p. 197). Family process becomes like a movie unfolding before the clergy. In a day, it is not unusual for clergy to officiate at the marriage of a parishioner whom they baptized 20 years before, counsel a couple having difficulties, and sit with a grieving family. The family life cycle plays out before them. Other professionals may concentrate on a specific population, but clergy touch people's entire lives.

In addition, the pulpit can be a major force in developing mature thinking. By transmitting what they have learned about systems thinking and theory to their congregants, clergy further reinforce and apply systems thinking to their own lives.

The awareness of the power and responsibility of the clergy's office is not without challenge. Many clergy confuse the Bowen theory practice of defining self with being selfish. This confusion often occurs because clergy frequently believe that they are responsible for saving the world, which predisposes them to overfunctioning for others. It prevents them from seeing the value in clarifying stances for self, prompting them to respond instead to the anxiety in the organization. It also makes clergy susceptible to getting on a treadmill of trying harder when things do not work and ultimately results in their ministries becoming identified with calming the anxiety of the moment (Friedman, 1999/2007, p. 176).

Here is a story to illustrate these principles.

A young clergyman who had been in a staff position had only recently returned to the pastorate. His new church had a reputation for being difficult, but he thought it would be a challenge. In the beginning, the minister did have a tendency to try too hard and respond to everyone's needs. He worked on this and began to define himself and handle the predictable sabotage. Perhaps things were going too well. At the beginning of his 2nd year, he decided to get married. The minister went away for a week to visit his fiancée. On the Sunday he returned, two women announced they were leaving the congregation, declaring that "he isn't fit to be a minister." The anxiety in the system started to climb and initiated a series of events culminating in the minister wanting to leave. The anxiety of the system was clouding his ability to think. In response to the attacks, all he could do was react and try to defend himself.

What happened to this minister? His vision got lost in the congregation's chronic anxiety. The implication of impropriety, even when not based on fact, is enough to get any congregation upset. A series of questions began to clarify the situation. Although the minister had told the senior layman of his marriage plans, no one else in the church "knew." But of course they knew, in the way kids in a family know something is happening. The two women who left the congregation were divorcees who were losing their fantasy husband. On an emotional level, the pastor's pending marriage threatened the church with a decrease of his attention (see Figure 14.1).

This story illustrates not only the personal lure of overfunctioning for the clergyperson, but also that the very nature of their work has clergy participating in three intense *interlocking triangles*: (a) in their own families, (b) within parishioner or congregation families, and (c) with the congregation itself, as an *emotional system*. In this story, all three triangles are affecting the clergyman and each of the other triangles. The clergyman and his family relationships were shifting as a result of his upcoming nuptials and decreased focus on the church, which allowed the women to become disruptive. The interlocking nature of the triangles of the pastor, his fiancée, congregants, and the church as a whole allowed the anxiety to flow from one part of the triangle

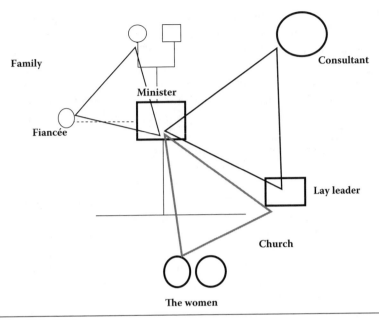

Figure 14.1 Minister genogram.

to the next. The shifting of these triangles was all it took to ignite the church members' chronic anxiety. Overfunctioning in any one of these three interlocking triangles can result in burnout as clergy become caught between emotional systems, with problems in one emotional system creating difficulties in other emotional systems. Enhancing this vulnerability to overfunctioning and burnout is that clergy lead the very people who have the power to hire and fire them.

How tempting for the consultant to be helpful. Overfunctioning is one of the most significant challenges clergy consultants face as they strive to retain their own self-regulation focus. It is as easy for the consultant, as for the clergy, to be caught up in the immediacy of the issues and with the chronic anxiety of the church. The focus on other rather than self can easily become a feedback loop between the consultant and the clergyperson. Friedman always emphasized the importance of managing self, which is an underlying theme of the seminars both for the consultant when working with the seminar participants and for the clergy with their congregations.

It is always easier to focus on others than to face one's own functioning (or lack of it). Working hard and meaning well, we get caught in the content, we see nothing but the need to fix a problem, or we blame clients or organizations for their resistance. It is difficult to monitor oneself and take leadership of the family, organization, or treatment session. It is also essential.

Leadership always takes place in an emotional field, and leaders can only navigate that challenging terrain if they can draw on a well-defined self. The ability to lead is directly proportional to one's willingness to define a self in the family of origin. Whatever the issue, shifting the focus to one's own family can clear the head, illumine previously unsuspected patterns, and strengthen the leader to act in new ways. That is what self-defining leadership is all about. Douglas Hester demonstrates this as a next-generation learner and teacher.

Hester's entrée into systems thinking came about through his reading of Friedman's (1985) book *Generation to Generation* in the late 1980s and his study of marriage and family therapy at St. Mary's University in San Antonio, Texas. He had been serving as a Lutheran parish pastor since 1980 and wanted to do more work in the area of pastoral care as a counselor in the church. After he discussed Friedman's book and his own course work at St. Mary's with area clergy, a number of colleagues came to him asking whether he would be willing to do some leadership training with them to apply some of these systems concepts to their work with families in the church and expressing their desire to become better leaders in the church. In the early 1990s, an initial group consisting of 10 Lutheran clergy began meeting monthly for 3 hours to discuss these concepts and to present their own family-of-origin work. As other area clergy heard about the group, they asked whether they might also participate.

In 1994, Hester received a brochure about Friedman's training program at the Center for Family Process in Bethesda, Maryland, and decided it would be a great opportunity to do further work in his development as a budding systems thinker and to deal with some of his own family and work systems issues. It was then that he came into contact with Crimone, who became his systems coach. With her coaching in his family-of-origin and work systems, and Friedman's focus on leadership through self-differentiation, Hester has been able to grow in his own ability to think systems. He has been able to work on his own differentiation of self in his family of origin as the younger of two sons and become more of an objective observer of emotional processes in the family. For example, he has become particularly aware of the reciprocal processes that occurred over the years between his mother and brother and how his mother presented as much of a problem for his brother as his brother presented for his mother, even though the family myth was that his brother was the problem. He has also become aware of how he participated in the triangle between his mother and brother and was thus a part of the problem. With the coaching of Friedman and Crimone, he was able to reposition himself in his family of origin by no longer playing the role of family chaplain.

Another part of the family myth was that Hester and his brother were as different as night and day and that Hester was the "good kid" who went on to seminary while his brother could not get his life together. Over the years, Hester had functioned in his family as an overresponsible youngest brother. Friedman once referred to Hester and his brother as the "straight arrow" and the crooked arrow. He once commented to Hester that "if you would just get a little more crooked, your brother would straighten up some." Armed with that comment after a visit to the Center for Family Process, Hester set out to reposition himself in his family of origin. He became a bit more perverse with his comments and irreverent at times in which he would be asked to put on his more reverent side. In fact, there were times when he became almost devilish. He was able to see the reciprocal processes going on between his brother and himself. By moving a few steps in his brother's direction and debunking the family myth about the two brothers, he was able to reposition himself with his mother by getting a little more distance, which actually allowed him to have a closer relationship with his mother.

Through his work in his family of origin, Hester was able to also see the reciprocal processes going on at the church where he was serving. He had been functioning in an overresponsible way in a triangle with the senior pastor and another staff member (similar to the triangle in his family with his mother and brother). He had been managing his anxiety by means of distance and avoidance. Hester began to reposition himself in the triangle at work as well. This view of reciprocity has enabled him to be a more responsible self rather than being responsible for others.

It was also during this time that Hester was working to redefine his position on the church staff where he was serving. After 13 years as associate pastor to the congregation, he was now finished with his studies, licensed as a marriage and family therapist, and ready to begin the counseling ministry at the church. Although there was a good deal of support at the beginning of this process, after he obtained his license, some of the church leadership changed and support lessened. He was also about to change from associate pastor to assistant pastor for counseling. With this change in call, Hester would become totally self-supporting financially, which would allow the congregation to call a new associate pastor to fill the vacated position. This also meant that his role with congregants would change from doing some of the everyday ministry tasks such as preaching, teaching, and visitation to a more defined role of counseling. This change in his call, and in his relationship role with the congregation, stirred a fair amount of anxiety in the congregation, as could be expected. Also during this time, Hester's brother was diagnosed with cancer, and his prognosis was not good.

A series of town-hall meetings was set up by the church leadership for members to come to voice concerns and ask questions about the change, because this was a new venture for the congregation. At the first of these meetings, which was held in 1998, one member suggested, "I don't know why the pastor continues to go chasing after some dead rabbi." Hester was a bit confused by this comment because he was not sure whether the congregant meant Jesus or Rabbi Friedman (this would have been about 2 years after Rabbi Friedman had died). A comment made by another congregant was that she felt as though the church were being cheated on, as though the pastor was having an affair by not doing his work. Again, these comments signaled a significant shift in the congregation's emotional processes.

During this time, it became apparent that Hester's brother was dying. For 4 months, Hester traveled once a week to see his brother in a hospital about 2 hours away from his home. It was difficult to monitor the family and the congregational systems with so much going on in both. Hester's brother died in August 1998. Crimone's coaching was extremely useful in navigating these uncharted waters. As it turned out, Hester stayed on in the congregation as assistant pastor for counseling for another 3 years and developed his counseling ministry program and the leadership classes based on Friedman's ideas about self-differentiated leadership. Again, without the lens of Bowen theory and Friedman's leadership ideas, it is doubtful that Hester would have been able to hold on to his nerve during such an anxiety-filled time as a shift in his call at church while his brother was dying.

Hester has seen an evolution in his own training of clergy over 16 years in which more than 400 clergy from 12 denominations and two faith traditions, as well as numerous leaders from the other helping professions, have participated in his groups across Texas and Arkansas. These groups include clergy who are just beginning their ministries, clergy who have been in parish ministry for more than 30 years, and even some retirees. Many of the more experienced clergy have reported that they wish they had come into contact with systems thinking when they were first starting out in parish ministry. Some of the newer clergy just starting out in ministry have reported that they read a book on systems theory, or perhaps it was presented as a kind of technique along with other counseling techniques that they learned in seminary. Very few have reported that there was much depth explored with systems theory. In most cases, the seminary professor teaching the class had not done much, if anything, in terms of his or her own family-of-origin work. It seems to Hester that many of the newer clergy who have come into contact with Bowen theory try to apply the theory to others rather than to themselves.

The classes offered by Hester meet once a month for 9 months, September through May. It has not been unusual for him to hear each September from returning class members that over the summer months they have missed the ongoing monthly contact with the theory. These comments have confirmed Hester's notion that ongoing contact with theory is vital to leaders today who are in what he likes to call the "splash zone of anxiety." It is easy for clergy, although not unique to them, to feel lonely and unappreciated in their leadership roles. Hester often likes to ask clergy in his classes, "Of the folks who served on your interview committee, how many of them are still members of your congregation 2 years later?" Many clergy report 50% or less. What is that about? How is it that the very things you heard from members of the interview committee and that you thought you were being called to do are the very things you seem to get criticized for? How is it that when you begin to pay too much attention to one part of the system, another part of the system begins to act out? Many of the clergy in the classes have reported that they think that Hester is talking about their congregations. It seems to be the nature of systems, however, that they have some of these commonalities. It is a natural part of life.

As stated before, clergy in particular have a unique interest in wanting to learn systems thinking and Bowen theory because they know and work with multiple generations of many families across those families' life cycles. In his own experience of 30 years of ministry, Hester has observed families at times of higher-level functioning and at times of lower-level functioning around these events. Knowing something about the history of these families from other ministry opportunities has proven to be extremely useful in working with them through such experiences. More important, Hester's own work on differentiation of self has provided him with a way to deal with the often seductive emotional processes that tend to hook one into the family's own unresolved issues. Being able to manage self, think systems, and observe emotional processes in these families has proven useful to these families in trying to work through difficult times. Hester has found that families become intrigued with systems thinking and want to know more. The interest in this way of thinking provides an opportunity for clergy to transmit what they have learned about systems thinking to their congregants and to be able to further apply systems thinking to their own lives and their own efforts at differentiation of self. When clergy can use a Bowen theory lens for viewing the church and the world, they tend to develop more mature perspectives about their leadership. They begin to see how differentiation in the leader begins to promote differentiation throughout the system they are leading, which often has a more positive influence on their congregation's health as systems concepts are passed on to and through many people. Clergy are able to use these concepts not only to lead, but also in other areas such as preaching, worship, teaching, counseling, and administration. Their work on differentiation of self even has an impact on their own health issues.

One of the early lessons Hester learned from Friedman and Crimone was the need to continually observe one's own family, one's work system, and the families in the system because they are all interconnected. The emotional processes in one are identical to those in the other two. On a practical level, this means that it is necessary for a leader to do his or her own family-of-origin work to be aware of the zapping effects of emotional processes in the work system. How one functions in one's family of origin influences how one functions in one's work system as a leader.

Hester came to realize through his own family-of-origin work how his overfunctioning role in his family was contributing to his overfunctioning as a leader in his church. As he began to reposition himself in the triangles with other staff, he began to get a lot of negative feedback from them. As the emotional processes in his family of origin were shifting, so were the emotional processes in his work system. One of Hester's most significant challenges during these times was retaining his self-regulation focus. He was able to keep in mind Friedman's challenge of hearing criticism as applause. Hester told the people who were highly critical of him that he appreciated how much they had missed him. Friedman's comment that criticism is a form of pursuit was useful.

Bowen theory provides clergy with a framework for clear thinking as they deal with chronic anxiety in all their emotional systems. This was another lesson that Hester has been able to pass on in the training he provides for clergy. The processes and learning transmitted to these clergy through their training are taken back into the congregation and practiced and then followed up the next month by processing what they did, with the focus being on their own self-regulation. Parallels to these experiences are also drawn to their functioning in their family of origin. By reporting their experiences each month, they are able to have ongoing contact with systems thinking that in turn affects the congregation they are leading. The clergy in the training programs Hester offers are encouraged to also examine their congregations as emotional systems. As they take a research stance with their congregations, they are able to get a more objective view of the emotional processes surrounding the congregations. By asking questions about the history of the congregation and their predecessors, they are able to obtain some factual information and to understand how the congregation has functioned as an emotional system.

The primary focus of the leadership training for clergy is based on Friedman's principle that the key to leadership is not how leaders manage others, but how leaders manage themselves. The notion of leadership through one's presence is difficult to hear. Some clergy hear that as too simplistic or that there has to be more to leadership. Clergy frequently believe that leadership has more to do with what they do, or what they know, than with who they are. There is a tendency to overfunction for others, which often leads to frustration, a loss of energy, and in some cases, a desire to leave the ministry. This overfunctioning position also prevents many clergy from seeing the value in clarifying their own position. The focus is often on how to change others. Both of us emphasize the need to clearly define one's position, manage one's own anxiety, and stay connected to the system one is trying to lead.

One outcome of Hester's clergy training is that he often gets asked to do further one-on-one coaching with class members. Many of these clergy are struggling with congregational issues (the organist is fighting with the altar guild about using a portion of the closet the altar guild has had all to themselves for years; the youth director is being attacked for storing leftover snacks from the last youth meeting in the refrigerator; the secretary had too many typing errors in the Sunday bulletin) that are draining their energy and consuming their time. Some are dealing with difficult pastoral counseling issues for which they want some coaching. Still others are struggling with their call to ministry and trying to think through their options. The focus of clergy when anxiety intensifies is often on how to change others rather than how to manage themselves. The questions asked by Hester in such struggles are "Who is this person [the one getting under the clergyperson's skin] in your family? And what gives him or her such power?" Many of the clergy can identify that their reaction to a troublesome congregant is similar to their reaction to their own mother, or their reaction to a staff member is like the reaction they have to their own father. In such instances, they are often encouraged to go back into their family and ask their mother's advice on how to deal with such congregational members or ask their father's advice on how to deal with such staff matters. A significant number of clergy will report that they have calmed down significantly after such conversations with family members. Other clergy dealing with significant congregational issues are often asked what they do for themselves or about their hobbies or play. What do they do for fun? Do they take their days off? In Hester's experience, many clergy have a kind of blank stare when asked about such self-care. It is almost as though it would be selfish to take care of self. And yet defining a self is crucial to leadership. As Friedman used to say, "A self is more attractive than a no-self."

Clergy trainees tend to draw parallels between systems thinking and theological concepts. Although Bowen theory is not a theological construct, it has been Hester's experience that clergy find it a bit easier to hear Bowen theory when it is considered from a theological perspective. Although a familiarity with biblical history or theology is not a prerequisite for understanding systems thinking or Bowen theory, it does offer insights into the functioning of families and larger systems over multiple generations and addresses how people define themselves while relating to others in their emotional systems. The biblical story, like Bowen theory, is a story about life and relationships. It is a story about how anxiety and reactivity are transmitted through relationships. Both systems theory and biblical history involve "matters of the soul," as Friedman used to say. These matters of the soul have to do with one's core self. They have to do with defining a self out of the multigenerational processes that have been passed along from generation to generation. God is continually defining self in relationship to others and to creation. One could say that God leads by means of his presence. It is God's presence that marks a defining moment in synagogue and church.

A part of the multigenerational transmission process in families is listening to the stories passed along from generation to generation. People experience the meaning of the stories by how the church and synagogue live them out and through the relationships that are formed. Faith gets passed along from one generation to the next through the connectedness of relationships. This begins to get to matters of the soul as one considers what one believes about one's core self. The ancient creeds of the church are defining statements about the church's "core self." Out of one's core self grow the principles by which one lives one's life. These principles are certainly influenced by the multigenerational processes passed along by one's family of origin, but at some point, a person must make those principles his or her own. The same could be said of a budding systems thinker or a theologian. At some point, people must make these concepts their own. A shift occurs when one goes from being able to speak a language to being able to think in that language. That same shift occurs for clergy when they can go from speaking the language of Bowen theory to thinking in the theory. As that paradigm shift occurs, it has a dramatic impact on their ministry.

Hester considers himself a third-generation systems thinker. He understands that the work he is doing today is a multigenerational process that has been passed along to him through the emotional processes of previous thinkers, and now through his own thinking with clergy in his training programs and beyond to their congregations. Both of us view the work with clergy as a multigenerational process that passes into our congregations and families and even into other work systems, into fourth and fifth generations. The goal is to present one's own thinking, not in such a way that others have to believe it too, but in a way that allows others to do their own best thinking about the issues and present their own ideas. In that way, we promote differentiation of self in others through their own differentiation of self.

References

Friedman, E. H. (1985). *Generation to generation.* New York, NY: Guilford Press.

Friedman, E. H. (2007). *A failure of nerve.* New York, NY: Church. (Original work published 1999.)

15
How Bowen Theory
Can Be Useful to People in the
Workplace: A Conversation Between
Kathy Wiseman and Daniel V. Papero[1]

Ms. Wiseman: Dan, once again you and I have the opportunity to think together about the application of Bowen theory in the workplace. If I remember correctly, we have been having this conversation informally since we met almost 25 years ago and more formally with the audiotapes that we began in 2000. To begin, I would like to ask you about your experience. You have been traveling throughout the country talking to people about Bowen family systems theory and its application to the workplace. What have you been talking about, and what are you learning from all of these different talks? Is it different than last year? What are you picking up from these audiences?

Dr. Papero: These are good questions to start with. I have been working on a more definitive statement about how Bowen theory can be useful to people in the workplace.

The element I have been looking at and talking more about has been, first and foremost, the idea of systems thinking. I'm trying to convey what an emotional and/or a relationship system is using fairly simple ideas, including Bowen's model of the electronic circuit. I've been talking more about the role of stress and anxiety and its impact on the individual and on emotional systems.

I have been talking about triangles. I don't think that people get triangles. People in business have a limited understanding of the concept, but not necessarily the depth of the emotional process at work in triangles. Maybe they don't need to. I wonder how much people really need to grapple with this and whether they can just take a few ideas and use them.

I also try to describe in these talks what I think are the general principles of working on differentiation of self at work. I describe

---

[1] Dan Papero and Kathy Wiseman regularly record their thinking about Bowen theory and the workplace. This conversation was held in 2003.

the concept and its relationship to anxiety and relationship sensitivity and the work it takes to manage self. I try to help people understand the kind of effort it takes to move toward differentiation of self.

I recently was involved in a series of talks in California on what I think leadership is from a systems perspective. There were a lot of questions from the audience. Those from the organizational development people are no different than those from the mental health people. They want techniques. They want to know, "What do I do when this happens?" I have no good answer for them because I don't think about it that way. It's not about techniques. From my point of view, technique is not the first thing to think about. The first thing you do think about is systems—systems theory and systems thinking—not about what do I do right now with this problem. As a consultant, my process is to "think alongside people" about the challenges in their world. I suppose you could call "thinking alongside" a technique, but I don't think of it that way.

For me, it is the process that goes on when interacting with another. The climate, the chemistry, whatever you call it, is being maintained in a way that reduces the level of anxiety and fear in people and increases the quality of the thinking that is going on. It's a back-and-forth exchange so that I am learning at the same time the people I am working with are learning. Is that enough for an organization or for a corporation? I don't have a good answer to that.

This isn't, I suppose, what you would do if you were an organizational consultant who was called in because there was a productivity problem on the line. I think it would work there, too, but I'm not sure that there aren't other ways that could work just as well and perhaps quicker.

I was in a 2-day meeting on organizations in San Diego, California. There were some very bright people in the audience. Several were organizational development people connected with universities. They could hear my point yet were also pointing out a different view of systems thinking than I do. I had to go back in my own mind to remember that many roads lead to Rome. While I have one piece of the elephant, I don't have the whole elephant. However, I think the piece of the elephant I'm talking about may be central to many of the other pieces of the elephant.

Ms. Wiseman: I have two ideas I want to explore. One is this idea of systems thinking that you were talking about. I'll tell you about my own dilemma lately with cases and would be interested in your response. I've got examples of a family business and a nonfamily business, where the leader has died within the past year and a problem has surfaced in both the executive leadership and in the family of both businesses. In the family business, one person's behavior is problematic. This person's behavior always tended to be a little different, but now the problem is focused on the symptom in this person, who is vital to the stability of both the family and business. It is everything I can do to keep thinking systems and not focus on the problem in that person.

Dr. Papero: The focus is on that person?

Ms. Wiseman: Yes, the focus of other family members is on this person. I know that after the death of an important person, people's thinking would go in different directions from high productivity. It is very hard not to think about the symptom, and to follow the thought "observe first." I am distracted from thinking systems by the behavior of this individual.

I find myself thinking, even after all these years of consulting and working on self, "What am I going to do here? Do I share my observations with these people? Do I keep asking questions?" I've been in situations in which the clients really don't care what your observations are. They say they want feedback but really don't. So, it can be very difficult for me to think systems when the client system is very anxious.

Is it enough to just keep observing and asking questions?

Dr. Papero: I don't know what the answer to that is, as that goes down to the core of the consultant, who he or she is, what he or she thinks is important, and where his or her values lie. There is a huge pressure in corporate consulting, including family businesses, because the reward to the consultant can be high. There's a lot of money tied up in it. There's a real tendency to do what the system wants as opposed to representing what one really thinks about the nature of the problem. In fact, I think a lot of corporate consulting, to the degree to which I have been able to watch it, actually is designed to do what the system in place already wants. That may or may not be wrong, but it also may or may not get at some of the basic problems.

How much do you say about what you really think to people? The challenge is to articulate what you think the nature of their dilemma is in the clearest way you can so that it can be heard but dismissed. In other words, the client feels free to take it or leave it.

Ms. Wiseman: And you still believe that kind of a presence in a system can fundamentally be a resource?

Dr. Papero: Yes, I do. Is it an important resource for a corporation? I don't know. They'll have to decide that. That's their task to think about the evaluation of the services they are receiving.

Ms. Wiseman: Here's a specific example you can help me with. A man has been working with his mother in a growing family business. His father died 6 months ago. In my opinion, there is probably no chance that his 60-year-old mother will turn over responsibility in her lifetime to her son. I think that's not possible. The son is talking about finding a way to have this happen.

    If you've got a viewpoint on a process, you do see some flexibility. However, my assessment, based on some of what I've observed about the nature of this system and what it is up against, is that any transfer of ownership won't make sense to the mother. She will die with her boots on at her desk. That's the nature of the beast of this business.

    If you have that belief or knowledge based on your experience, is there a responsibility to communicate that? I'm not sure that communicating these thoughts is a helpful way for a system to grow or for anyone in that group to think about its dilemma. I don't think this kind of consultant expertise is helpful to the client.

Dr. Papero: I don't think so either. When the expert comes in and gives opinions, and I want to be careful with how I say this because there are times to render opinions, it often has a way of setting the processes in stone so that the parties are not flexible. Typically, the expert comes in and whether he or she is aware of it, he or she has chosen sides in a triangle. And that choosing of sides somehow intensifies the rigidity of that basic relationship dilemma between the original two people.

Ms. Wiseman: How does that happen, choosing sides in a triangle? Is it because it's so easy to be caught in any triangle?

Dr. Papero: It happens mostly because people are unaware of triangles. They are unaware of emotional process. They are focused on issues. The transfer of control is the issue. Succession is an issue in the family you are talking about. Underneath that is the emotional process that has gone on between that mother and her son for as long as that son has been alive.

    At times, that process has been extraordinarily warm and close and at times extraordinarily distant and tense. Therein lies a basic misunderstanding for each of the other's position. There's a lot of sensitivity and reactivity. And perhaps coupled in it is the mother's lifelong concern that her son isn't up to being a functional human in life or in the business. So her message to the son is "You can be anything you want to be, but you don't have what it takes." Those are the two sides of the message. He comes out of it with this belief that he can do anything but underneath it he is unsure if he can do anything.

His role in this would be, on the one hand, mad at her because she doesn't go along with him, but on the other hand, acting in ways that, from her point of view, justify her reluctance to give up control.

From my way of thinking about this, a system approach would see this as a system of two in a period of high tension, since the father has been dead only 6 months. I don't know what anyone else in the family world would say about this, but I believe that the turbulence surrounding the death of a significant figure in the family has a half life of a year, minimum, before it really begins to settle down. And it can go on longer than that if during that year people do things that fuel the turbulence. During turbulent times such as that 1st year, people are much more sensitive and reactive. Inevitably, unless they are thinking about it, they will do things that increase the turbulence. The outcomes are impasses that are seen as personal rather than related to the turbulence and the loss of a very important family member.

Ms. Wiseman: The turbulence you describe is what?

Dr. Papero: Emotional sensitivity and reactivity. It is hard to describe this because it can be such a subtle process in people. It has to do with a sense that something has to happen, something has to be done.

Ms. Wiseman: When in fact it might not have to be done.

Dr. Papero: Yes, in fact it really might not need to be done. Things might be able to sail along for a while without anyone doing much. There's a sense of other people doing it wrong. There's also often an anxiety/ fear, which is often called by others "greed," where all of a sudden stability is no longer there and people start to get worried about their piece of the pie and then start grabbing for it. A grab leads to a countergrab, leading to a counter-countergrab. Then they're into it. And then, all it takes is to bring in a couple dozen attorneys or accountants or consultants and you've really got a stalemate.

And on it goes. It's emotional reactivity. It's not grief, although that may be a small piece of it. It's anxiety, it's uncertainty. Here is a system that has been in balance, then all of a sudden the balance is gone and constraints under which people have operated are no longer there. It's almost an overreaction to the loss of constraints. It's as if people go too far because the constraint they once had is no longer reining them in. They reach too far or make too big a demand or act too unfettered. In a sense, it is a lack of respect for the interdependence of the people. There is a lack of awareness of it. I say "lack of respect" as if people are doing this on purpose. They are doing it almost automatically, but the effect is to disrespect the power of the system and the interdependence of the people in it. And the minute you do that you begin to set up the reactive process.

Ms. Wiseman: When I think about this particular case, I think of how in hearing the one side of the story, the son's side, how much my thinking went toward the mother, the CEO, to make a change rather than believing that the son had the capacity to make a change for himself. I caught myself looking toward the other to soothe the situation and was surprised at how quickly I could go there.

Dr. Papero: That is, joining the son's side.

Ms. Wiseman: It happened in a nanosecond.

Dr. Papero: That's how it does happen. That it happened is not as important as recognizing it and working back out of it. It happens to all of us. I would like to say I sit in these corporate consultations and don't take the side of the person I am talking with. After all, the person makes perfect sense; they mostly always do. But you have to work on your head to remember that the person you're talking with represents just one view. What are the views of others? What are the people up against [who] have to deal with this character?

Ms. Wiseman: Is that the way you keep a systems view?

Dr. Papero: That's one of the ways I do it. I also try to watch my side-taking. I'm better at seeing it, but I don't always catch it.

Ms. Wiseman: What's the ability of that son to make a life for himself when he says, "This is not the path I want to go? If I don't have leadership in this, I'll find leadership somewhere else?" Where's the direction to the mother?

Dr. Papero: Go for it, go for it! How does that become a conversation between the two of them rather than a whine to a consultant? In other words, how can that dialogue get set up productively between the mother and the son, which is where it belongs?

Ms. Wiseman: So how would you think about doing that?

Dr. Papero: I think it can be rather difficult to do this. I might think about the tension between the two and that my role is to function as that neutral third position. That means I have to stay in contact with both of them about the emotional issue between them, without taking sides with either, and without disappearing myself, which can happen. Sometimes you get into these things, then all of a sudden the person in that third position just disappears, meaning they get emotionally reactive and withdraw or go silent or something. This is the basic model which informs my thinking when working within a system.

I then have to think, from a technique point of view, "How am I going to do this?" Would it be better to do separate meetings initially with the mother first and then the son? I probably would do that as a beginning point for two reasons: I want to get a sense of how each individual is thinking and how anxious he or she is. I'd like them to get a sense of me as well. And if I'm neutral, I'll seem different from other people. That might be enough to get them working on this. I might, if they want it, put the two of them together with me and then I would simply work on thinking along-side of each in the presence of the other so that they "overhear" each other. This is more likely to minimize attack/defend interactions between the two of them.

Ms. Wiseman: So the focus is on each of them defining their own thinking in that relationship.

Dr. Papero: Right. In other words, people can have the same conversation between the two of them, but when that third person is around and that third person is neutral, they often hear each one's viewpoint and position more clearly than when they try to do it between themselves. The reactivity and sensitivity is so hair triggered that they are into it before they know it and then become deeply frustrated.

Ms. Wiseman: What's helpful is that you're talking about maintaining a systems view. Observing and appreciating your tendency to get caught in it and then developing some techniques to get yourself out. So there is a technique part, but it is not based on solving the problem of another or the others.

Dr. Papero: The problem between the mother and the son can only be resolved between the mother and the son.

Ms. Wiseman: Not with me giving feedback to him or her?

Dr. Papero: Now, someone could come in with a technical business decision and could force it through. And this might actually be good for the business. The business could continue, but the problem between the mother and the son would not get addressed with that one. If the family still retains control of the business and that rift is there, it will keep surfacing through the years in the decision making of that company.

I'll give you an example of what I mean. I was in a large corporation that is family owned but not family run. The family owns the stock. They are in about the fourth or fifth generation in this family. In Generation 2, two brothers had been involved in developing this large corporation. After the death of their father, the two brothers got in a real battle with each other which ended up in court. Two siblings ganged up on one of the brothers in the lawsuit and the other brother lost.

To this day, the descendants of the one who lost have become irritants in the family processes around the business. They, in some ways, are the most irritating, make the most challenges, and so on.

Although the dispute was resolved legally, it was not resolved emotionally in the family, and the fight two generations ago continues to play out, hidden in the background to this day. The focus goes on in the behavior of those involved, yet misses the fact that this is a deep, emotional process in the family that has never been resolved. It repeatedly surfaces around business decisions/business interactions of the family and around some of the challenges the family throws at the management of the corporation.

Ms. Wiseman: What does one do when one has been invited to think alongside clients with deep emotional upset? I know it's not conducting a meeting where all the parties can vent at each other. It isn't helpful for them to say that they're still angry with each other.

Dr. Papero: No, it isn't.

Ms. Wiseman: I think that what has been happening in that corporation is that the management group has been communicating subtly by side-taking due to a lack of awareness of the emotional process in the family. If the management could get in a more neutral position with this family and with the two separate groups in the family, which would be a real challenging thing to do, it would over time lead to a resolution that would be in the best interest of the family and of the company. This may not be of interest to the management or the family in the short term but could evolve over time.

I know how I get neutral. But how do people begin to think neutrally about the people who cause them problems all the time rather than focus on what they're going to say to deal with the problem people?

Dr. Papero: First of all, they have to see the idea somehow.

Ms. Wiseman: The process and what is really happening?

Dr. Papero: Yes. Then, they have to begin to think about what would it mean to be neutral. This is where some sort of coaching could be very beneficial. I think most of us who have worked on this neutral position in our own families could not do it without coaching. At some point, and this is a tricky thing, does that businessperson need to start engaging his or her own family a little bit as a training ground for this? I think yes, but most people won't do that.

I don't think you can really get at neutrality, in your business life for example, unless you do some of that in your own family. I may be wrong about that. It's somehow leaning into the problem, not making it personal, keeping it focused on the relationship process, and staying in that neutral third position, when one can. There are times when one has to make decisions, obviously. And if you make decisions, you make them clearly and make them decisively.

Ms. Wiseman: Before we close, I'd like to touch upon this. Several people who have listened to our conversations wrote to ask if we could talk more about triangles and about the two "Cs" that are so prevalent in organizations: conflict and communication. What does a theory about human behavior have to add? I think that is an interesting way to think about the contribution that Bowen family systems theory can make. Can you think differently about conflict and communications if you are thinking emotional process?

Dr. Papero: I think so. Whether other people could see it and work with those ideas, I'm less sure of. But, yes, I think you can think about it differently.

Ms. Wiseman: What would be a different way of thinking about conflict?

Dr. Papero: First of all, I think people have to define very carefully what they mean by *conflict*. The term is used for all kinds of things that I would not call conflict. Any disagreement is called a conflict.

People disagree all of the time. Frans de Waal,[2] the great primatologist, points out in his book *Peacemaking Among Primates* that conflict is the root of cooperation. In other words, cooperation springs from disagreement or differing views of self-interest. It makes sense that conflict springs out of differing views of self-interest fueled by emotional intensity. Cooperation has to do with somehow finding ways of satisfying the self-interest of each in the name of the bigger whole. To do that, people have to have differing views of what's right, of what self-interest is, and be willing to represent that. At the same time, be aware that one's own self-interest is tied to some degree to the greater good. That is the step that is very hard in the modern world right now.

In 1986, Jack Calhoun[3] predicted that if population density rises, people will move toward a position of universal autism, which could be loosely described as the inability to respond appropriately to the situation of others. In other words, people will function with a "me-first" position, with a loss of awareness of the interconnectedness and lack of respect for the interconnectedness of the larger group.

Ms. Wiseman: Perhaps we should end on that. Thanks, Dan.

Dr. Papero: You're welcome, Kathy.

---

[2] de Waal, F. (1989). *Peacemaking among primates.* Cambridge, MA: Harvard University Press.

[3] Papero, D. V. (1996). Review of Calhoun, J. B., Universal autism: Extinction resulting from failure to develop relationships. In Sager, R. R. (Ed.), *Bowen theory and practice: Featured articles from the Family Center Report 1979–1996.* Washington, DC: Georgetown Family Center.

16
Bringing Bowen Theory to Family Business

JOANNE NORTON

As a member of the Family Business Consulting Group, the author specializes in working with large multigenerational families. Born into a second-generation family business in the Midwest, the author was very aware of the strong influences family businesses can have on a family. Her father and his two brothers worked together in a heating and energy business begun by their father, who had left a third-generation nursery business that is still thriving today. The seeds of cutoff, the comfort of the togetherness force, and the effectiveness of the triangle in relationships were sown very early in the author's life.

To better serve the third, fourth, and fifth generations of her employer's family business as vice president of shareholder relations, the author studied Bowen family systems theory and examined her own position in her family system and her employer's work system. Hired by a nonfamily chief executive officer (CEO) to work with the family shareholders primarily in the area of family governance, the author learned that to survive in the triangle made up of the CEO, the family shareholders, and herself, she would need to work at defining a self. She knew she would need to be clear about who she was, what she believed, and what she was going to do.

In an effort to define herself, the author began her family-of-origin study on her father's side, searching the roots of the Frese family. She made many trips from Southern California back to her hometown of Quincy, Illinois, and finally back to Bockholt, Germany, which used to be Prussia, where her great-great-grandfather, Anthonious Josephus Frese, and great-great-grandmother, Theresa Ank, had been born. The journey back to Bockholt ultimately inspired the author to earn a doctorate in organizational leadership at Pepperdine University.

The author was drawn to helping family owners succeed because family businesses are critical to the U.S. economy, and she believes that they are well worth the extra care it generally takes to make them work. Family firms constitute 80% to 98% of all businesses in the world's free economies, 49% of the gross domestic product in the United States, and more than 75% of the gross domestic product in most other countries. Family-owned companies are responsible for putting 80% of the U.S. workforce to work and more than 85% in the rest of the world. Of all the new jobs created in this country in the past 20 years, 80% were because of family businesses. Approximately 37% of the Fortune 500 companies are family controlled, and a total of 60% of all publicly held U.S. companies are also family controlled (Astrachan & Carey, 1994; Beehr, Drexler, & Faulkner, 1997; Daily & Dollinger, 1992; Dreux, 1990; Oster, 1999, all as cited in Poza, 2004, p. 4).

Although family businesses are both ubiquitous and critical to the world economy, they are also fragile. Ward wrote, "Keeping a family business alive is perhaps the toughest management job on earth. Only 13% of successful family businesses last through the third generation. Less than one-third survive into the second generation" (Ward [1987], quoted in Chaponniere & Ward, 2003, p. 54).

One of the most intriguing relationships is the one between family owners and the nonfamily CEOs families bring in to lead the family business when family owners are either unwilling or unable to take the top post; however, until recently there has been a dearth of research in this area. Poza (2004) wrote,

> There is little discussion of—or data on—the most productive way to manage relationships between family and non-family managers. Yet family businesses of any significant size depend on the quality and effectiveness of non-family managers to ensure their continued success and growth. (p. 121)

For her doctoral dissertation, the author studied the relationships between successful nonfamily CEOs and family owners of successful family businesses. It was her hope to find the factors that made the CEOs successful because she had developed her own hunches from observing the workings of four of them personally day after day. Until 2003, most of the research surrounding the relationships between nonfamily and family leaders had been anecdotal, based mostly on the stories collected by family business advisors.

Eckrich and McClure (2004) wrote, "One of the most challenging and confusing roles in a firm is that of the non-family supervisor or executive. And one of the least understood relationships is that between family members and key non-family employees" (p. 1). They went on to explain that nonfamily executives who come from the corporate world often become overwhelmed because they do not understand the inner workings of family firms and wish that the families would just get out of the way. Understanding that family businesses are different from public companies is critical to the success of senior executives serving in a family business. For the nonfamily CEO, understanding what makes for successful relationships with family owners is the difference between resounding success and utter failure.

That relationship between the family owners and the nonfamily executive is unique. Bringing a nonfamily CEO into a private company is not like introducing a new CEO in a public company—it is much more complicated. Rosplock (2003) claimed that "from family sabotage, to ownership and control squabbles, and compensation discrepancies, bringing in a non-family leader can generate a hotbed of jealousy and resentment especially from younger generations who feel entitled to the throne" (p. 1). Others have claimed that bringing in a nonfamily CEO is more like a marriage. Danco (1992) wrote, "When a family business owner hires a key manager, it's a lot like tying the marriage knot. More so than in a public company, employment in a family firm should be thought of as 'until death do us part'" (p. 2). Bringing in a nonfamily CEO affects the entire family system and all of the relationships in that system.

The better the relationships in family businesses are, the better the business will be. Hoover and Hoover (1999) theorized, "Relationships are the language of family business" (p. 197). Raymond claimed, "The company cannot improve unless the relationships among the members of the family are improving" (as cited in Senge, Kleiner, Roberts, Ross, & Smith, 1994, p. 57), an observation he made as the successful heir to the Raymond Corporation, which is now in its third generation of existence. Raymond explained that although there are enormous advantages to being in a family business, the complexities are also enormous, and that when relationships are ignored, it will sooner or later have a negative effect on the family business. Raymond recommended using systems thinking, specifically family diagrams, to help family members and top management understand the dynamics of the firm and the family (as cited in Senge et al., 1994, p. 473).

Family businesses definitely have special challenges when it comes to relationships and leadership. Hoover and Hoover (1999) asserted that "leadership is a relationship-first role" (p. 185) because leaders of family businesses have always had to deal with the three domains of family, business, and ownership. Systems thinking is actually more useful because succession is more of a linear approach and relationships are more systemic. Frishkoff (1994) asserted, "Family business succession is not about money; it is about relationships…. When in doubt, sell the business and salvage the family. While businesses can be replaced, families cannot, nor do they heal their wounds easily" (p. 70).

Astrachan, Keyt, Berry, and Lane (2002) found in their roundtable discussions with nonfamily CEOs that the family's wishes and objectives must be honored. Relationships with each other must come first. One nonfamily CEO explained how the owner of the family business instructed him to make the business more successful but without interfering with two historically underperforming divisions, which had been founded by the owner's grandfather. Sometimes profitability is risked in the name of family traditions or relationships. This is particularly difficult for nonfamily chief executives to deal with when their own compensation is based on profitability, and it is why it is so critical for them to understand the importance of relationships in family businesses.

Hoover and Hoover (1999) recommended using a systems approach for understanding relationships in family businesses, specifically Bowen theory. Lansberg (1999) also suggested Bowen's work (p. 130).

Hollender (1983) was one of the pioneers in the family business consulting field. She explained how she used Bowen's family systems approach: "In working with the family, it became necessary to see it as a unity rather than as individuals, echoing the systems concept that the whole is more than the sum of its parts" (p. 51).

In his 1986 book *Family Business, Risky Business: How to Make it Work*, Bork wrote that Bowen observed family members individually and began to look at the family as a system and to view the patient as a component of that system (p. 26). Although there are eight concepts in Bowen's theory, family business experts have agreed that the concepts most helpful to family business are *differentiation of self* and *triangles* (Bork, 1986; Hoover & Hoover, 1999). The author believes that of the four nonfamily CEOs with whom she worked, the most successful ones were not afraid to take a stand with the many family owners of the $2.5 billion company where she was an executive, and she decided to study differentiation of self in other nonfamily CEOs of family businesses as part of her dissertation.

The author found the work of Papero particularly helpful. Papero (1995) wrote about leadership, borrowing from both Bowen and neuroscientist Sapolsky. Papero's conclusions are as follows:

> First of all, effective leaders will likely have good control of their own emotional reactivity. They will have the ability to establish relationships and remain in contact with the various factions in the organization that push for rapid, fix-it change and the victory of narrow self-interest. (p. 51)

Whiteside, Aronoff, and Ward (1993) also recommended learning Bowen's family systems approach to understanding how family members need "to distinguish between the *feeling* process and the *intellectual* process" (p. 23). They explained that feelings include "contentment, satisfaction, aggression, anger, and sadness," in which the intellectual process would be "thinking, reasoning, and reflecting," giving family members and executives the opportunity to live their lives according to "logic, intellect, and reason" (p. 23).

After reviewing the literature on nonfamily CEOs and Bowen theory of differentiation of self, the author designed a methodology to be used in a qualitative study, including the development of interview questions using appreciative inquiry. She used a grounded theory study to design a specific theory that would deal with success factors of nonfamily CEOs of family businesses. A dozen nonfamily CEOs in Southern California were recommended by bankers; certified public accountants; executive directors of family business councils; and members of the Young Presidents' Organization, the World Presidents' Organization, and The Executive Committee.

Face-to-face interviews were held, and six questions were asked. The interview question regarding differentiation was as follows:

> According to Murray Bowen's family systems theory (Bowen, 1994), a person who is well defined, sometimes must take a stand that is not popular with a majority of those being led. Tell me about a time when you successfully took a stand that was unpopular with the family shareholders, but you continued to hold your ground. What were some of the ways in which you approached the issues?

After the interviews, the author and a second rater assigned a number—0, 1, or 2—to each of the codes. Then the author, along with two researchers, analyzed the content by forming axial categories for identifiable themes (see Table 16.1). Finally, hypotheses were generated.

Virtually all 12 of the nonfamily CEOs in the study had stories of times when they had to take a stand that was not popular. They were able to influence the family owners by outlining what they believed would be the consequences of the owners' decisions. Five of the nonfamily CEOs took drastic measures, drawing a line in the sand about some issues. Adam (pseudonyms are used for CEOs' names) explains the term *drawing a line in the sand*:

Table 16.1 Common Themes From Interview Question Regarding Differentiation

Theme	Mode	*M*
CEO reality check	2	2.00
Needs of the business	2	1.83
CEO line in the sand	2	1.75
CEO educating family	2	1.75
CEO success	2	1.50
CEO frequent stands	2	1.17
CEO consensus builder	2	1.00

Source: From Norton, J., *An exploration of the relationships between successful non-family CEOs of successful family businesses and the family owners* (Unpublished doctoral dissertation), Pepperdine University, Malibu, CA, 2005.

There were two or three instances of where I just had to stand my ground and say, "I don't care whether you want to do this or not; this is what we have to do, or you have to find somebody else to do it." Just draw a line in the sand, and say, "This is it." (Norton, 2005, p. 157)

Dave used a reality check to influence family owners and explained the meaning well:

I've had to go to the owners and try to explain to them that their vision or their understanding of what the business needs is very different from what the company actually needs, and create for them a vision of what this organization is, what's happening with it day to day. They usually have their own set of rose-colored glasses. I try to get that rose coloring off of them so they can see the reality of what they are....My tool has been, establish a vision. If we pursue their thought, this will be the result. If we pursue the current strategy, this will be the result, and preferably create a vision that combines the two, usually extending the time frame to accommodate it so that it's—you'll get what you want, it's just not going to be today. (Norton, 2005, p. 161)

Paul also has had to take frequent stands and sees it as part of his job:

There's so many, it's hard to lift out the particular one. That's my day-to-day—that's a large part of my job is to take on those factors, the old entrepreneurial approach, family business approach versus the modern, best-practice company. So it's pretty much a continuous thing. (Norton, 2005, p. 165)

C. J. stood his ground and helped the family owners understand his position by educating them. C. J. explained:

The current business that I'm running now is family-owned. I am in a situation where—it's a $200 million business, has four divisions to it—I am standing my ground right now that one of the divisions must be shut down, that the time and the dollars it's going to take to fix it [are] not worth it. The owner lives in another country. His reason for keeping it is non-business-related. His reason for keeping it is that this division currently employs about a hundred people. He doesn't want, in any way, to hurt those people, and he's afraid that if it's sold, the most likely buyers will not need the people and just need the assets of the company. He's correct. He's very proud of the fact that he puts food on their table, and he puts their kids through school. Extremely different paradigm than I would have, where his business is bleeding to death, and it's taking resources and talents and time from his other three divisions. (Norton, 2005, pp. 165–166)

At the conclusion of her research, the author hypothesized that successful nonfamily CEOs are able to take unpopular stands, preserving a degree of autonomy in the face of pressures for togetherness. In March 2007, the author also tested the hypotheses garnered through her research by surveying family CEOs of family businesses who are members of the California State University, Fullerton, Family Business Council. Using a Likert-type scale, she asked the 10 family CEOs who participated in the survey to rate how much, on a scale ranging from 0 (*not at all*) to 7 (*completely*), they agreed with her hypotheses.

The author used the following statement gleaned from her prior research to test her hypothesis regarding differentiation of self:

> To have a good relationship with the rest of the family owners, a family CEO must know when to take unpopular stands with family owners. This means they have to draw a line in the sand or give the other family owners a reality check from time to time even when the family does not want to hear what must be said.

The mean was 5.5, suggesting that the family CEOs "agreed a great deal" with the statement.

When asked for comments on their scores, one of the family CEOs commented: "You must always tell it like it is!" Another wrote, "The business comes first." And still another admitted, "This is perhaps one of the most difficult aspects of running a family business." Just how far to go gave one of the family CEOs pause. He wrote, "While an honest appraisal of the company's situation is always appropriate, drawing a line in the sand is too challenging a position to take. Part of the CEO's competency has to be diplomacy." This is also a good illustration of the difference between being a nonfamily CEO versus a family CEO. Whereas nonfamily CEOs can walk away from their jobs when family members choose to go a different direction in the business, as Adam explained earlier, family CEOs have a family relationship to be concerned about as well. For them, using diplomacy and being differentiated is a more difficult dance.

The author's research and experience has convinced her it is critical for those who are chosen by families to lead their legacy businesses to be more emotionally mature and better differentiated than most other leaders. In her consulting practice, the author works with both nonfamily and family executives to ensure that they are exceptionally focused and able to clearly articulate who they are, what they believe, and what they want to do. She also urges the executives to stay closely connected to the family owners, frequently communicating with them in person and via e-mail, informally and in more structured situations such as family meetings. In addition, she recommends that executives do family-of-origin work, knowing that understanding their own families will help them know themselves better but also be more understanding of the families they serve.

When working with family owners, the author helps them hold frequent family meetings, set up family councils, and organize annual family shareholder weekends so that family owners have ample opportunity to be very clear collectively about who they are, what they believe, and what they are going to do. She urges families who own businesses to honor the founders and their heritage and has produced, with the families, family videos of members of the older generation talking about their memories of the founder when the founder has already passed away. She believes that the most important work she does is aiding individual family members and nonfamily executives be better defined by explaining to them that conflict is inevitable when frequent meetings are held, and all are coached to stand their ground. She shows how the comfort of the togetherness force can sabotage even the best efforts at differentiation, and she helps families develop codes of conduct so they can fight fairly when necessary.

It is also important to remember that Bowen himself grew up in a family business that still exists to this day and that his early experiences must surely have shaped his thinking about families just as the author's early family business experience shaped hers. When Bowen (1994) described how "ideal family treatment begins," he could just as well have substituted *family businesses will be successful*

> when one can find a family leader with the courage to define self, who is as invested in the welfare of the family as in self, who is neither angry nor dogmatic, whose energy goes to changing self rather than telling others what they should do, who can know and respect the multiple opinions of others, who can modify self in response to the strengths of the group, and who is not influenced by the irresponsible opinions of others.... A family leader is beyond the popular notion of "power." A responsible family leader automatically generates mature leadership qualities in other family members who are to follow. (p. 243)

The implication for families choosing either family or nonfamily CEOs is that they must find someone who is differentiated, someone who fits the description of a family leader as described by Bowen. The implication for leaders of family businesses is that they need to continually work on defining a self, realizing it is not easy but certainly worth the work. In the quick-fix world of businesses today, this is not an easy accomplishment. Finally, the implications for families who own businesses together are that they must present a united front to their nonfamily employees and define and communicate their visions frequently. Families, owners, and nonfamily executives must be working toward the same goals to be successful, and bringing Bowen theory to family businesses helps families thrive and businesses succeed.

References

Astrachan, J., Keyt, A., Berry, J., & Lane, S. (2002, September). *Non-family CEOs in the family business: Connecting family values to business success.* Paper presented at the Family Business Network Academic Research Forum, Helsinki, Finland.

Bork, D. (1986). *Family business, risky business: How to make it work.* Bork Institute for Family Business.

Bowen, M. (1994). *Family therapy in clinical practice.* Northvale, NJ: Jason Aronson.

Chaponniere, C., & Ward, J. (2003). *Family business through Darwin's theory of species.* Geneva, Switzerland: Lombard Odier Darier Hentsch & Cie.

Danco, L. (1992). Before you get hitched to a hired gun. *Family Business Magazine.* Winter, 1992. Retrieved from http://www.familybusinessmagazine.com/index. php?/articles/single/before_you_get_hitched_to_a_hired_gun/

Eckrich, C., & McClure, S. (2004). *Working for a family business: A non-family employee's guide to success.* Marietta, GA: Family Enterprise.

Frishkoff, P. (1994). Succession need not tear a family apart. *Best's Review, 95*(8), 70–73.

Hollender, B. (1983). *Family-owned business as a system: A case study of the interaction of family, task, and marketplace components.* Unpublished doctoral dissertation, University of Pittsburgh.

Hoover, E., & Hoover, C. (1999). *Getting along in family business: The relationship intelligence handbook.* New York, NY: Routledge.

Lansberg, I. (1999). *Succeeding generations: Realizing the dream of family businesses.* Boston, MA: Harvard Business School Press.

Norton, J. (2005). *An exploration of the relationships between successful non-family CEOs of successful family businesses and the family owners* (Unpublished doctoral dissertation). Pepperdine University, Malibu, CA.

Papero, D. (1995). Anxiety and organizations. In P. Comella, J. Bader, J. Ball, K. Wiseman, & R. Sagar (Eds.), *The emotional side of organizations: Applications of Bowen theory* (pp. 47–53). Washington, DC: Georgetown Family Center.

Poza, E. (2004). *Family business.* Mason, OH: Southwestern.

Rosplock, K. (2003, November 3). Non-family CEO more common in family firms. *The Business Journal of Milwaukee.* Retrieved from http://milwaukee.bizjournals.com/milwaukee/stories/2003/11/03/editorial6.html

Senge, P., Kleiner, A., Roberts, C., Ross, R., & Smith, B. (1994). *The fifth discipline field book: Strategies and tools for building a learning organization.* New York, NY: Currency/Doubleday.

Whiteside, M., Aronoff, C., & Ward, J. (1993). *How families work together.* Marietta, GA: Business Owner Resources.

17
Bowen Theory and the Chain Reaction of Bad Leadership and Good Leadership

DENNIS A. ROMIG

Hogan and his colleagues measured leadership failure and success with objective measures of work and business performance. At the executive level, failure meant the organization lost significant amounts of money or went out of business. Hogan, Curphy, and Hogan (1994) documented that 50% of leaders were failing at all levels of the organization. In a more recent study, Hogan and Kaiser (2004) presented research that confirmed that the top leaders of organizations make a significant difference in their organization's performance. High-performing executives have been found to add an additional $25 million to their organization over the course of their leadership compared with lower performing executives. Hogan and Kaiser (2004) proposed that it was leadership personality and leadership style that made the difference in performance results.

The personality and leadership style approach to leadership improvement, however, has not produced significant business and organizational success. Organizations continue to send their low-performing managers and executives off to week-long leadership schools that drill into the leaders an awareness of current personality problems and deficits in leadership style. The leaders then troop back to their organizations with improved self-awareness but with no behavior changes or ensuing performance improvements.

The publication of the book *The Fifth Discipline: The Art and Practice of the Learning Organization* (Senge, 1990) introduced business leaders to systems thinking as another way to think about leadership success and failure. To teach systems thinking, Senge (1990) relied on physical systems like weather and mechanical systems like an automated factory to explain how parts of a system affect the whole system. *The Fifth Discipline* was enormously popular, and fifth discipline consulting and training programs were widely implemented in a variety of organizations. Unfortunately, the results of those programs were not as successful as Senge had hoped or predicted. After a string of business case study failures, he proposed that perhaps the field of leadership and management should consider *natural systems*.

This chapter presents two aspects of a systems theory of leadership success and failure that is built on Bowen's family systems theory. The author has been a leadership consultant and coach with global corporations for the past 25 years, endeavoring to promote leadership and organizational success. Two aspects of Bowen theory that the author has found useful in promoting leadership success are (a) the role of anxiety and stress in leader functioning, and (b) reciprocal overfunctioning and underfunctioning in leader–subordinate interactions.

In this chapter, the author describes how he discovered these two important concepts as triggers of leadership and organizational performance chain reactions. The two aspects of systems theory in the discovery of leadership chain reactions are

1. Leaders treat employees like children or like responsible adults.
2. Bowen's discoveries about his own leadership pattern.

Understanding these system concepts will be useful to leadership coaches, trainers, college and university professors, and researchers in communicating new insights that may promote greater leadership effectiveness.

Leaders Treat Employees Like Children or Like Responsible Adults

The senior vice president of the computer chip factory wanted to install breakthrough teamwork training in his manufacturing facility's work teams to improve the factory's quality and productivity. At the time, poor performance by the workers was pervasive, and the factory produced costly, low-quality computer chips that were often shipped late. The managers of the factory, however, opposed their vice president and did not want to train the workers in teamwork, which would allow them to make their own decisions about the work. The managers said the teamwork program would fail because the workers were like children who had to be told everything they are to do.

The managers also challenged teamwork because it involved having the workers set goals for the work rather than pursuing the goals the managers set for them. The justification for not empowering the workers to be involved in setting their own goals was that the workers regularly failed to do uncomplicated housekeeping tasks, including simple machine wipe downs. The managers believed that close supervision was required rather than empowerment because of the workers' seemingly irresponsible behavior.

Most of the managers at the time demonstrated high levels of stress and emotional reactivity, probably as a result of the poor factory performance. They worked 60 hours a week, charging from one meeting to the next. The senior vice president, however, was thoughtful and openly considered the managers' concerns about implementing something he wanted. His calmness was contagious and influenced the managers. After a vigorous but thoughtful debate regarding whether to implement the breakthrough teamwork program, the managers agreed to pilot the training program with two work teams, including each team's supervisor.

Surprisingly, after just 2 weeks, the productivity of those two pilot teams shot up so fast that managers throughout the factory requested the immediate expansion of the teamwork program. As each of the subsequent 100 work teams was trained, their weekly productivity and quality significantly improved. The initially anxious managers became calmer, more thoughtful, and more innovative in solving problems.

The improved worker and manager performance made a considerable amount of money for the computer chip factory, but there remained a big question: How did the improvements occur so rapidly and predictably? It was like a chain reaction. The managers, supervisors, and team members learned and applied improved listening skills. The leaders led their team members in participative goal setting, decision making, and problem solving. As each team and its leader learned and applied listening and the other skills, their work group productivity dramatically increased. But maybe something else was also happening.

A system has many interrelationships. In this case, the chain reaction resulted in the factory achieving 25% improvements in productivity per year for 3 straight years with no money for new equipment, just from the different thinking and working of the team members and their supervisors. The author documented 400 case studies of similar outstanding improved results from 10 other organizations. Some of the case studies are in the book *Breakthrough Teamwork* (Romig, 2000), which also includes a summary of the best of 1,200 published research studies and describes how organizations improved their results 20% to 40%. (See also the appendix to this chapter.)

The book reported the research and the stories, but not how the results were achieved so quickly and so predictably. The 400 case studies took place in factories and organizations in which work group and department performance was going down or at a flat level. After each department in the organization installed breakthrough teamwork, productivity significantly improved (Advanced Micro Devices, 1997; Asea Brown Boveri, 1993; K. Kemp (Sematech), personal communication, July 13, 2005; Moog Aircraft Group, 1998). The other departments continued to be flat until they brought in breakthrough teamwork. Then their productivity also went up. But there were still questions. What was going on, and what theory can explain how it happened?

In a separate case study, one division was literally the best in the world, receiving this recognition from its peer companies. On the basis of the great results, the vice president of the division, John,[1] a calm and relaxed leader, was promoted to lead a larger organization. To replace him, the company brought

---

[1] Names in this example are pseudonyms.

in a new leader, Tom, from outside the organization. As Tom took over leading the division, he demonstrated high amounts of stress and anxiousness. He was very impatient and interrupted people when they talked to him. He demanded to make all of the decisions himself. Tom believed that his employees were like children and that he was the only adult in the organization. Within 6 weeks, the morale and the productivity of Tom's new division plummeted. Performance continued to decrease monthly and almost bankrupted the whole organization.

The author wanted to solve the mystery of how replacing only the top leader of a division that previously nurtured 1,000 productive, motivated workers could result in such a dramatic downturn in performance. At that time, the author thought, "This was a negative chain reaction," but he still did not have a theory that could explain the phenomenon.

Bowen's Discoveries About His Own Leadership Pattern

This second section presents the results of two different leadership chain reactions that help uncover the mystery and begin to explain how certain leadership practices understood through the lens of Bowen theory influence work performance changes so quickly and so pervasively.

Bowen (1986) related the following discovery about his own leadership behavior pattern. As he was going home from work at the Georgetown Family Center where he was the executive director, he reflected on his day. Bowen thought to himself, "I didn't get any of my own work done today." He then asked himself, "Why didn't I get anything done?" He recalled the workday and remembered that employees from the family center came to his office throughout the day asking for his advice. They wanted him to make decisions for them. They wanted him to help solve problems for them. All day! Then he thought, "What's going to happen tomorrow when I go back to work?" He knew—the exact same thing unless something changed.

Bowen knew that his relationship system with each of his staff members was composed of three parts: (a) himself, (b) the other person or people, and (c) his relationship pattern with the other person or people. This is a different way to consider leadership because most leadership theories focus only unidimensionally on the leader doing things to followers. Rather than blaming and trying directly to change his employees' behavior, Bowen had a different idea.

Bowen thought that if he changed his own behavior pattern toward his staff, there might be subsequent changes in how the employees functioned. Bowen's breakthrough insight into his own behavior was that his overhelpfulness with his staff was unintentionally undermining their performance. He was too often helping them to solve their problems and make decisions. First, he was overfunctioning for his employees. Second, he was not getting his own job duties completed.

Bowen had previously discovered in family systems that when a husband or wife overfunctions in the marriage relationship, the other spouse underfunctions or underperforms. He called this a *reciprocal relationship pattern,* in which an overfunctioner produces underfunctioning behavior in the other. Bowen saw that he was overfunctioning for his employees. The reciprocal position for his employees would be to underfunction in their job responsibilities, especially in duties that overlapped or were interrelated to his responsibilities as the family center director. Inadvertently, Bowen undermined their confidence, their performance, and their ability to work by not giving them the opportunity to take fuller responsibility. Bowen thought through a conclusion—if he backed off doing other's work and started doing his own work, then his subordinates must start solving their own problems and making their own decisions. That is exactly what he did.

When the author heard about this application of family systems theory by Bowen to his own leadership of the family center, he thought, "Leadership is not *like* a chain reaction, leadership *is* a chain reaction." How the leader acts toward his or her subordinates directly influences their behaviors and thinking. When the leader does his or her own work and encourages the subordinates to do theirs, the subordinates' problem solving and decision making become more autonomous and timely. Such behaviors and patterns of thought improve work and organizational performance. The leader's relationship behavior pattern instigates the chain reaction.

The author remembered his own quest to find out how one leader, Tom, was able to destroy a 1,000-person organization. He now knew that Tom negatively influenced every person he came in contact with through his anxious, overfunctioning behavior pattern. Tom unintentionally produced a chain reaction of reciprocal anxious underfunctioning in his subordinates. Tom exhibited many anxious leadership behaviors that fit into a pattern that resulted in the underperformance of his employees. First, Tom did not listen to people. He never asked his managers or workers for advice. Tom did not involve people in setting goals. He did not involve people in decision making. He was a micromanager who consistently overachieved. He required that all the decisions be passed up to him for final review. Employee initiative was crushingly destroyed. Figure 17.1 shows the possible chain reactions of how anxious micromanager behaviors produce worker underperformance.

Overfunctioning top-down leadership results in a chain reaction that often, predictably, produces low performance. When leaders do all of the talking in one-on-one and group interactions, the followers respond in two distinctive ways. First, they shut down their thinking and they do not listen. They are not intellectually or motivationally engaged. Their minds become numb, and they actually go into a daze. The author's professor colleague, Steve Beebe, says that it is like the "student stupor" (S. Beebe, personal communication, 2008).

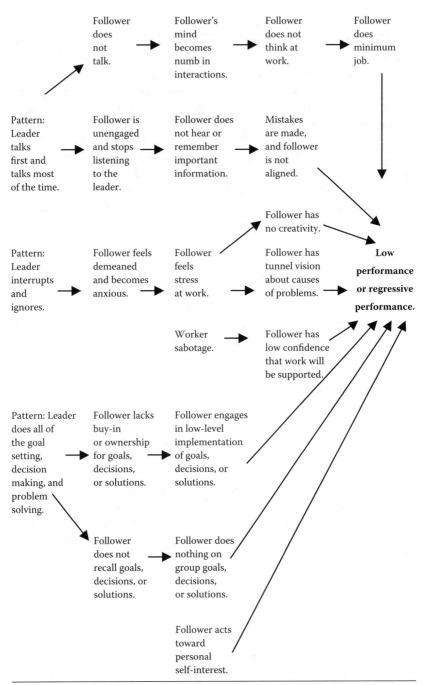

Figure 17.1 An overfunctioning top-down leader behavior pattern creates a continuous chain reaction for low performance.

Students look like they are paying attention, but they are not; their minds are 1,000 miles away. Because the subordinates do not hear their leader's assignments and directives for them, work is not done and mistakes are made.

The second leader pattern that Tom exhibited was interrupting and ignoring people. As a result, they felt demeaned, anxious, and stressed out. Work became a stressful place. Stress destroys creativity and innovation. It also creates tunnel vision, which destroys the ability to see the causes of problems. Finally, high stress kills brain cells in the hippocampus, which even causes the hippocampus to shrink (Doidge, 2007). The *hippocampus* is the part of the brain vital to short-term memory and the ability to be adaptable and responsive to change. The overfunctioning top-down leadership pattern destroys the very thing that every organization continually needs: the ability to respond to change.

A third top-down leadership behavior that has a negative chain reaction is when the overfunctioning leader makes all the decisions and sets all the goals. The result of unilateral decision making is no buy-in or ownership by the employees of the decisions or goals. In turn, this leads to a low level of implementation of the leader's decisions and goals. Even worse than that, when overfunctioning leaders make all the decisions and set all the goals and the employees are not involved, the employees do not even remember hearing the decisions or goals.

An example of this cause-and-effect relationship was reported in a study of a major oil company in Houston (Performance Resources, Inc., 1989). The executives conducted their annual goal-setting meeting in January. All of the employees trooped into the auditorium and were told, "Here are the goals for this year." Five months later, the company surveyed the employees to see whether they remembered the goals that were presented. The employees did not remember any of the goals. They did not even remember that they had been to a goal-setting meeting. The memory was gone because the overfunctioning relationship pattern of the meeting was all one way: top-down.

When the author discovered the negative chain reactions of overfunctioning leaders, he considered the implication: If one person can change things for the bad, one person can change things for the good. What does that leadership pattern look like? In pursuit of this quest to discover what leadership behavior led to improved performance, the author found and reviewed almost 3,000 leadership research studies (Romig, 2001). He began to uncover one theme of leadership practices that significantly improved work group and organizational effectiveness. The common elements in the practices that improved performance were skills and activities in which the leader involved the subordinates in sharing leadership with him or her. The leader and subordinates mutually led each other through team goal setting, decision making, and problem solving. I named this leadership approach *side-by-side leadership*.

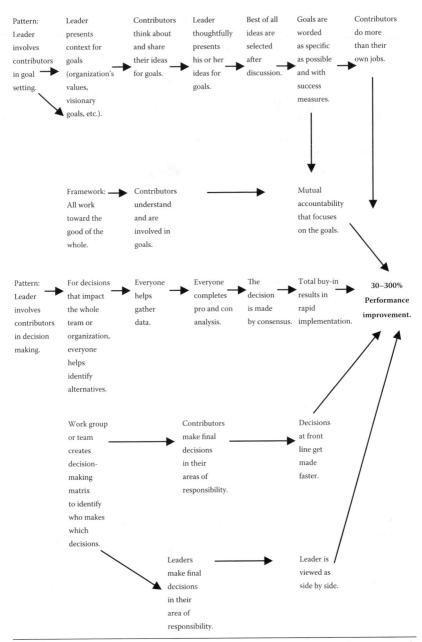

Figure 17.2 A side-by-side leadership pattern creates a chain reaction for continuous outstanding results.

Figure 17.2 shows the reciprocal leader chain reactions for a side-by-side leadership pattern for setting work goals and making decisions. When leaders involve their subordinates in goal setting, not only do the subordinates hear, understand, and remember the goals, but they also have ownership of the goals. When the leader asks subordinates what their ideas are for work goals or decisions, the leader is communicating calm respect toward subordinates. In turn, this draws forth subordinates' best thinking and ideas. The results of the breakthrough teamwork training presented in the first section summarized the subsequent dramatic improvements in business results after each leader involved his or her team in goal setting and decision making.

Conclusions

Bowen acknowledged that his natural systems theory was difficult for people to hear and understand. Since the author's first course in Bowen theory in 1995, he has endeavored to translate Bowen theory and concepts to business and industry leaders. Bowen's concept of the role of anxiety in relationships and of reciprocal under- and overfunctioning, communicated as leadership chain reactions, has assisted executives, managers, and supervisors in improving their leadership effectiveness.

References

Advanced Micro Devices Submicron Development Center. (1997). *Structured Teamwork Training Project evaluation*. Sunnyvale, CA: Author.

Asea Brown Boveri Power T&D Company Inc. (1993, April). *Relay Divisions News*, p. 10. Coral Springs, FL: Author.

Bowen, M. (1986). *Lectures by Murray Bowen* (audiotape). Washington, DC: Georgetown Family Center.

Doidge, N. (2007). *The brain that changes itself: Stories of personal triumph from the frontiers of brain science*. New York, NY: Penguin Group.

E-Systems Garland Division. (1992, July). *E-Systems: The Printed Circuit Newsletter*, p. 8. Garland, TX: Author.

Hogan, R., Curphy, G. J., & Hogan, J. (1994). What we know about leadership effectiveness and personality. *American Psychologist, 49*, 493–504.

Hogan, R., & Kaiser, B. (2004). What we know about leadership. *Review of General Psychology, 9*, 169–180.

Moog Aircraft Group Montek Division. (1998, December). *Continuous Improvement Newsletter*, p. 2.

Performance Resources, Inc. (1989). *Amoco Production Company communication follow-up studies*. Austin, TX: Author.

Romig, D. A. (2000). *Breakthrough teamwork: Outstanding results using structured teamwork*. Austin, TX: Performance Research Press.

Romig, D. A. (2001). *Side by side leadership: Achieving outstanding results together*. Austin, TX: Performance Research Press.

Senge, P. M. (1990). *The fifth discipline: The art and practice of the learning organization*. New York, NY: Doubleday.

Appendix

Case Studies of Successful Teams

Advanced Micro Devices Submicron Development Center (1997): Eighty-four teams with 728 participants were trained in team skills. Total estimated savings were $50 million while they were still in training.

Asea Brown Boveri (1993): Electromechanical Profit Center results: 97.3% shipments on time. A 20% improvement in cycle time. Substation Control/Communication and Eur Relays Profit Center results: 98% on-time delivery for Euro Relays and 65% reduction in cycle time.

E-Systems Garland Division (1992): Log Amp Team reduced labor costs by $85,000, experienced a 32% efficiency improvement in assembly time (savings of 5,300 hours), and improved average cycle time from 13 weeks to 6 weeks.

Moog Aircraft Group Montek Division (1998): Missile Fin and Maintenance-Machine Teams saved $32,000 in the first year with a procedure to communicate helium usage schedules and shutdowns.

18

Introducing Bowen Theory to Business Leaders

JOHN J. ENGELS

Broadly viewed, *Bowen family systems theory* is a research-based description of human emotional functioning. In this chapter, the author discusses how the breakthrough family systems ideas first taught by Bowen established a foundation for a successful advanced-level leadership course tailored to business owners, chief executives, presidents, managing partners, and other key leaders in business and industry. Before pursuing that end, it is important to understand some of the forces and factors that led to the design of a leadership course based on systems thinking.

The author's initial exposure to Bowen's principles came in 1994, when he attended a series of public presentations given by Edwin Friedman, a rabbi, student of Bowen's, and recognized therapist and thinker. Friedman's description of how the adventurous mindset of the Renaissance jolted Europe out of its insular thinking and "emotional stuckness" riveted this author's attention. At that time, the author had been consulting to business leaders for 9 years, coinciding with the first decade of his marriage and the arrival of three children.

Like most "helpers," the author's approach to leadership consulting centered around pleasing the client. His poorly defined theoretical base was drawn from the widely accepted standards of American business that still emphasize teamwork, consensus, harmony, and the leader's expertise. At that time, the author believed his job as a consultant was to dazzle clients by answering their questions and solving their problems. Looking back, he believes his professional consulting practice was every bit as lethargic as medieval Europe.

For the 4 years after his initial exposure to Bowen and Friedman, the author engaged in a serious effort to reconstruct his family history and study the multigenerational emotional patterns that governed his own functioning. This work was undertaken with help from the faculties at the Center for Family Process in Bethesda, Maryland, and the Georgetown Family Center (now the Bowen Center for the Study of the Family) in Washington, DC, and from the author's long-time colleague, Jim Edd Jones, a therapist based in Boulder,

Colorado, and an experienced theoretical thinker. Through these resources, the author also gained wide exposure to the research of evolutionary biologists, neurobiologists, and medical professionals whose data supported and expanded the ideas first postulated by Bowen.

The scientific facts and the depth of Bowen's insights about human functioning challenged the author to reorient his thinking about his consulting practice. The discipline of thinking calmly and neutrally led to genuine curiosity about his clients, ushering him out of the role of expert and into the role of learner. This posture enabled the author to observe his clients more objectively. He noticed four persistent patterns in his clients:

1. A bias toward emotional distance marked by superficial conversations in important relationships at work and at home
2. A chronic focus on others expressed by the leader's tendency to speak for others, overfunction in the space of others (micromanage), and blame others
3. A belief that the leader's subject-matter expertise and technical competence alone qualified the leader to coach and mentor others
4. A tendency for leaders to suffer from physical and emotional symptoms—diverticulitis, ulcers, heart problems, panic attacks, depression, and so forth—in the face of persistent business challenges

With its focus on emotional maturity and taking responsibility for self, systems thinking offered, in the author's view, science- and research-based principles he believed would be useful to motivated clients. The author began focusing on how to promote strategies and skills consistent with systems thinking to help his clients better understand and manage the patterns described earlier. He recognized that many delivery systems were available for communicating systems thinking to others. Those the author considered included presenting workshops for existing clients, giving keynote addresses at national business conferences, one-on-one coaching, writing articles and books oriented to business leaders, and working with leaders and their spouses. The most challenging possibility—designing and facilitating an in-depth leadership course based on systems theory—seemed the most likely to offer high potential value to participants.

The financial viability of such a program—a necessity given the scope of time and energy required—remained an important question. How would a multisession leadership course be promoted? How would it successfully compete with high-profile graduate business schools and expensive, well-established executive development programs? Would it be local, regional, or national in scope? Who would be the target audience?

Reasoning that most business leaders develop close relationships with their accountants, the author took the leadership course idea to several well-known accounting firms in three upstate New York cities. Partners in two of the firms enthusiastically endorsed the idea of an advanced leadership course for heads of small and medium-sized businesses. They provided examples of clients who needed help managing relationship challenges and told stories of other clients who understood the technical nature of their businesses but were often befuddled by their inability to develop people, retain talent, and execute succession. The accounting firm partners observed that executives of larger companies gravitate toward university-based executive development programs. Their endorsement of a focus on small businesses was clear and well supported.

Partners from the most enthusiastic firms agreed to collaborate with the author to help market the advanced leadership course to their business leader clients in exchange for a defined number of hours of leadership coaching by the author and his team within their firms. The author's commitment to win–win negotiating, and to staying connected with key influencers (a lesson from biological studies of leadership in nonhuman systems), contributed to this agreement.

Before designing the advanced leadership course, the author gave considerable thought to its strategic objectives. He decided that the course's overarching goal, consistent with Bowen's central concept of differentiation of self, would be "to promote maturity and responsibility among all participants, beginning with self." This focus compelled the author and his co-teachers to measure every decision related to course design and delivery by its predicted capacity to promote maturity and responsibility.

For example, many of the leadership course enrollees stated that their schedules did not allow for much thinking or homework between group sessions. After considering this point of view, the author decided that a learning process without between-session reflection would restrict the course's learning value and enable irresponsibility on the part of participants. During the first group session, the author took a position that practical-application homework would be assigned for every session and that participants would be expected to discuss those assignments at the beginning of every class session. Despite a few moans at the moment of this announcement, participants not only demonstrated a commitment to between-session reflection for the remainder of the course but also commented regularly on the value of that reflection.

Promoting maturity and responsibility in all aspects of the course also guided the author's request that participants speak only on behalf of self during class interactions, eliminating "we" and "you" language in favor of "I." The author explained that taking responsibility for one's own viewpoints and questions presented an opportunity for more responsible dialogue.

On the basis of the overarching strategy of promoting maturity and responsibility beginning with self, seven strategic objectives framed the course design:

1. Provide an opportunity for business leaders to explore and examine their respective multigenerational family histories in an effort to gain greater objectivity about their relationship strengths and vulnerabilities, at work and at home.
2. Convey in nonclinical language the basic tenets of systems thinking—differentiation of self, chronic anxiety, emotional reciprocity, triangles, family projection, and societal regression.
3. Help leaders think more broadly and deeply about the functions of leadership, particularly the distinction between higher maturity relationships and lower maturity relationships.
4. Assist leaders in developing a more strategic and skillful approach to mentoring the high-potential leaders within their organizations.
5. Explore the multifaceted implications of emotional courage in leadership, as contrasted with avoidance, superficiality, distance, and other forms of emotional fusion.
6. Provide a structured, carefully sequenced curriculum, animated by variation in teaching methodologies, to enhance the learning process.
7. To maximize robustness, impose four disciplines on the learning process: (a) Encourage variation in viewpoints by opening the course to all industries within the business sector, as well as not-for-profit and political heads; (b) require a stringent qualification process, ensuring that unmotivated prospects would be "disinvited"; (c) limit the group size to a maximum of 12 participants; and (d) engage the group in a self-designed pledge of confidentiality.

In 1998, 10 business leaders participated in the first Advanced Leadership Course. Participants included the chief financial officer (CFO) of an air cargo company, the president of a confectionary manufacturer, the owner of a 45-person law firm, the founder of a specialized printing company, the medical director of a large health care organization, the entrepreneurial head of a technology start-up, the third-generation president of a family oil business, the vice president of a photo finishing lab, the president of a truck lift-gate manufacturer, and the heir-apparent owner of a large commercial real estate firm.

Of the first 10 participants, 3 were previously known to the author. The remaining enrollees were referred to the course by the accounting firm partners. The promotional efforts of these partners turned out to be a critical element in the first 2 years. In the decade after those first 2 years, course graduates became the primary promoters of the course through word of mouth. As a result, course enrollment during each of the past 13 years has been maximized.

Over that time, the course has changed and grown. For example, during the first 8 years, only the author facilitated the actual course sessions; as of this writing, three others have co-taught or taught the sessions. Similarly, the number of sessions constituting the course was gradually reduced from 10 to 8, so that this learning model could be affordable to a wider range of leaders. A significant contributor to the course's cutting-edge reputation has been the author's willingness to revise course content on the basis of new research from science and his own continued thinking and learning. Moreover, the course's geographical reach has gradually widened. Leader participants from Dallas, San Jose, Chicago, Orlando, Charlotte, and other areas have enabled the advanced leadership course to morph from a local to a national stage.

One aspect of the course that has not varied is the precourse, individual family diagram consultation between each participant and the course facilitator. During this session, participants disclose the facts of four generations of family functioning—the participants' children; the participants' spouses and siblings; the participants' parents and the parents' siblings; and the participants' grandparents and the grandparents' siblings. Questions about their families' emotional patterns stimulate participants' thinking in what, for most, is a new and compelling arena.

At the conclusion of the precourse consultation, each participant is given an application assignment. This assignment might involve acquiring more data about little-known family facts or initiating a conversation with a specific family member with whom conversation has been sparse or altogether absent. Participants are asked to come to the first group session prepared to discuss their follow-up assignments.

Two courses are offered annually, beginning in August and ending in March. One course is offered for C-level leaders: presidents, chief executive officers, owners, CFOs, and other senior leaders. A second course is offered for high-potential or emerging leaders, who are often recommended to the course by their superiors who first participated. A maximum of 12 participants are accepted into each course.

Each course meets for 1 full day per month for 8 consecutive months. This format was judged far superior to an intensive week-long course for two reasons. First, the once-a-month format serves ideas and strategies in manageable portions, leaving space for thinking between sessions. Second, this format creates the opportunity for practical application assignments, reported by most participants as a valuable dimension of learning complementing the classroom.

The course content has been heavily influenced by the thinking of Murray Bowen and Michael Kerr, successive directors of the Bowen Center for the Study of the Family in Washington, DC, and Edwin Friedman, founder of the Center for Family Process and a renowned speaker, teacher, and therapist. Readers familiar with Bowen theory will note the intentional language changes in the listing of course topics in Table 18.1. This represents an effort on the author's part to make an important set of ideas, which historically has been restricted to the worlds of therapy and ministry, accessible to accomplished

Table 18.1 Advanced Leadership Course Sequence

Kick-off buffet (evening before Session 1)
- Confidentiality
- One-on-one participant introductions

Session 1: Clear thinking and clear talking
- Perspective in leadership
- Systems thinking
- The language of leadership
- Soliciting the perspectives of others

Session 2: Emotional maturity in leadership
- Functions of a leader
- Self-awareness and clarity
- Responsibility and maturity

Session 3: Roots of leadership
- Family emotional patterns
- Observing self in the family
- How patterns shift

Session 4: Coaching: A systems view
- Mentoring skills
- Managing triangles
- Coaching clinic: Live issues

Session 5: Presence in leadership
- Depth listening and keen observing
- Self-disclosure
- Calmness and accuracy

Session 6: Courage in leadership
- Forms of distance
- Handling conflicts
- Gumption, toughness, compassion

Session 7: Tending to yourself
- Beliefs and delusions
- Clarity about values
- Building a resource system

Session 8: The self-defined leader
- Course summary
- Continuous improvement

business professionals. The author's commitment to use business-friendly language instead of theoretical nomenclature is discussed later in this chapter.

The advanced leadership course has been designed to support and expand the overarching strategic goal of promoting maturity and responsibility, beginning with self. The sequence of topics shown in Table 18.1 characterizes the course's history.

Teaching methodologies in the advanced leadership course include stimulating presentations on theoretical principles and relationship strategies, reflection exercises, small-group discussions, large-group coaching demonstrations using participants' "live" issues, one-on-one "fishbowl" coaching clinics, and occasional guest presenters. The sessions are held in a comfortable lodge-style setting in upstate New York, featuring healthy food and natural surroundings. Business casual dress is the norm.

Because the author views systems thinking as a comprehensive set of ideas requiring continual exposure and practice, it became evident in the earliest groups that follow-up contact between group members and the course concepts would be a necessary dimension of the overall learning experience. To accomplish this objective, all course graduates are invited to a 1-day annual leaders' retreat. Consistent with the meaning of *retreat* ("stepping back"), this day is designed as a time of reflection and new ideas to reinforce the topics explored in the advanced leadership course. Themes have included "the language of self-definition," "parenting in the executive family," "crisis versus challenge: the importance of the leader's perspective," and "managing vexing relationship challenges." About 100 course graduates attend this refresher day; many make it an annual discipline.

The popularity of the advanced leadership course has made it the central focus of the author's successful consulting practice. An unplanned benefit of the course has been its marketing magnetism. A significant portion of graduates follow up their course participation with individual coaching or requests for a replicated leadership development course for their company management teams. The volume of requests generated by participating leaders has led the author to refer clients to other professionals who possess in-depth familiarity with Bowen theory. These professionals typically started their careers in mental health or ministry, gained exposure to Bowen theory through those professions, and eventually developed a desire to apply their knowledge and skills with business leaders. Those who have worked with the author have found business leadership consulting to involve a long, challenging, and satisfying learning curve.

The advanced leadership course has challenged the author to define himself clearly in the face of resistance and frustration. Virtually all aspects of theory challenge the prevailing societal norms. Most leaders are taught to supply answers, whereas theory asks them to recognize their ignorance and stay curious. Most leaders have been schooled to be "one with the people," but evolution and theory favor clear hierarchy. Most business leaders have been conditioned to expect quick, superficial, task-oriented exchanges with those who report to them, but fostering open dialogue and in-depth conversations better promotes subordinates' leadership development.

The author's experience suggests that only the most motivated leaders can sustain long-term interest in developing clarity and courage in self and in building strong connections with important others who avoid the trap of "globbed togetherness." Throughout the author's time teaching the advanced leadership course, he has predictably encountered a variety of issues, problems, and challenges. Two challenges stand out. The first is managing the resistance of busy leaders to the perceived tedium of learning new ways of thinking and behaving. Second, the author's concerted effort to make the language of theory user friendly to business leaders has exposed a tricky tension between language accessibility and theoretical accuracy. Each of these problems is discussed in succession.

The author has learned valuable lessons about managing others' resistance and discomfort. The most important is that clearly defining self can be relied on as a medicine for almost every form of resistance, recalcitrance, and low maturity in others. Lower maturity individuals, much like a child in a temper tantrum, often whine and complain interminably, even when it becomes clear the "child" is not really upset. Clients' emotional reactivity to the demands of a new way of thinking shows up in a spectrum of expressions:

"I don't know how to do this."
"I don't think you understand [the difficulty of] my situation."
"People are always pressuring me."
"I don't have the time to coach people this way—it's easier if I just do it myself."
"This is too expensive."
"I just want to solve the problem."

During the author's early learning days with systems thinking, he spent considerable time with Friedman, who often deadpanned to clients, "I'm not going to waste my time trying to stuff insight into unmotivated people." In a similar vein, it has become standard fare for the author to address whining, complaining, defensiveness, and resistance by defining himself to prospective course participants. Some of the common self-defined statements routinely delivered in the qualifying interview with course prospects follow. Note the provocative edge in each of these self-defined statements:

- "If you want answers, I can supply you with a list of less expensive consultants who will give you answers. If, on the other hand, you are more interested in questions that will get you thinking, you have come to the right place."
- "I am not too interested in working with the meek and easily offended. I do better with people who are up for a challenge and able to look at themselves."
- "I tend to attract avoiders who want to operate with more courage. I have noticed that real food looks especially inviting to someone used to bottle feedings."
- "I find it more meaningful to help the strong get stronger than to help the weak become less weak. Where do you see yourself on that spectrum?"

- "In my opinion, people who don't want to take on the challenge of understanding themselves and their reactions should get out of leadership. That includes parenting."

The author's second challenge, that of constructing a less theoretical language for teaching systems theory to business leaders without compromising theoretical soundness, presented an even greater test. The sharp minds that developed family systems theory functioned mostly in the context of academic and clinical settings. Business owners, particularly small business owners who hail from blue-collar backgrounds, tend to possess practical values and simple language. Many started with little or nothing and worked their way up to become successful owners and leaders. Using language that others understand is, for the author, an important ingredient in building strong connections. But strong connections must not come at the price of theoretical integrity. The author has managed this tension by carefully defining new terms, to the best of his ability, in ways that are accurately aligned with solid theory.

One poignant example of this "relanguaging" effort has been the author's decision to replace *differentiation of self* with the terms *emotional maturity* and *self-definition*. *Emotional maturity* is defined as a three-faceted idea: (a) a focus on promoting connection, rather than fusion, in family and other close relationships; (b) a focus on clear thinking rather than automatic (emotional) reactions; and (c) a focus on taking full responsibility for one's own daily life and destiny, including one's responses, needs, wants, and decisions, and one's part in the problems at hand, without blaming others or the circumstances.

Self-definition has been explained as "taking a clear position—through stated words or action—on an issue, belief or decision." Examples of self-definition include

"This is what I believe...."
"This is what I will do...."
"This is what I won't do...."
"This is what I expect...."
"This is what I need...."
"This is what I want...."

The author learned early on that terms such as *self-differentiation, family projection process,* and *multigenerational emotional transmission process,* although theoretically accurate, would not be easily understood by the layperson. For that reason, the author gave more thought to colloquial explanations. For example, the family projection process was explained as follows:

What one generation doesn't see clearly, what one generation won't deal with or refuses to address—that issue or problem will not go away. It will show up—in one form or another—for the next generation to deal with. The same thing can happen in businesses.

Translating theory to more user-friendly language is a work in progress. Discernment about the "right" or "best" way to put family systems theory into words will be an increasing necessity for those whose mission is, in the words of Bowen, "to bring the theory to the world." If the words *to the world* are accurate, and if others far and wide are to be able to hear and understand the theory, the language of teachers, consultants, and therapists must be marked as much by innovation as by loyalty to the original terms.

Small businesses employ most American workers. Leaders of these businesses wield considerable influence, not only within their businesses and families, but within the board and community leadership positions they occupy. The author chose this population as a target for his Advanced Leadership Course on the basis of the impact of business leaders on society as a whole. Although business leaders almost always understand the nature and craft of their businesses, they often lack exposure to high-impact knowledge about human emotional functioning. The author and his consulting team have successfully developed one format in which to teach systems thinking to business leaders. He views this as a modest contribution to the overall effort of advancing human functioning.

19

Misunderstandings From the Family Field: Selected Segments by Dr. Murray Bowen at the Minnesota Institute of Family Dynamics

Compiled and Edited by G. MARY BOURNE

Setting the Scene

My copy editor, who knew Dr. Bowen and his teaching style, said she sat in her office and laughed out loud as she read this chapter for the first time. Another colleague, who had been in that particular training session, recalled how overwhelmed she had been by the depth and scope of the questions raised. For me, it's an important reminder of the decades of time, and the many layers of research, that went into the development of Bowen theory. Dr. Bowen, for his part, simply said, "My whole goal would be to help you get your **thinking** straight." What follows is, verbatim, his effort to encourage thinking.

Dr. Bowen With Beginning Class of Trainees in Minneapolis, May 2, 1983

People, I don't know what I'll do today, or where I'll start or where I'll end up. In the past, I used to do a lot of diagrams. I started doing family diagrams back in the 1940s—as a way of seeing the situation. And it's become so simplistic I don't use 'em no more. Over the years in working with people I'd put a diagram up, and people'd copy it down and act like they'd know it. So I quit doing diagrams, and I've all but quit video tapes. People look at a video tape and say, "Aw, now I'll do it the way he do's it!" and screw it up royally. So I quit using video tapes, and I quit doing them damn diagrams.

My whole goal would be to help you get your **thinking** straight, and getting thinking straight would apply to all the various disciplines. How much have you read? How much have you read religion? How much have you read philosophy? How much have you read biology? How much have you read psychology? And are you able to separate psychology from philosophy, from biology, from religion, from medicine? And how you go about getting them separated?

Anyway, I used to do these diagrams, and then about 15 years later, one of my residents said, "Well, what you've been talking about is a **genogram**, isn't it?" I said, "But that's a new term. And I simply use the term Family Diagram—English words." I had a thing back then about never coining professional terms, 'cause when you coin new terms, people hear 'em in crazy ways. They hear 'em through their own heads, and then they're different. So I didn't want to coin any new terms. I put a lot of time on that.

But that resident came up with the term Genogram and popularized it, and now every damn body knows what a genogram is. And I don't know what the hell it means. Oh, when a person says "a genogram," I know what a person means when they say that. But now they want **me** to respond to it—something I developed as a Family Diagram. And they ask me what a genogram is. And now I'm expected to know what's in their heads. That's a simple old thing. Undo that. So that gets to be—gets to be the way things get changed by society.

Anyway, the world is the way the majority of the people out there say it is. And it fits the simplistic thinking of people. I've tried to stay ahead of the simplistic thinking of people. And I would hope maybe that you would—maybe you will. But you don't know the intensity of the societal pressure to think the way society wants you to think.

There are hundreds of unanswered questions. And the media runs one through as if the media knows the answers. And you are working in the mental health profession, and now **you** know the answer to that? And where did you get that answer? Off the media? Or did it come from something you know about people?

All it takes to get on a media show is to do a book. And then they'll ask you if you're an expert on the book that you wrote—inaccurate though it might be. Anyway, I think the media puts an incorrect tilt on a situation. But you're a part of the great majority that watches that media stuff, aren't you? Do you believe what you see? How much of what you see do you believe, and how much do you not believe? Do you have a way of accounting for your choices?

The family idea's really caught on these days—so much so it's become a popular fad. Are you going to pick up and ride that fad—get on that band wagon? Is what you know about families any better than the parents of the world? Is what you know about families any more than the mothers a hundred years ago knew? What's your evidence? You read it in a book somewhere? Well, ha! ha! Do you believe everything you read? Or do you throw out everything you read? What do you accept and what do you reject? What do you do about your framework? In other words, do you **have** a framework for being able to evaluate a fact? Or are you just going to pick up a belief?

I'll ask you some serious questions and let you break them down. Any one of these things you can put a lifetime on. And one would be: What's the difference between truth and fact? How can somebody louse you up with truth? What's truth? What's the difference between a belief and a conviction? How solid is philosophy as a way of thinking? Is mathematics a science? I'll let you struggle with that one—that'll be good for ten years, if you get **that** figured out.

In other words, these are things about which volumes have been written—all kinds of different ideas about it. Most of this stuff is in the libraries. Now when you go to a library, what do you take out? What do you read? There are volumes and volumes there. Do you read best-sellers? Where'd the author of a best-seller get it? Where'd it come from? In other words, if you were seriously asking the question, how did these people **know** what they were putting out was fact or truth? How did they know it?

Apparently as far as anybody knows, Freud was the author of modern day psychology. I think most people would give him credit for that. What is the basic operating premise of Freud? And how did Freud jibe with Adler or Jung, or with all the other early people? What kind of modifications in mental health have taken place over the last century? Freud came on the scene **about** a hundred years ago. When Freud developed his way of thinking, how well was he up on all of the *other* thinking that went before it? Where did Freud get his ideas? They had to come from somewhere. How has Freud been integrated with all the stuff that's come since? Who are the people who have influenced this?

Do you know all the terms that are used out there? When people say "mental illness" do you know what they mean? How many terms are synonymous with the term **mental**? Is it a good term? Are you gonna throw it out? You gonna throw it out because other people don't use it? You gonna do a substitute for it? What kind of a term are you gonna use?

Anyway, these are all background things. How does this all integrate with philosophy? It's easy to go back and quote a philosopher. But if you quote a philosopher is there a problem? You can go back and quote a philosopher who says almost anything.

Now I'd have you go back and get something that's **reasonably secure.** What is your most secure basis of all knowledge? Are you gonna be happy with using an author as a basis of something? There's a hell of a lot of people that don't go beyond putting an author in.

How 'bout the word "mental health"? Is that any good? What is mental health? Do you know what it is? If there's a mental health, there ought to be a mental illness, huh? Well, if you can define mental illness, you should be able to define mental health. Shouldn't you? What does "health" mean? What does "normal" mean? You know what normal is? You ever try to define it? This has to do with the squishy meaning of words. What are you gonna do? Go back to the dictionary? Have you got a dictionary that's right about all these damn things? You gonna make Webster your authority? Where in the hell did Webster get his ideas?

In other words, there has to be a basis for ideas. And there is a kind of a basis some**where**. But how far back do you gotta go? You could go beyond Freud and say "Darwin said...." But where'd he get his ideas? Or are you gonna start off with something the sociologists said? Or with something a philosopher said? And then, where'd the philosophers get their way of thinking?

Anyway, this has to do with facts. Where are you gonna take your text from? And what kind of a screen do you have to decide which points are the important ones—or the **most** important ones—and which are the least important ones?

In psychology these days, you're hearing all kinds of things about "cognitive" things. What the hell is cognitive? Do cognitive things have any influence on instinctual things? What is "instinct"? Does instinct apply to birds, or does it apply to you? You got any instincts in you? If you do, what the hell are they? Or does an instinct apply to a goose? What's the difference between a feeling and instincts?

You can find your author anywhere. You can say the basis is mathematics. Is mathematics a science? What's your evidence for that? Where'd you get that idea? What's your proof for it? What is a science? Can mental health ever be a science? Can human behavior be a science? If human behavior can be a science, then maybe there can be a science of ants. Is there a science of termites? If there's a science of termites, there ought to be a science of human behavior, shouldn't there? Or is only the ants a science, and not humans?

Is human behavior governed by a **brain?** Can the brain itself be scientific? Maybe the brain itself can be scientific, but what the brain **says** is not scientific, huh?

Anyway, you think this course is gonna be easy. It ain't gonna be so darned easy. Unless you're gonna take Mary's head as a basis of all knowledge. You take her head as a basis of knowledge, then maybe you'll be better off. It's easier to learn that way. Then you won't have to figure out where in the hell she got what she believes.

Or, I could put all kinds of stuff on the board. And you could copy it down, and then you could say "Bowen believes that." Or is that as squishy as everything else?

Or, you can take your own level of functioning now as a given. Who told you that you can trust your own level of functioning? Is it screwed up? Or do you think your own level of intellectual functioning is **the** level, and you're gonna judge all the world by it?

Anyway, what I'm trying to do is to say that a framework for these things is more complex than it seems. And **unless** you get a solid framework somewhere, your thinking is as squishy as the rest of the world out there. And we're living in a squishy world, in which people believe a hodge-podge. That's where a hell of a lot of people are—including people who teach courses in these universities. And if they are putting together a hodge-podge, where does that leave you?

There **are** some sources out there that are reasonably reliable. And there are people who have given thought to these things over the years. But nobody can give you a predigested outline of what the world is like. There are too damn many different kinds of outlines out there. So if there are all these outlines, then how can you trust **you**? Are you as suspect as everybody else? And how do you go about getting a basis in fact?

You know, 15 years ago I did a public presentation about **my family.** Still hearing about the damn thing. And everybody wants to pick that up as a beautiful example of what they're gonna do about their families, you know. And they go through all this junk, which has to do with presentations about your own family. Now you do a presentation about your own family; then see if all that stuff ain't in you, too. Well, I'll be damned! How about letting me hear what's in you and not what's out there in somebody else? How much is in you?

You can hear all this darn thing about families; you can make a diagram from here to kingdom come. And that's why I don't want to see too many of them diagrams no more. Because you get so good at putting in what's wrong with everybody else. Well, I'm interested in what the hell's wrong with you. I ain't interested in no more diagrams of what's wrong with your family— what's wrong with everybody else. But what's wrong with you? And the one that gets labeled with the problem is one's own family. So I want to know about you. What's wrong with *you?*

And this applies to you people who become mental health professionals, too, where you look down your snoot at the rest of the world, and you diagnose 'em. And what is your part in that? How are you contributing to that? This has to do with: whatever is in this world, you play a part in it. And you get off on the business of saying the problem is **over there.** Which means that I'm the center of the universe, and I'm good—I'm good, and you're bad.

I'm not gonna go into all the details about this stuff I tried to define about families; I'll let you read about that. And you're either gonna get it or you're not gonna get it. Everybody's gonna explain that stuff to you—**their** version of it. And their version is probably screwy somewhere. So you'll pick up a version that you **like** to hear. Well, **how do you do?** So that makes you different from everybody else! You're gonna believe them simplistic ways. So I won't be putting too much of that in any more.

You see, after I did this thing on one's own family—back 15 years ago— then it was picked up in all kinds of places and given media exposure. And now it is generally assumed that if you interest yourself in your own family, you learn a hell of a lot. Which you do. But that is no shortcut to knowing all these other things. And if you believe the popular magazines, all you gotta do is go home and say hello to the good people, and then you're automatically gonna know something. But you go back, and then you assume—you make contact with 'em, and you **assume something** from the contact with 'em. And then the more you do that, the more you don't know. That's one of the pitfalls of those who say, "Learn about **inter**generational stuff." I'd call it a pitfall, but it's also a horror story, of the way things get to be made simplistic.

I think one of the biggest problems people have to face is getting out of the position of being a therapist. There are so many people in this world—and that doesn't just have to do with a profession. It has to do with parents and all sorts of other people, too, who occupy the position of know-it-all. And that puts everybody else in a lousy position. Of course, I could spend a whole hour on the **disease** of being a therapist. And how do you get out of that disease? You'll spend the rest of your damn days on that.

That would be the equivalent of the guy who heard what I had to say about societal regression, and he wanted to set up a group of societal therapists. There was an immediate assumption that they know what's wrong with society, and they's gonna fix it. And they don't have the slightest notion of what's wrong—or what to do about it. Anyway, I'd hope that you would work on that—on how in the hell you get yourself out of the position of Mr. Know-It-All, who's the expert in everything. Because the more you get in that position, the harder it is for you to ask an honest question. Because you automatically assume you know it. No matter what they say, you know the answer to it. And that is a God-awful disease. Just try to fight your way out of that one.

You see, in families there's this tendency to do the same damn thing those people who wanted to be "societal therapists" were gonna do to society. And that is, the family people who are in charge project the problem to those who are **not** in charge. And now the ones not in charge become the labeled ones—the sick ones. And you see all that beautiful stuff up there in families. Only you're doing it, too. You're playing your part in it. And what are you going to do about it?

And child-focused-ness has to do with this, too. You say "There's a problem here somewhere," and you put the burden on the child. And you label it there, and you keep it labeled there, and then the child becomes sick. And you do the same damn thing to society, and to each other. And it couldn't exist out there without you playing a part in it. And what are you **going to do** about that?

Over the years, I've talked about my own effort with that sort of an orientation, and what you **do with it** in your own family. You're a human being, and they're human beings. And can you relate to 'em on a human level, without being assigned to either a superior position, or an inferior position?

You see, people's professional training has a way of, sort of, *amplifying* that problem—amplifying what the family already thought about them. What the family thought about you in the beginning is probably most important. And then what you've learned through the years is important. What you **assume** you know is important, too.

You've got a whole bunch of professional backgrounds in this class. And I suppose there's as many advantages to that as disadvantages to it. I suppose in some ways, the more you get involved in any one discipline the less you know about other disciplines. And the more you know whatever discipline you're in, you should know the bottom line of that discipline, where that discipline came from, how it stacks up with all the others, and how it defines science. For a lot of people—particularly for social workers—science is defined for them by a Ph.D. program.

I started out in medicine. And I had some qualms about movin' to psychiatry, and how psychiatry would fit in with medicine. The drift is still there; it's a mile wide and a mile deep. But I wondered from the very beginning why in the world psychiatry couldn't be recognized as a science. And I'll leave that as a question, with you. I don't have any answers to it, other than partial answers, about what will it take to make human behavior into a science? Is it possible for human behavior to become a science? I think it can.

Incidentally, I think that any of Carl Sagan's TV stuff that he's put out within the past two or three years is wonderful stuff. How did he get to be an astronomer? That was just his wonderings about the universe. What's the universe made up of? How'd it get to be the way it is? But I think anything you read of Carl Sagan is good stuff. That is not an answer **in itself**. But if you can know that Carl Sagan is not the answer, but he has good stuff, he'll give you a pretty good notion of the origin of science. And you absolutely cannot get a definition of science **from** anybody. But there is something solid about science, which has been solid for centuries, and it always will be.

Back in the early days, I decided I wanted to have a whirl at research. With a medical and psychiatric, and a psychoanalytic background, I was thinking: Well, if I'm gonna get into this, I've got to learn the scientific method as practiced by psychology. It would take me a long time to learn that. I didn't understand too much about it. Then, and after I'd had enough time with NIH and all those hot-shot scientists, I changed my mind. I began saying things like, "You can't chi square a feeling and make it into a fact." In other words, psychologists have their own ways to define science. They have lots of ways of taking a **thinking system** (which spins out of the head) and categorizing it and shaping it up, and making it **appear** scientific—which they call the scientific method. And as I see it, psychology dips over into philosophy, and then it attempts to make that into something which is **objectifiable.** Most of mental health is dominated more by psychology than anything else these days. So that makes psychology with its own problem.

I got off into this field back in the 40s, wondering if human behavior could not be a science. And **the whole of my theory** is based just as much on science as I could make it. **Everything in it** is based on science—and **facts.** And every single point has been labored and labored in microscopic detail. Well, all the stuff I've written on theory over the years has been based on that.

In my view, there are important ways in which **human behavior is exact.** I believe that human behavior is **factual**. Do you? Do you think that the behavior of monkeys is a science? Do you think the behavior of ants is a science? How about termites? How about the bees? Can that be a science? Then, how about human behavior? Can **that** be? Are there scientific facts about human behavior? What part of human behavior is **not** a science?

It is scientific fact that the earth is a planet, that it's part of the universe. That's fairly well supported by facts, by science. It is **a fact** that there are seasons on the earth, which has to do with the rotation of the earth in relation to the sun—the tilt of the earth to the sun. It is a fact that there's water on the earth. It is a fact—a **scientific** fact, I would say—that the tides go up and down. And this has to do with the rotation of the earth—with gravity. It is a fact that forms of life, animal life and plant life, reproduce themselves. It is a fact that seasons come and go, that the cycle goes through a growth period and then an inactive period, which is winter. It has to do with the seasons and the tides. And man is part of all this complex.

And there's two forms of life on earth. Can you separate those two forms of life? One's plant life, and one's animal life. They came from the same place, didn't they? As far as we know. And there's only one planet, as far as we know, that has water on it. And all life is made up of—one of the big components is water. So if in the whole damn universe, the only planet with water on it is Earth, that would make Earth different. Then if plant life and animal life are the two forms of life, then that makes you a cousin of the flowers, doesn't it? Then if the animal life on earth is part of —is related to plant life—then everything came from a common origin. And I think science is tending to support that.

When you get back to the origins of these things, there's one important fact of life, and that has to do with comparative anatomy. The human brain is not a hell of a lot different from an ape's brain, is it? How much is the human skeleton different from an ape's skeleton? And the next form below that, and below that, and below that? How much is a human **brain** different from other brains? Each brain in each form of life is a little bit different, but the basic nature of the brain is the same. We can take it on down to the brains of the lesser, lower animals. And how do these things fit together? It is a fact that the brain in the human is probably the most complex organ that separates the human from other forms of life.

How much of human behavior can be scientific? You could say it is **a fact**— you see, in lower forms of life the two sexes are involved in the same form—in the one celled forms, the lower forms. And these forms divide by simple division. But in the more complex forms of life, it takes two separate sexes. So would you want to debate **as a scientific fact** that the human being reproduces? That's a fact, ain't it? Reproduction, one generation after another, so I'd call that science. And it is a fact that in higher forms of life they are divided into male and female. Two sexes. Sex gets too complex to put it all into one form, so they get to be two forms. So we'd say it **evolved** into the two forms—too damn complex to have just one. That's a fact, ain't it?

Another one has to do with the **function** of the brain. I'll try to touch briefly on that today. I think one of the main things that distinguishes systems thinking from other thinking is that it entertains the notion of function. **Function, in contrast to structure.** I'll try to get into that a little bit more this afternoon.

You see, what I'm doing today is staying away from all them damn diagrams. They're a dime a dozen. You can buy those in sheet form. You can buy 'em in any music store. Set them to any damn tune you want. So, I'm staying away from them diagrams.

III
New Horizons for Systems Thinking and Bowen Theory

I'm trying today to put in the kind of thinking that had gone into the development of the theory in the beginning, and then an effort to extend the theory. Now that effort is not a clean one … it was as clean as I could get it at the time … anyway, I would just hope that you would have an inquiring mind, that you'd keep an open mind—always, always, always—always. And realize that there [are] always gaps in what you know.

Murray Bowen, MD, April 30, 1984
Minnesota Institute of Family Dynamics, Minneapolis, MN

Murray Bowen was concerned that without a sustained effort to build and maintain theoretical and research-based bridges back to and from the established natural sciences, his theory would be at risk of becoming a closed system of beliefs. This section features two such bridge-building efforts and a compilation of recent and innovative Bowen family systems theory applications that seek to extend systems thinking into new domains, disciplines, and cultures. It seems likely that Bowen would have welcomed such thoughtful and emergent applications of his theory, insofar as they foster a more comprehensive and robust way of looking at relationships, environments, and ourselves.

20

Integrating Bowen Theory With Academic Research, Teaching, and Service

CHERYL B. LESTER

In this chapter, a faculty member appointed in the College of Liberal Arts and Sciences at the University of Kansas reflects on her efforts at integrating Bowen family systems theory with her professional life.[1] As a theory and method for exploring the self in the context of emotional systems, Bowen theory has exerted a steady impact on the author's effort to define herself in relation to the three areas of her professional responsibilities: research, teaching, and service. Her efforts at emotional integration of Bowen theory in these areas and in the multiple systems to which she belongs have been advanced by systems thinking, an awareness of emotional process in self and other, and the effort to define self.

Integrating Bowen Theory With My Research

Reflecting on her career from a systems perspective, the author brings a broader view to bear on some of the professional pressures and limits that accompanied her initial appointment more than 20 years ago as an assistant professor whose research and teaching expectations were broadly defined in the areas of 20th-century American literature, critical theory, comparative literature, and modern poetry. This diversity of expectations reflected the need to explore rapidly changing assumptions and methods and emerging trends in the field of literary and cultural studies, and to fill multiple vacancies in a department that had not hired new faculty in literary studies for more than 15 years. The search for a candidate with a specialty in 20th-century American literature, a genre expertise in modern poetry, or both and professional training in critical theory and comparative literature reflected an effort both to reproduce traditional approaches to literary study and to move toward emergent theoretical and methodological trends. The job position was defined with

---

[1] Cheryl B. Lester thanks the College of Liberal Arts and Sciences at the University of Kansas for supporting the opportunities and efforts described in this essay, the Bowen Center for the Study of the Family for promoting the development of systems perspectives, and Philip Barnard, PhD, Associate Professor, University of Kansas, and Michael Sweeney, Ph.D., Lecturer, University of Missouri at Kansas City, for their editorial assistance.

one foot in the past and another in the future and, consequently, reflected systemic contradictions and transformations in the disciplinary field.

Because she completed her graduate training in literary studies 15 years after any of her colleagues had earned their doctoral degrees, the author entered a department with a loosening yet still outdated consensus on the object of study, protocols for interpretation, and boundaries of the field and discipline. Even as she was completing her own graduate training, most departments were suspended uneasily between older models that were idealist and relatively detached from historical reflection and newer, so-called post-structuralist and cultural–materialist models. In keeping with the period's critique of classical foundationalism, literary studies increasingly identified with critical and historical analysis and saw themselves and the broader field of the human sciences as more similar to than different from the social sciences.[2] In that period, as someone from the same era recently remarked of her own graduate training (with some exaggeration), training in social–scientific and philosophical theory was considered sufficiently important that it was possible to get a degree in English without reading a single novel. Although the author's graduate program was indeed focused on theoretically oriented research, the department in which she took a position at a time when jobs in higher education were scarce was alert yet not broadly attuned to "new" theoretical paradigms. Colleagues and graduate students in the department practiced a relatively traditional style of literary studies that focused on canonical literary history and was not yet realigned with broad disciplinary shifts then underway. Indeed, it would be several years before a critical mass of faculty members at the university approached texts and "textuality" in more contemporary terms as signifying systems whose meanings were constituted in fundamentally historical and social relations.[3]

As part of this general shift, the discipline's definition of its object of study was changing. Newer faculty drew on interpretive practices developed for literary texts and on other hermeneutic protocols to analyze not simply literary works and a broader range of written documents but nonalphabetic practices that also signify, like wrestling, parades, musical performance, and so forth. Through the influence of structuralism and poststructuralism, *text* was being redefined as an arena of semiosis, that is, in terms of the processes whereby all cultural forms, practices, and institutions produce meanings through multiple cycles, levels, and systems of signification. Linguistics, anthropology,

---

[2] For a discussion of the historical development of the social sciences and their transformation in recent scholarly generations, see Wallerstein (2004).

[3] For an introduction to these transformations from this period by the leading theorist of the Birmingham school, who died in 1988, see Williams (1989), especially Part II. For another review from the period by an author with an investment in the survival of literary values and a fear that we were approaching a crisis in meaning, see Birkerts (1994, pp. 189, 196), especially "The Death of Literature" (pp. 183–197).

psychoanalysis, and literary studies offered hermeneutic models that proved useful across a variety of disciplines in the human and social sciences, including history, sociology, and political science, to analyze additional phenomena that could be studied as cultural and historical constructions rather than as categories that are given before historical determinations. Categories such as gender, race, class, and sexuality and practices such as music, theater, dance, and communications lent themselves to new productive analyses aimed at revealing not only the internal rules and regulations that govern and circulate meaning in these diverse areas but also the extrinsic forces and relations of power that sustain these meanings or challenge and transform them.

Steadily, literature departments transformed the canons of literary study, broadened literary to cultural study, and asserted the political importance to the determination of values, norms, beliefs, desires, and so forth of cultural production in all forms of media (including the rapidly expanding new media). Faculty became more attuned to the role of cultural forms, practices, and institutions within broader formations and within complex and interlocking systems in a process that establishes hegemony by adapting to change and absorbing and neutralizing alternatives and opposition so as to generate and regenerate dominant values and beliefs. A cultural backlash took "tenured radicals" to task and used buzzwords and phrases such as "political correctness" and the "closing of the American mind" to condemn their advanced analytic models and emphasize their supposed failure to produce and reproduce "cultural literacy." This conservative response lamented the waning of the once dominant value of aesthetic prestige and the emergence of analyses that reveal the formative role of literature and culture in defining citizenship, social and cultural capital, political rights and representation, and so forth.

Rigorous questioning along such lines had some of its beginnings in the post–World War II era, when interdisciplinary theorists from the Frankfurt School for Social Research (1930s–1960s) who survived the war in exile drew connections between the emergence of mass media and the rise to power of fascist regimes. Like Bowen, these thinkers studied the forms and processes of persuasion and the social forces of conformity and dissent. The Frankfurt School, like the Birmingham School of cultural materialism (1960s–1980s), was especially alert to these issues in the context of rapid developments in the technology of communications and mass media. Such critical, oppositional thinking, in combination with other strands of materialist and formalist theory, informed the prevailing framework for scholarship in literary and cultural studies in the 1980s and shaped a new generation of faculty.

It is productive and rewarding to explore and analyze these conflicts and debates over values, practices, methods, and ideas not only as a hegemonic process but also, drawing on Bowen theory, as an emotional process. From this perspective, the author has a systematic way of thinking about the emotional challenges that were involved as she attempted to advance oppositional theories, methods, and goals in a department that was still guided by established aesthetic and political hierarchies. Just 15 years ago, some colleagues objected, for example, to shifts in the author's courses that opened the literary and cultural canon to the production of women, workers, non-Whites, youth, popular (lowbrow) culture, emerging media, and so forth. Differences of opinion regarding the appropriate scope of the curriculum contributed to a climate of emotional reactivity that must have affected everyone. Although the author understood intellectually that the period's methodological advances challenged habitual and ingrained beliefs, values, investments, and patterns of thinking and feeling, she had limited personal abilities and no theory or method for navigating this highly reactive emotional field. Having acquired her ideas and methods in academic communities of like-minded inquiry and practice, she was not adequately prepared for the challenge of defining herself in a climate of intellectual and political difference.

These challenges may have contributed to the author's interest in developing a deeper understanding of Bowen theory and its applications. Along with her successful application to the postgraduate program at the Bowen Center, the author undertook several research projects aimed at advancing her knowledge and emotional integration of Bowen theory. First, with the goal of finding practical applications for literary and cultural materials as they illuminate social relationships and forces, the author collaborated on a social work textbook. An anthology of first-person literary writings, case studies, and analyses by social work practitioners, the textbook guides students in social welfare to recognize and adapt to difference or diversity in their professional practice (Lieberman & Lester, 2003). Second, with the goal of learning how others apply Bowen theory in a variety of professional settings, the author collaborated to design, organize, and successfully submit for publication the prospectus for this volume.

Third, with the goal of setting out on the royal road to the emotional integration of Bowen theory, the author began to research her family of origin, make efforts to bridge emotional cutoff, and define herself within the emotional system of her large and widely dispersed extended family. Although these efforts were on some level ill-advised departures from the road to promotion to full professor, they provided the author with emotional resources that she needed in the short term and with new theoretical tools that she could apply over the long term to her research on American author William Faulkner (1897–1962).

For the author, Faulkner's stories and novels offer dramas about characters from the Deep South whose purchase on others and on their environment is narrow, whose freedom to think or act for self is constrained, and whose capacity for change is limited. She finds rich detail in Faulkner's writings about the experience of confronting a constraining emotional system and discovering the limits of one's own autonomy. At the same time, she wants to explore and demonstrate the ways in which his detailed observations, imaginative portraits, and expressive powers fall short of offering an adequate picture of the history and life of the segregated South. Using Bowen theory, the author explores in Faulkner's writings the expression of emotionally driven thoughts and feelings, bodily responses to heightened stress, emotional reactivity, and so forth as symptoms of societal regression in a region whose history of exploitation, oppression, and violence against Black Southerners earned it the nickname of "American Congo."[4]

Although she find less outright bias in writings and testimonies by Faulkner than by contemporary authors, landowners, and planters in the Delta, who fail to acknowledge or take responsibility for the systematic exploitation of their fellows, the author is nonetheless troubled by the blind spots and biases that occur in Faulkner. Some cannot tolerate the experience of reading Faulkner because of his one-sided presentation of the world that stretched from Memphis to Vicksburg along the Mississippi River valley. Scholars writing about the planters generally conclude that they must have been liars, victims of self-deception, or more or less knowing agents of larger market forces. Faulkner scholars, including the author, have relied on Freud's theory of defense mechanisms, such as repression, regression, projection, denial, and sublimation, to illuminate the processes through which characters in Faulkner avoid evidence or relationships that threaten their beliefs or condemn their actions. The author draws on concepts from Bowen theory to demonstrate how these fictions dramatize the ways in which emotional systems and networks of relationships transmit anxiety and restrict independent thoughts, feelings, and actions within an emotional field. An ongoing effort to think systems supports her goal of making a contribution to the scholarship that continues to proliferate in the intense emotional field that surrounds the study of Faulkner.

Integrating Bowen Theory With Teaching

As with her scholarship, the author's efforts to integrate Bowen theory with her teaching led her to move in new directions. First, she developed courses thematically focused on family and theoretically focused on Bowen theory; second, she collaborated on the development of a program in Jewish studies, to which she also contributed a new course on Jewish literature and culture in the United States; and third, she provided opportunities for students to engage in service learning in institutions, agencies, and programs outside the university.[5] These new directions reflect the author's efforts to place herself

---

[4] See Pickens (1921) and Woodruff (2003).

[5] For further reading and an introduction to scholarship on academic service learning, see Campus Compact's (2003) *Introduction to Service-Learning Toolkit: Readings and Resources for Faculty.*

in contexts that revive the challenges she encountered as a beginning faculty member and offer fresh opportunities for defining herself and holding her own course in an emotional field.

As a teacher, the author is accustomed to working with late adolescents or young adults at a formative stage of their lives. Most undergraduate students are in the early stages of moving away from their families for the first time, and most graduate students are not much further along in the process. Teaching courses that draw on Bowen theory offers the author an opportunity to meet one of the central goals of her teaching philosophy, which is to meet students halfway or, in other words, to match the knowledge that she brings to the course and classroom with the knowledge that students bring. Following radical pedagogy theorist Paolo Freire, the author rejects the "banking theory," a pedagogy that presumes that students are like empty piggy banks to be filled with knowledge deposited by the teacher. Instead, she aims to provide students with the tools to reflect on their own experience by developing critical consciousness (Freire, 1973). Leading students to approach their knowledge of and relation to family as a research question satisfies this goal. Offering students unfamiliar tools and methods for thinking about themselves and their families provides them with a chance to think for themselves, that is, to gather evidence, reflect on experience, grasp new theories for understanding, and consider methods for producing change. Studying the concepts of Bowen theory, constructing family diagrams, and exploring emotional process moves students toward new ways of thinking about relationships and emotional systems.[6] Students begin to see that the process of separating from their parents is one that involves many others. It also offers a rigorous method for challenging expectations, assumptions, and ideals about the family that saturate people's thoughts and feelings and the literary and cultural materials in the environment.

By drawing on her students' intimate knowledge about the process of separating from the family, the author is able to lay the groundwork for analyses of the transitions and processes that disperse families and social groups on a large scale. Modernity, migration and immigration, urbanization, globalization—all these social phenomena, the author believes, can be better grasped if students can approach them on a personal, smaller scale. From reflecting on the processes involved in their own separation from family, students can turn to the examination of readings about the transition from traditional to modern and postmodern or global societies, demographic movements or flows of capital

---

[6] Kerr (1999) and readings in Kerr and Bowen (1988), for example, introduce students to natural systems and to the concept of the family as an emotional system. In a collection of stories about ethnic families, TuSmith and Bergevin (2000) offer students a chance to analyze a variety of experiences and approaches to the family.

and labor, and the impact of these transitions and flows on family and other social networks.[7]

Integrating the content of Bowen theory into a variety of courses on literary and cultural studies of the family has also helped the author bring the concepts of Bowen theory into conversation with currently dominant cultural theories. As a scholar and teacher, the author views her teaching and research within the context of a community of inquiry dominated by prevailing beliefs and practices about culture, its social and historical construction, and the power interests that it serves. These prevailing beliefs and practices in literary and cultural studies have succeeded in opening to scrutiny a wide range of normative ideas, values, and practices. Debates over gender roles, sexual preference, marital rights, and so forth, for example, often hinge on claims as to what is natural and should thus be permissible, and unreflected ideas about so-called nature are habitually used in arguments defending prevailing or traditional cultural norms. Contemporary literary and cultural studies have noted that these claims are by and large social–historical constructions, rather than "natural" or transhistorical givens. Consequently, the entire category of nature and the natural is often equated with a naïve sense of phenomena that are pregiven or unhistorical and is thus met with skepticism, emotional reactivity, and defensiveness. As academics in literary and cultural studies increasingly turn to studies of the environment, the body, and other aspects of "nature" that interface with the cultural world, they seem to be developing more carefully nuanced theoretical perspectives with regard to the concept of nature. As this thinking progresses, Bowen theory's inquiry into nature, natural systems, and emotional process may offer avenues for research and discovery.

The author's efforts to connect with a large network of extended family intensified her activity in local Jewish organizations and with Jewish organizations and groups at the university. She collaborated with a small group of faculty to advocate for resources to support research and teaching in the field of Jewish studies, and a program in Jewish studies was established in 2008. In connection with the approval of a proposal to establish a minor in Jewish studies in spring 2001, the author developed a course in Jewish American literature and culture, which she teaches regularly. The author's interest in Jewish studies was a logical outgrowth of efforts she began in the early 1990s when, in keeping with a national trend toward multiculturalism, she introduced multicultural surveys of American literature since the Civil War. In connection with her research on the underrepresented history and life of African Americans in the segregated South, she also developed undergraduate and graduate courses in African American literary and cultural studies. These courses aimed at correcting the narrow viewpoints that governed not simply the literary writings of canonical authors like William Faulkner but

---

[7] Shapiro (2001) provided a view of the family as a moving target in political debate.

also the broader views of the American past presented in historical writings, textbooks, and the popular narratives of Hollywood and network television.

Courses informed by an effort at cultural pluralism or multiculturalism attempt to provide students with a historical understanding of social group formation, of the processes that produce the specific and varied meanings of social groups, and of the challenges of defining self within and among groups. The author guides students to think about group identities as influenced by historical forces and social relationships as well as by emotional process. In the case of the Jewish people in the United States, the history of persecution and the Jewish Diaspora, the Holocaust or Shoah, the establishment of the state of Israel, the revival of Yiddish culture, and Jewish assimilation exert broad pressures and limits on individuals as members of social groups. Some of these emotional pressures are felt in the classroom, which attracts students who are either emotionally invested in a naïve and unreflected sense of their Jewish identities, which they hope the course might reinforce, or who have an interest in exploring and perhaps moving toward Jewish identity, which they hope the course will define. The author's goal is to teach both groups of students to view assertions of Jewish identity as an ongoing multigenerational process with a unique focus on the challenge of defining self in the context of an inhospitable environment.

The author's efforts to integrate Bowen theory at a deep emotional level guided her decision to provide opportunities for students to integrate the learning of the classroom with reflections and actions in the field. She developed the community service or service learning component of her teaching in connection with this course on Jewish literature and culture. Collaborating with public libraries and agencies that provide audio-reader services for people who are visually impaired, the author offered students opportunities to engage with the ongoing process of defining self and to put theories and readings from class to the test of experience and reflection. Working with seniors, families, cultural activities, homeless people, immigrants, children, Holocaust survivors, and so forth, students confront the challenge of making an effort to emotionally integrate material from their coursework with real life. The author works at strengthening the alignment between the focus of learning both inside and outside the classroom and at providing students with opportunities to integrate their learning.

Bowen theory explores the processes through which living beings develop, flourish, and die in the context of natural systems. It focuses on the processes rather than the content of cultural transmission, and it offers novel ways of thinking about conformity and resistance in the context of this transmission process. Emotional process, as presented in Bowen theory, addresses a level of cultural transmission distinct from the traumatic and ideological particularities of culture transmitted within that process. To gain the benefits of Bowen theory, it is not enough to incorporate ideas intellectually; integrating Bowen theory at an emotional level engages a deep level of learning. For those who wish to advance in their capacity to resolve competing ideas, proposals, desires, values, and beliefs, within self and in relation to emotionally significant others, emotional integration of Bowen theory offers an opportunity for growth. The practice of decision making and position taking is an emotional process that involves not just intellectual but also physiological, psychological, emotional, and social processes. From this perspective, the author's efforts at integrating Bowen theory into her professional life have involved more opportunities and emotional effort than are represented by her integration of Bowen theory into the content of her research or teaching.

Integrating Bowen Theory With Service

When the author applied for admission to the Postgraduate Program in Bowen Family Systems Theory and Its Applications, which she attended from 1997 to 2001, she explained that she expected to assume more administrative leadership at the university in the coming years and believed that more training in Bowen theory would be helpful. Indeed, while she was a participant in the postgraduate program, the author was given an opportunity to assume an administrative role as graduate director in one of the two units in which she holds a faculty appointment. Over the next decade, she assumed increasing responsibilities in that unit and 5 years ago became the chair. She also assumed service obligations at the college, university, and local, regional, and national levels. Besides contributing leadership to the development of a new academic program in Jewish studies, the author served on the board of the regional association in her field, hosted a regional conference on campus, and held the office of president of the regional association. She is currently completing a 3-year term and serving as chair of a standing committee in the national association in her field.

The role of chair, which the author assumed in January 2006, offered her the most challenges and the greatest opportunities to learn systems thinking. Assuming leadership required the author to develop her capacity to be present and accountable to a system that was experiencing a difficult transition. With senior members moving toward retirement and junior members joining the program, the system was vulnerable to stress and became intense and emotionally reactive. Three senior members lost parents during this period; another senior faculty member was on leave while her partner's mother passed away; and one of the two staff members was forced to take family leave to care for her terminally ill husband until his death in January 2008. All told, when the author became chair, she and the two staff members had four teenagers at home finishing high school, and a fifth already in college. Three of the junior faculty members are parents, with seven children among them, and the youngest is 2 years old. Another junior faculty member is caregiver for her elderly grandfather. At 89 years the author's mother is a source of worry and concern.

Broader forces in the administration of the university also contribute stressors. In fall 2006, the university hired a new provost and a new dean of the College of Liberal Arts and Sciences, a new dean of the Law School, a new dean of libraries, and a new dean of the School of Social Welfare. Two years later, in fall 2008, two of the four associate deans in the college moved to higher positions and were replaced by first-time deans from within the faculty. This spring, the chancellor (of 14 years) announced his plan to retire, and the provost (of 2 years), after replacing three key staff members in his office, accepted the position of president at another university. With the goal of appointing a new chancellor by July 1, 2009, the dean of the college was appointed interim provost. The new provost would be appointed by the new chancellor. The governor of the state of Kansas, a key figure in the overall state university system, accepted an appointment as the Secretary of Health and Human Services. These transitions in leadership also occurred in the context of critical transformations linked to a world-wide economic crisis.[8] In this challenging and emotionally reactive environment, thinking systems has helped the author stay afloat.

Systems thinking has provided guidance to the author as she navigates the emotional field of her professional responsibilities and opportunities. It has provided her with a model for observing emotional reactivity, triangles, fusion, emotional distance and cutoff, projection processes, and the forces of togetherness and individuality in group process. Attention to emotional process has transformed the everyday challenges of the author's professional life into opportunities for doing a better job of observing and regulating self, achieving emotional neutrality, charting the best available course, and making an effort to differentiate self. Systems thinking reminds the author to constantly bear in mind the deep origins of emotional reactivity and thus to keep a broad perspective on its ebbs and flows. Although difficult to sustain in the moment, a broader and more neutral perspective on emotional flare-ups reduces the author's sensitivity, focus on the other, and tendency to triangle; it contributes to reducing the anxiety of the system and enhancing her capacity to "stay cool."

The author has become more alert to the processes of togetherness and individuality, the operation of triangles, the potential for rapidly escalating emotional reactivity, the occasional emotional regressions, and the variation in relationship patterns. She continues to observe the difference among faculty members driven by fusion or isolated by distance and attempts to learn as much as she can from those who demonstrate the greatest ability to maintain emotional contact with others while continuing to think for themselves. She is more aware of the impact of these forces on emotional process in the group, the opportunities for differentiation of self, and challenges to regulate herself

---

[8] For an analysis of the changes affecting public universities, see Newfield (2008).

in this climate. The effort to gain greater clarity about her role and to establish and maintain person-to-person contact with each member of her system improves her ability to listen to others and to define her own expectations and goals. Getting clear about her own expectations, goals, and limits helps the author hold others accountable for fulfilling their roles and responsibilities. In a videotape about his experience at administration, Bowen speaks of having been the "go-to guy," applying himself to the solution of everyone's problems and allowing every matter to pass through his hands. Making oneself less important, he advised, should be the goal of an effective administrator.

Leadership has grown more interesting to the author in the context of systems thinking, which has given her a way of thinking about her professional development and about the challenges of being effective as a member of multiple systems. From an automatic focus on the responses of others aimed at seeking agreement and minimizing conflict, the author has come to focus on more thoughtful concerns, such as clarifying her roles, responsibilities, goals, and expectations. Gaining emotional neutrality enables the author to grapple with broader and more significant questions about the contribution she hopes to make in her professional life through her research, teaching, and administrative service and about her responsibilities to multiple systems outside of my profession.

Although the capacity to participate in complex organizational efforts comes easily for some people, the author attributes her own increased level of participation to the modest progress she has made in differentiating self and in managing emotional reactivity. Such progress has enabled her to be more observant of and less bogged down by the emotional process that accompanies all relationships and group activity. Learning to stay connected with others without becoming mired in emotional process requires training and vigilance.

References

Birkerts, S. (1994). *The Gutenberg elegies: The fate of reading in an electronic age.* Boston, MA: Faber & Faber.

Campus Compact. (2003). *Introduction to service-learning toolkit: Readings and resources for faculty.* Providence, RI: Brown University.

Freire, P. (1973). *Education for critical consciousness.* New York: Seabury Press.

Kerr, M. (1999). Applying systems thinking to human behavior. In Georgetown Family Center (Producer), *Bowen family systems theory and its applications* [DVD]. Available from http://www.thebowencenter.org

Kerr, M. E., & Bowen, M. (1988). *Family evaluation: An approach based on Bowen theory.* New York, NY: W. W. Norton.

Lieberman, A., & Lester, C. (2003). *Social work practice with a difference: A literary approach.* New York, NY: McGraw Hill.

Newfield, C. (2008). *Unmaking the public university: The forty-year assault on the middle class.* Cambridge, MA: Harvard University Press.

Pickens, W. (1921). The American Congo—Burning of Henry Lowry. *Nation, 112,* 426–428.

Shapiro, M. (2001). *For moral ambiguity: National culture and the politics of the family.* Minneapolis: University of Minnesota Press.

TuSmith, B., & Bergevin, G.W. (Eds.). (2000). *American family album: 28 contemporary ethnic stories.* Forth Worth, TX: Harcourt College.

Wallerstein, I. (2004). *World-systems analysis: An introduction.* Durham, NC: Duke University Press.

Williams, R. (1989). *What I came to say.* London: Hutchinson Radius.

Woodruff, N. (2003). *American Congo: The African American freedom struggle in the Delta.* Cambridge, MA: Harvard University Press.

21

The Critical Reader as Scientist: Approaching Literature From the Perspective of Bowen Theory

DAVID S. HARGROVE

Psychological approaches to the teaching and criticism of literature have largely been confined to psychoanalytic theory. Freud's own use of literary accounts of the personal development of historical or fictional figures has provided rich perspectives on the lives of these individuals and their times. Psychoanalytic interpretation of Faulkner's life, portrayed in Kartiganer and Abadie (1991), adds useful insights to Faulkner studies.

Psychoanalytic studies of literary figures, however, contain a significant subjective quality that diminishes their contribution. Psychological theory can offer a broader method of reading and interpreting literature, offering perspectives based on objective information. Although no psychological theory will bring absolutely objective data to the interpretive process, some theories are better grounded than others.

Bowen family systems theory is a perspective on human experience and literature that is based on objective information and is contextually relevant. As a systems theory, it is placed within the context of present and past human relationships. Moreover, the theory offers a useful framework from which literature and writing are taught, offering both teachers and students experiences that may be interpreted according to the theory.

This chapter describes three university psychology classes that are focused on literature and writing and are based on Bowen theory. The classes represent three distinctly different times and levels of college experience: one in the freshman year designed to enhance writing skills, another upper-level undergraduate course consisting of an intensive study of prominent American writers, and the third a graduate seminar in family systems requiring detailed attention to one particular writer. The important focus of each of these courses is developing a critical reader who can work toward objectivity in the analysis of literary work and gain an understanding of self that is both related to and separate from that which is in the literature. Descriptions of the common factors and differentiating characteristics among these classes follow.

Merging the learning of Bowen theory with reading and writing about literature requires the student to become a critical reader according to a specific criterion. The reader–writer must find some point of identity with the literature without becoming reactive to it as a means of understanding and analysis. Accomplishing this goal requires different expectations and goals at each level of education—in this case, first-year, upper-level undergraduate, and graduate.

Freshman Writing Class

The University of Mississippi developed a broadly based freshman writing class that could substitute for one of the two required English composition courses. This course was taught by faculty from the perspective of the discipline that the faculty member represented. The semester-long class required completion of at least six papers of moderate length. Class time was balanced among instruction in writing and composition, critical thinking, and the relevant academic discipline of the faculty member.

Psychology faculty members who taught this particular course focused either on one particular theory within psychology or on specific issues of concern in the discipline (e.g., nature versus nurture in human development). Reading, classroom discussion, and writing were in response to the material related to these themes. The particular section of the freshman composition class devoted to Bowen theory required reading the theory, writing a series of papers on certain aspects of the theory, providing family diagrams that are incorporated into written products, and reading a specific piece of fiction selected from a predeveloped list that served as the basis for writing and interpretation from the perspective of Bowen theory.

As they developed family diagrams, students were encouraged to talk with their parents and other family members. This enabled them to gather objective data about the family and develop initial perspectives about relationships within the family. At this point, objectivity was stressed by assisting students to assess the reliability and validity of the various family members' points of view, particularly when they discovered conflicting perspectives. Helping students remain neutral by not taking the side of any given individual was important to assist them in developing more objective, critical thinking.

A rudimentary knowledge of Bowen theory was necessary for the students to carry out the tasks of the class. This was gained in two ways. First, reading Roberta Gilbert's (1992, 2004) *Extraordinary Relationships: A New Way of Thinking About Human Interactions* and *The Eight Concepts of Bowen Theory: A New Way of Thinking About the Individual and the Group* was required. Students were also referred to the Web site of the Georgetown Family Center (http://www.thebowencenter.org) for further information about the theory. Second, several class periods were devoted to learning the eight concepts of Bowen theory. These class periods were organized around the reading.

Characteristically, the concepts of the theory were addressed in the order in which they were presented in the books and were integrated with the assignments.

Early in the semester, readings and class discussion were focused on the development of rudimentary concepts of Bowen theory. These activities typically took the form of encouraging students to think systems or in relationships, then using examples from literature. Thinking systems is difficult for most people because, consistent with Bowen's prediction, they think "individually." Moreover, as they became frustrated with themselves or their families, or with characters in novels, they would revert to individual thinking, claiming that the consequence of a behavior lay in a specific cause that can be identified. Reciprocity of behavior between people was frequently missed because of individual thinking. Also, classroom time devoted to a discussion of the students' contacting their families was particularly helpful as they observed each others' efforts to get and interpret information from family members.

Knowledge of Bowen theory was further developed in the students' writing. At least one writing assignment was based on an interaction with a family member. The student was asked to discuss the attempt to remain neutral during the conversation and in the interpretation of the information. Discussion of these experiences revealed the subtle ways in which emotional reactivity influenced interpretation and presentation of information. This assignment required students to observe their own behavior, attempting to reach some level of objectivity about themselves.

Upper-Level Undergraduate Class

The upper-level undergraduate class in psychology and literature was taught in the Honors College of the University of Mississippi. Students enrolled with the expectation that it was an intense, individually based, writing-intensive class that required substantial reading. There was, then, considerable self-selection in the class. Some of the students who enrolled in this class had completed the 1st-year writing class and had previous exposure to Bowen theory, but most had not.

Requirements of this class were familiarity with Bowen theory, developing one's family diagram and writing about one's own family, and the intense study of one particular American writer about whom sufficient public information about family and life circumstances was available. Examples included William Faulkner, Anne Sexton, Sylvia Plath, William Styron, Charlotte Perkins Gilman, Robert Lowell, Tennessee Williams, and Walker Percy. Readings of the assigned authors consisted of all their writing and any available biographies and autobiographies. Some critical work was assigned when it was useful for interpretations that related to the author.

The first sessions of this class were characterized by viewing the basic series of the Bowen tapes and reading both Gilbert books (Gilbert, 1992, 2004).

Class discussions revolved around these tapes and the readings from Gilbert. Moreover, Bowen (1978), Kerr and Bowen (1988), and Papero (1990) were used as reference works. The grounding in Bowen theory in the first 3 to 4 weeks of the class set the context for the students' approach to their own families and the beginning of the readings of the assigned author. Particular attention was paid to the interrelationships of the concepts of Bowen theory and the function of differentiation of self. There typically was considerable discussion of differentiation of self in the context of one's own family and social groups at the university and in relation to the readings in which the students became immersed.

Each student was required to submit a series of papers designed to address the constructs of Bowen theory. Material for these papers came from the writings, biographical and autobiographical information, and criticism of the author's works. These papers were structured to lead to a final, comprehensive perspective of that writer. This paper was given in a formal presentation to the entire class at the end of the term.

The personal work that each student did with family members was viewed as a learning experience for the application of theory. This involved such things as the proper way to construct a family diagram, recognizing themes within diagrams, managing conversations with family members around the development of the diagrams, and working toward some degree of objectivity in this work.

Graduate Seminar in Family Systems

Family systems theory was an elective seminar in a doctoral program in clinical psychology at the University of Mississippi. Portrayed originally as a family psychotherapy seminar, it was reconstituted as family systems to include the broader perspective of systems thinking beyond simply the clinical application. The foundation of the seminar was the systematic reading of Bowen (1978) and Kerr and Bowen (1988), supplemented with Papero's (1990) and Gilbert's (1992, 2004) work. The basic series of Bowen theory tapes was presented in the first seven meetings of the seminar. Additionally, students were to read one piece of fiction to which they would apply Bowen theory.

Each student was expected to make a presentation every 2 to 3 weeks, depending on the number of students in the class, on any topic that was of interest. The intent was to encourage systems thinking about personal situations, clinical application, observations of social behavior, or virtually any other topic that a student might find relevant. The common expectation was that the presentation had to reflect systems thinking. Examples of the kinds of presentations that were made were native American ecology, personal family situations, clinical involvements in practicum experiences, and students' teaching experiences.

The end-of-term presentations by the students were treatments of the authors they had read over the course of the semester. These presentations reflected the students' work with the theory in relationship to their own families and their understanding of the families of the authors on whom they had focused. The final examination involved the presentation of a commercial film that reflected specific family situations for interpretation according to Bowen theory.

Bowen Theory and Teaching

Each of these classes offered students the opportunity to begin to learn Bowen theory, initiating efforts to use its principles in understanding self and literature. First, the concepts of Bowen theory were presented in a systematic way and demonstrated the theory's interrelatedness. Each student and the faculty member presented a family diagram with some interpretation early in the course. Assistance was provided in interpreting the diagram that was consistent with Bowen theory. Students were encouraged to maintain consistent contact with their families to continue this process. Second, the class was described as a system along with the roles of each person. For example, the positions of over- and underfunctioning were described and interpreted as possibilities for the behavior of both students and faculty in the group. This was typically viewed as related to the functioning of people in their families of origin and extended families, further elaborating on Bowen theory. These attempts to assist students to think in systems rather than individually were designed to reinforce the efforts to see the authors that they studied as parts of larger contexts of relationships.

The level of functioning of the teacher of these classes is an important aspect of the learning process, both of Bowen theory and of the literature. The teacher's activity concerns both the learning of material and managing the emotional reactivity of both him- or herself and the students. The value of recognizing reactivity in the interpretation and discussion of literature is important to the learning process. The teacher who functions at a higher level of differentiation of self is more likely to be able to manage his or her own reactivity in such a way as to enhance students' learning, both in their own functioning and in their understanding of the literature of the class. Both the reading and the writing involved in the classes offered the teacher and students opportunities to view self, particularly in important relationships. Parker Palmer (1993) underscored the importance of teacher and students reaching beyond superficial appearances of learning to something more substantial. He pointed out "two of the most difficult truths about teaching. The first is that what we teach will never 'take' unless it connects with the inward, living core of our students' lives, with our students' inward teachers" (p. 32). He affirmed the reciprocity of the teaching process in the connection between the teacher and the student. "The second truth is even more daunting: we can speak to the teacher within our students only when we are on speaking terms with the teacher within ourselves" (p. 32).

Several common factors bind these classes in an approach to reading and writing from the perspective of Bowen theory. First, each contains a basic understanding of the substance and structure of Bowen theory. This requires that students attempt to think in systems of relationships rather than from an individual perspective. Second, each person in the class becomes aware of the importance of the functioning of self as a part of the process of teaching and learning, including learning literature. Third, each person develops and presents a family diagram as a part of the process, further emphasizing the importance of the system. This presentation enables each person to examine personal functioning and learning in the larger systems context. Fourth, the teacher participates in the process of discovery with the students by developing and presenting his or her own family as a part of the classroom activity. Fifth, evaluation of student performance is a significant aspect of the classroom experience. It is not possible to evaluate the student's experience by means of examination alone; rather, it requires participation and engagement in the total process of the course. This requires significant interaction between teacher and student, enabling the faculty member to accurately assess the student's progress. The faculty member must avoid using emotional reactivity or a student's inability to manage anxiety as components of the evaluation process. The components may or may not translate into positive or negative academic progress.

Two essential components distinguish these classes from one another. First is the level of understanding of psychological theory in general and Bowen theory in particular that may be expected of students. First-year college students are typically younger than 20, about the time at which differentiation of self solidifies but is still tenuous. Most of them still are financially dependent on their parents. It appears that the degree of differentiation of self that enables a person to understand Bowen theory is quite variable at that age, influencing the degree of receptivity and participation in activities involving the theory. Second is the variability among people in the intensity with which they choose to engage in the activities that support the theory. Clear and straightforward contact with their families, for example, is frequently more difficult for younger students who are still dependent than for older students, perhaps in graduate school or with some life experiences.

The study of Bowen theory becomes intense as the personal involvement of students and faculty grows. It is impossible to avoid this intensity because the study of characters in families in literature and the study of one's own family progress simultaneously. Although there is no pressure to reveal personal information, it is rare for students not to discover important aspects of their own relationships to their families. This thoughtful contact with their families creates both opportunities and difficulties for both students and faculty. Respect for boundaries, the levels of functioning, and individual variation are important as a part of the content and process of teaching.

These courses that require reading and writing teach Bowen theory directly in the content of the material and indirectly in the process by which they are taught. They demand that students become scientists, studying themselves as they develop understanding of fictional characters, their own families, and the social systems of which they are a part.

References

Bowen, M. (1970). Differentiation of the self or the "I" position. In Georgetown Family Center (Producer), *The Basic Series* [DVD]. Available from http://www.thebowencenter.org

Bowen, M. (1978). *Family therapy in clinical practice*. New York, NY: Jason Aronson.

Gilbert, R. (1992). *Extraordinary relationships: A new way of thinking about human interactions*. Falls Church, VA: Leading Systems Press.

Gilbert, R. (2004). *The eight concepts of Bowen theory: A new way of thinking about the individual and the group*. Falls Church, VA: Leading Systems Press.

Kartiganer, D., & Abadie, A. (Eds.). (1991). *Faulkner and psychology*. Jackson, MS: University of Mississippi Press.

Kerr, M. E., & Bowen, M. (1988). *Family evaluation: An approach based on Bowen theory*. New York, NY: W. W. Norton.

Palmer, P. (1993). *The courage to teach*. Hoboken, NJ: Wiley.

Papero, D. (1990). *Bowen family systems theory*. Boston, MA: Allyn & Bacon.

22

A Supervision Model Based in Bowen Theory and Language

THOMAS J. SCHUR

The purpose of this chapter is twofold: (1) to present this author's model of clinical supervision as an example of a practical and well-developed use of Bowen family systems theory, and (2) to show how this model can offer ways to further develop the theory itself. Part 1 begins with a definition of *supervision* from the model, then link each of the elements in the definition to major components of Bowen theory and describe those elements in terms of language, which is fundamental to this supervision model. Part 2 begins with a brief description of the specific theory of language that underlies this model and then delineates how language actually enhances this model's foundation in Bowen theory. The chapter concludes with suggestions of areas for further exploration and development of Bowen theory that follow from these enhancements.

Part 1

The Self-Based Supervision model (Schur, 2002, p. 399) defines *clinical supervision* as

> an activity in which supervisor and supervisee engage one another in conversation about clients with whom the supervisee is working, while maintaining a self-focus in an effort to allow the least constricted flow of movement in the system for the supervisor, supervisee and clients as they all experiment with acting differently. (p. 405)[1]

Embedded in this definition are the following elements of Bowen theory: the differentiation of self in the emotional system of the supervision; self-focus as an essential characteristic of higher levels of functioning of basic self on the scale of differentiation; the flow of the emotional system as a natural system; and the emphasis on behavior or action.

---

[1] The reader is encouraged to review the article for a more comprehensive presentation of the model.

Differentiation of Self

In the conversation that makes up the activity of supervision, the supervisor works constantly to monitor the fusion of self in the system of the relationships between supervisor and supervisee and between supervisee and client, as well as the third relationship in the triangle between supervisor and client who may or may not ever meet. There is always anxiety in this set of relationships that make up the activity of supervision. The client comes to the therapist with a problem that a Bowen therapist would understand in terms of reactive patterns that are attempts to deal with the anxiety from the family system. The supervisee–therapist brings patterns from his or her family to the anxiety presented by the client system, along with habitual ways of dealing with that anxiety, to the supervisor, who likewise has his or her own reactive patterns. The supervisor's task is to maintain self in the emotional field in this set of relationships that comprise supervision.

For example, a supervisee may present a case in which his client is struggling with a conflictual relationship with his father. The client is angry with his father for refusing to cosign a loan for the client's new business. There is a history of the son starting businesses that do not succeed and of the father investing in them and then getting angry when the businesses fail, blaming his son as incompetent. The supervisee–therapist tells the supervisor that he gets angry with his client for constantly complaining about his father, wanting to tell the client to grow up and not be so caught in this dependency on his father. The male supervisor then works to hold his own in his relationship with this supervisee, first working to understand the pattern of the client around the fusion with his father and then how the supervisee gets caught in that dynamic by getting angry with his client.

For the client, the work is to understand the pattern of his anger toward his father and control the reactivity of constantly asking his father for financial help and then having businesses fail, maintaining a pattern of continual conflict with his father. This is the work of differentiating a self for the client. For the supervisee, the work is to understand his reactivity to the client's conflict with his father, which means having to understand the links of the client's anxiety to the supervisee's experiences in his own family. For the supervisor, the task is to work with the supervisee to think through the client's patterns of conflict with his father and the supervisee's reactivity to the client's reactivity. This would involve staying neutral in the triangle with the supervisee and his client, and working with the supervisee to understand the patterns in the client's family and those in the supervisee's own family that provoke the reactive response of anger toward the client.

This conceptualization of the role and functioning of the supervisor is consistent with Bowen theory but is in sharp contrast to an individual, nonsystems model of supervision that would see the process of supervision in a more linear way when there is a goal or desired outcome of the supervisor's activity. Here the work is on differentiation of self for all parties, through efforts to understand and control the reactivity of acting on feelings, which can then lead to the possibility of better functioning for all three parties.

Self-Focus

Because of the specific foundation of this model of supervision in Bowen theory and the differentiation of self, attempts on the supervisor's part to focus on the supervisee or the supervisee's client are incongruent and would actually reflect a lower level of differentiation. Bowen theory would understand this as the functioning of the supervisor's pseudoself focusing on the relationship systems in an attempt to relieve his or her anxiety by working to change the supervisee or client.

In the ongoing example, the supervisor may find himself getting anxious and then angry with the supervisee, who continually talks about his frustrations with his angry client. The tendency might be for the supervisor to confront the supervisee about his issue of anger with this client, which would be an other-focused action, disguised as an appropriate supervisory challenge. The supervisee indeed needs to deal with his reactivity to his client's anger, but if the supervisor raises this issue from an other-focused attempt to calm his own anxiety, the supervisor has yielded self and made it more difficult for the supervisee to think through his reactive patterns with the client because he now has to deal with the supervisor's reactivity as well. The supervisor's lower level of differentiation interferes with the possible increase in differentiation of the supervisee and the client.

For more traditional, other-focused supervision models, this confrontation by the supervisor might be appropriate, as the reactivity of the supervisor would not be problematic because the selves of supervisor and supervisee are seen as more autonomous.

Flow and Adaptation

In this model of supervision, the supervisor attends to the extent of momentum in the flow of the conversation. When it flows, it is easy for the supervisor to listen and understand what is going on in the therapy with the clients. The narrative makes sense because the supervisor can understand the client's struggles, history, and patterns and what the supervisee is doing with the client on the basis of the supervisee's understanding of the case. However, there are inevitably breaks in this momentum in which the client, the supervisee, or both get stuck. The flow of the conversation is disrupted as the supervisee reports getting upset, confused, frustrated, or lost and does not know what to say next about the case. This model assumes this is a reflection of the client being caught in a reactive pattern and not able to make changes and resolve the problems for which he or she came to therapy. Likewise, the supervisee is caught in the relationship with the client and the patterns in that family system.

The task for the supervisor is to work with the supervisee to understand the supervisee's reactive responses to the client's therapy that are part of maintaining the fusion in the therapeutic relationship, which is inhibiting the momentum. Because the supervisor can engage the supervisee from a self-focused position in this effort to understand this reactivity, both supervisor and supervisee can experiment with different ways of thinking about the case that can facilitate momentum as one idea leads to another. This is an adaptation to the problem of being stuck in talking and thinking about the case. However, if the supervisor takes an other-focused approach of trying to get the supervisee to understand, there is less opportunity for the adaptation of different ways of thinking, which will continue to limit the momentum in the flow of ideas.

As the supervisor raises questions with the supervisee about his angry responses to his angry client, instead of confronting him, the supervisee can begin to self-focus and reflect on his patterns around anger. As he thinks about his own history, he recognizes his long-term struggle with his mother, who was always complaining about her husband and what was wrong with him, but never did more than complain. This continual behavior of his mother upset the supervisee as a youth, and he would respond to the anxiety in this situation with anger.

With this understanding, the supervisee can allow the anxiety generated by the client's anger and continue to listen through the client's complaints about his father to get to a better understanding of how this conflict functions in the family system and how the client is part of it. This perspective opens up the flow of the conversation in supervision because the supervisee has a sense of direction with the case and can use the supervision to maintain his clear thinking about the therapy.

The notion of flow in this model derives from its foundation in Bowen theory as natural systems theory. The momentum described in this process of supervision is the "life force" that Kerr and Bowen (1988) described well as "that which propels the grass to grow, bears to hibernate, a newborn kangaroo to crawl to its mother's pouch, humpback whales to migrate, etc." (p. 28). Supervision from this model is not about an other-focused attempt to change the supervisee or client, but rather, is the work of defining a self in an ongoing process that enables one to participate in the flow of life and adapt in ways that allow the best functioning. This approach contrasts clearly with individual models of supervision that deliberately work toward established goals.

Behavior

Fundamental to this model is the focus on experimentation. As the momentum flows, all three parties—supervisor, supervisee, and client—can experiment with different ways of acting to allow for better adaptation and more productive functioning.

Bowen often referred to his work as an attempt to develop a science of human behavior. He was very interested in the phenomenon of how people act differently from what they say they do or will do. This discrepancy between language and behavior reflects anxiety and fusion between thinking and feeling. At higher levels of differentiation, there is more congruence between the thinking and the action. This model of supervision assumes that with better thinking, one can experiment with less reactive behaviors.

Once the supervisee realizes he is stuck in the therapy with the client and understands how he is caught, based on his reactive patterns prompted by the client's family and the supervisee's own family, he can experiment with different behaviors. The supervisor's role at this point is as an overseer of the experimentation. Because the supervisee knows he needs to tolerate his own anxiety about his client's complaints about his father, he might experiment with just being quiet when the client is caught up in telling the supervisee about something his father has done again and how angry he is. Because the supervisee stays quiet, it gives the client a chance to realize how caught he is in this cycle of anger and think about what he might do to change the pattern. This can be an opening for the supervisee to engage the client in this direction in which there is the possibility for some momentum to develop. In addition, the understanding can lead to experiments of ways of acting differently with his father.

For this flow to happen with the supervisee and his client, the supervisor must be able to allow this flow in the supervision with the supervisee. This means that as the supervisee presents his struggles with the client and with himself, the supervisor must monitor his or her own reactivity as the conversation proceeds. If the supervisee's frustration with the client annoys the supervisor, who wants the supervisee to just move on and stop getting so caught up in this pattern, then the supervisor needs to self-focus, understand his or her own annoyance, and then find ways to experiment with acting differently in his or her supervision with the supervisee.

Just as the client's work in therapy enables him to raise his level of differentiation, so can the therapist's work on self as the therapist enable a higher level of differentiation for him. Similarly, to the extent that the supervisor is able to allow the momentum of the supervisee's work with the client and the client's work with his own family, the process of the supervision can enable the supervisor to raise his or her level of differentiation. This model contrasts with more linear models of supervision that operate in a teaching or training mode, assuming that once the supervisee understands the ideas, he or she can implement them and change will happen. It also differs in the notion that the process of supervising itself enables the supervisor to grow.

Language in Links With Bowen Theory

Although it may seem trivial to say that what happens in almost all supervision is that supervisor and supervisee talk, conversation is an explicit component in the definition of this model of supervision because of its foundation in a theory of language. In this model, language is an essential component of each of the four elements of the definition presented earlier, which together reflect the model's grounding in Bowen theory as just described. Language is the mode of defining self (differentiation of self). The parties focus on self as they talk with each other and reflect on what they have said and done (self-focus). The momentum of the process of supervision and therapy happens as the conversation flows, as the parties continue to talk and think, and one idea leads to another (flow and adaptation). In the recursive loop of thinking and doing, language is inseparable from how people act (behavior).

To return to the ongoing example, the supervisee may get caught up in his reactive frustration with his client's complaints and tell him to let go of this constant focus on his father. Whenever the supervisee says this, the client then protests and says words to the effect of it not being fair that his father never understands. This prompts the supervisee to try other ways of saying the same thing, which results in the client responding with the same idea about unfairness. Each provokes the other's reflex statements. This is what they say to each other. Inside, each keeps thinking the same thing. The supervisor basically thinks that the client is going nowhere until he lets go, and the client thinks that his therapist just keeps telling him the same thing over and over.

The conversation, including the reflection that is an inherent part of it, actively maintains the fusion. The automatic responses are physiological. The anxiety generated in the relationship between supervisor and supervisee as they discuss the case triggers their brains, which respond with particular words, spoken in certain tones and with certain gestures. This physiological dynamic of stimulation and response becomes coordinated as a pattern in their talking and thinking. Controlling this reactivity requires controlling how they speak and think, which is done in language. For this author, this is differentiation of self in the emotional system.

Part 2

This model of supervision has been presented as a model grounded in Bowen theory and conceptualized in a framework of language. Now this chapter uses this model of supervision to demonstrate the possibility of expanding Bowen theory through the inclusion of language as a concept. It is relevant to note here that Bowen himself defined the self in terms that can hardly be understood as anything other than language, although he did not explicitly identify them as language. He said, "The solid self is made up of clearly defined beliefs, opinions, convictions and life principles" (Bowen, 1978, p. 365).

In addition to the description offered in Part 1 of how language operates generally in the model, in this section the author uses the presentation of a specific theory of language to make a case for the inclusion of language in Bowen theory. Although this particular theory of language is the one that undergirds the author's model of supervision, and although its congruence with Bowen theory is powerful, it is presented here simply to stimulate thinking about the place of language in Bowen theory.

A Specific Theory of Language

Humberto Maturana has developed his theory of language around the concept of cognition, which he identifies with life. "Living systems are cognitive systems and living is a process of cognition" (Capra, 1996, p. 267). *Cognition* is a process of a living system recurrently interacting with its environment in such a way that a structure develops and is maintained. In this process of cognition, the living system "brings forth a world" through a process of continually making distinctions. As the immune system detects a pathogen, it brings forth a world of a threat that was not there before. Deer discovering berries in some bushes distinguish a world of food. Humans walking on a sidewalk toward each other make the distinction of an obstacle.

However, this basic process of cognition, or knowing, for all living systems can rise to a different level in the case of the human. Although each person on the sidewalk becomes a distinction of an obstacle for the other initially, they most likely will coordinate their behavior to not collide as they get closer. If those two people happen to move to the same side and then realize they may indeed bump into each other, one may move deliberately to the other side and say, "Sorry," smiling about the situation they both understand while the other says, "No problem." At this point, the cognition has become language. "In the flow of recurrent social interactions, language appears when the operations in a linguistic domain result in coordination of actions about actions that pertain to the linguistic domain itself" (Maturana & Varela, 1987, pp. 209–210). Out of their behavioral interactions, they bring forth a world but then interact in coordination about that world itself, the linguistic domain, as they exchange words.

Because language is cognition for the human as a living system, it involves bringing forth a world as it does for all living systems. As humans interact in language, however, they can bring forth worlds together that have a sophisticated coordination they would call reality. This process of cognition with recurrent interactions in language between humans Maturana saw as the basis for consciousness that one could call a self. Language as cognition, a process he identified with life, enables humans to interact and thereby bring forth the world of separate selves, each aware of itself as a self. Referring to the self in their coauthored book, Maturana and his colleague Francisco Varela (1987) said that "we are constituted in language in a continuous becoming that we bring forth with others" (pp. 234–235).

This theory of language can seem unnecessarily complicated to explain this common phenomenon of language that people take for granted. That, however, is exactly the point about this model of supervision, with its foundation in Bowen theory and the self. Bowen theory cannot just presume the self. This essential element of the theory, namely the self, needs to be defined and explained for the theory to develop further. Language offers a way to do that.

What Language Does for This Model of
Supervision Based in Bowen Theory

The foundation of language in this supervision model provides a way to use the existing and potential power of Bowen theory in the practice of supervision. It does this in three ways: (a) by distinguishing the role of the supervisor through the dynamic definition of the self as a function of language; (b) by basing the understanding of the supervision process in the concept of a narrative, which incorporates the physiology of the brain and theories of neuroscience; and (c) by providing a concrete and practical way to manage self in the emotional system by monitoring one's use of language.

Understanding the self as an entity that is created and maintained in the relationship system of recurrent interactions in language frees the supervisor from restrictive conceptualizations of the role. The systems-based supervisor does not have to struggle with reductionist and linear conceptualizations of the role like teacher, consultant, boss, therapist, gatekeeper, peer, or outside observer, which conflict directly with systems theory. This freedom liberates the supervisor to raise his or her level of functioning and to affect the level of functioning of the systems involved because the objectivity of the role is no longer constrictive as a goal in the work of differentiation. Attempts to be more objective pull in the direction of other-focus on both one's own self and on the supervisee. In this model, self-focus allows the supervisor to engage more fully in the supervisory relationship in the constant process of differentiation through more effective coordination. Thus, the power of differentiation of self as a concept makes this model of supervision powerful in a way that other-focused ones are not.

In this model of supervision, language functions not just as a process of coordination in the present interactions, but as coordination that includes the recurrent interactions over time. The notion of narrative captures this familiar process. People easily understand the idea of a story, whether it is the history of a people or the biography of one person. The theory of language behind this model of supervision is embedded in physiology, so that the narrative is a process that happens in the coordination of brain function, both within individual brains and between brains.

The conversation that happens in supervision as the supervisee presents the case by telling the story of the client, aware of his or her own personal story and the story of the history of the supervision to date, is understood here in terms of brain function. Conceptualizing the supervisory conversation as an ongoing narrative that is a function of brain processes accesses the foundation of Bowen theory in nature and expands the perspective about defining a self to include the field of neuroscience, especially with its focus on memory. Some neuroscientists have speculated that narrative provides a way for the brain to remember experiences, from both explicit and implicit memory. "Because narratives require the participation of multiple memory networks, these stories serve as ways of enhancing memory through linked associations" (Cozolino & Sprokay, 2006, p. 16). Then, differentiation is about how reactive one's current thinking is to the anxiety embedded in the narrative, for both individuals and the members of that system.

The model's foundation in language provides a practical way to differentiate self in the supervisory relationships as supervisor and supervisee monitor their use of language in the process of supervision. They can recognize reactivity in the patterns of language they use and can experiment with ways to control that reactivity by distinguishing thinking and feeling as they learn to tolerate the anxiety. This use of language as a tool of differentiation provides an effective way to achieve higher levels of functioning for self and for the system, particularly because it is based in physiology, so that one could hypothesize that changing language patterns is changing brain patterns.

What Language Could Do for Further Development of Bowen Theory

This author's position is that differentiation is a process that occurs throughout nature, at all levels of living systems, and that for the human, there is an additional component of differentiation, that of the self, which happens through the use of language.

Although this author believes language is inherent in the differentiation of self, language is not a useful concept if it is not understood as a process in nature. This is consistent with Bowen's clear and deliberate effort in the development of his theory to formulate it "on the model of 'systems' in nature" (Bowen, 1978, p. 398). With this congruence, the inclusion of language, understood as a physiological process as demonstrated in this model of supervision, then provides for a rich, new dimension of the foundational concept of differentiation of self in Bowen theory.

Bowen distinguished two aspects of the differentiation of self: the differentiation of thinking and feeling within a person and the differentiation of self and other (Bowen, 1978, pp. 362–366). Language as presented here provides a powerful conceptual way to understand these two dimensions and how they interact. In this regard, it is helpful to simplify a person's use of language as internal and external, where *internal* refers to reflection and *external* to conversation. Because *differentiation* refers to the extent to which an entity has the ability to maintain integrity in the face of anxiety in the system, this author postulates that one can assess differentiation in a person's use of language, both in reflection and in conversation.

The criterion for reactivity in reflection is the extent to which the thinking can be distinguished from the feelings. An example is how much a person can sort out internal reactions to an upsetting event by allowing the feelings while thinking through what actually happened, instead of going over and over the recollection, thereby maintaining a state of being upset. Repetitive patterns of thoughts reflect fusion of thinking and feeling, a manifestation of the underlying physiological process of language.

The criterion for reactivity in conversation is the extent to which talking with others leads to the expression of ideas that allows interaction, in which each person can state what he or she thinks and be heard, versus fusion, in which people are primarily responding with more reflex responses in attempts to manage their own anxiety. Repetitive patterns of words and phrases that evoke feelings reflect fusion of self and other, again a manifestation of the physiological process of language.

Of course, these two domains of internal and external are inextricably linked in a dynamic of constant recursion. Statements made by oneself and others in conversation lead to reflection and then to expression of those reflections and on and on. This author has found it helpful to use the idea of narrative to conceptualize language as the underlying phenomenon in this ongoing interaction of reflection and conversation. The self can be understood as a person's biography. The story of that self is remembered over time and is often accessed in the present in reflection. That story of an individual self is also understood by others in the family as part of the narrative of the family and its history understood over time, but is also often accessed in the present in conversation. Both narratives are part of maintaining the dynamics of that system as members interact in language, talking with each other as they continually reflect on what is said.

This inclusion of language as a physiological process that is a major component of the differentiation of self opens up an additional range of research domains in which Bowen theory can be tested. One area would be the exploration of consciousness and the self in which narrative is a current interest in the field of neuroscience. Siegel (2001) talked about the importance of a "coherent narrative" for integration in the brain (p. 79). This corresponds to the internal, reflective domain of differentiation.

Another area would be the study of language and the brain in the evolution of the human. In her article, Wylie (2004) quotes Siegel: "The capacity and need to tell stories is not only part of our culture, but part of our evolutionary heritage, built into our genetic code and embedded in the circuits of our brains" (p. 34). With another focus, Deacon (1997) posited that symbolic language has played such a critical role in the management and evolution of human social relationships, with its capacity for "representing a social contract" (p. 401), that it has actually driven the evolution of the human brain.

> Symbol use itself must have been the prime mover for the prefrontalization of the brain in hominid evolution. Language has given rise to a brain which is strongly biased to employ the one mode of associative learning that is most critical to it. (p. 336)

This area corresponds to the external, conversational domain of differentiation.

Conclusion

This chapter is both a validation of Bowen theory and a challenge to further develop the theory. The concepts of Bowen theory inform and guide the practice of supervision from my systems model, which is organized around the self and in which language is understood as a phenomenon of nature. At the same time, language as this physiological process offers the opportunity for the theory to become more powerful in the call to experiment with the inclusion of language as a major component of human interactions in the emotional system.

References

Bowen, M. (1978). *Family therapy in clinical practice.* New York, NY: Jason Aronson.

Capra, F. (1996). *The web of life.* New York, NY: Doubleday.

Cozolino, L., & Sprokay, S. (2006). Neuroscience and adult learning. *New Directions for Adult and Continuing Education, 110,* 11–19.

Deacon, T. (1997). *The symbolic species.* New York, NY: W. W. Norton.

Kerr, M. E., & Bowen, M. (1988). *Family evaluation: An approach based on Bowen theory.* New York, NY: W. W. Norton.

Maturana, H. R., & Varela, F. J. (1987). *The tree of knowledge.* Boston, MA: New Science Library.

Schur, T. J. (2002). Supervision as a disciplined focus on self and not the other: A different systems model. *Contemporary Family Therapy, 24,* 399–422.

Siegel, D. (2001). Toward an interpersonal neurobiology of the developing mind: Attachment relationships, "mindsight," and neural integration. *Infant Mental Health Journal, 22,* 67–94.

Wylie, M. S. (2004, September/October). Mindsight. *Psychotherapy Networker,* 29–41.

23
Introducing Adolescents to Systems Thinking: Learning to See the Self as Part of a System

DONNA G. KNAUTH

The lifelong developmental process of *differentiating a self*—defined as a person's ability to regulate emotional reactivity, to think clearly under stress, and to achieve an autonomous self within one's family relationships while staying connected (Bowen, 1978)—accelerates during adolescence. During this developmental period, adolescents work toward establishing autonomy from their family and becoming gradually more responsible for their own decision making. Adolescents' decisions in a rapidly expanding era of behavioral choices often leave much to be desired. Many choose high-risk sexual behaviors and alcohol and other drug (AOD) use, placing themselves at major health risks. Patterns of risky health behavior established during this critical developmental period often continue into adulthood, with problematic physical, emotional, and social consequences (American Academy of Pediatrics, 2001; Centers for Disease Control and Prevention, 2006).

To arm adolescents with better information for making responsible decisions and enhancing educational engagement, many states mandate a health education curriculum in junior and senior high school to provide students with education about human sexuality and reproduction, sexually transmitted diseases, teen pregnancy, and AOD use (Botvin, Baker, Dusenbury, Tortu, & Botvin, 1995; Durlak, 1997). Although these courses deliver science-based facts about how high-risk behaviors affect the brain and body, long-term behavioral change has not been achieved (U.S. Department of Health and Human Services, 2001).

Convincing arguments exist for including the family as a focus for prevention efforts in multicomponent programs to reduce early-onset sexual intercourse, teen pregnancy, and AOD use (Kumpfer & Alvarado, 2003). Epidemiological and etiological studies have shown that family processes mediate links between adolescent AOD use and deviant peers (Conger & Rueter, 1996; Patterson, Reid, & Dishion, 1992; Center for Substance Abuse Prevention [CSAP], 1997). This has also been shown in longitudinal studies of family risk and protective factors (e.g., Brook & Brook, 1992; Loeber & Stouthammer-Loeber, 1986) and empirical studies of family-focused treatment for adolescent drug use (e.g., Santisteban et al., 2003; Szapocznik, Kurtines, Perez-Vidal, Hervis, & Foote, 1990). Yet, despite evidence that positive family processes are associated with lower levels of risky behaviors, most programs designed to prevent or reduce adolescent risky sexual behaviors and AOD use tend to overlook the family system as a major focus of intervention efforts, particularly for youth in the upper grades (CSAP, 1997; Kumpfer & Alvarado, 2003; Walker James, & Partee, 2002).

A different approach is needed to achieve long-term behavioral change. This researcher asked the following question: If adolescents are introduced to the principles of Bowen family systems theory, which would provide them with a systems framework on which to make decisions, would their efforts to differentiate a self be supported and would they be better able to make more reflective and responsible life decisions? This chapter elaborates on this researcher's program of research. The chapter is divided into sections on (a) Family diagram and adolescent mothers: a pilot study; (b) testing the Differentiation of Self Inventory (DSI; Skowron & Friedlander, 1998; Skowron & Schmitt, 2003) for use with ethnically diverse high school adolescents; (c) testing the theoretical model that guides the FaMILY intervention; and (d) recommendations for further research.

Family Diagram and Adolescent Mothers: A Pilot Study

To begin to answer the research question, the author developed and implemented the curriculum for the 16-week Families Matter in the Lives of Youth (FaMILY) educational program in a small pilot study in an inner-city Maryland high school and a rural Pennsylvania community adolescent program. The FaMILY program is based on Bowen theory (Bowen, 1978; Kerr & Bowen, 1988), which views an adolescent's family relationship system as an important etiological pathway to risky health behaviors (e.g., Gilbert, 1999; McKnight, 2003; Rosen, Bartle-Harting, & Stith, 2001; Titelman, 1998). The program introduces adolescents to basic principles of Bowen theory, provides guidance for them to explore their own multigenerational family processes through construction of a multigenerational family diagram, and enhances awareness of the emotional and behavioral patterns in the family system that influence one's behavior in the present.

Adolescence is an ideal time to introduce people to systems thinking because this developmental period marks the intersection of physiological maturation (i.e., puberty) and emerging cognitive and emotional development (Thompson et al., 2000), and therefore appears to be the earliest time one is likely capable of conscientiously working toward differentiating a self in relation to one's family of origin. This educational program is expected to prevent or delay initiation of high-risk sexual behaviors and AOD use and enhance academic engagement among urban, ethnically diverse adolescents by promoting their ability to function at higher levels of differentiation of self (Knauth, Skowron, & Escobar, 2006).

Method

Gaining Access to the Study Site To gain access to the high school, this researcher obtained approval from the Research, Evaluation, and Accountability Officer and Health Education Curriculum Specialist at the city public school system. She then met with the principal and the head of the counseling department at the high school. All were supportive of the study and suggested that participants for the pilot study be adolescent mothers who were attending the school. Institutional Review Board approval was obtained from both study sites and the university.

Study Purpose and Design The pretest–posttest two-group experimental pilot study (a) evaluated the efficacy of the FaMILY program intervention for enhancing health behaviors (i.e., reduce repeat teen pregnancies, enhance parenting skills) relative to controls, and (b) assessed feasibility issues, including the sampling plan, assessment protocols, intervention implementation strategies, and the participants' responses to the intervention. Participants were randomly assigned, within their respective sites, to the experimental group, which included the FaMILY program plus parenting education ($n = 8$) or the control group, which included parenting education alone ($n = 7$).

Sample Participants were adolescent mothers ($N = 15$) and ranged in age from 15 to 19 ($M = 17$, $SD = 1.33$). Most teen mothers (84.6%) had one child, and the remaining 15.4% had two children. In terms of ethnicity, 67% were White and 33% were Black. Forty-seven percent of the adolescents lived with their mothers, 20% lived with their grandmothers, 20% lived with their partners, and 13% lived with other relatives. The majority (75%) reported yearly household incomes under $20,000. Of the 15 participants, 2 from the community adolescent program dropped out of the study—1 from the control group and 1 from the experimental group. The participant from the control group dropped out because of work-related problems, and the participant from the experimental group decided to place her child for adoption. The remaining 13 adolescent mothers completed the intervention and made up the study sample.

Procedures All 24 adolescent mothers attending the high school were invited by their academy counselor to attend the initial meeting during which the purpose of the study was to be explained. Seven students came to this initial meeting. After learning about the study, all 7 students agreed to participate, signed the consent form, and then completed the three study instruments. This researcher then met with the director of the Community Adolescent Program in Pennsylvania to invite all of the adolescent mothers who were attending the program to participate in the study. Eight adolescents responded to the invitation and attended the initial meeting. After learning the purpose of the study, all 8 adolescent mothers agreed to participate, signed the consent forms, and completed the study instruments.

The 16-week intervention began in October and ended in mid-April. Each session lasted 60 minutes. The experimental group was given 30 minutes of instruction in parenting and 30 minutes in the FaMILY program. The control group had only parenting instruction for 60 minutes. As the study's principal investigator, this researcher taught both the parenting and the FaMILY program curriculums.

Intervention Design   The control condition consisted of an existing parent education program, *1,2,3,4 Parents!* (Popkin, Gard, & Montgomery, 1996). *1,2,3,4 Parents!* is a part video, part group discussion, multicultural program for parents of children in the 1- to 4-year-old age group. The program teaches parents basic developmental stages from ages 1 to 4, nonviolent discipline skills, problem-prevention techniques, encouragement skills, the importance of a child's self-esteem, and parental self-care. It includes an easy-to-read *Parent's Workbook* that offers examples, charts, and worksheets so parents can practice their new skills at home.

The experimental condition consisted of the parent education program and the FaMILY program. The FaMILY program is made up of 16 weekly classes and consists of PowerPoint presentations, group discussions, class handouts, films, and role-play and other experiential exercises. In preparation for each class, an outline of the class was written on a flip chart to help students focus and learn the content presented. Throughout the class sessions, family case examples (not related to participants' own families) were used to illustrate and clarify concepts. Adolescents participated in role-playing exercises on how to express their thoughts and ideas in the presence of their family members and peers, with the goal of improving communication, increasing spontaneous feelings and positive regard for self, and enhancing family and peer relationships. Formulations about the part the adolescents play in their own family were discussed. The adolescents were encouraged to relate to as many members in their family as possible, to check the accuracy of the formulations, and to evaluate their ability to relate within their family. Discussion focused on how to develop person-to-person relationships with as many living persons in one's nuclear and extended family.

Participants in the experimental condition began each class session with 30 minutes of the parenting program followed by 30 minutes of the FaMILY program. Additional private time (10–15 minutes) was provided after the session if an individual participant had specific questions about the content covered or about their family. As the principal investigator, this researcher taught the FaMILY curriculum, serving as a coach to the adolescents in their efforts to modify their functioning in ongoing relationships and work toward higher functioning levels of differentiation of self.

Information about Bowen theory was introduced to the adolescent mothers in an environment in which a free exchange of thinking could occur. No specific instructions were given to the adolescents on how to respond in the class. An atmosphere of calm acceptance was established in which the adolescents felt comfortable discussing the principles of Bowen theory. No agenda existed about what the adolescents would do with this new information or how they would apply it to their own families. This researcher went into each class session with an open mind and curiosity. The order of topics covered in the FaMILY program is presented in Table 23.1.

Measures The study instruments were administered to the participants pre- and postintervention. These self-report instruments included the Differentiation in the Family Systems scale (Anderson & Sabatelli, 1992), Costello and Comrey's (1967) scale for anxiety, and the Adult-Adolescent Parenting Inventory (Bavolek, 1984).

Table 23.1 Families Matter in the Lives of Youth Program Outline

Class	Topic
Class 1	Introduction to Bowen family systems theory: Constructing your family diagram
Class 2	Differentiating a self in one's family: "The responsible self"
Class 3	Sibling position
Class 4	Nodal events and their effects on family functioning
Class 5	Family boundaries and anxiety: In the family system
Class 6	Family functioning and triangles
Class 7	Triangles and interlocking triangles
Class 8	Detriangling: Steps to differentiating a self within your relationships
Class 9	Nuclear family emotional system: Patterns of emotional functioning
Class 10	Understanding one's multigenerational family
Class 11	Universal patterns of family interaction: Conflict and distances
Class 12	Universal patterns of family interaction: Overfunctioning/underfunctioning, reciprocity
Class 13	Universal patterns of family interaction: Projection of anxiety to one or more children
Class 14	Emotional cutoff
Class 15	Societal regression
Class 16	Review: Differentiating a self in your family and making healthy, responsible decisions

Results

FaMILY intervention and control group participants were statistically equivalent on baseline measures. At postintervention, results of the Wilcoxon signed-ranks test indicated that FaMILY intervention adolescents reported more realistic expectations of their children than did control group mothers ($z = -2.032$, $p < .05$) and greater interest in trying new parenting strategies. Moreover, no pregnancies occurred among intervention group mothers, whereas 2 teen mothers in the control group became pregnant over the course of the study. In terms of study feasibility, participant responses to the FaMILY intervention were positive. Adolescents expressed strong interest in learning how family systems function and how they function in their own family systems. They were eager to create their family diagrams, noting it was a helpful guide to learning about their family. Their comments suggested they were able to understand basic concepts in Bowen theory and apply them to their own lives.

Limitations of the pilot study included the small sample size and an exclusive focus on adolescent mothers. This unique population of adolescents may have greater motivation to study their families because they are now in the adult role of a parent and may be a little more emancipated from their parents. To illustrate the application of theory and the adolescent mothers' responses, dialogues between 2 of the participants and the author follow.

Vignette: Nicole's Multigenerational Family

Nicole was 15 years old when she began the study, and her son was 5 months old. During the initial meeting, she was very quiet. She never looked up and only answered questions when asked. She was dressed all in gray clothes and never smiled. As the classes progressed, she became more talkative, more interested in her personal appearance, and showed great interest in drawing her family diagram and learning about how families function.

Nicole lived with her maternal aunt and uncle, who served as her foster parents, and with their son and her child. The aunt and uncle had taken custody of Nicole after a judge ordered Nicole's mother to choose between her ex-husband and Nicole. Her mother chose her ex-husband and moved with him and their son to Greece. Nicole did not know who her biological father was, nor did her mother, who had had relationships with three men before marrying Nicole's stepfather. Nicole's older brother was fathered by one of these men. This brother was married and lived with his wife and two children in California. Nicole had not heard from him in more than 2 years.

Nicole was cut off both geographically and emotionally from her mother and stepfather. She stated that she had been physically abused by both of them. Her mother and stepfather had borne a son, whom Nicole stated they favored over her. Nicole continued her relationship with the father of her baby. He had dropped out of high school and was working as a car mechanic.

After the 13th class session, Nicole remained to ask how to draw some of her cousins on her family diagram. After explaining, this researcher asked her if she had learned a lot about her family. She looked up, raised her hands, and with a smile said, "Oh, yes! I have learned so much about my family!" She stated that there was a lot of violence in her family. "All the women in my family live with abusive men." She stated that she had been abused by her mother and stepfather. Her aunt had been abused by her second husband (the one before her present husband), and her cousin was married to an abusive man ("drinks a lot, too").

Nicole then related a recent incident with her partner. While having an argument, he hit the door and broke a bone in his hand. When Nicole asked him why he had hit the door, he stated he did not want to hit her. This researcher talked about the importance of thinking about this pattern of abuse when the time came for her to choose her life partner. The next week, Nicole came to class and was very quiet. After the following class, she came to this researcher and stated, "I plan to continue my friendship with my baby's father so that he and his parents can spend time with and know their grandchild. But my boyfriend will not be my choice of my life partner." Toward the end of the course, Nicole stated that she had written to her brother who lived in California and that they planned to write to each other often. (Figure 23.1 depicts Nicole's drawing of her family diagram.)

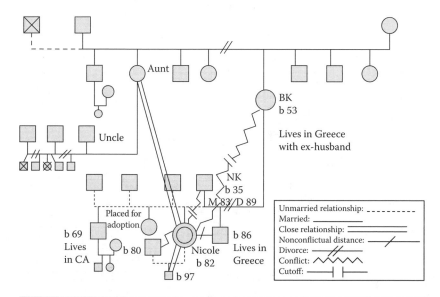

Figure 23.1 Nicole's family diagram.

Vignette: Leslie's Family Diagram

Leslie was 16 years old when she began the study and her daughter was 20 months old. Leslie was friendly, outgoing, and very talkative. She lived with her maternal grandmother. She stated that she had lived with her boyfriend for a short time after her baby was born, but "did not like it." She preferred to live with her grandmother. She explained that she was interested in participating in the study because her daughter had bad tantrums, and she was not sure what to do. Throughout the study, Leslie showed active interest in learning how families function and how she functioned in her family. She eagerly met with her extended family members to learn more about her family. She stated that her family "occupied the entire block" on which she lived. She had close relationships with her grandmother, her brother, and her cousins. She explained that the whole family regularly got together.

During one class, which happened to be on April 1, she came up to this researcher and said that she had something to tell her. When asked what it was, she said that she was pregnant. With a smile, she quickly stated, "April fools. I have learned a lot about myself in this class." In Leslie's family, there were many relationships that produced babies, but few marital commitments. Leslie could easily see this on her family diagram. She stated that she had different plans for herself. (Figure 23.2 depicts Leslie's drawing of her family diagram.)

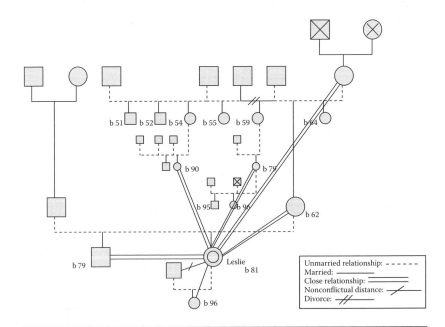

Figure 23.2 Leslie's family diagram.

Discussion

All of the participants in the FaMILY experimental group had made great progress in drawing their family diagrams. In applying the basic principles of Bowen theory to their own family diagrams, they were able to engage in more reflective thinking about their family systems, their multigenerational patterns, and their own patterns of behaviors. In the class discussions, they demonstrated an enhanced understanding of themselves, their families, their environment, and the emotional and behavioral patterns in their family system. They could see themselves as part of a family system, in which they were influenced by other family members' behaviors and others were influenced by theirs. Bowen (1978) stated that "a little knowledge about broad principles of emotional systems can help the motivated one reach a calmer and more contained level of functioning" (p. 234). The FaMILY program had presented them with a new systems framework with which they could better understand their families and their part in them and make more reflective and responsible life decisions.

By the end of the course, FaMILY participants had completed a personalized 5-inch × 7-inch card identifying reflective rather than reactive behaviors, which they had identified during the course as helping them manage their anxiety and work toward being a more differentiated self within their family. Adolescents were encouraged to continue to use these cards as cues to reinforce reflective behaviors.

The participants' evaluations were very positive. Comments included, "I enjoyed the family diagram class. It gave me a sense of where I came from"; "I wish the study would just keep going"; "Our discussions about family were very helpful. I learned a lot about my family. It made me think about my own behavior"; "Everything was very helpful and explained very well. There was nothing that needed to be improved. Everything was great"; "It helped me become a better mom"; and "I enjoyed participating in the family diagram because it gave me a chance to reflect on my family relationships. I also enjoyed the socialization, time away, and advice that I got from the program. What I liked least was that it had to end." The positive responses encouraged this researcher to continue her research in introducing systems thinking to adolescents.

Testing the Differentiation of Self Inventory for Use With Ethnically Diverse High School Adolescents

It was evident from this first pilot study that a psychometrically sound instrument was needed to measure differentiation of self. Therefore, in a second preliminary study, Knauth and Skowron (2004) examined the suitability of the DSI (Skowron & Friedlander, 1998; Skowron & Schmitt, 2003) for use with ethnically diverse high school adolescents. Skowron and her colleagues had developed and revised the DSI into a reliable and valid measure of differentiation of self for adults and had empirically tested the central tenets of Bowen theory (Skowron, 2000; Skowron, Holmes, & Sabatelli, 2003).

To evaluate the psychometric properties of the 46-item self-report DSI for use with adolescents, the DSI, the State–Trait Anxiety Inventory (Spielberger, Gorsuch, Lushene, Vagg, & Jacobs, 1983), and the Symptom Pattern Scale (Gurin, Veroff, & Feld, 1960) were administered to an ethnically diverse sample of 363 adolescents ages 14 to 19 from the same Baltimore high school. The DSI full scale demonstrated good internal consistency reliability, with a Cronbach's alpha coefficient of .84 for the full DSI scale and alphas of .82 and .73 for the Emotional Reactivity and the Emotional Cutoff subscales, respectively (Knauth & Skowron, 2004). Factor analysis yielded a six-factor structure, representing the multidimensionality of the DSI items among adolescents. Tests of two hypotheses derived from Bowen theory were also supported. Differentiation of self mediated the relation between chronic anxiety and symptom development ($p < .001$), indicating that greater differentiation of self predicted fewer symptoms over and above chronic anxiety and lending support to the construct validity of the DSI in adolescents. The results of this study provided support for using the DSI with this population.

Testing the Theoretical Model That Guides the FaMILY Intervention

A third preliminary study was then conducted in preparation for the FaMILY intervention. The primary goals were to evaluate (a) reliability of measures in the assessment protocol, (b) response distributions on the intervention outcomes of interest, and (c) relations among adolescent differentiation of self, chronic anxiety, social problem solving, risky health behaviors, and academic engagement in this urban, ethnically diverse population of adolescents (Knauth et al., 2006). Data were collected from 161 adolescents ages 14 to 19 in the same Baltimore high school.

Findings provided support for the credibility of the theoretical model that guides the FaMILY intervention model. Consistent with the model, higher levels of differentiation of self related to lower levels of chronic anxiety ($p < .001$) and higher levels of social problem solving ($p < .01$). Higher chronic anxiety related to lower social problem solving ($p < .001$). A test of mediation showed that chronic anxiety mediated the relationship between differentiation of self and social problem solving ($p < .001$), indicating that differentiation influences social problem solving through chronic anxiety. Higher levels of social problem solving were related to less drug use ($p < .05$), less high-risk sexual behavior ($p < .01$), and an increase in academic engagement ($p < .01$).

These findings provide evidence that differentiation of self is a cognitive factor that enables adolescents to manage chronic anxiety and motivates them to use effective problem solving, resulting in less involvement in health-compromising behaviors and an increase in academic engagement. This study and the previous study of the DSI's psychometric properties provide further evidence of the cross-cultural applicability of Bowen theory. A one-way analysis of variance showed no significant differences in levels of differentiation of self on the basis of race or ethnicity.

Recommendations for Further Research

On the basis of the preliminary work and pilot intervention, empirical support exists for theoretical relations between aspects of differentiation of self, chronic anxiety, social problem solving, risk behaviors, and academic engagement among this population of ethnically diverse adolescents. This knowledge emphasizes the importance of studying adolescent risk behaviors from a family systems perspective. Continuing to focus on the adolescent as the problem prevents health care providers from accurately assessing the contribution of the family relationship system to the problem and developing interventions that work.

The introduction of systems thinking, and how families function as systems, in the early high school years is expected to help teens to engage in more reflective thinking about their family systems, their multigenerational patterns, and their own patterns of risky health behaviors. This includes ways to avoid reenacting maladaptive family patterns in their current lives, enhance health behaviors, and strengthen academic engagement and success. An effective and economic way to introduce systems thinking to adolescents is to offer a program, taught by a consultant in family theory, to small groups of adolescents in their high school or community adolescent program. The importance and many benefits of bringing Bowen theory to adolescents cannot be overstated.

References

American Academy of Pediatrics. (2001). Adolescents and human immunodeficiency virus infection: The role of the pediatrician in prevention and intervention (RE0031). *Pediatrics, 107,* 188–190.

Anderson, S., & Sabatelli, R. (1992). The Differentiation in the Family Scale (DIFS). *American Journal of Family Therapy, 20,* 77–89.

Bavolek, S. (1984). *Adult-Adolescent Parenting Inventory.* Eau Claire, WI: Family Development Resources.

Botvin, G. J., Baker, E., Dusenbury, L., Tortu, S., & Botvin, E. M. (1995). Long-term follow up results of a randomized drug abuse prevention trial in a White middle-class population. *JAMA, 273,* 1106–1112.

Bowen, M. (1978). *Family therapy in clinical practice.* New York, NY: Jason Aronson.

Brook, D. W. & Brook, J. S. (1992). Family processes associated with alcohol and drug use and abuse. In E. Kaufman & P. Kaufman (Eds.), *Family therapy of drug and alcohol abuse* (pp. 15–33). Boston, MA: Allyn & Bacon.

Centers for Disease Control and Prevention. (2006). Youth risk behavior surveillance—United States, 2005. *MMWR, 55*(SS-5), 1–108.

Center for Substance Abuse Prevention. (1997). *Selected findings in prevention: A decade of results from the Center for Substance Abuse Prevention.* Washington, DC: Author.

Conger, R. D., & Rueter, M. A. (1996). Siblings, parents, and peers: A longitudinal study of social influences in adolescent risk for alcohol use and abuse. In G. H. Brody (Ed.), *Sibling relationships: Their causes and consequences* (pp. 1–30). Westport, CT: Ablex.

Costello, C., & Comrey, L. (1967). Scales for measuring depression and anxiety. *Journal of Psychology, 66,* 303–313.

Durlak, J. A. (1997). *Successful prevention programs for children and adolescents.* New York, NY: Plenum Press.

Gilbert, R. (1999). *Connecting with our children: Guiding principles for parents in a troubled world.* New York, NY: Wiley.

Gurin, G., Veroff, J., & Feld, S. (1960). *Americans view their mental health.* New York, NY: Basic Books.

Kerr, M. E., & Bowen, M. (1988). *Family evaluation: An approach based on Bowen theory.* New York, NY: W. W. Norton.

Knauth, D., & Skowron, E. (2004). Psychometric evaluation of the Differentiation of Self Inventory for adolescents. *Journal of Nursing Research, 53,* 163–171.

Knauth, D., Skowron, E., & Escobar, M. (2006). Effect of differentiation of self on adolescent risk behavior : Test of the theoretical model. *Nursing Research, 55,* 336–345.

Kumpfer, K. L., & Alvarado, R. (2003). Family-strengthening approaches for the prevention of youth problem behaviors. *American Psychologist, 58,* 457–465.

Loeber, R., & Stouthammer-Loeber, M. (1986). Family factors as correlates and predictors of juvenile conduct problems and delinquency. In N. Morris & M. Tonry (Eds.), *Crime and justice: An annual review of research* (pp. 29–149). Chicago, IL: University of Chicago Press.

McKnight, A. S. (2003). The impact of cutoff in families raising adolescents. In P. Titelman (Ed.), *Emotional cutoff: Bowen family systems theory perspectives* (pp. 273–288). New York, NY: Haworth Press.

Patterson, G. R., Reid, J. B., & Dishion, T. J. (1992). *Antisocial boys.* Eugene, OR: Castalia.

Popkin, M., Gard, B., & Montgomery, M. (1996). *Parenting your 1- to 4-year-old.* Atlanta, GA: Active Parenting.

Rosen, K., Bartle-Harting, S., & Stith, S. (2001). Using Bowen theory to enhance understanding of the intergenerational transmission of dating violence. *Journal of Family Issues, 22,* 124–142.

Santisteban, D. A., Coatsworth, J. D., Perez-Vidal, A., Kurtines, W. M., Schwartz, S. J., LaPerriere, A., & Szapocznik, J. (2003). Efficacy of brief strategic family therapy in modifying Hispanic adolescent behavior problems and substance use. *Journal of Family Psychology, 17,* 121–133.

Skowron, E. A. (2000). The role of differentiation of self in marital adjustment. *Journal of Counseling Psychology, 47,* 229–237.

Skowron, E., & Friedlander, M. (1998). The Differentiation of Self Inventory: Development and initial validation. *Journal of Counseling Psychology, 45,* 235–246.

Skowron, E. A., Holmes, S. E., & Sabatelli, R. M. (2003). Deconstructing differentiation: Self regulation, interdependent relating, and well-being in adulthood. *Contemporary Family Therapy: An International Journal, 25,* 111–129.

Skowron, E., & Schmitt, T. (2003). Assessing interpersonal fusion: Reliability and validity of a new Fusion With Others subscale. *Journal of Marital and Family Therapy, 29,* 209–222.

Spielberger, C., Gorsuch, R., Lushene, R., Vagg, P., & Jacobs, G. (1983). *Manual for the State–Trait Anxiety Inventory.* Redwood City, CA: Mind Garden.

Szapocznik, J., Kurtines, W. M., Perez-Vidal, A., Hervis, O. E., & Foote, F. H. (1990). One person family therapy. In R. A. Wells & V. J. Giannetti (Eds.), *Handbook of brief psychotherapies: Applied clinical psychology* (pp. 493–510). New York, NY: Plenum Press.

Thompson, P., Giedd, J., Woods, R., MacDonald, D., Evans, A., & Toga, A. (2000). Growth patterns in the developing brain detected by using continuum mechanical tensor maps. *Nature, 404,* 190–193.

Titelman, P. (Ed.). (1998). *Clinical applications of Bowen family systems theory.* New York, NY: Haworth Press.

U.S. Department of Health and Human Services. (2001). *Healthy people 2010: Leading health indicators.* Retrieved from http://www.healthypeople.gov/LHI/

Walker James, D., & Partee, G. (2002). *No more islands: Family involvement in 27 school and youth programs.* Washington, DC: American Youth Policy Forum.

24

Bowen Theory in Russia: A Training Program for Russian Psychologists

KATHARINE GRATWICK BAKER and PETER TITELMAN

In October 1999, the Russian Society of Family Consultants and Psychotherapists invited Katharine Gratwick Baker and Peter Titelman to present a training seminar on Bowen family systems theory to a group of 40 Russian psychologists, clinicians, academics, researchers, and business consultants in Moscow. The seminar was conceptualized as 2 full days of theoretical and practical training, taking place every 6 months for 2 years. Between sessions, participants were to meet monthly in small groups to discuss translated material from the professional literature on Bowen theory and to prepare writing assignments on specific concepts from the theory. The program began in April 2000 and continued through October 2001.

The goals of the program were (a) to develop a group of Russian clinicians and business consultants solidly grounded in Bowen theory who could themselves become teachers or trainers for other interested Russian professionals and (b) to develop a theoretical framework for understanding the multigenerational effects of trauma on individuals, families, and larger social systems.

Background of Presenters

The first author has long had an interest in Russia and Russian culture. She first traveled to the Soviet Union in 1962 as a student and received a master's degree in Russian studies from New York University in 1965. She also has a doctoral degree in social work and extensive postdoctoral training in Bowen theory, including 4 years at the Bowen Center for the Study of the Family in Washington, DC.

During the glasnost period, the first author went to Russia a number of times with groups of psychologists who presented brief workshops on family therapy. In the early 1990s, she developed a small consulting company, Intercultural Training Associates, with Boris M. Masterov, a Russian psychologist. The company was based in both Moscow and Washington, DC. Its purpose was to provide intercultural training programs for Russian–American joint ventures, with a focus on improving mutual cultural understanding and behavioral change among Russians and Americans working together. Cross-cultural approaches to team building, decision making, communication, and conflict management were some of the topics addressed by the company.

During this period, Baker published several articles in *Voprosy Psikhologii,* a widely distributed Russian journal of psychology. One of the articles gave an overview of Bowen theory as a theoretical and therapeutic approach to family clinical practice. In 1993, Baker undertook a research project on the impact of Stalin's Purge on three generations of Russian families, collaborating with a Russian coinvestigator, Julia B. Gippenreiter, and with the cooperation of the Memorial Foundation and financial support from the International Research and Exchanges Board. The results of this research were published in the United States and in Russia in 1994 (Baker & Gippenreiter, 1995, 1996).

Peter Titelman's interest in Russia and the wider central European region stemmed from his own family background. Ancestors on both sides of his family had migrated from the Russian Empire to the United States in the late 19th century. Although he knew of no relatives still living in Russia, his belief in the importance of understanding the multigenerational history of one's family of origin first led him to travel in Russia and Lithuania in the late 1990s. He, too, is deeply grounded in Bowen theory, which he has practiced as a clinical psychologist for many years. He has also edited four books on Bowen theory and therapy.

For both authors, the opportunity offered by the Russian Society of Family Consultants and Psychotherapists to provide a substantive 2-year seminar in Bowen theory in Moscow was exciting and challenging. They knew that short weekend workshops usually have very little carryover effect, especially because it is so easy to forget the new ideas one has learned when there is no structured support for ongoing application and practice. It is also difficult to maintain a systems way of thinking in a world driven by linear cause-and-effect thinking. Development of a 2-year program that would include readings and small Moscow-based consultation groups for participants offered a potentially more effective alternative. In addition, they were intrigued by the possibility of offering a seminar in Bowen theory to professionals from a different cultural background. Cultural variation might be observed in the specific ways in which the concepts manifest themselves, but the underlying family relationship patterns should be similar if the theory is accurate and truly grounded in natural processes.

The Model

In consultation with the directors of the Russian Society of Family Consultants and Psychotherapists, the authors planned a series of weekend seminars that would be repeated in April and October for 2 years. On Saturday and Sunday mornings of the seminars, each author presented a didactic lecture on a concept from Bowen theory, which was followed by discussion with the participants. On several of the seminar mornings, the first author also conducted a live family interview with a participant volunteer, followed by discussion. The ground rules for the discussion were that no questions were to be directed to the person interviewed, all questions and comments were to focus on the interview process rather than its content, and absolute confidentiality was to be preserved. The person being interviewed was, of course, not a clinical client, and the purpose of the interview was to demonstrate a systems approach to interviewing. After a lunch break, the seminar participants divided into two groups, each facilitated by one of the authors. Three participants presented material on their own families and clinical cases that reflected some of the issues raised in the readings and didactic lectures.

During the 6-month intervals between seminars, the participants met once a month in small groups of 6 to 8 people, discussed articles translated for them, and presented clinical cases or their own families to each other. Participants were also asked to complete one writing assignment during the 6-month interval that they would turn in at the beginning of the next seminar. Some participants chose not to complete the writing assignments.

During the first weekend seminar in April 2000, the authors described the origins of Bowen theory and presented an overview of its eight concepts. The importance of understanding one's family of origin as a starting point for clinical and consultation work was emphasized. The authors then both presented their own families of origin, using family diagrams to describe the members of their families, family relationship patterns, and family functional levels over 3 or 4 generations.

Before the first seminar began, the authors sent participants a written overview of the program describing the expectations for participants, including the completion of readings and written assignments as well as participation in small monthly discussion groups:

> This is a program for adult learners. Our hope is that you may begin to learn to think in a different way about human relationships and behavior in general, and about your *own* relationships and behavior in particular. Each participant is encouraged to read as much as possible in Bowen theory and related fields, such as evolution, biology, and ethology. Participants are also encouraged to keep a journal, in order to provide continuity between meetings. There will be no grades.

The authors also sent participants an explanation of what a family diagram should look like and a list of family facts to include in the diagrams. Participants were asked to identify patterns of functioning that had occurred over several generations and to describe at least three major emotional triangles in their family system and one or more triangles in the family system with which they would like to start a detriangling effort. In addition, they were asked to use symbols to indicate where there was cutoff or fusion in the family.

The authors asked participants to respond to the following questions:

1. What is your sibling position?
2. How would you describe yourself in the triangle with your parents?
3. How would you describe yourself in triangles that include your spouse and your children?
4. How would you describe yourself in terms of overfunctioning–underfunctioning with your parents, your spouse, or both?
5. What does your anxiety look like within family relationships?
6. Do you have any emotional, social, or physical symptoms that might be expressions of anxiety?
7. Can you describe issues of emotional fusion or cutoff across several generations that would help you understand your own basic functioning?
8. What is the relationship between your choice to be a psychologist or business consultant and the way you function in your family of origin? Are there any parallels?

Participants were also given an outline for preparing written case reports, in which they were asked to provide, in the following order, (a) the presenting problem; (b) a brief history of the nuclear family; (c) a brief history of the extended family; (d) an initial summary assessment of sibling positions, the multigenerational process, triangles, the projection process, patterns of over- and underfunctioning, and an estimate of the level of differentiation of the family; and (e) the plan and process of therapy, including observing the self in the system, planning change, taking action, evaluating the impact of action, and planning additional change.

In preparation for the monthly small-group discussion meetings, participants were given the following guidelines:

1. The leader of the group should encourage confidentiality, mutual respectfulness, neutrality, thoughtfulness, and connections with Bowen theory, and discourage advice giving.
2. The meetings would not emphasize traditional group process (i.e., relationship building among group members); rather, they were to provide an opportunity for individual participants to present thoughtful observations about their own families or clients and for the other members of the group to listen and learn.
3. After each presentation, group members might wish to comment. If asking questions, participants were encouraged to focus on facts rather than interpretations. In other words, they were encouraged to ask who, what, where, when, and how questions and avoid why questions.

4. Individuals presenting their families should start with a focus on themselves, their spouses, and their children and then move toward observations about their families of origin and multigenerational families; however, there was no rigid format for presentations.
5. Participants were encouraged to first focus on facts of chronology and nodal events and then to identify patterns and themes in family relationships across generations.

The full 2-year program was as follows: an overview of Bowen theory with presentations of the authors' exploration of differentiation of self in their own families of origin (April 2000), followed by an introduction to assessment in clinical practice and business consulting (October 2000); clinical practice approaches and business consultation approaches (April 2001); and organizational, societal, and natural systems concepts and a review of the concept of cutoff (October 2001). Throughout all these meetings, the eight basic concepts from Bowen theory were continually revisited and discussed.

Underlying the seminar model was an emphasis on differentiation of self for presenters and participants. High levels of self-observation and responsibility for self in meeting the expectations of the program were assumed. Reference was often made to what was called *the adult learner model of education,* implying that the participants were autonomous professional adults enrolled in the seminar because they wanted to be there, to be responsible for themselves and the effort they put into their learning, and to be independent evaluators of the usefulness of the program.

Undoubtedly, these expectations may have generated some anxiety for the participants, and each person met the expectations at the level of his or her capacity. Anxiety may have occasionally impeded free discussion during the first few seminars. It may also have interfered with some participants' ability to complete the written homework assignments. Toward the end of the meetings, there appeared to be more active, energetic engagement because participants openly expressed their thoughts with regard to theoretical concepts and cases, and more written assignments were received during the last meeting than at any previous meeting.

The presenters expected that they would hold themselves to similar standards of responsibility and self-observation, doing the best job they could to present Bowen theory clearly, without imposing "right" answers on the participants. They tried to raise questions more than give answers. They were interested in participants' perspectives and responses during discussions of concepts and of cases. Monitoring their own anxieties about their ability to present Bowen theory effectively was important. They presented within the limits of their own competence and understanding, acknowledging that neither of them could speak for Bowen but that they could only explain the theory as each of them personally understood it at that point in time. Managing their relationship with each other as they prepared for the seminar and then presented their own best thinking was also a significant area of responsibility. The presenters gave themselves room for disagreement in their understanding of the concepts. They took turns presenting and leading discussions and tried not to interrupt each other's presentations unless asked to make a contribution.

The necessity of translation was an interesting element in all presentations and discussions. A Russian psychologist fluent in English provided excellent consecutive translation for all the verbal interactions, and she was occasionally assisted by a number of participants who spoke excellent English. The first author speaks some Russian and was therefore able to develop more direct interpersonal connections with participants who did not speak any English. Consecutive translation naturally slows down a presentation process, with mixed results. Because every paragraph is repeated in the second language, the presenter and the listeners have time to think about and absorb the material without pressure. Consecutive translation does, however, mean that all presentations require double the amount of time, and therefore the amount of material that can be covered in a given time period is cut in half. This limitation was frustrating to participants who spoke English well. It was, of course, necessary for those who spoke no English and could access the material only through translation.

Outcome

At the end of the seminar in October 2001, a director of the Russian Society remarked, "One of the most satisfying aspects of the whole program was that everyone did what was expected." The Russian Society provided space for the meetings and highly effective logistical support. The presenters came to the seminars prepared with the appropriate plans and materials. The participants attended all meetings regularly and arrived on time. It was their choice to complete the homework assignments or not. Slightly fewer than half of them did so and received certificates of participation.

There were several mechanisms for evaluating the substantive outcome of the seminar. First, almost 75% of the participants completed a written evaluation of the course after the final class meeting. Second, a group of participants met in Moscow in December 2001 for a roundtable discussion of the seminar's usefulness. Third, during the fall of 2001, 8 participants who spoke and wrote English well enrolled in a distance-learning program to continue their study of Bowen theory through the Western Pennsylvania Family Center in Pittsburgh. There were also efforts to apply for grant monies to send individual participants to the United States for continued study of the theory, but these applications were not successful.

Written Evaluations

The evaluation consisted of 10 substantive questions and some specific questions about the participants' demographic information. In terms of age, 80%

were in their 30s and 40s, 10% in their 20s, and 10% in their 50s. Ninety percent were married. Almost 50% were only children in their families of origin, 24% were oldest children, and 24% were youngest children. There was 1 twin. Eighty percent had received the highest level of education in psychology, and almost all of these individuals had taken some other courses in family therapy. One person was a student at the Moscow Psychological Institute, and 2 people had received pedagogical training. Years of professional experience ranged from none to 25, with most having 6 to 10 years of experience. Fifty-nine percent said they had completed all the homework assignments. Twenty-four percent said they had done no homework, and 17% said they had done "some" homework. Ninety percent wanted further training in Bowen theory.

The first substantive question was, "From your experience in this seminar, has anything changed in the way you think about yourself and your own functioning?" There were many thoughtful answers to this question; participants shared, for example, that they were "beginning to think of myself as part of a large system of many generations," developing an interest in family history, lowering their own anxiety, working on cutoff, gaining objectivity, becoming more observant of their own functioning, and realizing that their own levels of differentiation were lower than they had thought. One noted that "the changes have only just begun. It is evident that it will be a long road."

The second question asked, "Has anything changed in the way you think about and function in your family?" Several noted that their thinking had changed, but that changes in their behavior would take longer. Many noted that they were working on bridging cutoffs in their families. Several had observed their own overfunctioning and were trying to rein themselves in. Many were working to develop more open connections in specific relationships with parents, siblings, and spouses.

The third question asked, "Has anything changed in the way you assess your clients?" Several described themselves as more neutral. A number described themselves as more systematic in the way they gathered information about their clients' multigenerational families. Some were more attuned to the issue of cutoff in client families.

The fourth question asked, "Has anything changed in the way you plan interventions in your clinical work?" More than a third reported that they collect information more systematically and thoughtfully, using the family diagram. A number had started to focus on their own functioning with clients. Several found themselves paying more attention to those who appeared to be higher functioning members of client families. A number found that Bowen theory provided them with a framework for working with one or two adult family members rather than with the whole family group.

Next they were asked, "What were the most useful concepts in Bowen theory for you?" Most participants listed a number of concepts. Most frequently listed were cutoff, the emotional triangle, and differentiation of self. Also listed were projection, societal process, fusion, sibling position, multigenerational process, nuclear family process, and the transmission of anxiety.

A follow-up question asked, "What were the most difficult concepts in Bowen theory for you?" One person said that all of them were difficult because of their complexity and the fact that she had to think so much about each one. Almost 50% said that differentiation was the most difficult concept to understand: "It is a mystery," "It is complicated to understand and recognize in practice," "It isn't completely clear how to use it with clients," and "It is difficult for me to understand the precise levels of differentiation with a precise measure." Two mentioned that the concept of societal process was too superficial and not well thought out.

Questions 7 and 8 asked, "Which aspects of the seminar were most interesting to you?" and "Which aspects were least interesting to you?" Most said that all aspects of the seminar were very interesting to them, with the live interviews, readings, group meetings, and case presentations receiving the most positive responses. Twenty-eight percent thought that the lectures were less interesting than the rest of the program, and several thought the lectures repeated much of the material in the readings. Seventeen percent thought the readings were not useful, particularly because the participants received them irregularly and the books they came from were not listed, so they could not pursue the topics further. Seventeen percent did not find the group meetings particularly interesting.

The ninth question asked, "How would you describe your relationship with the trainers in terms of the effect on your learning Bowen theory?" This question was not particularly well phrased, and so the answers were not clear. Several said they would have wanted more contact with and more clinical supervision from us. A number commented on the training style, which was different from what they were used to. Most thought the presenters communicated the theory clearly and effectively and were open, respectful, and approachable.

The 10th question asked, "What were the positive and negative aspects of a long-distance program on your own learning process? What about learning through translation?" Only 1 participant said that the translation was a problem. All the others said it posed no problem to them and did not interfere with their learning, although some said it slowed down the transmission of content in the lectures. Many commented that the distance, both in time and in geography, gave them more time to think about the materials and to function more independently with regard to their learning. One wrote that "the long distance gave me time to develop my own rhythm in absorbing the material." Another noted that "long-distance learning requires more organization and initiative. I did not always succeed in being completely organized, but when it happened, I considered it progress." Another wrote that "this learning process required more maturity and independence in study."

Negative aspects of the program were that 2 days per seminar was too short; there was not enough feedback on their writing, not enough supervision, and too little clinical analysis; and the 6-month breaks between seminars were too long.

This brief summary of the responses to the evaluation questions does not begin to do justice to the thoughtfulness and care that participants put into them. Most of them spent a significant period of time reflecting on the impact of the seminar and then writing their answers in great detail, for which the authors were very appreciative.

Discussion Meeting

In December 2001, 2 months after the seminar ended, all the participants were invited to get together for a roundtable discussion to explore their impressions of and reactions to the 2-year training course in Bowen theory. Thirteen participants attended this meeting. For the purpose of discussion, the organizers of the meeting proposed five topics: (a) the cultural specifics of the Bowen approach in Russia, (b) participants' personal experiences of the adult model of training with Bowen theory, (c) the most interesting aspect of the theory and what made the deepest impression on participants, (d) the place of Bowen theory among other systemic approaches, and (e) perspectives for using Bowen theory in Russia. The first and fifth topics seemed to be the most interesting to the group. But several participants also spoke of the theory as a whole and its influence on large societal groups.

Summary and Conclusions

The Moscow seminar on Bowen theory had many positive aspects, as well as some difficulties and potential areas of misunderstanding. The seminar provided an opportunity for the presenters to clarify their thoughts and present the theory over a 2-year time period to a motivated group of professionals from a different part of the world. The presenters had time to build the connections among the concepts, to have a sense of continuity in the didactic content of their presentations, and to create a learning environment that they hoped would reflect high levels of differentiation. The idea of an adult learning model was based on the assumption that participants would be functioning at a reasonably mature level and would take charge of the way in which they wanted to engage with the new ideas of Bowen theory.

Generally, this assumption proved to be true. Participants attended regularly, and their written assignments, as well as their family and clinical presentations, were thoughtful, complex, and deep. Although 1 participant in the December discussion group said that Russians do not have access to information about their families because of Russia's long history of societal trauma, the authors were impressed by the many careful family diagrams of 3 or more generations that they received. On the basis of their understanding of Bowen theory, the authors assumed that the functioning of Russians, like that of all other humans, varies along many dimensions. Knowledge of past-generation family members is undoubtedly one of these dimensions because some people know nothing about their family history and some people know a lot, and there is a large group in the middle with some family information, regardless of societal trauma (for a study of societal trauma in Russia, see Baker & Gippenreiter, 1996). Discussions with the whole group were slow at first, perhaps because the learning model was somewhat different from and more informal than what the participants were used to in their own educational system. By the end of the seminar, however, almost all participants seemed to be actively engaged in thinking and speaking about the theory and its relevance to their personal lives and to their professional practices.

A major challenge to the whole learning experience was the fact that neither of the authors speaks Russian fluently. Although participants did not define the need for translation as a problem in their written evaluations, the authors did experience this as a problem. Consecutive translation slowed down the process and limited the amount of material they could cover in lectures. The first author had some free-flowing conversations with the non–English-speaking participants, although she is not fluent enough to present didactic lectures in Russian. The second author does not speak any Russian, and therefore all his formal and informal communications had to be translated. Inevitably, there was less development of a relationship between the presenters and the participants, and therefore the real substance of the theory came through translation and reading materials. This can be seen as both an advantage and a disadvantage.

Translation of the reading materials also posed a problem. There was not enough time nor were there financial resources to produce professional translations of the readings at the time the seminar took place. Therefore, many of the participants received only brief summaries rather than the full chapters written by Bowen and his followers. Their initial understanding of the theory was based on these summaries, although the summaries were, of course, supplemented over time by the lectures and discussions. A collection of articles on Bowen theory was translated into Russian and published in Moscow in 2005 for future seminars (Baker & Varga, 2005).

It was interesting to the authors that participants in the December 2001 discussion group continued to focus on the question of whether Bowen theory is relevant to Russia. Throughout the seminar, Bowen theory was presented as a universal species-wide theory grounded in natural systems and the biological sciences. Although it is a theory of human behavior and relationship systems, many of its theoretical concepts and patterns can be observed in other social mammals, such as other primates, dolphins, and elephants. The concepts of emotional process and anxiety, as described by Bowen, are observable throughout the animal kingdom.

The cultural variations and diverse historical experiences of different human populations are highly significant for understanding specific human groups. However, variations on the themes described in Bowen theory, such as triangles, cutoff, projection, and differentiation of self, can be seen in all human populations. They may look slightly different on the surface, but underneath, they are emotionally similar. The authors regret not having made this point clearly enough because there was some continuing anxiety and concern about whether Bowen theory is applicable to Russia.

An example of universality is provided by the concept of *cutoff*. This concept describes variations in the range of distance or closeness that humans have with their parents as they grow into adulthood and form their own families. There is a great deal of cultural variation in the way cutoff manifests itself. In the United States, an anxious young person at the more distant end of the range might move from New York to California and rarely connect with his or her parents. In Russia, an emotionally distant or cutoff young person might continue to share an apartment with his or her parents but rarely communicate personal thoughts or feelings to them. Long-term emotional cutoff across generations usually leads to the development of emotional, social, or physical symptoms in some members of the succeeding generations. In different cultures, these symptoms may appear to be different, but they are linked to the underlying pattern of cutoff as a way of managing anxiety in families from all cultures.

One might have thought that growing up and living in a repressive, intrusive, totalitarian society (as did all the Russian participants under the old Soviet system) would lead to a sense of inhibition about examining intimate family relationships in a somewhat open setting with colleagues. Here the authors observed a range of responsiveness as they encouraged participants to do their own family-of-origin work. Many participants explored their family relationships in depth, but others did so only partially or not at all. The authors believe that the decision as to whether to engage in this work was determined more by the individual's level of differentiation than by a societal history of mistrust. However, the authors do not have any way to prove that belief.

References

Baker, K., & Gippenreiter, Y. B. (1995). Vliyaniye stalinskikh repressii kontsa 30-kh godov na zhizn' semei v trekh pokoleniyakh [The impact of Stalin's repression at the end of the 1930s on family life over three generations]. *Voprosy Psikhologii, 2,* 66–84.

Baker, K., & Gippenreiter, J. B. (1996). The effects of Stalin's purge on three generations of Russian families. *Family Systems, 3*(1), 5–35.

Baker, K., & Varga, A. Y. (Eds.). (2005). *Teoriya semeinykh system Murray Bowen: Osnovnyye ponyatiya, metody i klinicheskaya praktika* [Murray Bowen's family systems theory: Basic concepts, methods, and clinical practice]. Moscow, Russia: Kogito-Tsentr.

25
Restless Bedfellows: Taking Bowen Theory Into a Child-Focused Adolescent Treatment Unit in Australia

JENNIFER A. BROWN

It is a challenging task to bring systems thinking to life for professionals working in a program underpinned by medical and child-focused frameworks. Although much value is given to thinking about the family in addressing symptoms in children at the Adolescent and Family Unit (AFU) in Sydney, New South Wales, Australia, the program is predominately structured to treat the symptoms of the adolescent patient. Bowen family systems theory, which views symptoms as residing in the emotional process of the relationship system, inevitably brings dissonance to learners who wish to apply systems thinking on top of an individual focus. The medical approach, which pervades societal thinking about mental illness, treats the pathology as residing in the young patient. Bowen theory sees the symptom as emerging from an adaptation common to all relationship systems that serve to contain the anxieties of surviving as a unit. Rather than seeing illness residing in an individual, Bowen theory considers symptoms in terms of adjustments made in a relationship network. Hence, the treatment focus is on reducing the anxious intensity in the family unit.

This chapter has grown out of the author's involvement over 10 years as a consultant to a treatment program for adolescents with protracted mental health issues. The author describes some of the challenges to thinking systems when the main frame of reference is seeing the symptoms in the child. Survey feedback from mental health professionals who have attended the training is used to highlight hurdles encountered in endeavoring to apply a systems lens. Learning opportunities that arose in the training process, the anxious workplace, and the worker's own families are also discussed. Additionally, the author describes her retrospective appreciation of initial limitations in understanding Bowen theory and how this affected her conduct of consultations.

Setting and Role

Ten years ago, an adolescent mental health service in Sydney, New South Wales, Australia, contracted the author to facilitate weekly meetings to explore the use of family therapy in the treatment of adolescents. The program is located within the grounds of a major teaching hospital in the most populated region of Sydney, which includes a spectrum of socioeconomic neighborhoods. Given the socialization of much of Australia's health system, patients are drawn from the full range of social groups in the region. The clinical team is made up of psychiatrists, trainee psychiatrists, clinical psychologists, and social workers who operate within a multidisciplinary unit that also includes a school and a nursing department. To be admitted for a school term (10 weeks) into the AFU, the young person must already have been in treatment at a primary level for mental health symptoms. Each patient attends the unit school and regular individual therapy with their case manager to set behavioral goals. Community and therapy groups that focus on social skills and self-regulation techniques are also part of treatment. Psychiatrists, who are positioned as leaders on each team, review medication and hold primary medical–legal accountability for treatment decisions and safety assessments before discharge. Most patients are on psychotropic medication with a range of diagnostic categories applied.

The inclusion of the term *family* in the unit's official title speaks to a strong premise that family involvement is important to the treatment of a child's symptoms. Along a continuum of mental health services for adolescents in Sydney, the AFU program sits a long way from the intensely child-focused end of the scale, where families are excluded from the child's treatment. Within the AFU team, individuals are committed to bypassing an emphasis on diagnosis and to thinking about multiple factors influencing the young person's symptoms. The influence of cybernetic systems models over the years has meant that problems are not always thought of in terms of linear causality, with ideas about reciprocity in relationships being considered. Although these trends toward thinking systems are recognized, the focus of treatment remains geared to reducing the individual's symptoms, which logically extends to attention being directed to the child.

There is an imperative on the unit to bring some fast relief to very severe symptoms that are often life threatening for adolescents. It is not uncommon for patients to have made regular suicide attempts such as jumping from the roofs of school buildings. Some young people make significant gains through their therapeutic relationship with workers; yet, team members acknowledge that any changes in the child are superficial unless there are some changes in the family. This view underpins the strong motivation of clinicians to improve their ways of engaging and working with the parents of the symptom bearer.

Barriers to Thinking Systems for the Team

Many approaches to treating symptoms in the individual often bring observable improvements. The effort goes into correcting the fault that is believed to have caused the problem and to symptom reduction. When focusing on diagnosing and treating the symptom bearer, attention goes into monitoring the signs of disorder. In contrast, seeing the symptom as an expression of the entire relationship system requires a different frame of reference. Rather than asking what causes this symptom, the systems thinker asks, how is it that the symptoms landed in this part of the system when others who have experienced similar stressors are able to function better? The focus is not on the individual's internal state but on where anxiety, generated by relationship insecurities, gets channeled. To assist the whole system's functioning, the therapist often works to engage the less symptomatic adults, who have some capacity to reduce the intensity they bring to interactions.

The challenge of bringing this way of thinking into the work of the AFU was brought into focus at the first consultation 10 years ago, which involved viewing a case from behind the one-way screen. A psychiatric registrar was meeting with two parents and their 15-year-old son who was exhibiting extreme anxiety in the form of paranoid delusional thinking. The parents had emigrated from China some years earlier with two young children and spoke of their distress that their eldest son was not able to take advantage of the educational opportunities available in Australia that had motivated their move. This concern appeared to have been intensified by increased daytime drowsiness as a side effect of the boy's medication. The trainee psychiatrist, with the use of an interpreter, answered the parents' questions about the nature of their son's diagnosis and his medication. The key issue for team deliberation was how to implement early intervention for psychosis and the efficacy of increasing the boy's medication.

If systems thinking was to be incorporated in the understanding of this clinical problem, questions would explore the challenges to the family's functioning and the variations in the coping of the older sibling compared with that of the younger child. The focus would extend beyond the role of medication to consideration of the family's anxiety about perceived threats and how the concerned parents might increase their self-in-the-system awareness. Discussions would consider how the treating systems, in becoming the decision makers about the problem, may be taking away functioning from family members. Despite the family involvement in treatment, this example highlighted how the thinking informing treatment decisions often presents challenges to seeing the broader emotional process behind a patient's diagnosis, particularly when symptoms are seen as predominately biological. Survey responses from team members about their exposure to Bowen theory often noted the confusing challenge of getting their thinking clear when holding onto disparate ways of viewing the clinical problem:

It can be hard not to step into the system and function within it. Expectations of families and referrers can be very forceful. I experience a strong push to pathologize the identified patient, to be able to access a diagnostic label, or to be able to treat the problem with medication or individual therapy. Clinical practice is structured and prioritized in such a way that is not always compatible to managing families by applying systems thinking. (J. Brown, personal communication [team survey], December 2008)

Team members who are thinking about anxiety forces in the family as the fuel of the adolescent's symptoms have made many changes over the years to their interviews with families. Increasingly, they report being mindful of managing their own anxiety in sessions and resisting invitations to be an "expert" on fixing the child. The focus on the child, however, is very difficult to shift when it is embodied in both program structures and social trends. Although parents are being included in discussions about the child's progress and are often given suggestions for how they can assist their child, the main frame of reference for thinking about the problem is one of explaining and treating the symptoms in the young person (Brown, 2008). This frame is embedded in society as a whole, which tends to respond to problems in a child through an anxious increase in attention, as opposed to thinking about the responsibilities and thoughtful functioning of the concerned adult (Bowen, 1978, pp. 273–276; Kerr & Bowen, 1988). Those wishing to use Bowen family systems thinking will be challenged to make the paradigm shift from asking why and correcting the problems of the individual to asking what, how, when, and where and to reducing the fusion ("stuck togetherness") in the system by inviting family members to be better observers of self in reaction to others.

Reflections on the Evolution of a Systems Approach to Training

At the time of commencing consulting at the AFU, the author had received only 2 years of postgraduate training in a version of Bowen theory. After leaving the United States, she had continued independently over a number of years to apply the thinking to her own family interactions and clinical practice. The author recognizes that it would have been ideal to remain in coaching with more experienced proponents of Bowen theory before teaching others. It is interesting to reflect, however, that even a partial understanding of this very different way of thinking about interdependence was sufficient to begin to open up a research attitude in working with other professionals.

Over the 10 years of weekly visits to AFU, the author assumed the role of trainer and used teaching methods that have not always been conducive to encouraging self-directed live learning for team members. Early consultations reflected the predominant didactic model of teaching that she had experienced. This style met the expectations of the team, who wanted to know how to do family sessions rather than how to think about family emotional process. The author met the anxious requests for techniques, giving the team a suggested framework for a family session and being willing every 3 months to conduct sessions for the team to observe. When team members saw their cases in front of the screen, they were eager to receive questions to ask via phone. This style of teaching encourages others to borrow functioning from the trainer and bypass developing their own independent thinking about their work with families. Additionally, it replicates the unidirectional pattern inherent in the medical model in which an expert tells the learner how to think and behave with the family. Bowen (1978) spoke of the traps of this approach in consultations: "When the therapist allows himself to become a 'healer' or 'repairman' the family goes into dysfunction to wait for the therapist to accomplish his work" (pp. 157–158).

The author became increasingly uncomfortable with the invitations to demonstrate how to do therapy as she grew in her awareness of the detrimental impact within her own family of her tendency toward overresponsibility. The trainer's endeavors to regulate her propensity to overfunction seem to have caught on as a useful effort for other team members, as is reflected in the following survey response: "I have become committed to the importance of a collaborative approach whereby you work with the family to create a curious, evidence-finding environment. Overfunctioning for the family does not result in larger or faster gains" (J. Brown, personal communication [team survey], December 2008).

Although the method of teaching may, at times, have been flawed in terms of a systems understanding, theory remained the bedrock of any preparation for family sessions, with clinicians presenting their ideas about key triangles in the family, how the therapist could stay out of triangles, and what ideas would invite family members to think for themselves and not others. This appears to be an example of the thinking behind the training carrying more weight in teaching theory than the technique used to teach. Conversely, if the technique is compatible with a systems view but the thinking remains individually focused, it is unlikely to expand the frame of reference.

After the first 18 months of consultations, the team was no longer asking the trainer to demonstrate family sessions. The focus in clinical work shifted somewhat from how to fix the problem to trying to make sense of it in the system of relationships.

What the trainer had not anticipated in the early phase of teaching was that the arenas of workplace dynamics and the clinician's own family would emerge as offering more assistance to team members in learning to think systems than the context of clinical practice. When asked what systems ideas have persisted after exposure to Bowen theory, respondents all stated that the awareness of the impact of their own anxiety and the consciousness of triangles in their professional dynamics have been retained. Those who have participated for longer periods add to this their appreciation of how instinctual programming from their family of origin affects their reactions to clinical family members, as suggested here:

> Being able to see how the concepts were relevant to my own life was a key step in integrating Bowen theory into my practice. This was partly achieved through the general process of supervision where the assumption was clearly stated that the therapist's family of origin influenced his or her therapeutic approach. (J. Brown, personal communication [team survey], December 2008)

A nodal point in the thinking effort of the AFU team came 18 months into the consultations with a decision to prepare a presentation on a family systems understanding of adolescent anxiety for a national conference. In their presentations, clinicians were motivated to include the key lenses from which anxiety was viewed by the team. These were cognitive–behavioral therapy, attachment theory, and biological and systems theory. The work to distinguish these models from a Bowen approach appeared to assist in understanding systems thinking. The trainer has made an effort not to criticize other models or to convince team members that they should work from a Bowen systems framework, but rather to make the distinctions clear enough for individuals to make their own choice about what framework best fits the facts of clinical presentations.

Over the next year of systems training, the questions that were asked revealed evidence of a growing interest in how anxious patterns of triangling, distancing, fusing into groupthink, and over- and underfunctioning were part of the organization itself. As team members took their own initiative to research ideas about adolescent anxiety, they began to bring more of their independent thinking to weekly case discussions. This lift in team members' functioning was reciprocal to the trainer regulating her tendencies to think for others. Increased collaboration bore much fruit, with various individuals making efforts to look at cases and workplace dynamics through a systems lens. Such an evolution illustrates well the goal of differentiation of self in a training context in which "the goal for the instructor is to be in contact with the thinking of the learner without responding emotionally to it. The goal for the learner is to move towards greater differentiation of self" (Papero, 1990, p. 102).

The Workplace as a Context for Learning Systems Thinking

The awareness of workplace patterns became a primary learning vehicle for systems ideas. The complex professional system in which each clinician works provides daily opportunities to draw on an awareness of emotional systems. With the multiple disciplines involved in implementing the child's treatment plan, there is inevitable tension about how this occurs. With the most symptomatic adolescents, the team anxiety intensifies around safety issues, and with this comes a spread of interlocking triangles around the correct way to handle the difficult young person. Conflicts also surface about who is pulling their weight and who is not. This environment has become the most active laboratory for testing Bowen theory. Most team members report that their ability to think systems has been enhanced by refraining from taking sides and considering their potential to overfunction. Additionally, systems learning has been enhanced by being alert to patterns of distancing in the workplace and the pull of togetherness within certain groups. This is reflected in the comments of a social worker: "I have become aware of how much gossip goes on and I make every effort to avoid being part of it. I am trying to lower my reactivity to my colleagues' anxiety, which I am so sensitized to" (J. Brown, personal communication [team survey], December 2008).

The involvement of families in once-a-week sessions does not provide the same repetitive experience of managing self in an anxious system as does the workplace. As a result, clinicians often struggle to see triangles in the identified patient's families, whereas they can readily identify the involvements of third parties to defuse tension in their work system. Managing self in the workplace does not have the pressure inherent in clinical work to treat symptoms. Hence, the dissonance of individual analysis and systems analysis is not as high.

With the growing awareness of how each team member operates in his or her workplace, some clinicians became interested in exploring their family of origin to gain more understanding of their predictable reactions when under stress. This resulted in the permanent members of the team using one out of every four of their systems consultations to present their own intergenerational families and discuss how Bowen theory might shed some light on themselves and the functioning of others. Members of this group have each reported that the exploration of their own families, with the experience of verifying that the same patterns are present in each of their colleagues' families, has enhanced their ability to see the emotional system at work in their client families. The following survey response reflects this learning:

> Being able to see how the concepts were relevant to my own life was a key step to learning. A number of my family members used to be "hard work" but they no longer are, because of the shift in my thinking. I have avoided being triangled in my family on a number of occasions, but I still get caught of course. (J. Brown, personal communication [team survey], December 2008)

Importance of a Systems Leader

A key ingredient of the application of systems thinking in the clinical team and in their relationships with other units and disciplines was the leadership that emerged from the team director. As she increasingly considered Bowen theory to shed light on her functioning in the workplace, she used this learning in discussions about cases. Her systems leadership in this area was highlighted by a presentation she gave at an outside conference in which she shared her family-of-origin understanding of how she operates as a peacemaker in the workplace at the expense of other aspects of her functioning. It is likely that such a focus on self in relationships greatly enhanced the systems understanding of other workers that went beyond what could be achieved in the short meetings with her. Just as in Bowen systems therapy, success is driven by the emergence of a family leader who is willing to understand and work on his or her part in the relationship system difficulties; so it is in a workplace that is struggling to deal with anxiety about demanding clients, symptoms of staff burnout, internal conflicts, and variables in professionals' functioning.

The organization provides rich fodder for systems thinking and action that enables workers to live the experience of how an adjustment in one person, who focuses more on his or her own functioning and less on others, can affect the entire system. Such a change assists others to achieve a greater sense of calm and to operate more from thinking as opposed to emotional reactions.

Challenges to Thinking Systems in Psychiatry

In an organization that is inherently anxious because of the severity of symptoms being managed, it will be particularly difficult to tolerate the de-skilling impact of experimenting with new thinking. Added to this is the anxiety generated by increasing medical–legal risks, which heighten the bureaucratic requirements for diagnosis and a record of all treatment protocols. Bowen acknowledged the huge effort required for a clinician in a medical environment "to avoid diagnosing the patient and to focus on the family emotional process that creates the patient" (Bowen, 1978, p. 290). Longer term team members report that they struggle to find a way to meet the program requirements while still incorporating Bowen theory. They regularly ask how the models might find a way to coexist. As one survey respondent reflected,

> I have to keep reviewing medication and do risk assessments to determine if it is safe enough for a young person to return home. I need the medical model to meet these responsibilities but at the same time I can't let go of Bowen theory because it fits my lived experience too well. I hope to find a way to hold onto both. (J. Brown, personal communication [team survey], December 2008)

Bowen's example of changing diagnostic language about illness to systems terms such as *functional collapse* and referring to the patient as the "collapsed one" (Bowen, 1978, p. 133) may be helpful for practitioners dealing with these paradigm tensions.

It remains a challenge, particularly for psychiatrists in the AFU, to walk the tightrope of representing their medical expertise and obligations while integrating a systems view. Such a work in progress is reflected in the following comments from a psychiatrist who had trained with the team:

> I still struggle with integrating the Bowen ideas into an overarching medical framework. How can I work with the psychiatric model and still speak for self? I'm not sure that just practicing according to the Bowen model and distancing myself from the mainstream is necessarily helpful. I'm not sure how to pursue this, other than to constantly reflect on where I am in my thinking. What I am sure about, however, is that my focus on the process of how people relate and function, rather than just the content of the clinical history, enriches my experience of work. (J. Brown, personal communication [team survey], December 2008)

Conclusion

At this juncture in experimenting with systems thinking in the AFU, family therapy sessions have evolved into research opportunities to see what transpires when the therapist refrains from asking about symptoms but rather asks about each person's view of his or her functioning. Parents are being asked about how they would define their own job description and what is required for them to work at expressing these responsibilities. Invitations to engage in discussion of the complaints about the adolescent's behavior or symptoms are not being accepted as often. Team members are often monitoring their own functioning with the following questions: Am I exploring the relationship process instead of the problem content? Am I blaming anyone? Am I working harder than any member of the client family to address the problem? Am I thinking, feeling, or behaving for the other, rather than expressing myself to the other? Am I making adjustments in my own thoughts, feelings, or behavior to lower tension?

Without exception, all present and past participants in consultations speak of how difficult they have found the model to implement clinically and that they have often felt overwhelmed endeavoring to get a handle on how symptoms emerge in families. The appeal of approaches that give the clinician a clearer prescriptive role with the patient and parents is understandable. Many, however, have come to appreciate through their own research of self in the workplace and in their family of origin, as well as from clinical observations, that the quick fix is rarely sustainable and that change that does not come at the cost of someone else's functioning requires smaller shifts that lay the groundwork for a family member's longer term effort.

References

Bowen, M. (1978). *Family therapy in clinical practice.* Lanham, MD: Jason Aronson.

Brown, J. (2008). We don't need your help but will you please fix our children? *Australian and New Zealand Journal of Family Therapy, 29*(2), 61–69.

Kerr, M. E., & Bowen, M. (1988). *Family evaluation: An approach based on Bowen theory.* New York, NY: W. W. Norton.

Papero, D. (1990). *Bowen family systems theory.* Boston, MA: Allyn & Bacon.

26
Learning Bowen Theory From a Distance

ANNETTE KOLSKI-ANDREACO

After considerable research and exploration, the Western Pennsylvania Family Center (WPFC) launched the first distance-learning course in Bowen family systems theory in November 2001. In keeping with the center's mission to develop and provide resources for the study of Bowen theory, a self-guided distance-learning course was viewed as an opportunity to extend resources to individuals in parts of the world where these materials were limited or nonexistent. Launched with seed funding from the Richard King Mellon Foundation obtained by the center's director, the course has attracted 31 students from Africa, Australia, Canada, Chile, France, India, Japan, Russia, Sweden, and the United States.

Before creating the course content, WPFC faculty member Catherine Rakow led a small committee through an examination of the feasibility and advisability of using online technology to teach Bowen theory. Having understood that the relationship with a faculty member was an important element in a student's learning, the faculty took some time to decide whether teaching Bowen theory could be achieved online. They identified several other concerns rooted in shifting to the new medium—principally, how the course would adhere to principles of differentiation of self if presented in a distance-learning format.

- Would the theoretical content be applied by the trainees to their own functioning in family and organizational settings using this type of learning environment?
- Would the essentially impersonal nature of the format reduce emotional togetherness and actually enhance individual learning and differentiation of self?
- Would all concepts be able to be learned as easily in this format when the social cues that are observed in physical settings are absent?
- Because this is a self-guided course, what would the pace of learning be, and would it be as variable as that observed in the basic seminar taught in the core postgraduate program?

Rakow guided the exploration of the feasibility of managing such a course and the decisions concerning the best technology for the purpose. Arthur

Zipris, another faculty member working with board member Sandra Caffo, designed and wrote six of the modules; the others were authored by other faculty members. Another board member who had created an online master's-level nursing course as dean of a local university nursing school consulted with the team. She provided invaluable first-hand knowledge about distance-learning technology and the learning experience from the point of view of the student and the faculty. To address the concern that the WPFC emphasize the coaching relationship between student and faculty member, it was decided that a volunteer faculty member would interact with an assigned student, answering questions, asking questions to challenge the student's understanding, and qualifying the student to advance to the next module.

The initial course offering included the following modules:

- Module 1: Thinking Systemically—The Origins and Evolution of Systems Thinking
- Module 2: Differentiation of Self Scale and Anxiety
- Module 3: The Family as a Natural System
- Module 4: Triangles
- Module 5: Family Projection Process
- Module 6: Multigenerational Transmission Process
- Module 7: Emotional Cutoff
- Module 8: Sibling Position: Its Impact on Personality Development and Social Behavior
- Module 9: Spirituality and Religion
- Module 10: Emotional Process in Society

Each of the 10 modules was designed with a focus on applying the theory in life. It was left to the working group to design the mechanics of online registration application, fee, and payment procedures; bibliography; faculty participation; and advertising and marketing. Once the course was posted on the center's Web site and without a promotional campaign, applications began to come in. Several Russian students were referred by two Bowen theory faculty at the New England Center.

One year later, the faculty's review of the first distance-learning course in Bowen theory elicited several questions:

1. How is the experiment going?
2. What technical or coordination problems exist?
3. What role does the center have in providing required reading materials?
4. Does the course application need to be revised since it was first designed?
5. Is the application a detriment to enrolling interested students?
6. Is there additional information that needs to be given to students?

7. Under whose name will distance-learning materials be copyrighted?
8. Have all the modules been developed?
9. What is the faculty support for this course?
10. What, if any, changes are needed in program coordination?

Committee members wrote a fact sheet to clarify center, student, and faculty responsibilities and a course evaluation to gauge the students' learning experience.

In the summer of 2006, Linda Fleming, associate professor of psychology and director of the doctoral program in counseling psychology, and two of her doctoral students in the psychology program at Gannon University in Erie, Pennsylvania, conducted a survey of the students' experience. Fleming had previously completed 2 years of the WPFC Basic Seminar.

After discussion with faculty director Jim Smith, they identified the following four areas of inquiry that their survey instrument would explore: (a) the degree to which the relationship between distance-learning students and faculty mentors (coaches) supported learning; (b) the course's impact on the learner's personal and professional development; (c) issues arising from the distance-learning format and hardware and software technological limitations; and (d) emergent general recommendations from course and faculty participants. They constructed questionnaires using a Likert scale, and these questionnaires were sent to all students; the response rate was 29.6%. The data indicated that 45%, or 14 students, had not moved beyond the first module despite being enrolled from 6 months to 6 years. Of this group, 7 individuals were the original Russian students who had experienced significant language difficulties. From the applications, the researchers reported that the average student's age was 43.4, 66.7% were married, 37% were psychologists, 26% were clergy, 78% worked with families, 63% had had prior exposure to Bowen theory and thought it useful, 78% had never previously participated in an online course, and only 11% of respondents had completed the course.

Only 8 individuals who responded to the questionnaire were at Module 3 or higher or had completed the program. However, all of those who responded were more likely to have had some previous familiarity with Bowen theory as contrasted with the other students. People with no history or familiarity with online coursework were less likely to have moved beyond Module 1. Clergy were more likely to have moved beyond the first module than psychologists.

All respondents answered positively that the course was what they expected. They further stated that the course helped them to develop a deeper understanding of Bowen theory, was applicable to family or professional life, and included valuable resource materials. They stated that they believed that more interaction with their mentor would have helped them to complete the modules. Although the technology did not seem to be an impediment for these students, other life responsibilities and obligations were obstacles to completing the course. Overall, these students stated that they would recommend the course to others.

Students' open-ended comments further uncovered the strengths and weaknesses of the course. Although flexibility, convenience, accessibility, faculty coaching, and overall quality were highlighted as course strengths, respondents identified definite limitations. These limitations included the lack of interaction and personal connection with the coach, the absence of a systematic application of materials to self or clinical cases, the use of complex language, limited access to additional resources, and, for some, technical difficulties. Challenges to completing the course were unavailability of the coach, topic difficulty, motivation, and time, English fluency, and materials slanted toward mental health professionals. Aiding course completion were such factors as interest, persistence, goal focus, and contact with the mentor. From these data, the evaluators made several recommendations. Key suggestions included designing the course for increased contact with mentors via phone, videocamera, and instant messaging; more opportunities to read and apply material to their own lives and cases; more clearly written and printer-friendly modules; reorganization of modules into smaller learning chunks; ongoing program evaluation; and alerting prospective students to the amount of time needed to complete the course.

When comparing the goals in launching this experiment in teaching Bowen theory with the conclusions of the participant survey 6 years later, one central issue clearly emerges: the importance of a relationship with a coach in learning and applying theory to life. Respondents identified contact with the coach as a major factor that supports the learning process, one that needs to be more robustly incorporated in the course going forward. Another finding, that there are insufficient experiential opportunities during the learning, presents a challenge in redesigning the course, one that designers of most online courses face. Repurposing instructor-led learning to self-directed learning is an ongoing task in online education when an exchange with the coach and other students is limited by the inability to read nonverbal cues.

Both of these conclusions are related to the key variable of Bowen theory—differentiation of self. To pursue the course to its conclusion is at some level related to *differentiation*, or the relative ability to push forward with a goal and enlist one's own motivation as fuel despite the technical and life challenges. However, there is at least a shared responsibility on the part of the course's designers to create an environment that is more supportive of the learning process. To that end, several efforts are now underway to address the recommendations of the survey:

- Experiential opportunities for each module are being designed.
- There will be more points of contact with the coaches.
- Psychological jargon is being removed from the modules.

- The scientific context of Bowen theory and other contextual materials are being added to the course's introduction.
- In the near future, the center intends to test the redesign of the course, offering it at no fee to all previous students who have not completed it.

The evaluation of the pilot course and preliminary survey results proved useful in discovering and addressing the challenges in designing an online distance-learning course in Bowen theory. Even with the survey's low response rate, this experiment in online pedagogy suggests that this approach can efficaciously teach what was thought to be content dependent on in-person interactions. As with all formats, refinements are needed to eliminate barriers that have to do with software and hardware limitations, access to supplemental reading materials, and basic rewriting of some of the modules. Important additions are sections that incorporate ways to apply newly learned concepts. Like all learning experiences, indeed as in basic differentiation itself, the center continues to incorporate the information from the student evaluations to make adjustments so as to present an experience more aligned with a theoretical understanding of how humans change their thinking and behavior.

27

Bowen Theory and Zulu Understanding of Family

MICHAEL J. NEL

Social science theories are primarily crafted in the West and then often used to explain relationship processes in non-Western cultures. Often overlooked or ignored is the fact that these theories assume Western, and in particular North American, values and beliefs. This is evident in the way that individualism has influenced the understanding of kinship and family relationships. In Africa, there has been a reaction to the imposition of Western social theories and thought forms on African cultures. Social science theories, including Bowen family systems theory, need to be scrutinized and validated within the context of African cultures if they are to have credibility as being comprehensive and universally applicable to family systems.

Bowen theory acknowledges the importance of culture (Kerr, 1986, p. 3), but culture alone does not sufficiently explain relationships, especially the universality of certain relationship processes. Culture shapes or "stains" (Friedman, 1999, p. 246) the emotional processes that Bowen theory describes. This chapter explores the relationship between Bowen theory and one particular African culture, the Zulu, and examines the correlation between Bowen theory and the Zulu understanding of kinship and family relationships.

The Family as an Emotional Unit

An initial connecting point with the Zulu understanding of kinship and family relationships is the assumption of Bowen theory that the family is an emotional unit that includes the nuclear, the extended, and the multigenerational family. "Bowen theory describes the human family as an emotional unit, and uses systems thinking to deal with the complex, interdependent processes that occur in the unit" (Kerr, 1994, p. 1). This concept of family is congruent with the Zulu understanding of family, and it demonstrates a cross-cultural application.

According to Krige (1936/1962), the Zulu kinship pattern is more inclusive than the Western understanding of kinship. Krige wrote, "Among the Zulus, as in most primitive societies, the bonds of kinship are very extensive and serve to bring together and knit into a group, people that in European society would not be regarded as related at all" (p. 23). The Zulu understanding of kinship, however, does not minimize the importance of either the nuclear family or the individual. It is characterized by its inclusiveness and complexity, as Krige stated:

> But though the classificatory nomenclature provides every Zulu with a number of fathers and mothers and a very large circle of brothers and sisters, the individual family, consisting of a man and his wife and children, is no whit less important than among Europeans and must be considered the most important unit in Zulu society. (p. 23)

As Krige (1936/1962) has pointed out, this understanding of the family, especially as it relates to brother, sister, mother, and father, is both foreign and confusing for those raised in the West, where *family* is usually assumed to refer to the nuclear family. This view of family creates confusion for Westerners, particularly as it relates to birth order. In the West, birth order is usually associated with membership in the nuclear family. For the Zulu, birth order relates to the person's place in the extended family in which cousins are referred to as brothers and sisters. Because the focus of Bowen theory is on the emotional processes that shape family relationships, it is not tied to any particular understanding of kinship.

The Zulu understanding of family relationships is reflected in every aspect of life, even in the design of the traditional homestead (also referred to as a *kraal*) and in their relationship to their cattle. The homestead consists of circular huts surrounding a circular cattle byre.

> This circle of huts surrounds a circular cattle enclosure at the very center of the village. This inner circle is also called a kraal. So, in effect, you have a kraal within a kraal, a cattle enclosure within a human enclosure. (Lawson, 1985, p. 19)

By placing the cattle byre at the center of the homestead, the Zulu affirm the importance of the family as a unit because the cattle are not the possession of any one individual but belong to the household, which includes the ancestors (Berglund, 1976, p. 110). The unity of the family is also affirmed by the burying of the lineage heads in the cattle byre, where the ancestral spirits dwell (Lamla, 1981, p. 18).

Family Membership

As important as the nuclear family is to both the Zulu and Bowen theory, it needs to be understood within the larger context of the extended and multigenerational family. For the Zulu, the multigenerational family is not limited to those who are living but includes the dead. Death does not end family relationships and kinship ties. The Zulu acknowledge through their rites and practices the ongoing important function of those who have died. This understanding of the importance of ancestors is reflected in the multigenerational transmission process in Bowen theory.

Family Harmony

Living systems, whether an ant colony or a human family, seek homeostasis (Friedman, 1999, p. 238). In such systems, each individual member has functional importance for restoring and maintaining the balance of the whole relationship system. As anxiety increases, each family member functions more and more for the system, ceding individuality for the sake of family harmony and togetherness. Anything that creates discomfort or disharmony or undermines family togetherness has to be dealt with. Natural systems, such as the family, are constantly in a process of rebalancing. Zulu families describe this process of seeking homeostasis as establishing "harmony." Much of the rebalancing takes place at family gatherings, and attending these gatherings is very important. The Zulu will travel great distances to attend. As in Western families, the extent of the commitment required of family members to the restoration of harmony or balance is a function of the family's level of differentiation.

For the Zulu, the holding of grudges and resentments reflects a disturbance of family harmony and is dealt with through a process of reconciliation. Those holding a grudge may participate in the traditional feasts only after reconciliation (Berglund, 1976, p. 246). Reconciliation restores harmony and balance and brings a renewed openness and flexibility to the family system (Berglund, 1976).

Maintaining and restoring harmony is stressed in every aspect of Zulu culture, whether it is in the architecture and layout of the homestead, in the feasts, in the dancing, or in the drinking of beer. In all of these aspects of Zulu family life, the ancestors also have an important function in maintaining, preserving, and restoring family harmony. A disturbance of the togetherness increases anxiety and the level of emotional reactivity that then threatens family peace and harmony. It is during occasions of increased anxiety that Zulu families turn to the extended and multigenerational family, and particularly to the ancestors, for assistance. It is then that they traditionally welcome the "brooding" of the ancestors (Berglund, 1976, p. 129). The brooding of the ancestors increases the family togetherness, level of comfort, calmness, and peace. However, once the crisis has passed, Zulu families are quite clear that they would prefer that the ancestors no longer brood with them.

It is important to note the distinction between *ukuba kona*, to be present, and *ukufukamela*, brooding. Although the former, the presence of the shades, is a necessity for a normal and prosperous life, the latter is required only at very special times of crisis when the presence of the shades is changed to brooding. But when the brooding of the shades is no longer required, or when the crisis is over, the shades are shaken off and the appropriate distance between them and the living, which is understood in *ukuba kona*, returns (Berglund, 1976, p. 127).

The extended and multigenerational families, and particularly the ancestors, function for the Zulu nuclear family as anxiety binders (Lamla, 1981, p. 17). By binding the nuclear family's anxiety during times of increased anxiety, the extended family—as well as the multigenerational family and ancestors—provides stability, balance, harmony, and unity. Togetherness is restored.

Function of Zulu Family Rites and Rituals

Rituals have an important function for Zulu families because family rituals offer the resources of the extended, and particularly the multigenerational, family to the nuclear family. The rituals associated with family gatherings allow the nuclear family's anxiety to dissipate into the larger system.

Rituals and ceremonies, especially those associated with Zulu "rites of passage" (Plog & Bates, 1980, p. 371), are an essential part of the process of dealing with the imbalance associated with the disturbance of family togetherness. For example, traditional funeral rites, which include the *ukubuyisa,* or bringing home of the dead, help the family to process their grief. Puberty rites in which the whole family and clan participate assist the child and the family to renegotiate family relationships. According to Berglund (1976), "While ceremony is a conventional and sometimes an elaborate form of voicing one's feelings, ritual aims at a communion with the shades which is efficacious" (p. 28). The repetition of these rituals from generation to generation underscores the importance of community, the sense of belonging and communion among the generations (Lamla, 1981, p. 16).

The family homestead functions as the center of the clan or community. Its design reflects the importance of belonging, community, and togetherness that includes the living and the dead. Zulu family rituals assist not only in maintaining the family togetherness but also in preventing cutoff. The family homestead, where all ritual slaughtering is done, functions as "the primary locus for ritual" (Lawson, 1985, p. 17). Failure to attend and participate in these family rituals is understood as cutting off from the family and considered a sign of disrespect to the family, including the ancestors.

The concept of connectedness with previous generations is reflected in the *umsamo,* where the family has communion with its ancestors. "Its particular purpose is to provide a ritual ground for communing with the very present family ancestors" (Lawson, 1985, p. 19). Like the *umsamo,* the ritual spear and cattle also emphasize the connectedness of the members of all generations of the homestead. Berglund (1976) noted the importance of these items: "They do not belong to any one person but they belong to *umuzi* (homestead, of which the shades are family members)" (p. 103).

Traditional Zulu celebrations, as noted, involve feasting, dancing, the slaughtering of cattle or goats, and the drinking of beer. Every one of these actions reinforces the sense that the living and dead form a single community. Hammond-Tooke (1981) referred to the communion of the living and the ancestors in the ritual feasting and beer drinking as the participants being of a "single heart" (p. 26). Berglund (1976) wrote that "informed Zulu are emphatic that the ritual dance performed by the officiant aims at exciting the shades to action" (p. 236). Cattle and goats that are part of the ritual celebrations are slaughtered at the homestead "because that is where the shades are" (Berglund, 1976). Beer drinking is a community activity and is an expression of the communion of the living with their ancestors.

By emphasizing the unity of the family, ritual brings the Zulu family into positive contact with its roots and the resources of the extended and multigenerational family. The strengths of the generations become available to the anxious nuclear family and function as anxiety binders.

Belonging, Communion, and Emotional Cutoff

Communion and belonging are powerful forces that shape Zulu family life. These two forces correlate with the togetherness force in Bowen theory. According to Bowen theory, the togetherness force is part of the emotional system. There can be no family or community without the influence of the togetherness force. The counterbalancing force to togetherness is individuality, which is often confused with emotional cutoff. Emotional cutoff is rooted in reactivity to the intensity of togetherness in the family when members react by distancing themselves emotionally or geographically. Being part of the family satisfies the Zulu's deep-rooted need for belonging, or communion. *Belonging* is more than membership in the family; it is a relational concept that allows for ongoing communion among family members, which includes the dead, because the Zulu do not view death as "terminal," or an end to the relationship.

When the author researched the Zulu's relationship with the ancestors, the following dialogue was among those recorded:

Interviewer: And if you don't follow the customs?

Mr. B.: You lose the concept of belonging.

Interviewer: Going back to the washing of the hands on Saturday, is it really about belonging?

Mr. B.: Absolutely. Even here today there was a burial of a pastor. When there is a funeral here in the urban areas in Christian settlements, when there is a funeral, people going to the funeral, you find two basins of water. People wash their hands before they go in to have the feast. They don't eat from the graveyard without having washed their hands. Even if they didn't touch the soil you go there and stand while people are digging and burying and singing. But before you go to eat you pass the big basin of water and everyone washes in that basin of water. You don't open your own tap and wash. That would have no sense of togetherness, of communion. I am stressing my understanding of ancestors' spiritual communion relationship. Not something to see, study, as spiritual as the very Christian belief. Because the Christian belief is spiritual. Those who worship, God is Spirit, those worship God in Spirit, a spiritual communion.

Interviewer: Which would be another way of defining belonging?

Mr. B.: Which is another way of defining togetherness, belonging.

This concept of belonging was expressed differently by Mr. A. When directing his children as a parent, he would remind them that they belonged to a larger family unit, just as his father had reminded him of this same fact. He would introduce what he was going to say with "In my father's house," explaining that the saying expressed connectivity between the generations, reminding the child of his or her belonging to the generations of this family, the father's house.

When questioned by the interviewer as to what satisfaction he gains by reintroducing certain cultural practices previously rejected by the Christian church, Mr. B responded,

Mr. B.: I think that I am not removed from them, not alienated from them, I am still a part of the community. Hmmm. Because when something happens to you, you need this people you live with. So I think that you do things, other things, which you understand that to you have no meaning but because you live with this people you do that.

Interviewer: So relationships become very important?

Mr. B.: Yes.

Interviewer: The cultural practices are really about keeping good relationships in the community?

Mr. B.: Ja, that is what I think.

Togetherness is a powerful part of humankind's phylogenetic heritage. As part of the deep-rooted life force, it is a neutral force. According to Kerr and Bowen (1988),

Togetherness is a biologically rooted life force (more basic than being just a function of the brain) that propels an organism to follow the directives of others, to be a dependent, connected, and indistinct entity. A human being has various biological and psychological systems that incline him to function as part of a group and to follow the group's compass.

These internal systems not only orient the person to the directives of the group, but also send out signals that orient others to self. This force to be connected is reflected in the striving to act, feel, and think like others, as well as in the striving to have others act, feel, and think like oneself. While the togetherness force is rooted in biological processes, its intensity in a given person is heavily influenced by learning. This learning ranges from the conditioning of emotional and feeling responses to the acquisition of values and beliefs. (p. 65)

Humankind has an instinctual need for togetherness, for belonging to family and community. The Zulu's need for community and belonging is reinforced and affirmed by their returning to the family homestead as an expression of the emotional force of togetherness. At the family homestead, they are assured that they belong and have communion. To be absent, then, from the family gathering is not only a cutting off from and a sign of disrespect but also an ignoring of one's emotional significance with the family system. Failure to attend means that other family members will be expected to accommodate and fill that vacant functional position in the system to bring about a "dynamic equilibrium" (Kerr & Bowen, 1988, p. 65). Other members are then expected to commit more energy and resources to the rebalancing process. Zulu family rituals seek to prevent this process from occurring.

The traditional expectation of the Christian church was that new Zulu Christians were to reject any association with their ancestors. This was akin to asking them to cut off emotionally from their families and community. It meant that they no longer had access to the family resources, especially during times of heightened anxiety, and had to find new ways to fulfill their need for togetherness, communion, and belonging. Theological beliefs and practices of the church community could not overcome the social and psychological implications of this loss. Being Zulu Christians meant social and cultural alienation from their families as they abandoned their family relationships. Cutting off from their families also meant the loss of identity. Unfortunately, the Christian church became the instrument of emotional, physical, and cultural cutoff, which ran counter to traditional Zulu society in which everything possible was done to prevent such cutoff. The requirement to leave their past left Zulu Christians caught between two loyalties: to family and to the church. On one hand, to separate from the family and its traditions meant isolation, the loss of communion with the generations, and showing disrespect for their forebears. On the other hand, they were informed that to participate in family rites that included the ancestors was to compromise, and even deny, their faith in Christ. Either decision meant loss and anxiety for Zulu Christians. In response to the question about what it meant to him not to be able to participate in the traditional family rites and customs, Mr. B. said, "You lose the concept of belonging."

Umuntu and the Development of the Self

There are significant similarities between the Zulu concept of *umuntu* and the Bowen concept of differentiation of self. Kerr and Bowen (1988) described differentiation as "the ability to be in emotional contact with others yet still autonomous in one's emotional functioning" (p. 145). During a lecture in 2003 in Vancouver, British Columbia, Michael E. Kerr defined *differentiation* as "being self-focused without being selfish. Being other-focused without the loss of self." For the Zulu and Bowen theory, the self is never shaped in isolation but always within emotionally significant relationships such as the family.

The Zulu concept of *umuntu umuntu ngabantu* can be translated as "a person is a person in relation to other persons" or as "I am because you are." This Zulu expression indicates the essential process by which the self is always defined in the connectedness to others, especially to the family. According to the Zulu and Bowen theory, the family is not limited simply to members of the nuclear family but also includes the extended and multigenerational family, which is the arena for the process of differentiation. This concept of *umuntu* also provides insight into the variations of differentiation within and between families, which Bowen described in his scale of differentiation.

The scale of differentiation describes patterns of behavior that cross the generations and display "a remarkable orderliness and predictability" (Kerr, 1997, p. 64). These multigenerational patterns have a profound influence on the level of differentiation of the nuclear family.

The basic level of differentiation of the offspring will be largely shaped by the basic level of differentiation of the parents. One implication of the multigenerational emotional process is that between any two generations, little variation in basic levels of differentiation is to be expected without unusual and unpredictable life circumstances (Comella, 1994, p. 3).

The level of attachment within the nuclear family is also a product of the attachment level between the generations. The more fused the selves of previous generations, the higher the chronic anxiety level, the more permeable the boundaries, and the more relationship systems influence behavior and functioning (Holt, 1989, p. 84).

Depending on the level of differentiation, not just of the nuclear but also of the multigenerational family, *umuntu* can be used as a process that leads to greater differentiation or greater fusion. During times of increased anxiety, families may use the concept of *umuntu* to promote more togetherness at the cost of individuality. *Umuntu*, a concept that is descriptive of a relational process, can be transformed into a relational force acquiring functional importance for Zulu families. Variation in levels of differentiation is illustrated by Berglund's (1976) comment: "Like fertility, anger is innate in the lineage and clan, and peculiar to each individual member of the lineage" (p. 255).

Ancestors and Emotional Triangulation

Bowen theory assumes that when anxiety increases, families maintain the homeostatic relationship balance by intensifying the triangling process of family members or by triangling other people into the family process. Family members may also form triadic relationships with substances like alcohol, prescription and nonprescription drugs, gambling, fantasies, and beliefs. The most effective anxiety binders, however, are relationships (Kerr & Bowen, 1988, p. 119), which become more important as anxiety increases in intensity (Kerr & Bowen, 1988, p. 142).

A live third person is not required for a triangle. A fantasied relationship, objects, activities, and pets can all function as a corner of a triangle. For all the facets of a triangle to be played out, however, three live people are usually required (Kerr & Bowen, 1988, p. 136).

Interlocking triangles are formed when the nuclear family triangles can no longer accommodate the increased anxiety (Kerr & Bowen, 1988, p. 124). According to Bowen theory, triangles are part of humankind's evolutionary heritage. They are neither good nor bad, neither right nor wrong; they just are part of life. It is what humankind does when anxious. The process of emotional triangulation is dynamic and takes many different forms. This section describes just one such process.

During times of heightened anxiety, especially those occasions associated with family transitions, Zulu families triangle in the extended, multigenerational family members, including the ancestors. These emotional triangles stabilize the anxious family, at least for a while. They dampen the anxiety, thus allowing for greater flexibility and time for the nuclear family to rebalance. The ancestors have an important function during these intensely anxious times of transition. The description of the "brooding" of the ancestors during these occasions is the Zulu way of describing their function in the family triangles. Kerr and Bowen (1988) described this multigenerational triangling process:

> Triangles are forever, at least in families. Once the emotional circuitry of a triangle is in place, it usually outlives the people who participate in it. If one member of a triangle dies, another person usually replaces him. The actors come and go, but the play lives on through the generations. Children may act out a conflict that was never resolved between their great-grandparents. So a particular triangle was not created necessarily by its present participants; nor does it form anew or completely dissolve with the ebb and flow of anxiety. (p. 135)

These multigenerational triangles can facilitate family togetherness without the loss of individuality and promote belonging and the unity of the generations by preventing emotional cutoff.

Triangling of the ancestors into the family emotional process was referred to by a number of interviewees as "reporting" to the ancestors. This distinction is important because it describes a very different process than prayer for Zulu Christians. Reporting, from a systems perspective, describes a triangling process rather than a religious act.

Conclusion

In interviews with Zulu families, the author was impressed by the correlations between Zulu understanding of family process and Bowen theory. This strong association suggests that perhaps Bowen did not discover anything new but rather described what was already an integral part of nature. The Zulu, who have traditionally lived close to the Earth, were aware of these natural relational processes that the Western world, through Murray Bowen, is now uncovering. As Bowen theory seeks to become a science, it must provide explanation and understanding of human relationships in all cultures. This study is an example of its potential for universal application.

References

Berglund, A. (1976). *Zulu thought-patterns and symbolism.* Cape Town, South Africa: David Philip.

Comella, P. A. (1994). A brief summary of Bowen family systems theory. *Family Center Report, 15*(2), 2–4.

Friedman, E. H., with Treadwell, M. M., & Beal, E. W. (Eds.). (1999). *A failure of nerve: Leadership in the age of the quick fix.* Bethesda, MD: Edwin Friedman Foundation.

Hammond-Tooke, W. D. (1981). Ancestor religion. In H. Kuckertz (Ed.), *Ancestor religion in southern Africa* (pp. 22–23). Transkei, South Africa: Lumko Missiological Institute.

Holt, R. B. (1989). Reproduction, survival and extinction. *Family Center Report, 10*(4), 1–2.

Kerr, M. E. (1986). Significance of Murray Bowen's scientific contributions. *Family Center Report, 7*(4), 1–4.

Kerr, M. E. (1994). Challenging assumptions. *Family Center Report, 15*(3), 1–2.

Kerr, M. E. (1997). Significance of Murray Bowen's scientific contributions. In R. R. Sagar (Ed.), *Theory and practice: Feature articles from the Family Center Report 1979–1996* (pp. 3–13). Washington, DC: Georgetown Family Center.

Kerr, M. E., & Bowen, M. (1988). *Family evaluation: An approach based on Bowen theory.* New York, NY: W. W. Norton.

Krige, E. J. (1962). *The social system of the Zulus.* Pietermaritzburg, South Africa: Shuter & Shooter. (Original work published 1936)

Lamla, C. M. (1981). The dead: Prepared to live in the spirit world. In H. Kuckertz (Ed.), *Ancestor religion in Southern Africa* (pp. 14–21). Transkei, South Africa: Lumko Missiological Institute.

Lawson, E. T. (1985). *Religions of Africa: Traditions in transformation.* San Francisco, CA: Harper & Row.

Plog, F., & Bates, D. G. (1980). *Cultural anthropology.* New York, NY: Alfred Knopf.

Acknowledgment

This chapter is based on a thesis completed for the DTh in Practical Theology at the University of South Africa. Copyrighted material is used with permission from the University of South Africa.

28
Building Bridges to the Natural Sciences: Field Research on Harvester Ants

LEANN S. HOWARD

Bowen family systems theory conceptualizes the human family as an emotional unit in which interdependence among family members significantly influences the emotional, social, and physical functioning of each. In addition, a fundamental assumption of the theory is that the human is a product of evolution and is regulated in important ways by processes found throughout all of life.

To test the fundamental assumptions of Bowen theory in other living systems, I moved toward the biological sciences. This chapter is a report on that ongoing process extending over 20 years and concludes with efforts to apply and extend Bowen theory to research on the more ancient natural system of harvester ants.

Beginning Moves Toward Science

After several years of formal study at the Bowen Center for the Study of the Family (formerly the Georgetown Family Center) in Washington, DC, I decided to enroll in two beginning biology courses: ecology and insect behavior and ecology. The courses were carefully chosen to help me gain a clearer understanding of Darwin's theory of evolution by natural selection (Darwin, 1859/1964) and how the theory accounts for the evolution of highly integrated social systems and the diversity of life forms in nature. Worster (1977) stated the significance of Darwin's impact on the study of ecology and social relationships as follows:

> The single most important figure in the history of ecology over the past two or three centuries is Charles Darwin (1809–1882). No one else contributed as much to the development of the idea of ecology into a flourishing field of science, and no other individual has had so much influence generally on western man's perception of nature. (p. 114)

> The bedrock idea upon which Darwin built, though he never isolated it as such, was that all survival on earth is socially determined. (Worster, 1977, p. 156)

I began the process of study with an early speculation that other species are more constrained by environmental conditions and humans are more constrained by emotional process (automatically driven relationship process). In time, I came to believe that all species are engaged in an ongoing effort to adapt to changing physical conditions and in the struggle to successfully manage social interactions.

Through the coursework on insect behavior, I was exposed to the work of Hamilton (1964), who developed a model of natural selection based on the concept of inclusive fitness that could account for the evolution of sterile castes in social insects.[1] Central to Hamilton's genetically based theory was the premise that sterile workers, operating within a colony, can pass their genes to the next generation through a closely related relative rather than themselves. Through this process, surviving genes are more important than surviving offspring.

I was confused and perplexed by this lens because it offered a plausible theoretical explanation for a link between specific behaviors, such as altruism, and specific genes and was not able to reconcile this lens with Bowen theory. It would be several years before I would be able to put this confusion to rest.

Early dialogue with a PhD student in biology and an associate professor of biology helped me to distinguish Bowen theory from Hamilton's (1964) alternative model. I established contact with Mary Greenberg, who at that time was a PhD student in biology at the University of Kansas. Greenberg, also a longtime student of Bowen theory, was developing a relationship systems model for understanding social behavior within the context of evolutionary theory. Her speculation follows:

> In conclusion, a general social behavior model derived from the study of human behavior can be used to directly bridge the field of human behavior and animal behavior in order to 1) create a more comprehensive paradigm to investigate social behavior and 2) to place human social behavior within the context of natural social systems. (Greenberg, 1998, p. 34)

A second early contact with Cynthia Annett, associate professor of biology at the University of Kansas, was also beneficial in my efforts to compare and contrast Bowen theory with other models of social behavior based in genetics. Annett had been studying variation in gull pairs in their capacity to successfully reproduce and fledge offspring (Annett, 1989, pp. 222–223). She was open to considering Bowen theory as a way to account for variation in adaptiveness

---

[1] Darwin had formerly proposed that natural selection could operate at the level of the family.

between gull pairs. Through dialogue with both Greenberg and Annett, I was able to see that the theory of inclusive fitness is not a proven theory. Although I was still unclear about where I stood with regard to the two lenses, I was becoming more able to distinguish one lens from another.

In that early phase, I also found the writing of Michael Kerr, director of the Bowen Center, useful. His seminal book *Family Evaluation: An Approach Based on Bowen Theory* (Kerr & Bowen, 1988) articulated differences between sociobiology theory (a genetic theory of the group) and Bowen theory, a theory that assumes all organisms are fundamentally affected by life processes possibly more basic than genes. In later writings, Kerr distinguished Bowen theory, a theory of how relationship systems function, from natural selection, a theory of how relationship systems evolve (Kerr, 1998, p. 119).

Through continued coursework, speculation, study, and dialogue, I determined to keep Bowen theory and other biological models separate from one another and separate from a direct study of nature. My perspective was moving closer to that of a scientist. That is, when a model of how nature operates is kept separate from nature, it becomes open to scientific test.

Fieldwork Research

In 1995, 7 years into my study of biology, I took early steps in the direction of testing Bowen theory in other species for myself. I established a relationship with Johanna Foster, an ecologist working at the time at Johnson County Community College in Overland Park, Kansas, and began assisting her in researching the role of a mound-building ant (*Formica subsericea*) in biodiversity on a native prairie.

Through 10 years of fieldwork research, I was exposed to the importance of each species' creating an environmental niche and competing and cooperating for the purpose of survival and reproduction. I observed firsthand the ever-changing physical environment to which species must adapt. I also learned about the specific details of field research necessary to garner valuable knowledge regarding the natural world. I began to consider how I might conduct field research on social behavior in another species.

In 1997, Deborah Gordon, then associate professor of biological sciences at Stanford University, was the Distinguished Guest Presenter at the Annual Georgetown Family Symposium. Gordon's presentation focused on her fieldwork research on harvester ant behavior conducted in the Sonoran Desert over many years. I followed her presentation with a reading of her book, *Ants at Work* (Gordon, 1999), which I found to be one of the most important books I had read on social behavior in another species. Its significance to me was that it was a book by a biologist about social behavior in a more ancient system based on a systems perspective. I contacted Gordon directly to inquire about the possibility of becoming a part of her research team, and she agreed.

The study of harvester ant behavior was the beginning of a side-by-side comparison of Gordon's complex systems perspective (developing discipline in biology) on harvester ant behavior and Bowen's family systems perspective on human behavior. Each lens is a developmental perspective, and each is based in the view that behavior is not genetically preprogrammed but is established through ongoing relationship processes that also include genes.

Harvester Ants (Pogonomyrmix barbatus)

To apply Bowen theory to the study of harvester ant behavior, I begin with an overview of Gordon's research on the ecology, development, and functioning of harvester ant colonies (Gordon, 1999, 2010; Gordon, Holmes, & Nacu, 2008; Greene & Gordon, 2007). Harvester ants are located in the southwestern United States and Mexico in the Sonoran Desert region. Gordon's 25-acre research site is located between the Chiricahau and Peloncillo Mountains along the state line between Arizona and New Mexico. Many other species of ants live on the site, and one species, *Aphenogaster,* is a major competitor.

Harvester ants evolved approximately 140 million years ago. Each ant is 1 centimeter in size and lives for 1 year. Colonies live up to 20 years, based on the survival of the queen. Complex chambers inside the nest, connected by tunnels, house the queen, brood, ants, and seeds.

Reproduction

The mating season for harvester ants is in late July and August around the time of the monsoon rains. Many thousands of fertile reproductives, winged males and queens, engage in the mating flight. On the 1st day after the flight, about 2,000 new colonies, founded by a mated queen, survive. One year later, only approximately 20 to 50 of the colonies remain. Although each individual worker ant lives only 1 year, the queen continues to reproduce ants for up to 20 years until the time of her death. Once the queen dies, the colony will slowly die as well. The queen does not control the process within the colony and instead is one functioning part of the whole. Mature colonies that survive the first few years and grow large enough to reproduce may consist of as many as 12,000 workers. It is average for a mature colony to consist of 10,000 workers.

Colonies exist within a neighborhood of other colonies. Where a queen founds her nest is a factor in whether the new nest will survive or is outcompeted by established colonies. Once a colony reaches adulthood, it generally survives for many years in the neighborhood in which it was first established.

Patterns of Behavior

Harvester ant colonies display tremendous flexibility and do not function simply as an outcome of preprogrammed genetic instruction. If seed availability is greater on a given day, more ants will forage. If a storm leaves debris at the entrance to the colony, more workers will engage in nest maintenance. Workers also switch tasks on the basis of what other workers are doing. The more workers an ant encounters doing a different task, the more likely it will be that the ant will shift tasks. Ants respond quickly to shifts in interaction patterns with one another and to moment-to-moment shifts in the environment.

Simple interactions between ants lead to patterns of interaction. Harvester ants navigate their world by touch, mediated by chemical exchange. The pattern of contact conveys one of three messages to the ant contacted: become active, keep the same task, or switch to a different task. Simple interactions between two ants alter the state of each ant and affect the position of each in relation to one another. This ripples out to affect all other ants in the unit. With 10,000 ants in a mature colony, thousands of simple interactions between individuals generate the very complex colony behavior of the unit.

Networks of individual interactions lead to waves of ants leaving the nest in search of seeds and waves of ants returning to the nest carrying seeds. The waves of ants in and ants out are tuned to one another and operate in synchrony. When the flow of foraging is disrupted, colony activity is affected. Ants respond rapidly to a shift in the expected patterns of ant return with a slowing of foraging activity.

When colonies of the same age, adjusted for size, are studied side by side, there is vast variation in the basic patterns between the colonies. Variation is observed in sensitivity, reactivity, stability, and recovery of active foraging after disruption. These variations may ultimately demonstrate a link between variation in fundamental pattern and reproductive success. Research is being undertaken to study how variation in patterns and variation in reproductive success may be linked.

The complex process of the colony as a unit is guided by each individual ant responding to simple cues. No ant is in charge of the process or directs the unit as a whole. The unit is a self-organizing, interdependent system in which simple patterns lead to the functioning of the unit as a whole. Frequency of contact regulates the activity level of the colony. When there is more food available, ants will return to the nest more frequently with a seed, and inactive ants will in turn leave the nest on a more frequent basis. Frequency of contact regulates the intensity of colony behavior.

Once contact between two ants is made, there is immediately movement away from one another. Contact and distance are continuously balanced. When an ant accidentally meets an ant from a different colony, there is an automatic springing apart. At times, conflict between two ants leads to fights that are always fatal for one ant. The signs of the fight are evident when ants are seen walking on the desert floor carrying the heads of other ants in their mandibles. Gordon speculates that ants regulate their interaction rate to keep the interaction within an appropriate range. Uncontrolled interaction rates might contribute to heightened reactivity within the unit.

Expansion of Bowen Theory to the Study of Harvester Ant Behavior

I now make an effort to apply and extend Bowen theory to the study of harvester ant behavior. Kerr (1998) applied Bowen theory to the understanding of the much older nonhuman naked mole rat (*Heterocephaus glaber*) of East Africa (pp. 136–147). In the following speculation, I apply Bowen theory to the nonmammalian, more ancient species of harvester ants and use research from Gordon's work to discuss my views. However, I do not intend to speak for Gordon or any other researcher of social behavior whose views may not coincide with my own.

A fundamental premise of Bowen theory is that all species sense and respond to the environment and to the social process through an emotional guidance system that is very ancient in the history of life. It is also hypothesized that the balance of the two life forces of individuality and togetherness is central to variation in adaptiveness of human and other species. Furthermore, it is hypothesized that variation in anxiety and reactivity, a form of anxiety, is of fundamental importance in the overall functioning of all emotional units in nature (Bowen, 1978; Kerr, 1998; Kerr & Bowen, 1988; Papero, 1990).

The togetherness force in harvester ants can be observed through the study of smell. Ants coat one another with a greasy substance (hydrocarbons) to mark the sameness of the unit. Ants that smell different from the colony odor are fought with, avoided, or killed. Brood from an unrelated colony can be "adopted" into a different colony only if this occurs before taking on the characteristic colony smell. There is a very brief window of time in which this can occur. After sameness with the colony is established, no movement to another colony can occur without loss of life.

Other manifestations of the togetherness force can be viewed in the dependence and tight, integrated functioning of the unit of the colony. A change in the functioning in one part of the system leads to change in another part. Task switching is an example of such a change. The tight tuning of ants to one another and to the group process is another such change.

The individuality force in harvester ants is believed to be observed through the uniqueness of individual ants. Some individuals within a colony are especially active and may contribute more to the overall functioning of the unit. Individual ants will also "go their own way" in the choice of trail on the basis of foraging choice the day before, if the characteristic patroller smell is blocked (*patrollers* regulate the choice of daily foraging direction; Beverly, McLendon, Nacu, Holmes, & Gordon, 2009). That is, relationship-governed processes have the capacity to inhibit the presence of individually determined action. During the mating flight, females who need to mate with many males to acquire the necessary genetic materials for establishing a new colony will not, however, wish to mate with all males. Females will strenuously resist mating with certain males deemed "unacceptable." This background level of conflict reflects rudimentary signs of individuality in the ants.

A balance of contact and distance is fundamental to the functioning of all harvester ant colonies. Without contact, a colony will not function, but too much contact threatens to disrupt optimal functioning of the unit. A balance of individuality and togetherness is seen to underlie this fundamental pattern harvester ants share with human beings.

The regulation of reactivity is fundamental to the functioning of harvester ant behavior. Within the colony, the functioning positions of patroller and early forager serve regulatory functions in the management of the reactivity required for the initiation and persistence of foraging. The regulatory functions ensure an orderly process of movement through the various stages of ant behavior in the course of the daily round (the daily foraging process leading to the collection and storage of seeds). Each individual ant, in addition, regulates reactivity by moving toward another ant and then moving immediately away. Human beings must also regulate contact and distance and the anxiety and reactivity that accompanies group living.

Established colonies also regulate reactivity with other colonies through a process of "making room" for other established colonies by carving out trails that reduce intersection with other colonies. Although there are points of intersection, these are carefully managed between adjoining colonies. Under conditions of crowding, ants may turn away from one another on the trail to reduce the reactivity of excessive contact. Under the opposite conditions, ants may establish greater contact to manage difficulties of underreacting. A middle-ground level of reactivity appears necessary for optimal functioning. Both over- and underreacting would leave ants and humans less adaptable to changing conditions.

Studies by Gordon are currently underway to identify variation in the fundamental patterns between colonies that are linked to adaptiveness as measured through reproductive success. This research speculates that colonies that are less sensitive are able to collect more food and have more offspring that survive to reproduce. I also speculate that colonies that are more able to regulate reactivity during heightened periods of challenge such as extreme conditions of drought are more adaptive. Many more studies are required before these preliminary studies are proven or disproven.

When each basic pattern of behavior in the harvester ants is reviewed, it is clear that there is a fundamental similarity to basic patterns of behavior in the human family. In both units, members move toward one another when contact is too little and move away to avoid excessive contact. Both systems use conflict to manage closeness and distance. The forces for individuality and togetherness are readily observed. There is interdependence and reciprocal functioning in both units. The management of anxiety in both systems can be observed through patterns of contact, distance, conflict, and reciprocal functioning.

A fundamental hypothesis of Bowen theory is that variation in fundamental patterns leads to variation in overall adaptiveness to changing conditions. Although genes are considered a part of this process, they cannot be separated from these fundamental patterns.

Conclusion

A distant goal of long-term students of Bowen theory is to move toward a science of human behavior. Central to that goal is the assumption that the human is an evolved form of life driven and regulated by the same fundamental life forces governing all natural systems on the planet.

Research from many areas of investigation supports the view that the family plays an important role in individuals' level of sensitivity to the social environment. Such sensitivity is seen to relate to overall adaptiveness of individuals and family units. Although research in animal behavior is continuing to uncover links between the processes in human families and those found in other species, it is a stretch to consider common processes between human families and distantly related nonmammalian species such as harvester ants.

Speculation regarding fundamental processes across all forms of life is not proven. However, long-term field research such as that conducted by Gordon may one day raise new areas of study concerning fundamental processes and forces governing all of life. Such study would be very interesting and potentially contribute to new perspectives on evolution. Bowen theory may play an important role in developing such insights.

References

Annett, R. (1989). Foraging theory. *Condor, 91,* 222–223.

Beverly, B., McLendon, H., Nacu, S., Holmes, S., & Gordon, D. M. (2009). How site fidelity leads to individual differences in the foraging activity of harvester ants. *Behavioral Ecology, 20,* 633–638.

Bowen, M. (1978). *Family therapy in clinical practice.* New York, NY: Jason Aronson.

Darwin, C. (1964). *On the origin of species by means of natural selection.* (Facsimile of first edition; Ernst Mayr, Ed.). Boston, MA: Harvard University Press. (Original work published 1859.)

Gordon, D. M. (1999). *Ants at work: How an insect society is organized.* New York, NY: Free Press.

Gordon, D. M. (2007). Control without hierarchy. *Nature, 4468,* 143.

Gordon, D. M. (2010). *Ant encounters: Interaction networks and colony behavior.* Princeton, NJ: Princeton University Press.

Gordon, D. M., Holmes, S., & Nacu, S. (2008). The short-term regulation of foraging in harvester ants. *Behavioral Ecology, 19,* 217–222.

Greenberg, M. (1998). *Application of relationship systems model on social birds and mammals* (Unpublished doctoral dissertation). University of Kansas.

Greene, M. J., & Gordon, D. M. (2007). How patrollers set foraging direction in harvester ants. *American Naturalist, 170,* 943–948.

Hamilton, W. D. (1964). The genetical evolution of social behavior, I–III. *Journal of Theoretical Biology, 7,* 1–52.

Kerr, M. (1998). Bowen theory and evolutionary theory. *Family Systems, 4*(2), 119–177.

Kerr, M. E., & Bowen, M. (1988). *Family evaluation: An approach based on Bowen theory.* New York, NY: W. W. Norton.

Papero, D. (1990). *Bowen family systems theory.* Boston, MA: Allyn & Bacon.

Worster, D. (1977). *Nature's economy: A history of ecological ideas.* New York, NY: Cambridge University Press.

29

Social Behavior in Nonhuman Animals: A Behavioral Model of Proximate Mechanisms Based on Bowen Theory

MARY GREENBERG

The author proposes a structural framework built on Bowen family systems theory to investigate social behavior in nonhuman animals. Conundrums posed by traditional models of animal behavior need an alternate theory or framework to provide solutions and suggest new mechanisms for investigating social interactions. Such an alternate theory or framework needs to (a) be structurally simple; (b) allow for a history of interaction, or shared experience between and among individuals; (c) be applicable to behavior regardless of the degree of relatedness of the participating individuals; (d) explain positive and negative interactions, how these come to occur, and how they are resolved; and (e) incorporate interactions involving more than two individuals. Such a theory exists in the literature of human family functioning (Ackerman, 1958; Bateson, Jackson, Haley, & Weakland, 1956; Boszormeny-Nagy, 1965; Bowen, 1960; Lidz & Fleck, 1960; Minuchin, 1974; Weakland, 1960; Whitaker & Malone, 1953).

In this chapter, the author reformulates Bowen theory (Bowen, 1978) into a structural framework of proximate mechanisms for applying this theory to social animals. The model, known as the *relationship systems model* (RSM), emphasizes relationship bonds in keeping with the Bowen theory suggestion that "the individual is often incomprehensible out of context of the individual's relationship to the group" (Kerr & Bowen, 1988, p. 30), which is often neglected in animal studies (Das, 2000; Wielebnowski, 1998). The RSM is a behavioral model placed within the context of evolutionary theory, and the entire model has not previously been applied to social animals. Animal models are common in biology, although the names of researchers are not used to identify them; rather, this designation is limited to an exceptional few such as Darwinian theories. Bowen family systems theory has been renamed in keeping with this viewpoint and because Bowen theory was developed specifically to study human, not animal, behavior.

The Relationship Systems Model

The major question for the evolution of social behavior has been, "If natural selection acts primarily or exclusively on individuals, why do many species spend so much time together engaging in cooperative-appearing interactions with conspecifics?" A wide variety of solutions have focused on ultimate explanations that include group selection (Lorenz, 1966; Wynne-Edwards, 1965), kin selection (Hamilton, 1964; E. O. Wilson, 1975), reciprocal altruism (Trivers, 1971), and delayed return altruism (pseudoreciprocity; Rothstein & Pierotti, 1988). Ultimate explanations focus on the consequences or outcome of behavior and the long-term historical causes of distinct abilities with an emphasis on questions of survival value and evolution (Tinbergen, 1963).

Many suggested ultimate explanations contain limitations based on simplifying assumptions. For example, group selection has long been controversial (Maynard Smith, 1964; Williams, 1966; D. S. Wilson, 1980) because it tends to deemphasize the role of the individual in social situations and concentrates on the group as the object of natural selection. Many models reveal logical flaws behind the concept of group selection and, thus, appear to work only in certain restricted situations (Aoki, 1982; Levin & Kilmer, 1974; D. S. Wilson, 1980). Kin selection is also limited because it assumes that certain cooperative behavior should take place between only relatives; however, this is not the case in many situations (Kaplan, 1977; Ligon, 1978; Rothstein & Pierotti, 1988). Reciprocal and delayed-return altruism can clearly be applied to situations involving nonrelatives, but these models have limited support (Butovskaya, 1993; Kaplan, 1978) and also assume that interactants are initially unfamiliar with one another. The best solution to cooperation under reciprocal altruism appears to be a game of tit-for-tat (Axelrod & Hamilton, 1981), which assumes that the interacting individuals know nothing about the other's tendency to behave in a certain manner in conflict situations.

An individual's survival depends on day-to-day behaviors that are explained by proximate mechanisms. *Proximate mechanisms* focus on immediate sources of behavior or on questions of how an organism is designed to behave in a given circumstance (Gubernick, 1996; Tinbergen, 1963). "Proximate explanations include, but are not limited to, immediate sensory stimulation (e.g., sounds, visual cues, etc.), past experience, hormonal and neural mechanism, emotions, and cognitive processes" (Gubernick, 1996, p. 113). Known proximate explanations are unsatisfactory in many cases as when dominance hierarchies (Allee, Emerson, Park, Park, & Schmidt, 1949; Lorenz, 1966) are invoked; evidence for dominance rank is limited, that is, many groups appear to lack a true hierarchical structure (Brown, 1975; Hand, 1986; Hinde, 1976; Ralls, 1976). *Game theory*, which determines the best tactic or set of tactics for conflicts, is probably the best solution posed currently; however, game theory assumes that all interactions are dyadic, that is, they involve only two individuals in any single encounter (Lowentin, 1970; Maynard Smith, 1976; Maynard Smith & Price, 1973).

The RSM provides solutions for challenges posed by traditional models and suggests new proximate mechanisms for investigating behavior. The foundation for the RSM is the research of Bowen, an originator of family therapy during the 1950s and 1960s. An assumption of Bowen family systems theory is that human behavior is shaped by an emotional process that is both instinctual and learned in character and predates human development (Bowen, 1966; Kerr & Bowen, 1988). The RSM emphasizes acquired behavior, the predictable nature of the nonhuman social environment and how constancy in relationships is maintained in patterned behaviors over time.

Social environment is a factor that contributes to an individual's stress. How an individual behaves in response to a stressful situation, a situation in which "the usual pattern of maintenance activities becomes more or less disrupted" (Rowell & Hinde, 1963, p. 235), is likely to indicate the level of anxiety he or she experiences. The level of anxiety is a functional category of behaviors given in response to stressful situations (e.g., agonistic interactions). Anxiety takes one of two forms: first, *acute anxiety*, which is associated with short-term effects, and second, *chronic anxiety*, which is associated with long-term effects (Kerr & Bowen, 1988). An example of acute anxiety is the response of a prey to being chased by a predator, which requires immediate physiological changes and actions for the prey to survive (Sapolsky, 2001). The prey experiences acute physical stress that subsides if it successfully evades the predator.

A likely example of chronic anxiety in monogamously breeding birds is when an adult offspring's dispersal changes the parents' relationship if that offspring's functional role served as a buffer in their relationship. A disturbance in the parental relationship can generate more stress responses than the initial triggering event of the offspring leaving home. By impairing relationship stability, anxiety can potentially reduce reproductive success, which has important evolutionary consequences.

The RSM consists of six major components: (1) triangles, (2) differentiation, (3) natal unit process, (4) natal unit projection process, (5) birth or hatch order, and (6) the multigenerational transmission process. An assumption of the RSM is that components direct attention to functional equilibrium rather than to dysfunction; as a consequence, behaviors are identified that can be observed and measured to facilitate empirical studies. Detailed descriptions of these components may be found in Chapter 1 of this volume. The author has collected reports with data on captive and wild species. Parts of the data are from studies that catalogue other behaviors: Frequently, each component's behaviors are pointed out only in the context of other social interactions such as aggressive conflicts and dispersal of offspring from the natal home range.

Triangles: Nonreproductive or Nonnatal Units

According to Hinde (1976), a *relationship* in nonhuman animals is a series of interactions between two individuals that is influenced by the history of past interactions between them. An assumption of this definition is that the basic social unit is two individuals. The basic social unit of two individuals provides explanations of interactions as the following example shows: When more than two individuals interact, for example, A and B chase C, interactions are broken down to two animal units such as A chases C and B chases C (Rowell, 1967). These explanations are incomplete because the possible social bond between A and B is lost and the fact that both chase C together is lost, also. The RSM provides an alternative explanation for the actions of A, B, and C by identifying the basic social unit as a triangle.

The *triangle* is a complex process that consists of three positions (Kerr & Bowen, 1988). Relationships between two individuals are stable only in low-stress situations; these relationships can easily become unstable by disturbances (internal or external) to an individual. The process of activating a triangle is observable during relationship disturbances, but the process cannot be observed if there is no disturbance. During no disturbance, observing the close twosome may give the mistaken impression that the basic social unit consists of only two individuals. Outcomes of activating a single triangle may range from relationship balance of the original two participants to continued relationship instability with increased numbers of stress responses by all three individuals.

A relationship among three individuals has emergent behavioral properties. The triangle should be more stable than a dyad because three individuals can sustain more anxiety than two (Bowen, 1976, 1978). A triangle allows for the spread and shift of anxiety (with attendant behavioral stress responses) through interconnecting relationships. No fewer than three individuals should be able to minimize social anxiety if the relationship of two individuals has been disturbed. This leads to the following prediction: Triangles should be activated by individuals in response to relationship disturbances. A successful triangle reduces social anxiety and preserves the relationship of the original two participants. In the following examples, only the featured component, for example, the triangle, is fully described to demonstrate its characteristics and how it operates. However, it is assumed that other components of the RSM may be contributing to the observed behavior as well.

Baboons (*Papio* spp.) are large-group–living Old World monkeys with diverse social structures that occupy a wide range of habitats in East and Central Africa (Altmann, 1980). In baboon societies of the savanna, a group may consist of several adult males, a greater number of adult females with infants, and subadult and juveniles of mixed age–sex classes. Group members do not ordinarily interact with one another, although close proximity can provide opportunities for social interactions (Altmann, 1980).

A troop of yellow baboons (*Papio c. cynocephalus*) in Ruaba National Park, Tanzania, was observed for 445.6 hours over a period of 84 days (Collins, 1986). Of the approximately 70 individuals in the troop, data were collected on 31 subjects, which included all 8 adult males (6 residents and 2 newcomers or immigrants), subadult males, adult females, and 14 infants under 1 year of age (Collins, 1986). The male newcomers were not the fathers of any of the infants (Collins, 1986).

Results showed 381 interactions between adult males and infants; 57 interactions involved 1 male carrying an infant during one or more interactions with other males (Collins, 1986). Males did not limit contacts with only their own offspring and possibly did not recognize them (Collins, 1986). Twenty-two (39%) of the 57 interactions included episodes between resident and newcomer males in which the resident males carried infants; the newcomers never carried infants. Twenty-five (44%) of the 57 interactions between resident males included episodes of infant carrying. The "most frequently recognizable context was when a male was involved in agonistic interaction with other males nearby or there was obvious tenseness between them" (Collins, 1986, p. 433). Carrying behaviors cannot easily be mistaken for protective behavior of infants because there were no indications of distress by any infant (Collins, 1986).

At other research sites, interactions between adult males rarely escalated to the level of fighting, and the male carrying an infant was less vulnerable to aggression (Busse & Hamilton, 1981; Packer, 1980; Strum, 1984). Males that carried infants were likely to be fathers of those infants no more than 40% of the time (Packer & Pusey, 1985). Depending on the male's circumstances, he could be the infant's protector, exploiter, or possibly its father (Altmann, 1980; Collins, 1986; Smuts, 1985).

Behavior of yellow baboons has been subject to various interpretations (see earlier), but the RSM likely provides the most parsimonious explanation. RSM predicts that feuding males, with infant carrying, activate a triangle. A relationship disturbance between two males triggers behavior to include a third party, the infant. Including a third party allows for the spread and shift of anxiety among all individuals, thus potentially reducing the anxiety between the original two opponents. Because any infant may be carried, a degree of relatedness between a youngster and a male is unnecessary; rather, the choice of an infant may be one of convenience. Activating a triangle may avoid conflicts regardless of the status of a male, such as resident or newcomer, or the kinship status between individuals. How better to ensure one's survival than to establish patterns of non-aggressive behavior in advance of a potential conflict? As a consequence, survival is likely accomplished by maintaining one's position in a group.

Maintaining one's position may be inextricably linked to maximizing one's fitness gain. Without being able to fulfill the requirement of maintaining a position, an individual may not reproduce successfully. For example, an adult male who is ostracized from the group may not find an appropriate breeding partner outside the group context.

Differentiation

Natal units as emotional systems tend toward togetherness or undifferentiation, especially during stressful situations (Bowen, 1966). The range of differentiation is from togetherness or undifferentiation to individuality or differentiation of self (Bowen, 1966). Low-functioning individuals tend toward togetherness or intense emotional closeness and rely on others for making decisions. High-functioning individuals tend toward individuality or high levels of differentiation and can make decisions without relying much on others. According to the RSM, as an offspring grows and develops, it interacts with related and unrelated individuals to master social skills that are species specific and age appropriate. The level of differentiation may be identified by behaviors characterized by social skills or the lack of them. Levels of differentiation are influenced by the level of chronic anxiety within a family (Kerr & Bowen, 1988). Chronic anxiety should have a detrimental influence on the process of differentiation.

This leads to the following predictions:

1. In species in which variation exists in social autonomy from parents, an association should exist between the levels of differentiation of parents and offspring.
2. Natal units (including all members) with low levels of differentiation should be characterized by low levels of social autonomy, high levels of chronic anxiety, and low reproductive success.
3. High levels of anxiety suggest that more situations than expected should be responded to as disturbances to social relationships.
4. Natal units (including all members) with high levels of differentiation should be characterized by high levels of social autonomy, low levels of chronic anxiety, and high reproductive success.

A population of approximately 160 eastern or long-haired chimpanzees (*Pan troglodytes schweinfurthii*) was observed in the Gombe National Park, Tanzania (Goodall, 1986). In chimpanzee societies, mothers care for their dependent offspring, and fathers may or may not provide any care (Goodall, 1986).

Five chimpanzee mothers with offspring under 24 months of age were studied for social independence in infants (van de Rijt-Plooij & Plooij, 1988). The process of developing independence occurs in a series of five maturational stages during the first 24 months (van de Rijt-Plooij & Plooij). When a new developmental ability emerged in infants where the process preceded normally, the mothers were clear about their demands. In observations of 3 mothers, once a mother refused to suckle her infant when she was busy, she always refused to do so consistently. These mothers encouraged their infants' "independence by training them to adapt to other individuals and to the physical world when using the new ability" (van de Rijt-Plooij & Plooij, 1988, p. 307). In contrast, 2 mothers were both inconsistent in their behavior and unclear in their demands. These mothers refused to suckle their infants but then rewarded them the same day by allowing the infants to suckle. Their infants became ill; one had symptoms of a cold and cough, and the other developed red spots and a lump on its chest. Both infants recovered. The authors suggested that the behavior of these two mothers created prolonged periods of social stress for the infants, which resulted in their being susceptible to disease. No conclusions were made regarding the possible links among social independence, the mother–offspring relationship, and illness in offspring.

Variation in parent–offspring relationships should indicate variation in the levels of differentiation in each offspring (Bowen, 1978). Inconsistent behavior of a mother may indicate a low level of differentiation; as a consequence, she does not encourage the infant's increased independence. The infant develops physically but does not develop increased independence or social autonomy.

Natal Unit Processes

The natal unit is a combination of emotional (see earlier) and relationship systems and likely has a strong influence on the behavior and social development of an offspring (Bowen, 1966). It is also probable that the importance of the natal unit in behavioral ontogeny is responsible for most of the evidence that has been used to support the concept of kin selection because in most animals, early social experience is primarily with close relatives, for example, parents and siblings, so cooperative behavior will be observed most frequently within family groups.

Primary Natal Triangle   A *primary natal triangle* consists of a monogamous breeding pair, with biparental care, and at least one offspring. The offspring is included in the relationship of both parents, who repeatedly activate the triangle, and overlapping triangles are created if there is more than one offspring (Bowen, 1978).

There are three possible relationships in a primary natal triangle:

1. A stable relationship of parents can become unstable by the inclusion of an offspring, for example, when young are born or hatched. The ability of the parents to maintain a stable relationship may be depleted by the time and energy required for the care of the young. In gulls, genus *Larus,* conflicts between parents sometimes occur over who sits on the nest after young have hatched (Hand, 1986).

2. A stable relationship of a duo can become unstable by the removal of a third individual. In seabirds, pair bonds can break after the death of offspring (R. Pierotti, personal communication, February 4, 2002).
3. An unstable relationship of a duo may be stabilized by the inclusion of an offspring (Kerr & Bowen, 1988).

This leads to the following prediction: When the natal unit is a stable reproductive unit, the primary triangle should include the two parents and one offspring. Either parent or offspring can activate a primary triangle.

Natal Unit Projection Process   A significantly important aspect of the projection process is the mother–offspring bond. Interactions between the two, and at times with the father, are characterized by high parental anxiety and by parental behaviors associated with lower levels of differentiation (see earlier; Kerr & Bowen, 1988). The offspring's attempts toward age-specific behaviors and social autonomy fail. Consequently, dispersal, reproductive success, or both are likely at risk. This leads to the following prediction: In natal units in which the mother–offspring bond is characterized by the parent's high level of anxiety and low level of differentiation, an offspring is likely to develop (a) a low level of differentiation, and (b) few social behaviors required for reproductive success.

Birth or Hatch Order

When the natal unit is a stable reproductive unit with multiple offspring that overlap in their social development, birth or hatch order shapes an individual's behavior. Variations in behavioral characteristics are likely when multiple offspring are born or hatched into a natal unit (e.g., litters or clutches). Siblings that are born or hatched in less than 24-hour intervals may not exhibit behavioral differences and, therefore, among-litter or clutch variability may be measured. Siblings born or hatched at greater intervals may exhibit behavioral differences and, therefore, within-litter or clutch variability may be measured. Birth or hatch order can inform future relationships with breeding partners. Depending on each partner's sibling position in its original family, partner bonds can be complementary or noncomplementary (Kerr & Bowen, 1988).

This leads to the following predictions: (a) Stereotypical behaviors associated with birth or hatch order may contribute to the functioning role of an offspring; (b) an offspring should duplicate behaviors characteristic of its sibling position in breeding relationships; and (c) breeding partner relationship bonds can be complementary or noncomplementary.

Multigenerational Transmission Process

The natal unit projection process (see earlier) is central to the multigenerational transmission process (Bowen, 1978). Parental transmission of varying levels of differentiation is repeated between parent and one offspring in each successive generation (Bowen, 1966). Parent and offspring interactions can include attempts—both successful and unsuccessful—by the offspring to increase independence or social autonomy. This leads to the following predictions: (a) The natal unit projection process in one generation is duplicated in subsequent generations, and (b) parental transmission of varying levels of differentiation repeats itself with different individuals.

Van Schaik et al. (2003) raised the issue of material culture such as nest building and tool use by orangutans (*Pongo pygmaeus*). Material culture (Van Schaik et al., 2003) likely results from the mother's own interactions with her mother (Whiten et al., 1999). One area that is neglected in this work is the recognition that the complexity of multigenerational relationship bonds increases the likelihood that genuine transmission occurs in this species.

A *multigenerational relationship* in orangutans is best defined as a sequential series of mother–offspring interactions that creates close bonds in each generation. In each generation, young orangutans and other primates acquire maternal behavioral patterns and other skills from their mothers (Berman, 1990; Fairbanks, 1996; Van Schaik, 2004; Van Schaik & Van Hooff, 1996). For example, captive female offspring rejected by their mothers often reject their own young, and similar behavior has been noted in other primates (Altmann, 1980; Berman, 1990; Goodall, 1986; C. Sodaro, personal communication, March 20, 2001). Rejecting young may indicate low levels of differentiation transmitted across generations. Clearly, understanding orangutan relationships should include maternal levels of differentiation that may be transmitted by the multigenerational effect.

Summary

The RSM

- provides a comprehensive framework for examining the often-neglected social environment in animal studies
- functions within the context of evolutionary theory by including variation in behavior among individuals, genetic or nongenetic inheritance of behavior, and the transmission of behavior (tendencies and functional roles) across generations
- identifies likely proximate mechanisms that occur across species, and age–sex classes, that are more parsimonious explanations than traditional approaches; RSM proximate mechanisms are argued to be critical to survival and reproductive success
- can be applied to both field research and statistical analyses (Greenberg, 1998). The statistical analyses of fight interference of a

rhesus monkey (*Macaca mulatta*) group suggested that only some group members had functional roles as interveners, a novel result made possible by using the RSM (Greenberg, 1998).

References

Ackerman, N. W. (1958). *The psychodynamics of family life*. New York, NY: Basic Books.

Allee, W. C., Emerson, A. E., Park, O., Park, T., & Schmidt, K. P. (1949). *Principles of animal ecology*. Philadelphia, PA: W. B. Saunders.

Altmann, J. (1980). *Baboon mothers and infants*. Cambridge, MA: Harvard University Press.

Aoki, K. (1982). A condition for group selection to prevail over counteracting individual selection. *Evolution, 36*, 832–842.

Axelrod, R., & Hamilton, W. D. (1981, March 27). The evolution of cooperation. *Science, 211*, 1390–1396.

Bateson, G., Jackson, D. D., Haley, J., & Weakland, J. (1956). Toward a theory of schizophrenia. *Behavioral Science, 1*, 251–264.

Berman, C. M. (1990). Intergenerational transmission of maternal rejection rates among free ranging rhesus monkeys. *Animal Behaviour, 39*, 329–337.

Boszormeny-Nagy, I. (1965). A theory of relationships: Experience and transaction. In I. Boszormeny-Nagy & J. L. Framo (Eds.), *Intensive family therapy* (pp. 33–86). New York, NY: Hoeber.

Bowen, M. (1960). A family concept of schizophrenia. In D. D. Jackson (Ed.), *Etiology of schizophrenia* (pp. 346–372). New York, NY: Basic Books.

Bowen, M. (1966). The use of family theory in clinical practice. *Comprehensive Psychiatry, 7*(5), 345–374.

Bowen, M. (1976). Theory in the practice of psychotherapy. In P. J. Guerin (Ed.), *Family therapy: Theory and practice* (pp. 42–90). New York, NY: Gardner Press.

Bowen, M. (1978). *Family therapy in clinical practice*. New York, NY: Jason Aronson.

Brown, J. L. (1975). *The evolution of behavior*. New York, NY: W. W. Norton.

Busse, C., & Hamilton, W. J. (1981, June 12). Infant carrying by male chacma baboons. *Science, 212*, 1281–1283.

Butovskaya, M. (1993). Kinship and different dominance styles in groups of three species of the genus macaca, *M. arctoides, M. mulatta, M. fascicularis*. *Folia Primatologica, 60*, 210–224.

Collins, D. A. (1986). Interactions between adult male and infant yellow baboons (*Papio c. cynocephalus*) in Tanzania. *Animal Behaviour, 34*, 430–443.

Das, M. (2000). Conflict management via third parties: Post conflict affiliation. In F. Aureli & F. B. M. De Waal (Eds.), *Natural conflict resolution* (pp. 263–280). Berkeley, CA: University of California Press.

Fairbanks, L. A. (1996). Individual differences in maternal style: Causes and consequences for mother-offspring. In J. S. Rosenblatt & C. T. Snowdon (Eds.), *Advances in the study of behavior* (pp. 579–611). San Diego, CA: Academic Press.

Goodall, J. (1986). *Chimpanzees of Gombe*. Cambridge, MA: Belknap Press.

Greenberg, M. (1998). *Application of the relationship systems model on social birds and mammals* (Unpublished doctoral dissertation). University of Kansas.

Gubernick, D. J. (1996). A natural family system. *Family Systems, 3*(2), 109–124.

Hamilton, W. D. (1964). The genetical evolution of social behaviour, I–III. *Journal of Theoretical Biology, 7*, 1–52.

Hand, J. L. (1986). Resolution of social conflicts: Dominance, egalitarianism, spheres of dominance, and game theory. *Quarterly Review of Biology, 61*(2), 201–219.

Hinde, R. A. (1976). Interactions, relationships and social structure. *Man, 11,* 1–17.

Kaplan, J. R. (1977). Patterns of fight interference in free-ranging rhesus monkeys. *American Journal of Anthropology, 47,* 279–288.

Kaplan, J. R. (1978). Fight interference and altruism in rhesus monkeys. *American Journal of Physical Anthropology, 49,* 241–250.

Kerr, M. E., & Bowen, M. (1988). *Family evaluation: An approach based on Bowen theory.* New York, NY: W. W. Norton.

Levin, B. R., & Kilmer, W. L. (1974). Interdemic selection and the evolution of altruism: A computer simulation study. *Evolution, 28,* 527–545.

Lidz, T., & Fleck, S. (1960). Schizophrenia, human integration, and the role of the family. In D. D. Jackson (Ed.), *Etiology of schizophrenia* (pp. 323–345). New York, NY: Basic Books.

Ligon, J. D. (1978). Communal breeding in birds: An assessment of kinship theory. *Symposium on Altruism in Birds, 6*(6), 857–861.

Lorenz, K. (1966). *On aggression.* New York, NY: Harcourt Brace & World.

Lowentin, R. C. (1970). The units of selection. *Annual Review of Ecology and Systematics, 1,* 1–18.

Maynard Smith, J. (1964, March 14). Group selection and kin selection. *Nature, 201,* 1145–1147.

Maynard Smith, J. (1976). Evolution and the theory of games. *American Scientist, 64,* 41–45.

Maynard Smith, J. P., & Price, G. R. (1973, November 2). The logic of animal conflict. *Nature, 2,* 15–18.

Minuchin, S. (1974). *Family and family therapy.* Cambridge, MA: Harvard University Press.

Packer, C. (1980). Male care and exploitation of infants in *Papio anibus. Animal Behaviour, 28,* 512–520.

Packer, C., & Pusey, A. (1985). Asymmetric contests in social animals: Respect, manipulation and age-specific aspects. In P. J. Greenwood, P. H. Harvey, & M. Slatkin (Eds.), *Evolution: Essays in honor of John Maynard Smith* (pp. 173–186). Cambridge, England: Cambridge University Press.

Ralls, K. (1976). Mammals in which females are larger than males. *Quarterly Review of Biology, 51,* 245–276.

Rothstein, S. I. P., & Pierotti, R. (1988). Distinctions among reciprocal altruism, kin selection, and cooperation and a model for the initial evolution of beneficent behavior. *Ethology and Sociobiology, 9,* 189–209.

Rowell, T. E. (1967). A quantitative comparison of the behaviour of a wild and a caged baboon group. *Animal Behaviour, 15,* 499–509.

Rowell, T. E., & Hinde, R. A. (1963). Responses of rhesus monkeys to mildly stressful situations. *Animal Behaviour, 11,* 235–243.

Sapolsky, R. M. (2001). Physiological and pathophysiological implications of social stress in mammals. In B. S. McEwen & H. M. Goodman (Eds.), *Handbook of physiology IV* (pp. 517–532). Oxford, England: Oxford University Press.

Smuts, B. B. (1985). *Sex and friendship in baboons.* New York, NY: Aldine.

Strum, S. C. (1984). Why males use infants. In D. M. Taub (Ed.), *Primate paternalism* (pp. 146–185). New York, NY: Van Nostrand.

Tinbergen, N. (1963). On aims and methods of ethology. *Zeitschrift fur Tierpsychologie, 20,* 410–433.

Trivers, R. (1971). The evolution of reciprocal altruism. *Quarterly Review of Biology, 46,* 35–59.

van de Rijt-Plooij, H. H. C., & Plooij, F. X. (1988). Mother-infant relations, conflict, stress and illness among free-ranging chimpanzees. *Developmental Medicine and Child Neurology, 30,* 306–315.

Van Schaik, C. P. (2004). *Among orangutans: Red apes and the rise of human culture.* Cambridge, MA: Belknap Press.

Van Schaik, C. P., Ancrenaz, M., Borgen, G., Galdikas, B., Knott, C. D., Singleton, I., ... Merrill, M. (2003, January 3). Orangutan cultures and the evolution of material culture. *Science, 299,* 102–105.

Van Schaik, C. P., & Van Hooff, J. A. R. A. M. (1996). Toward an understanding of the orangutan's social system. In W. McGrew, L. Marchant, & T. Nishida (Eds.), *Great ape societies* (pp. 3–15). Cambridge, England: Cambridge University Press.

Weakland, J. H. (1960). The "double bind" hypothesis of schizophrenia and three party interactions. In D. D. Jackson (Ed.), *Etiology of schizophrenia* (pp. 373–388). New York, NY: Basic Books.

Whitaker, C. A., & Malone, T. P. (1953). *The roots of psychotherapy.* New York, NY: Blakeston.

Whiten, A., Goodall, J., McGrew, W. C., Nishida, T., Reynolds, V., Sugiyama, Y., ... Boesch, C. (1999, June 17). Cultures of chimpanzees. *Nature, 399,* 682–685.

Wielebnowski, N. (1998). Contributions of behavioral studies to captive management and breeding of rare and endangered mammals. In T. Caro (Ed.), *Behavioral ecology and conservation biology* (pp. 131–162). New York, NY: Oxford University Press.

Williams, G. C. (1966). *Adaptation and natural selection: A critique of some evolutionary thought.* Princeton, NJ: Princeton University Press.

Wilson, D. S. (1980). *The natural selection of populations and communities.* Menlo Park, CA: Benjamin Cummings.

Wilson, E. O. (1975). *Sociobiology.* Cambridge, MA: Belknap Press.

Wynne-Edwards, V. C. (1965, March 26). Self-regulating systems in populations of animals. *Science, 147,* 1543–1548.

30

A Science of Human Behavior for the Future: Selected Segments by Dr. Murray Bowen at the Minnesota Institute of Family Dynamics

Compiled and Edited by G. MARY BOURNE

Setting the Scene

This session pairs well with that of May 2, 1983 (Chapter 19 of this volume), because the questions Dr. Bowen asked the class in 1983 so closely resemble the questions he had been asking himself in the early decades of his own research. The stories are not new ones; yet the particular juxtaposition of facts makes them appear so. Dr. Bowen spent 10 years or more on very basic questions, and on cross-discipline study, as well. He looked everywhere for facts. And from the very beginning, he hoped to make a contribution, not only to a new **theory,** but to a new **science** of human behavior for the future. What follows is, verbatim, the story of his research, beginning in the 1940s and projected into the future.

Dr. Bowen With Beginning Class of Trainees in Minneapolis, October 30, 1984

Back in the early days—that was back in the 1940s—I was wondering why in the world human behavior couldn't be a science. It was as if the only way we could deal with human behavior was with the scientific method. That would be to take a whole bunch of incongruent variables, with no way to put 'em together with a **thinking** model. So we'd use a scientific method on a bunch of subjectivity—a bunch of **feeling** things.

So then Freud ended up with the only theory, or the best known theory, about human behavior, which was taken from a psychological model—a feeling model, in which he used segments of the theory made up of feelings. And I was wondering why in the world human behavior couldn't be a science—I had a way of saying, "like the rest of medicine." So that was **always** in the background. I was thinking, "Human behavior could be a science **if** we could stick to the rules that go with science." And then, of course, I got off into psychoanalysis. So Freud had used a lot of feeling stuff—a lot of imagination. He'd used a lot of concepts that came out of literature, which were feeling concepts—and he'd used a lot of mythology. So he ended up with a theory made up of an ego, and an id, and a superego, and an unconscious. And nobody's ever seen an id or a superego or an unconscious. Nobody's ever had a way of measuring it or knowing whether it's there or not, except what somebody else says. This resulted in most of our theories about mental health being called a "non-theory" by most people in the accepted sciences.

So I got to thinkin' about **all** those things that went into this. I read all kinds of things, like philosophy. And there's no such thing as one philosophy, for which there is not a counter-philosophy—a philosophy of the opposite side. So this is all feeling stuff. And Oedipus, of course, came from a play, which was dreamed up by the brain. Anyway, I got off on the notion of—that if we could think of the human being as being related to all other forms of life, rather than being separate from all other forms of life, it would move human behavior closer to the sciences. Well, **why** move human behavior to the sciences? It's gonna' be the same, isn't it always, whether it's a science or not? But I would say that if human behavior could ever be related or could be considered to be a part of all the sciences—and this has to do with biology, anatomy, physiology, all of the known sciences—that when one science makes a breakthrough, it can contribute to all of them. The same if human behavior is a science, it can contribute back to chemistry, neurophysiology, physiology, and all that good stuff. So if it could ever be a science, there is something to be said for that.

Anyway, my thought then was, "Good Lord, this is gonna' take 200 years." But if I can make a little progress on this, I'd like to do whatever I can toward it. Anyway, I got off on this thing of evolution, largely because the human brain is similar to the subhuman brain and right on down the line. So that, if you look at it that way, you could say the human is unique and different from all other forms of life and still be inaccurate. Most of the libraries is filled with ways in which the human is **different** from all other forms of life, which just doesn't go along with my argument—except you do end up in the non-science up there. And I was trying to think of the human brain as being—and it's absolutely amazing that this is there [GOES TO THE BOARD] and traces back to the lowest forms of life. Any form that is mobile will have some kind of a nervous system, which directs the mobility of the form. So it will have some kind of specialized cells. And that gets back even to animals like insects and worms and what-have-you. They **do** have a nervous system which directs the activity in this. And this starts at lowest forms of life and comes right on up through the human. And this form is like this, and like this, and like this, and like this, and like this and like this. I thought, "Boy, that is **one** way to begin and it would be worth an effort." Whether or not it pays off, I just thought it would be worth an effort.

And up until that time, human behavior had been conceptualized by Freud. Freud developed the first theory about human behavior, which was a **psychological** theory. And psychology comes from a product of the mind. Well, when you think of psychology as a **product** of the mind, then you're free to put in all this stuff about imagination, dreams, and mythology. But you end up with something that you don't know whether it exists or not. Somebody can **say** it exists, but you can't—you got no way of provin' it.

Anyway, nobody can tell you why psychology went for 75 years using a scientific method which is a non-theory way. Nobody knows why we went 75 years. See, originally people using Freudian theory, what they did—is they **conceptualized the problem in the person**—as being within the person. And treatment involved a relationship with them, through which a **big** bunch of details come into play, called a "transference." So that the treatment of these pathological problems in an individual could be treated by a transference. And then **why** did we go 75 years before anybody thought of working on family?

Now when you bring a family into it, for the first time ever, you bring in the relationship **between people**. Now, individual theory had a way of thinking, which could see the problem as in the person of the patient. And the **treatment** of the problem is a relationship with that person. And successful treatment is a resolution of that problem conceived to be in the patient, through a relationship with another person or a therapist, or what-have-you. Now, when you think about a family instead of the individual, then a **group of people** becomes the patient—**and the relationship between them.**

So, that was the state of the world back in the 1950s, when a half a dozen or so of us, working on the problem in isolation from each other, began to write about characteristics of the family. Up until that time, there was absolutely nothing in the literature which dealt with relationships—the relationship of one person to another person, **except** in terms of the transference. A fair amount was written about the relationship between the therapist and the patient—the transference. But that was the **only** relationship thing in conventional theory. And why did we go so long before we moved the focus from the gun barrel, which is the patient, or the patient and the therapist, to seeing the whole family, which influenced the beginning of a new literature?

Well, at that time, I'd been fooling around with reading evolution, and philosophy, and mathematics, all these things—getting an idea here, an idea there, and putting some of them together. But that didn't have any great influence on me until I started this family research back in the 1950s. And then years ago, we picked up the ball game where you see **the individual as part and parcel of his family.** That was really the beginning of "Family Therapy." I think that was much less important than **thinking** of the individual as connected with all the other people in the family. And I thought, "Boy, oh boy! It probably won't happen for another couple hundred years, but if we can **think** of the individual as part and parcel of the family, rather than being a contained unit within himself, this would be a way to go." So I had this notion about **a different theory** from the very beginning.

Now amongst all the people who were involved in family research back in the 50s, most of the people conceptualized what they saw within the family **through** their teaching about the individual. Now I thought, "Boy, that is a short-sighted way to do it, because if we can see **the whole family as a unit**, it is a different way of thinking."

Now let me put this one in, which has to do with therapy. And first, last and always, you will hear about something that I've written about—tried to write about—about being able to get a more distant view of the family, as a way to **see** the family. I believe something more than that necessary, because there is **one big chasm** between seeing the human being as unique and different from all other living things, and seeing the human being as part and parcel of all things.

So back very early, I was thinking, "Well, there's not a heck of a lot I'll be able to do with this in **a lifetime**. But if I can **think** of the family in terms of the family being related to all living things, it will be a better way of thinking than thinking about the human being as a unique form of life. I think if you can have that kind of a view about the families you see, that enables you to back up and to see them in a different way than you would if you thought **through** another way of thinking. Which is my viewpoint on it. See, most of the theories about family are sort of watered down versions of conventional theory—what there was of it. And I would say, if you can think about the human being in different terms, you can see different things in the family than you would see if you had another way of thinking. This was back in the early days of family research.

I had quite a few research assistants. And they would do observations on the family and **see** individual theory, which is what they have been **taught** to see in their original thinking. And that is difficult for them, to **change** a way of thinking. Now you got some notion of how difficult it is to change a way of thinking once it gets embedded into a life. The other is out there, only you can't see it. And back in those early days, I used to say to my research assistants, "The greatest scientific discoveries are still to be made. They're right in front of your eyes all the time. They've been there. The discoveries for the next century—two centuries—are right in front of your eyes. Now all you gotta' do is open your eyes so you can see. Well, you cannot open your eyes to see until you have re-programmed your head. You're still blind to everything that's right in front of your eyes." So I used to say things to my assistants like, "What do you do with your blindness?" It's an impossible question. But it applies to them and also applies to me. Maybe I've been working on this thing longer than them and maybe I can get a little better view of it. But it applies to everybody.

So, one of the things that I would say is: I wanted to put together a theory which I hope will hold water for a century from now—two centuries from now—and not just be an **extension** of Freudian theory. That was sort of a background motivation. And you get into another one in that. Part of it has to do with your way of **thinking** about it. If you could change your way of thinking, you could see things that you couldn't see otherwise, so how do you go about that?

Back in those days, I was fairly close to the University of Maryland. Used to go to periodic football games up there, and I used to be thinking things like: Here are these people jumping up and down and doing all this stuff. And what would the ducks think about the human phenomenon if they could look down on a football game and see cheerleaders jumping up and down and going crazy, and people sitting around? Wouldn't this be a wonderful observation for the ducks? [LAUGHTER] In other words, that would be an effort to make all that blindness a universal characteristic, rather than something different. And that was just part of it—that one.

So one part gets to be: How much do you include regular psychological theory in this? And my basic way of thinking would say that if you mix up your observations—if it is true that "family" provides a different view of the human phenomenon but you conceptualize from old theory—you end up with old theory. So a command to my research people would be: "I'm not going to use no more 'ids, egos, superegos, repression, suppression,' all the stuff that goes into psychoanalysis, because once you use it, you got psychoanalytic theory. And right in front of our eyes is a new way of thinking. So I'll put the next years on trying to—trying **not** to use old concepts."

And every concept, you better believe it, has been researched back and forth, back and forth, to the origin of the word and the origin of the development of concepts. Point by point, by point by point—being **very** careful not to use anything that belonged to psychological theory—in this effort to describe the human phenomenon. And I would say, if we could think of the human being as another form of life, and if we can avoid using anything from psychological theory within this, we will be a few decades closer to having a real, honest-to-goodness theory than if we mix it up and leave it to the future to un-mix it.

So that basically is what I did. And I had a lot of people who were doing a lot of reading in the libraries about every concept. So what I was trying to do was to move back to biology—to see the human as a biological phenomenon **and** a psychological phenomenon. We've always had this concept of a **psycho**-somatic illness. What's a **psycho**somatic illness? Well, all we know is that is a descriptive term which says that this illness—we don't know what it is—but it has **psychological** aspects to it, and it also involves the organ system. So we call it psychosomatic. We don't know what the word means. It's a dumping ground. It's a wastebasket. We still haven't gotten around that corner.

Another one I got into then—for instance here would be one. Right now in our society, we get off into this business about the differences between men and women, which are real. There they are. So you could spend your time debating the advantages or disadvantages of males, or the advantages or disadvantages of females. And you could spend the rest of your days arguing all the details in it, like you could spend the rest of your days arguing the details that gets into Republicans and Democrats. You can never finish. You can never finish arguing the details that go into a philosophy. Because one defined one viewpoint and another the opposing viewpoint. That's what I tried to put in with that inductive, deductive stuff. It's not "either-or." It's both and the interplay between them.

One of the very simple ways that the professions do, they call "interfaces." I've never used that word. An interface is a way to take one tiny step toward systems thinking. But we think of interface as some kind of way of—in other words, we got something called biology, and psychology. We don't know how they go together. So that becomes the interface. So that is just a big catchword for it. It doesn't mean a durned thing, except we know there's a **problem** in it. And that means [WRITING ON BOARD] there's something over here, an analogy that is like that over there—a similarity. But a similarity don't let you bridge that gap. And a gap will be bridged by finding a way of thinking that can operate on both sides of this. So what I've tried to do, instead of picking up analogies—"similarities"—will be to get a way of thinking which supersedes it. For instance, I put in that one about male-female. That can be superseded by saying that men and women are both human beings. So that you don't get **caught** on laboring the polarities. You don't get caught in that debate. Same as interfaces. I don't—I try not to get caught belaboring this. It'd be to go back and find something up there. [BLACKBOARD]

For instance, I wouldn't get **caught** in trying to labor the difference between plant forms of life and an animal form of life. These are **both** forms of life. And they're both made up of genes and they're genetic. In other words, insofar as we know, we've been able to define the origin of the universe. How did it start? How'd it get to be the way it is? Which is another way of thinking about evolution. The universe started four thousand million years ago. And then it went seven eighths of that time, as far as we can know it, before life appeared. And, as far as we know, the Earth is the only planet in the solar system with water on it. And water combined with the elements of the earth, which over a period of millions and millions of years evolved into life. And now life has been created in a laboratory.

So that would be water, plus the elements of the earth, plus the heat of the sun, as far as we know. Then over a period of about five hundred million years, as well as we know it, these forms of life—a characteristic of **all** forms of life, plant and animal, is that they reproduce **almost** exactly like the previous generation—which is so in **all** plants, all animals. Each generation is almost the same, but a little bit different. And the difference between the generations, as it goes through the multiple centuries—millions of years—is what you call evolution. So life on earth is constantly changing—man included in it.

So when you think about—we are cousins of all plants, on that level of thinking. So you could get out of thinking about animal forms by moving back, and that is another form of life. Plant forms are in it, too, and the universe, and what-have-you. That would be my way of trying to supersede this thing. In other words, I'd go back—if you put animal and plant on one side— you get up here, then you'd have **both** forms of life. They're both living, as far as we know, **only** on planet earth. We don't know about the others. Those are still to be discovered. "Yay or nay"—one way or the other. But as far as we know, the earth is the only one with water on it. And water is the essential ingredient for life.

Well, when I was thinking about that back then, and as you go along here, you will be hearing that Bowen theory is different from all other theories. It is. That depends on the people who use it. Because I've been working very hard at making it different.

And if we can think of the human with a systems frame of reference, and **if** we do not use psychological theory, we will eventually end up with something that goes in the direction of **a new theory**. Anyway, that's all I tried to do back in the beginning, would be to pick up universals as much as possible, and to work it into a new way of thinking.

Well, there are an awful lot of things in the theory which I've described that are different from everything else—but not necessarily in terms of the way people use it. People can say that all of these concepts which I tried to develop are mere extensions of conventional theory. That's one way of thinking. I tried very hard to create something new. I think I did, and I think the future will recognize that, even though for now, it's considered to be part of the old.

Appendix

Bowen Theory Training Centers and Contributor Organizations

Bowen Center for the Study of the Family / Georgetown Family Center
Michael E. Kerr, Director
4400 MacArthur Boulevard NW, Suite 103
Washington, DC 20007-2521
Phone: 800-432-6882 / 202-965-4400
Email: info@thebowencenter.org
http://www.thebowencenter.org

The Center for Family Consultation
Sydney Reed, Director of Training
1167 Wilmette Avenue, Suite 201
Wilmette, IL 60091-2643
Phone: 847-866-7357
Email: sydneykreed@gmail.com
http://www.thecenterforfamilyconsultation.com

Center for Family, Organizational, and Natural Systems Education
Charles M. White, Founder and Principal Associate
Ellen Rogan, Principal Associate
PO Box 875
Westfield, NJ 07091
Phone: 908-451-5818
Email: charlesmwhitejr@gmail.com / ellnrogan@gmail.com
http://www.centerforfamilyorganizationalandnaturalsystemseducation.org
http://www.cfonse.org

The Center for Family Process
Mickie W. Crimone, Partner and Faculty
10601 Willowbrook Drive
Potomac, MD 20854
Phone: 410-799-7774 / 301-299-7475
Email: contactus@centerforfamilyprocess.com
http://www.centerforfamilyprocess.com

Center for the Study of Natural Systems and the Family
Victoria Harrison, Director
PO Box 701187
Houston, TX 77007
Phone: 713-790-0226
Email: vaharrison@sbcglobal.net
http://www.csnsf.org

Center for the Study of Natural Systems and the Family
Programs at the Border (El Paso, TX and Ciudad Juárez, México)
Louise Rauseo, Director
PO Box 1387
El Paso, TX 79948
Phone: 443-623-4021
Email: louise@rauseos.net / rauseo1@verizon.net
http://www.csnsf.org/borderprograms

The Family Systems Institute
Jenny Brown, Director
Grosvenor Cottage
30 Grosvenor Street, Neutral Bay
Sydney, NSW, 2089 Australia
Phone: 02 9904 5600
Email: info@thefsi.com.au
http://www.thefsi.com.au

The Florida Family Research Network, Inc. /
Bowen Theory Postgraduate Training Program of South Florida
Eileen Gottlieb, Education Director
232 SW 28th Avenue
Delray Beach, FL 33445
Phone: 561-279-0861
Email: ebgfamilycenter@comcast.net
http://www.ffrnbowentheory.org

Kansas City Center for Family and Organizational Systems
Margaret Otto, Director
3100 NE 83rd Street, Suite 2350
Kansas City, MO 64119
Phone: 816-436-1721
Email: motto@kcfamilysystems.com
http://www.kcfamilysystems.com

Leadership Coaching, Inc.
John Engels, President
63 Klink Road
Rochester, NY 14625
Phone: 585-381-9040
Email: emily@leadershipcoachinginc.com
http://www.leadershipcoachinginc.com

The Learning Space
Priscilla J. Friesen, Founder
4545 42nd Street NW, Suite 201
Washington, DC 20016
Phone: 202-966-1145
Email: priscilla@thelearningspacedc.com
http://thelearningspacedc.com

Living Systems
Randall Frost, Director of Training and Research
Lois Walker, Faculty
209-1500 Marine Drive
North Vancouver, BC, V7P1T7
Phone: 604-926-5496
Email: livingsystems@telus.net
http://www.livingsystems.ca

New England Seminar on Bowen Theory
Ann V. Nicholson, Chair
25 Medway Street
Dorchester, MA 02124
Phone: 617-296-4614
Email: ann.nicholson@verizon.net
http://www.bowentheoryne.org

Princeton Family Center for Education, Inc.
Joan McElroy, Director
PO Box 331
Pennington, NJ 08534
Phone: 609-924-0514
Email: joanmcelroy@princetonfamilycenter.org
http://www.princetonfamilycenter.org

Programs in Bowen Theory
Laura Havstad, Executive Director
120 Pleasant Hill Avenue N # 370
Sebastopol, CA 95472
Phone: 707-823-1848
Email: info@programsinbowentheory.org
http://www.programsinbowentheory.org

Side By Side, Inc.
Dennis Romig, CEO
9506 San Diego Road
Austin, TX 78737
Phone: 800-204-3118 / 512-288-0416
Email: dromig@sidebyside.com
http://www.sidebyside.com

Southern California Education and Training in Bowen Family Systems Theory
Carolyn Jacobs, Director
625 Third Avenue
Chula Vista, CA 91910
Phone: 619-525-7747
Email: info@socalbowentheory.com
http://www.socalbowentheory.com

Vermont Center for Family Studies
Monika Baege, Faculty
PO Box 5124
Essex Junction, VT 05453-5124
Phone: 802-872-1818
Email: info@vermontcenterforfamilystudies.org
http://www.vermontcenterforfamilystudies.org

Western Pennsylvania Family Center
James B. Smith, Executive Director
733 North Highland Avenue
Pittsburgh, PA 15206
Phone: 412-362-2295
Email: info@wpfc.net
http://www.wpfc.net

Index

Note: *Italicized* page references denote figures and tables.